CANAN

The superwarriors

The
Superwarriors

THE
SUPER

James W. Canan

WARRIORS

The Fantastic World of Pentagon Superweapons

WEYBRIGHT and TALLEY
New York

To my wife Joan
and
my parents

Weybright and Talley
750 Third Avenue
New York, New York 10017

Library of Congress Cataloging in Publication Data

Canan, James W
    The superwarriors.

    Includes index.
    1. United States—Military policy. 2. United
States. Dept. of Defense. 3. United States—Armed
Forces—Weapons systems. I. Title.
UA23.C235   355.8′2′0973   75-9575
ISBN 0-679-40126-1

Manufactured in the United States of America

Contents

The
Superwarriors

1

Whispering
Death

A favorite parable of mine, one which I have found useful to keep in mind while writing about the Defense Department and its research and development of weaponry, comes from Benjamin Franklin. It is titled: "How to Make a Striking Sundial, by which not only a Man's Family, but all his Neighbors for ten Miles round, may know what a Clock it is, when the Sun shines, without seeing the Dial." It goes like this:

Chuse an open Place in your yard or Garden, on which the Sun may shine all Day without any Impediment from Trees or Buildings. On the Ground mark out your Hour lines, as for a horizontal Dial, according to Art, taking Room enough for the Guns. On the Line for One O'Clock, place one Gun; on the Two O'Clock Line two Guns, and so of the rest. The Guns must all be charged with Powder, but Ball is unnecessary. Your Gnomon or Style must have twelve Burning Glasses annex't to it, and be so placed that the Sun shining through the Glasses, one after the other, shall cause the Focus or Burning Spot to fall on the Hour Line of One, for Example, at One O'Clock, and there kindle a Train of Gunpowder that shall fire one Gun. At Two O'Clock, a Focus shall fall on the Hour Line of Two, and kindle another Train that shall discharge two Guns successively: and so of the rest.

Note, There must be 78 Guns in all. Thirty-two Pounders will be the best for this Use; but 18 Pounders may do, and will cost less, as well as use less Powder, for nine Pounds of Powder will do for one Charge of each eighteen Pounder, whereas the Thirty-two Pounders would require for each Gun 16 Pounds.

Note also, That the chief Expense will be the Powder, for the Cannon, once bought, will, with Care, last 100 Years.

Note, moreover, that there will be a great Saving of Powder in Cloudy Days.

Kind Reader, Methinks I hear Thee say, That is indeed a good Thing to know how the Time Passes, but this Kind of Dial, notwithstanding the mentioned Savings, would be very Expensive; and the Cost greater than the Advantage. Thou art wise, my Friend, to be so considerate beforehand; some Fools would not have found out so much, till they had made the Dial and Try'd It.

Let all such learn that many a private and many a publick Project, are like this Striking Dial, great Cost for little Profit.

The curious thing about the long, nasty war in Vietnam was that it proved our weapons worked. Hardly anyone except the weapons makers and the military took note of this, and there was no way for the military and civilian chiefs of the Department of Defense to put it across to the public. Weapons, whether fighter planes, attack bombers, missiles, rifles, bayonets or clubs, are for killing the enemy. Vietnam probably was the only war in American history where killing the enemy never caught on with the American people, who could not get worked up about the Vietcong and the North Vietnamese regulars the way they had the Germans, the Japanese, or even the North Koreans and the Chinese, in wars gone by. In 1966 and 1967, when the United States was still optimistic about its chances of wearing down the enemy, Secretary of Defense Robert S. McNamara held weekly press briefings which he would begin by giving out the latest "body count" statistics. Four Vietcong for every one American. Five Vietcong for every one American. Nobody really believed these body counts, and even if they had, would have taken no solace from them. It was obvious that the war had soured.

By 1972, with American withdrawal well under way, Vietnam had become a nightmare to be forgotten. The less said about it, the better. The Pentagon, that tawny, squat command center beside the Potomac, was staffed by self-conscious, even sheepish, people. As the war had dragged on, year after year after year, the verve and the military bearing had been drained out of the place. My memory may be overly impressionistic, but I recalled the Pentagon as it had been in the early 1950s, during the Korean War and not long after World War II, when I had done a short tour there as a young officer. Military men and civilians alike strode the halls with a sense of purpose. They worked amid an aura of American giants and their heroic deeds. Eisenhower. Marshall. Patton. Bradley. Nimitz. King. Halsey. Forrestal. Lovett. MacArthur. Ridgeway. Van Fleet. Taylor. Gavin. Anzio. The Rhine. Remagen. North Africa. Sicily. Normandy. Coral Sea. Midway. Iwo Jima. Guadalcanal. Heartbreak Ridge. Pork Chop Hill. V-E Day. V-J Day. This atmosphere persisted even into the early 1960s, when the Cuban missile crisis reminded us that Thor can be comforting to have around, and when brisk Bob McNamara called cadence like a Secretary of Defense who knows how to fall out the troops. The military services didn't much like McNamara's drive to bring them more tightly under civilian control. But they acknowledged his command presence, and they did their work on the double. By the end of the 1960s, all this was gone. The Pentagon's "Hall of Heroes" might as well have contained a single-spaced display of old Congressional Records, for all the attention anyone paid to its name-plated galleries of military greats. Who could forget, who witnessed it, the spectacle of the Pentagon under siege in 1967, when companies of soldiers bivouacked in its halls in anticipation of a peace marchers' assault on the building? Now, the Pentagon was being called "Fort Futility," "The Puzzle Palace." All its weapons cost too much and were being built to line the pockets of the defense industry, or so the wisdom went. All its soldiers—except maybe for Lt. William Calley—were unknowns. We had broken our lance in Vietnam. Our military had become a disestablishment.

Representative Otis Pike, a New Yorker on the House Armed Services Committee, got to the heart of the matter: "The trouble that a lot of us seem to be having in rethinking a coherent defense posture really stems from the trouble we're having shaking off the spell of Camelot. Who can forget the exhilaration on hearing John F. Kennedy's great declaration: 'We shall pay any price, bear any burden, meet any hardship, support any friend, oppose any foe to assure the survival and success of liberty.' But that was 1961, and the ensuing decade has made it abundantly clear that we will *not* pay *any* price, we will *not* bear *any* burden, we will *not* meet *any* hardship, and we will most certainly *not* oppose *any* foe to assure the survival and success of liberty, at least as liberty is defined and practiced in Vietnam, Cambodia or, for that matter, Greece." Pike made the point that much of our weaponry had been devised—and was still being devised—for the kind of war, like Vietnam, that we would not fight again for a long time to come, if ever. "Our defense policies," he said, "don't accord with our diplomatic initiatives, and as time goes by, they seem to be diverging ever farther. What's a Joint Chief to do when he doesn't know from one day to the next on what continent he's to be fighting in defense of what kind of liberty—in jungle swamp, frozen tundra or high sierra, against sophisticated mechanized armies supported by nuclear weapons or guerrilla bands armed only with AK-47s? He's going to ask for more of everything, that's what he's going to do. We have looked backward for our threats, and it's time we looked forward. If we're going to look backward anywhere, let's look backward to the toughness and leanness and meanness of the military establishment we used to have—and can have again, if only some tough, mean people in the Pentagon and some tough, mean people in the defense industry and some tough, mean people in Congress would only have the guts to say 'No' once in a while."

It was difficult, at the time Pike spoke out, to find any people in top jobs at the Pentagon, let alone tough, mean ones. Melvin Laird, who had been Secretary of Defense for the four years of the first Nixon administration, was gone, claiming to have accomplished what he set out to do: "pacify" Vietnam and get our troops out of there. Along with Laird went nearly all the men in key second-level posts, including the bosses of the budget, of procurement and of research, and two of the three service secretaries. Unlike McNamara, Laird, often preoccupied with Vietnam, had given the services a fairly free hand to go their separate ways in pursuit of pet weapons projects without much supervision from above. To replace Laird, Presi-

dent Nixon appointed Elliot L. Richardson, who had performed competently as Undersecretary of State and as Secretary of Health, Education and Welfare, but who knew next to
nothing about the Defense Department and admitted it. In
three months, with the Watergate scandal skyrocketing
through the administration, Nixon plucked Richardson from
the Pentagon and made him Attorney General. At his final
press conference as Secretary of Defense, Richardson was
asked what he thought he had accomplished during his brief
tour. "Not a hell of a lot," he replied. Only five months later,
Richardson resigned as Attorney General after refusing Nixon's order that he fire Archibald Cox, the special prosecutor
whom Richardson had promised complete freedom in his
investigation of White House involvement in the Watergate
affair. Meanwhile, James R. Schlesinger had taken over at the
Pentagon. An economist by training, and with much experience in defense-related government leadership posts, Schlesinger was well prepared for his new job. Right off, he
emphasized that it was his duty, as Secretary of Defense, to
keep the national security up to snuff, and leave the peacemak-
ing to others, who got paid for it. It was proper posture. But
it seemed, at the time, out of step.

Peace was sprouting. An American President had gone to
Peking, heralding a new era of social, political and economic
relations with a nation we had feared and ostracized since
World War II, and which we had fought in Korea. Strategic
Arms Limitation Talks (SALT) with the Soviet Union had
been fruitful. The American President and the Soviet Secre-
tary-General were practically champagne-drinking buddies,
toasting détente. The Russians and the Chinese were openly
more hostile to one another than either was to the United
States, which had come to look upon both more as prospective
partners in trade, less as opponents in the field. The irony of
this struck me forcefully at Central Intelligence Agency headquarters in McLean, Virginia, just outside Washington. Talking with CIA economists, I felt as if I were turning into Alice:
clearly, the agency was spending more and more time studying
and worrying about the plans and pursuits of our military
allies—Japan and the Common Market countries of Europe—
in world trade. In the context of our worsening balance of
trade and payments, these countries, highly competitive with

us in the mercantile world, had become, in a very real sense, our enemies. Our national security was increasingly being equated with our economic health, and they—far more than the Russians or the Chinese—were being regarded as threats to that health. I had known many CIA men personally and professionally for two decades, and this was the first time I had heard any of them speak openly of China and the Soviet Union as prospective helpmates in any sort of endeavor. Did the cold war have a future? Sure, the CIA would always keep an eye on the missiles and the marching orders of Moscow and Peking. But now, early in 1973, the watchword was wheat, not weapons; détente, not defense. Put Vietnam and the cold war behind us. Peace. Let us never have another Christmas like the one we had just gone through.

During the twelve days of Christmas, 1972, eighteen years after the American people had thrilled to our gallant stand against the Germans at Bastogne in quite a different kind of war, savage U.S. air strikes were perpetrated on North Vietnam. The U.S. Air Force, trying to bomb Hanoi back to bargaining for peace, unlimbered giant B-52s by the hundreds to pound military targets in the Hanoi-Haiphong area and the Red River Delta. President Nixon was lashing the North Vietnamese for not having delivered on a peace agreement which his agent, Henry Kissinger, had promised the American people during the Presidential campaign of the previous autumn. It was dirty going. B-52s were being blown out of the skies by surface-to-air (SAM) missiles made in Russia. There were reports of many civilians killed, homes destroyed. Americans winced, turned their heads and hollered to halt it, to get the hell out of Vietnam and, if it made us feel any better, to take the advice of Senator George Aiken of Vermont and simply say we'd won. Congress became bellicose toward the White House. Senator William Saxbe of Ohio said Nixon "must have taken leave of his senses." The *Los Angeles Times,* reflecting the mood of much of the American press, editorialized: "There sits the President, consulting with few, explaining to no one, directing against a small Asian country a rain of death and terror that to the whole world makes the United States of America appear a barbarian gone mad." Now, of course, we know it was not Nixon sitting in isolation. Henry Kissinger has surfaced as the smart bomb Santa Claus, according to recent Watergate testimony.

Making my reportorial rounds at the Pentagon during that period, I headed one day along the third-floor corridor, over-looking the building's Potomac River entrance, which housed top Air Force generals. I noticed, for the hundredth time, the photographic display of flyers who had been awarded the Medal of Honor, most of them posthumously, in American wars. I was struck once again by the difference between those who had been honored in World Wars I and II, and in Korea, and those who had earned the medal in Vietnam. The former were household names; the latter, well . . . it had been that kind of war, and it was still that kind of war, nearly eight years after we had made the plunge.

Brigadier General Robert Ginsburgh, an air warrior of scholarly bent and soft voice, received me, and we talked about the bombing of the north. He was frustrated. Sure, it hurts to lose the B-52s, and God knows, no one wants to bomb North Vietnam back to the Stone Age, but why do the press, the Congress and the public keep on emphasizing the negative? Why don't they look on the positive side for a change, and take some pride in military achievements? The bombings, from the Air Force viewpoint, were a resounding success. Indeed, as the Air Force saw it, Vietnam had vindicated air weapons and tactics. All those hundreds of millions (those billions, if you want to take it back far enough) spent on weapons research and development had been proved worth the candle in combat, the only crucible where you can ever tell for sure. This should have been reassuring to the American people. But they weren't being told about it. And they probably didn't even care. We had won the war, damn it, and our weapons, the weapons McNamara had been banking on 'way back when, had finally done it for us, once we decided to go all out and use them the way they should be used. The point, however much you may have hated the war, was well taken. Let us look back.

In April 1972, the North Vietnamese struck south in their first full-scale onslaught since the Tet offensive of 1968. This strike required huge tonnages of gasoline, shells and trucks to keep tanks, heavy artillery, flak batteries and mobile radar units in action on the move. But now, for the first time, the United States had new weapons that stripped the cover of darkness and camouflage from the armor and artillery in the field, and from the truck convoys running from Haiphong to below the Demilitarized Zone. Air Force and Army helicopter

gunships went into combat equipped with electronic and infrared sensors which enabled them to zero in on truck and tank
motors running at night. Bombs guided by lasers and television signals knocked out bridges, railroad lines and supply
dumps with sharpshooter precision. Until this time, pumping
stations along the enemy's fuel pipelines into the south had
been invincible in the protection of antiaircraft batteries.
Now, the flak counted for nothing. American fighter-bombers
and attack bombers no longer needed to fly through it to get
at the pumping stations. They launched their laser-guided
bombs from outside the flak belts. In a matter of days, the
stations were destroyed. U.S. aircraft also sowed North Vietnamese ports with new types of mines which could sense the
surface passage of enemy ships with unbelievable accuracy.
They choked off the flow of Chinese, Russian and Eastern
European supplies by sea. When freighters from these Com-
munist-bloc countries anchored outside the minefields and unloaded their cargos into lighter, smaller boats, U.S. air strikes
and naval shelling blasted the boats before they could reach the
cover of estuaries along the North Vietnam coast. By early
autumn of 1972, Hanoi was up against economic and military
disaster. Virtually all the tanks, artillery and mobile radar
units had been destroyed. U.S. air cover had made their replacement impossible. Not only that—stockpiles of SAM missiles had been exhausted. At the beginning of the offensive,
SAM batteries had fired up to two hundred missiles a day. In
the end, they were firing only sparingly, at targets they
thought were sure. So Hanoi began suing for peace, and Kissinger passed the word to the American people, prematurely,
that the suitor was serious. With Hanoi in deep trouble, China
and the Soviet Union temporarily put aside their own grim
concerns about the warlike intentions of one another and
cooperated in a grand-scale, overland resupply of the armies of
the north. Soviet ships delivered the goods around the clock to
Chinese ports. Freight trains with Russian and Chinese equipment clogged rail lines through southeastern China, heading
for Hanoi. When U.S. bombers knocked out rail lines in the
north, the supplies were transferred to trucks and sampans. By
November, Hanoi felt sinewy again. Peace negotiations turned
into nitpicking, and then into nothing. Kissinger had to take
to TV again to tell Americans that peace was "at hand" no

more. Hanoi's negotiators left the conference table, probably figuring on some U.S. military reaction but counting on the thick monsoon weather that blankets the north in the winter to work against any precision bombing there for months to come. And then, coursing above the weather, came the B-52s. From first light to twilight, for twelve days, with only a twenty-four hour respite at Christmas itself, they hammered at Hanoi and Haiphong, unloading twenty-four tons of bombs on each and every one of their one thousand raids. The laser-guided iron bombs plunged from on high to bull's-eyes nearly all the time. It was not the indiscriminate, murderous "carpet bombing" that its critics said it was, but Air Force protestations were drowned out in the antibombing emotion back home.

In the first few days of the twelve, the toll of B-52s was high, a dozen downed. North Vietnamese SAM crews, probably the best (Russian) trained and certainly the most combat-tested anywhere, picked up impulses from the electronic equipment aboard the bombers which was designed to jam the SAMs' radar. By triangulating these electronic emissions from the bombers, the SAM crews could compute the bombers' flight paths and then fire salvos of SAMs, sometimes a hundred at once, along the bombers' courses. Radar stations remote from the battles also relayed bomber-tracking data to SAM crews whose radar had been jammed. These tactics attained peak effectiveness in the third and fourth days of the bombing; six B-52s were downed.

Then the bombers turned it around. They gave up the tactic of approaching targets in continuous waves and thundered in, instead, from different points around the compass, at various altitudes. This foiled the defenders' practice of computing flight paths and firing salvos along them. B-52 jamming techniques also were improved. Fighter-bombers were sent north, hurtling through the wintertime murk at sea level, to savage the SAM sites between the sorties by B-52s from on high. By the sixth day, the bombers clearly had won the air. None were lost on that day, for the second day in a row, and losses thereafter were only random. By December 28, the blue yonder no longer was wild for the B-52s. Hanoi's radar had been demolished. MiG-21 interceptors could not take off from shattered airfields. SAM batteries lay in ruins. The industrial capacity of the north was gone, along with power plants and their transmission grids. Rail marshaling yards lay pocked and gnarled. The air force amassed hundreds upon hundreds of aerial photos authenticating all this damage, but made little use of them. Americans were in no mood for them, and would have taken no comfort. Inside Fortress Pentagon, however, there was grim satisfaction that our weapons and tactics had shown their worth. Even that laughing stock, the F-III . . .

In the early 1960s, Robert McNamara persuaded the Air Force and the Navy to buy—grudgingly—his notion that both services should use the same fighter-bomber. Commonality for Cost Effectiveness. The plane was called the TFX (the X being a designation for a plane in the experimental stage) and it was being promoted by General Dynamics, its builder, as the hottest bird to come along in the jet age. It was the first swing-winger: its wings could be swept back for greater speed in the dash, or forward for fancier wheeling around the sky, depending on the pilot's needs of the moment. It also came equipped with an electronic device called TFR—Terrain-Following Radar—which was supposed to enable the pilot to fly blind at ground-hugging altitudes, even in the filthiest weather, keeping his hand off the stick and letting the radar's computer plot his path up and down hillsides (pilots call it "skiing") on his way to target. But the plane, by now called the F-III, quickly acquired a reputation for gremlins. The Navy's version was too heavy to operate off carriers, and was canceled. The Air Force model developed airframe problems, mostly involving metal fatigue, and had a tendency to crash. General George S. Brown, then the CO of the Air Force Systems Command and now Chairman of the Joint Chiefs of Staff, cited the F-III as a prime example of asking for trouble by putting technology into service without fully understanding it: "The Watts steam engine, for example, was in operation for a full seventy-five years, powering the Industrial Revolution, before Clausius and Kelvin developed the laws of thermodynamics that explained its behavior. Once that was understood, all types of heat engines could be designed with improvements in both effectiveness and efficiency. Even today, such artifacts as rocket motors, aircraft engines, load-bearing structures, electronic circuits and other products of modern technology operate quite effectively without a full understanding of all the chemistry, physics and other basic sciences involved. They could be made to operate more efficiently, and be designed a great deal closer to the optimum, if we *had* such understanding. This in itself is a powerful argument for strong and sustained support of scientific research. A convincing case can be made that our experience with the F-III would have been far different if our basic knowledge of metal fatigue, fracture mechanics and metallurgy in general had been more advanced."

The Air Force kept the F-III in production because it was the only new bomber around. The B-52 production line had long since been shut down, and the B-1 bomber, envisaged as the eventual replacement for the B-52, was still an engineer's dream, many years from production. The bomber model of the F-III could range the Atlantic without refueling, fill up from a flying tanker, and proceed to east of the Urals, with a nuclear payload. Its metal-fatigue difficulties had been worked out. The only time it made news, however, was when it crashed, and it had become known as a nice idea with no future. But wait. It still had TFR, and a scenario was building in Indochina . . .

In September 1972, the 474th Tactical Fighter Wing ferried its forty-eight F-IIIs to Takhli Air Base, Thailand, and immediately went into action over North Vietnam, testing the tactical theory that enemy aircraft defenses could be penetrated at long range by fighter-bombers flying too fast and too low to be hit. The story went around that when one of the F-III pilots was asked, on arrival in Thailand, whether the 474th had "smart bombs," he replied: "No, but we've got smart airplanes." Right off, his words seemed to boomerang. Of the first two F-IIIs sent into combat, one failed to return. The reaction ran true to form. Headlines proclaimed "Another F-III lost," this time in action, a setting which might have been considered conducive to the loss of any other plane. But this one was an F-III. The notion had taken hold that F-IIIs were foredoomed to crash wherever they went. Even Seventh Air Force Headquarters had grown skittish about it.

In the first few weeks of combat, F-III crews routinely kept radio silence after they got airborne, to keep the enemy unaware that they were heading north. But by November, with F-III missions being intensified, and after a few had been shot down, Seventh Air Force ordered a change of radio procedure. Radio silence had precluded clues as to why the F-IIIs had been lost. Had they been hit? Or had they simply fallen out of the sky? So the F-III pilots were ordered to check in by radio at position points along their routes to the north. They dutifully did so for a while. But they soon determined that the radio checks distracted them from the business at hand, especially as they flew nearer and nearer to target, and they began ignoring the order. Through an article in *Air Force* magazine, Captain Jackie Crouch spoke for his fellow pilots: "We never could figure why the generals went straight up when an F-III failed to return. Navy could lose an A-6, which was just as expensive and almost as sophisticated in navigation, radar and bomb delivery as we are, yet nothing was said. The same attitudes were evident when Air Force or Navy F-4s went down, almost every day. Even with the B-52s, when they began hitting Hanoi, those shoot-downs were more or less accepted. But let an F-III be lost, and everybody seemed to go right through the roof. It wasn't realistic."

By the completion of the heavy bombing of the north, in January 1973, the F-IIIs had piled up an astounding record. They had flown 3,500 sorties, each dropping salvoes of twelve to sixteen bombs at a time. Their accuracy was nearly as good as that of the planes which had dropped the "smart bombs," guided by TV or laser. Lone wolves, too. Lethal. Time after time, one F-III was all it took to punish SAM sites, airfields, bridges, railroad yards, ammunition dumps beyond repair. Only once in four months did weather cause an F-III mission to be scrubbed—and that, during one of the fiercest monsoon rains. Through it all, only six F-IIIs were lost: one-sixth of 1 percent of all the F-IIIs exposed to enemy fire. You can't hit 'em if you can't see 'em. The North Vietnamese called the F-III "whispering death." If you've ever watched a fighter jet approach at high speed, on the deck, you'll know why. All you hear is the rush, the whisper, of air into the engines, building in intensity to a whistle, and then to the roar of the exhaust as the fighter whooshes by. And the sudden blast of the afterburners as the F-III hauled up out of there.

"Think," said Captain Crouch in *Air Force* magazine, "about flying around in daylight and good weather only two hundred feet above the ground, and going up and down over hills and into valleys, keeping this height. Now, do this at night, in mountains and in heavy cloud, when you can't see anything outside the cockpit. That is really, really exciting, even without the enemy threat. It takes real discipline to come up over those mountains, as we did at night, out on top of the cloud layer in the moonlight. We'd see those jagged peaks all around us, poking through the cloud tops, and we'd have to put the nose down back into that mist. And as we went down, the moonlight would fade and the clouds would get darker, and we'd know we were descending below those peaks and depending on our radar and our autopilots—and with Hanoi coming up. One night, when the weather was very bad, I was in cloud for the last eleven minutes before bombs away—and that means at the lowest levels of the whole flight, going up and down hills and keeping our clearance, still at two hundred to two hundred and fifty feet above those obstructions. We didn't see a thing outside the cockpit, not even after the bombs left us. For me, this thing was really remarkable. Even now, I can't explain how fantastic it was, what extraordinary instrumentation we have, what systems. The confidence I gained in the airplane—it made a believer out of me. I'll tell anyone in the Air Force that, given a choice on a night strike of going in high or going in low, I'll go in low every time. And I'll go anywhere in an F-111."

Now comes a twist in the saga of the F-111, a change of direction by the Air Force of the sort which leads the public to lose confidence in the certainty and steadiness of weapons development. If Captain Crouch was ready to go anywhere in an F-111, the Air Force wasn't about to let him. In its budget for fiscal 1974, beginning in June 1973, the Air Force included not a dime for buying any future F-111s. This meant that the production line at the General Dynamics plant in Fort Worth, Texas, would be shut down in 1974, after current F-111 orders, running at a rate of only one a month, were ended. There were howls in Congress, mostly from powerful Texas politicians in key spots on the Armed Services and Appropriations committees. They were heeded. Congress forced the Air Force to take enough money to keep F-111 production going at least into 1975. Among those who lit into the Air Force was Representative Samuel S. Stratton of New York, veteran member of the House Armed Services Committee. Stratton is a former Navy commander, and is regarded as among Capitol Hill's staunchest allies of the Pentagon. He'll vote for nearly everything the military wants, but on occasion, he gets his dander up. He had no personal or political stake in saving the F-III, so his dudgeon rang true. "What is most appalling about this," he said, "is that the Air Force made its announcement at the very time that our committee was seriously deliberating whether to come up with the money to keep the F-III line open for another year, until the Pentagon gets around to making a final decision on putting the B-I into production. The Defense Department people knew what was going on in the committee, so this is just plain arrogant defiance. The real truth of the matter is that the Air Force is so desperate to build the B-I that it is trying to leave us with no alternative by the time 1975 rolls around and Congress has to make a decision on approving or disapproving B-I production. So the Air Force has to kill off the F-III right now. If there is anything that inflates defense budgets these days, it's this weird logic that you should abandon weapons systems which finally have been made to work, and sink all your billions into dream weapons of the future. And they generally prove to involve costly overruns and all kinds of operating bugs. You watch. Congress is going to make the Air Force keep on building the F-III."

Stratton was right about that. Congress not only stuffed 200 million unwanted F-III dollars into the Air Force wallet, it added about the same amount to salvage still another production line of a veteran attack bomber which the Air Force had planned to scratch from its supermarket list in the year ahead. This plane was the LTV Corp. A-7D Corsair. Like the F-III, it had performed surprisingly well in Vietnam in a role for which it had not been designed. So well, in fact, that it embarrassed the Air Force's long-cherished plans for a plane called the AX. The AX story shows some of the pitfalls along the tortuous trail of a weapon system from inception to production. Forget about cost. There can be enough other troubles. But again, let us go back.

The problem, from the beginning, was air power in close support of ground troops. During the Korean War, I was trained at Fort Benning, Georgia, as a platoon leader. I recall our instructors, officers and noncoms who had been in combat, telling us horror stories about the infantry calling in the Air Force to bomb and strafe enemy troops, either in support of an assault or in defense of a position, only to cringe and take casualties, all too often, from the misdirected strikes of jets which zipped into the fray too fast to be accurate. When the Air Force, in 1967, decided to develop a jet tailored specifically to the support of infantry, it sounded like a good idea. There hadn't been such a plane since the advent of the jet age. Prior to that, propeller-driven planes did the job because they were slow, their pilots could circle the battlefield and pick out targets, and they were fairly accurate. But they had become too vulnerable. They simply could not go up against jet interceptors or the antiaircraft missiles and cannon that came along in the 1960s. In 1970, the Air Force pushed ahead with its plan to build a jet for the job, the AX. It contracted with Fairchild Corp. and Northrop Corp. for competitive prototypes of a heavily armored jet, bristling with machine guns, cannon and ten thousand pounds of bombs, loitering over battlefields up to two hours, delivering thunderous firepower on call of the infantry. The companies were told to work full speed. The winner could reasonably expect a production contract for maybe 750 planes, at $2 million or more apiece. The Air Force was urgent. It was running behind. Early in the Vietnam War, the Army, with its helicopter gunships, had assumed a big chunk of responsibility for the dirty work down low with the riflemen. This threatened the Air Force with loss of a mission which traditionally had been its own, and which the Army long had wanted to preempt. Northrop and Fairchild responded to Air Force prodding. In 1972, after "flyoff" competition between the AX prototypes, the Air Force chose the Fairchild model, called the A-10 now that it was to go into production. Immediately the flak hit the fan.

William P. Clements, Jr., a Texas oil-drilling multimillionaire who had been Deputy Secretary of Defense for less than a month, blew up at his chieftains for choosing the Fairchild plane and for drawing up a production contract without first having given him time to assess the situation. Clements was especially upset that the chieftains—a panel of high-ranking Defense Department officials called the Defense Systems Acquisition Review Council (DSARC)—had not waited to be briefed on the department's own estimate of what the A-10 program would cost. With good reason, Clements did not fully trust the Air Force cost estimate, on which the production approval had been based. He wanted it cross-checked by the Defense Department's (meaning, civilian cost analysts') figures. Air Force cost estimates had fallen into the "Can You Top This?" category of incredibility ever since the $2-billion-dollar overrun of the Lockheed C-5 transport-cargo plane in 1971. To make sure he would not be the fall guy in any more Air Force budgetary tomfoolery, Clements forbade the service to sign its contract with Fairchild while he took two months to go over every fact and figure. Finally, he said okay. Costs looked better than those of most other big weapons programs, in fact. Fairchild was commended.

Now that the A-10 seemed safely on its way into the arsenal, the Air Force told Congress that it would need no more A-7s. It already had more than four hundred of them, and it planned to restore those planes to their original mission: bombing *behind* enemy lines, not *on* enemy lines. But Congress wouldn't play. From Texas, home of the A-7, and from Capitol Hill, where the powerful Texas lawmakers came again to the fore, a campaign was mounted to shoot down the A-10. Why sink billions into a new plane, so the argument went, when you already have one which has proved it can do the same job, even though it wasn't designed for that job?

Once again, here was an instance of a weapons system—the A-7—confounding the Air Force with its effectiveness. A-7s had been deployed to Vietnam in 1972. Between September of that year and the following March, they flew 6,500 combat sorties. Only two were lost. Pressed into the close-support chore, they struck their targets nearly all the time. Forward air controllers reported an average "miss" distance of only ten meters in their attacks. They also achieved what the Air Force calls "a high secondary explosion rate" in their pinpoint bombing of supply dumps and depots. What made it possible? An electronic target-selection and bomb-guidance system which enabled A-7 pilots to approach targets at 600 miles an hour (half again the speed of the A-10 on the attack), release bombs without poking the plane down into the thick of antiaircraft fire, and get out safely. This bombing system was developed after the Air Force first got its idea, back in 1967, for the close-support plane which was to become, in 1973, the A-10. And it may have rendered the A-10 obsolete while still embryonic.

The F-111 and A-10 affairs are among many examples of the services seeming to fall all over themselves—and over each other—in a game of weapons, weapons, who's got the weapons.

The Navy, the Army—and the Marine Corps, too—often appear to be more concerned, helter-skelter, with outdoing one another in rushing new weapons into their inventories, and in protecting their individual budgets and prerogatives, than they are with cooperating on a mix of the most effective things that sail, fly and shoot. Service pride helps explain the fierce insistence of the Air Force, Navy, Army and Marines that each have its own close-support aircraft. The Defense Department has gone along with them, claiming that the attack planes and chopper gunships spread through all the services complement one another and do not duplicate missions. But the ranks of believers have been dwindling. Senator Barry Goldwater of Arizona, reserve Air Force general and strong Pentagon supporter, complained: "We have four tactical air forces. . . . Our last figures show a total inventory cost of around $13 billion, and I think a total inventory that would do just as good a job could be had for under $5 billion."

The notion persists—and grows—that there are too many weapons for now and maybe too few for the future, that they all cost too much, and that an awful lot of them do pretty much the same jobs, with slight variations. Comptroller General Elmer Staats, who runs the Pentagon-watchdogging General Accounting Office, had this to say: "Even though the public doesn't fully understand the complexities of modern weapons, it knows that they are exceedingly expensive and that many mistakes have been made, resulting in enormous waste of their taxes. This has led to a credibility gap of sizable proportions. The public's confidence in the ability of government and industry to provide modern weapons without excessive waste has been shaken." GAO, a sprawling agency of lawyers, accountants and cost analysts, has called the turn on many a weapons cost overrun. In recent years, it has been engaged in a running battle with the military over waste, not only of money but of weapons themselves. The Pentagon has come to regard GAO as one hell of a pest, or worse, peeking here and probing there every time some congressman or senator wants it to pick apart a particular weapon program. In 1973, for the first time, GAO stood back and surveyed the whole wide world of weapons systems. It reported 116 of them in development at an estimated eventual cost—probably conservative—of $153 billion. This figure did not include production costs. At the time,

Congress had appropriated only $89 billion of the total, and had no clear idea of what the remainder might involve. On reading the GAO report, Representative William Dickinson, an Alabaman on the House Armed Services Committee, sighed: "We can't afford war anymore. We can't afford the technology we're capable of developing."

Like Dickinson, the public was becoming aware of a frightening fact: soaring costs of all new weapons projects shrink dramatically the number of planes, ships, tanks and missiles which the Pentagon can buy and field in any future war. They also shrink the dollars available for development of the whole new family of weapons—robot planes and, very likely, laser guns—which could well be imperative. A Senate Armed Services Committee report laid it out: "If the geometric cost increase for weapon systems is not sharply reversed, then even significant increases in the defense budget may not insure the force levels required for our national security. . . . The present rising trend of manpower and weapon system unit costs means that we will soon see either striking increases in defense budgets, a sharp decline in force levels and readiness, or reform of the weapon system development and procurement process. If defense budgets are to remain more or less constant, as now seems likely, and consume an ever smaller part of the nation's resources, then the present development and procurement policies are no longer open to us. They only point the way to burdensome increases in defense spending, inadequate forces for defense, or to both of these unacceptable alternatives." In the year that followed this report, the Pentagon budget increased by $5 billion—to $85 billion—over that of the previous January, 1972. And the grab bag of weapons goodies just seemed to spill out all over.

The reasons for weapons confusion at the Pentagon really go much deeper than service pride. Inside each service, factions run riot. Admiral Hyman Rickover, the Navy's curmudgeon nuclear propulsion boss, has warred for years with the surface-ship admirals, whom he accuses of "wishing that submarines would just go away" so they could lay hands on more millions for their own kinds of ships. The bomber men in the Air Force feud with the fighter men for bigger pieces of the pie. Both types disdain the proponents of pilotless planes, and work against them, too. But the principal pulling and hauling takes place between the Air Force and the Navy, much of it centered in research and development of weapons. Sooner or later, this will have to be brought under control. McNamara had a shot at it. But Vietnam distracted him, and then defeated him.

The Air Force has been pushing since the early 1960s for a new, front-line intercontinental bomber to replace the B-52, which will become obsolete in the mid-1980s. First came the B-70. McNamara shot it down so fast that the prototype B-70 was relegated to the Air Force museum at Wright Patterson Air Base in Ohio practically right off the assembly line. Up popped plans for the B-1. None too soon. With its land-based Minuteman missiles becoming ever more vulnerable to the multiple-warhead Soviet ICBMs, the Air Force regards the bomber as its last bastion against the Navy's challenge to become the service primarily responsible for the nation's strategic missile deterrent. Air Force generals promote the B-1—in the halls of Congress and in the sanctums of the Defense Department's civilian chiefs—with a fervor bordering on desperation. Building $80-million bombers in an age of submarine and land-launched intercontinental missiles makes little sense to many lawmakers. What makes better sense to a growing number of them is the Navy's concept of strategic-strike submarines.

Shortly after Schlesinger took charge at the Pentagon, he talked about the changing missions of the services and the squabbling among them. "I hope to get the services to look at the longer view more than they have," he said. "They are different today than they were before the Vietnamese war. Take the Air Force. It was formed in 1947, and it has this dandy little toy—an atomic bomb that somebody developed two years earlier. Two years after the Air Force is formed the Soviets detonate something, and people go into a minor panic. Then the next year—in the interim, by the way, they run the Berlin airlift—then the next year, you have Korea. The next year, the Soviets—before we do—have a workable hydrogen bomb. By this time everybody is in a panic, and so the defense budgets just escalate. The Air Force comes away with 46 percent of the budget—the upstart service casting the senior services into shame. The national strategy is Air Force strategy. Massive retaliation. You step across the line in Iran, and by God, you lose every city in the Soviet Union. It's not a hell of a lot more sophisticated than that. If you believe in massive retaliation, then certainly this is a plausible threat during a period that the Soviets don't have a counterdeterrent. You really don't need anything else. The Navy is sort of irrelevant in the time frame we're talking about. But then you come along to 1960, and you begin to see the rudiments of the Soviet intercontinental strike capability, and that's beginning to shake up the Air Force doctrine. Then Kennedy brings Curtis LeMay on as chief of the Air Staff, and he's not going to change his view of the world dramatically just because he's moved from Omaha [Strategic Air Command Headquarters] to Washington, right? So you get a built-in fight within the Kennedy administration. The years go by, and gradually some of the importance of maintaining general purpose forces—as opposed to strategic forces—is perceived by the Air Force. They fight their second war since the atomic bomb with all their aircraft, developed as nuclear bombers, being used to drop iron bombs, including the B-52s, which would have been regarded as sacrilege in an earlier period of time. And they have been cuffed around, rather badly, by McNamara. By the end of the 1960s, you've got an entirely different Air Force in terms of its fundamental attitudes. It's bedraggled in many ways. It's lost a lot of steam. But I think that it's coming back now in a very dramatic way."

Pressures against the B-1 prompted the Air Force, in 1973, to go one step beyond. Acknowledging the vulnerability of the hard-silo Minuteman missiles, the Air Force had proposed making Minutemen mobile, on the ground. Nothing doing. So why not try to have the best of both worlds? The new concept: "M-X," for "Missile System X." It would involve the launching of intercontinental missiles from aircraft. Actually, the idea had been around for years, thwarted, however, by poor prospects for hitting targets. But advances in electronics, sisters to those which made the F-111 a-radar-wizard fighter-bomber and the A-7 a super-sharpshooter attack plane, had come together in an airborne ballistic missile-guidance system of potentially pinpoint accuracy. *Air Force* magazine called the embryonic M-X "the missile system for the Year 2000." Lieutenant General Otto Glasser, then Air Force deputy chief of staff for research and development, told the magazine that if, in the past, the Air Force had not put sufficient emphasis on air-mobile missile systems, "then we must attribute this to the only defect in Air Force thinking that we might be guilty of —our concern about cost and, therefore, the desire to incrementally and inexpensively improve what we already have, rather than go after brand new, completely innovative systems such as the Navy's Trident submarine." Glasser was begging the question somewhat. Even laymen have wondered for a long time why the Air Force did not explore combining long-range missiles with long-range, high-flying heavyweights such as the C-5. In fact, the concept had caught the fancy, years ago, of even some of the toughest Capitol Hill critics of the intercontinental bomber. If the Air Force had made a hard decision to explore the idea in the 1960s, chances are that its exploration would have led much more swiftly to the development of the very guidance systems which now make the concept feasible. As is so often the case in defense research planning, the tail chased the dog. The gut reason the Air Force was slow to get into airborne ballistic missiles was the feeling among many of its senior officers that this would detract from efforts to push the B-1. Not until the B-1 began to get hurt anyway did they move. They grew up in a world of fighters and bombers, the stuff of pilot legends, of aces. They do not want to let go of that world, and they sometimes rationalize its reality. They have never been all that attached to missiles. (Hell, even the Army has missiles. You give missiles names like Minuteman or Titan, which are kind of defense-neutral, but you name planes Phantom, Black Widow, Tomcat, Eagle, Thunder, Lightning, Crusader, Sabre, which stand for speed, spunk, superiority). The Air Force generals also have had in hand for several years the technology, based on computers and electro-optics, to turn pilotless planes into attack bombers, even fighters. They did not turn on this technology. The reason, again, was partly romantic. But now, like it or not, the Air Force must doff its crushed cap and go forward with the electronics which can give the humdrum drone a brain of its own—and a capacity for performance in the air unlimited by the inhibiting physical presence of a human pilot.

Perhaps the Pentagon can be pardoned for getting bogged down in conventional weaponry and for not having concentrated on weapons which could revolutionize warfare. Sometimes it is hard to believe the weapons we already have, to say nothing of the weapons we will see in the later years of this century. After all, existing weapons are based on technologies which were unknown, or barely perceived, only a generation ago. World War II was fought with reciprocating engine aircraft. They were guided by a new invention—radar, which relied on vacuum tube computers, marvels of the 1940s, museum pieces of the 1970s. Our micro-circuited radars of today can see over the horizon, steer a supersonic F-111 through a thicket. The atomic bomb that ended World War II was a crude pipsqueak alongside the hydrogen horrors which nest with today's Minutemen. Our guidance systems today can take men to the moon, with never a miss, our missiles to Moscow, with their margin of error measured in feet, not miles. Our bombing systems can make a fighter-bomber pilot an expert marksman at Mach 2. Our nuclear submarines can range under the seas, never surfacing, for months on end. Our fighter planes fly at two and a half times the speed of sound. The Navy's newest, the $20-million F-14 Tomcat, carries six computer-guided Phoenix missiles which it can fire simultaneously at six different targets, ranging ahead at various speeds, distances and altitudes, and hit them all, all at once. In one test over the Pacific Missile Range, an F-14 Phoenix struck a supersonic drone 100 miles distant. The Tomcat was flying at 40,000 feet when it fired the Phoenix. The Phoenix arced to 100,000 feet on its deadly course to the target drone, which was simulating the Soviet "Blinder" bomber. The new Air Force fighter, the $12-million F-15 Eagle, has neither the range nor the long-range striking power of the Tomcat. But with its highly advanced, experimental engine, the Eagle is almost certainly the swiftest, tightest-turning interceptor in the air. On takeoff, it can stand up on its tail and go out of sight before you blink twice. Its Sparrow missiles, no slouches either, are high-average hitters up to 70 miles.

Still, the impression persists that weapons are nothing but trouble. The events of two weeks in August 1973 lent themselves to that impression. The engine for the F-15 blew up in a 150-hour endurance run at Pratt & Whitney's ground-test chamber in West Palm Beach, Florida. The Pentagon announced that a special management team was being set up to investigate what was wrong with the B-1 prototype construction at Rockwell International's plant in California. And Congressional testimony revealed that the Navy's submarine-launched Poseidon ICBM had been failing at an unusually high rate in tests throughout the summer. All these malfunctions eventually were overcome. But like many others before them, in the development and testing of many other weapons systems, they left their mark on public confidence. And if you believe that there are too many of them for today's national security, but not enough of the right kinds of them for tomorrow's, then they may all cost too much, collectively and individually—the cost measured beyond dollars.

Some outright failures are, of course, inevitable. The routes to space or to national security are strewn with the rubble of ambitious technical enterprises which preoccupied, for years and years, enormous energies of America's best scientists and engineers, and cost billions—the B-70, the Manned Orbiting Laboratory (which came back in another form, and which still has the technological seeds of a superweapon), the nuclear airplane, DynaSoar, the Skybolt missile, the Main Battle Tank, the Cheyenne helicopter, to name but a few. These have been magnets of Congressional and public criticism, and have contributed to the pervasiveness of the notion that nothing really works and nobody really cares, just so long as the military and industrial maws are fed and their managers, wedded in unholy alliance, get fat in the nuptial. The truth is a long way from that.

Still more provocative, however, is the notion that even the weapons which seem wondrous today may be obsolete tomorrow morning. Dr. John S. Foster, Jr., worries a lot about that. If Foster worries, maybe we all should worry. For nearly eight years, he was in charge of the Defense Directorate of Research and Engineering (DDR&E), which innovates and supervises the research and development of weapons, and coordinates the services' research shops. Foster's critics charged that while he did a good job keeping Capitol Hill aware of the need for research dollars, he allowed himself to become too preoccupied with Vietnam. He may have had good reason. When he came to the Pentagon in 1965, Vietnam had, in his words, "sneaked up on our technology" and had posed a wide range of new requirements for fighting guerrillas. It came as a shock to a nation accustomed to regarding its technology as omnipotent that the U.S. arsenal did not contain the gadgetry needed just to find Vietcong infiltrators. Radar and mine detectors worked well enough in the open, but not in the jungle. How, for instance, did you detect cobras tied by their tails in tunnels, booby traps hung from trees, thousands of bicycles wheeling Vietcong supplies along narrow trails under cover of triple-canopied jungles, constantly moving targets that defied U.S. photo-reconnaissance planes? Foster managed to meet the Vietnam challenge—but at a high price in money and use of U.S. research talent. Vietnam R&D funds stood at some $70 million when he took over. He pushed them up to ten times that amount, annually, even though his total budget remained fairly constant at about $8 billion a year, and bought less with every passing year. Apart from Vietnam research, Foster's biggest problem lay in allocating research money and emphasis between two priorities: improving on existing strategic systems and development of an entirely new generation of weapons. Some critics said he put too much emphasis on product improvement and systems development, not enough on making big leaps in weaponry, such as the previous ones from planes to missiles, from fission bomb to fusion bomb. It is not enough, the argument ran, to be satisfied with a better Minuteman or a better Poseidon. We needed to intensify our work on lasers, robot planes, nuclear propulsion of aircraft, airborne missiles. We needed to think far out, and be willing to risk a whole lot more unproductive research. Foster deeply resented charges that he had permitted defense R&D to rest on a technological plateau. But he was stuck, pretty much, with a nondefense. There was plenty of esoteric research going on under his wing, but much of it was superclassified, and he could not make speeches about it. One such project was "Strat X," which led to the Trident submarine.

Foster left DDR&E in 1973 to become a vice-president of TRW Inc., a top defense contractor. He had served in two administrations—one Democratic, one Republican—and under five different Defense Secretaries. He believed he had done a good job, but he had grown weary of it. And he was uneasy. In his final testimony before the House Armed Services Committee, Foster delivered a grim message: "I am seriously concerned that within the next several years we may be faced with one or more Soviet technological advances which will change the balance of security, and for which we will have no immediate counteraction." He posed two tough questions which may or may not have been rhetorical. "What happens," he asked, "if the Soviet Union is first to succeed in developing a laser system which can knock airplanes out of the sky? What would happen if they were able to find most of our submarines at sea?" The Pentagon is concerned that the Soviets, in the 1980s, will be able to do just those things. If they had been able to in October 1973 . . .

The sabre-rattling of the superpowers in that crucial month of the Arab-Israeli War served as a reminder that the cold war had not come to an end. James Schlesinger's words of caution about the Russian Bear, words which had seemed out of place only four months previously, were appropriate, after all. The road to détente can fork abruptly to the brink. We would have to keep on improving our swords, postponing our plowshares.

2

Tally Ho
in the Pentagon

Sir: Mr. Walcott, director of the Geological Survey, has just been in to see me, having seen the president. He has shown me some interesting photographs of Professor Langley's flying machine. The machine has worked. It seems to me worth while for this government to try whether it will not work on a large enough scale to be of use in the event of war. For this purpose I recommend that you appoint two officers of scientific attainments and practical ability, who in conjunction with two officers appointed by the Secretary of War, shall meet and examine into this flying machine, to inform us whether or not they think it could be duplicated on a large scale, to make recommendation as to its practicability and prepare estimates as to the cost. I think this is well worth doing. This board should have the power to call in outside experts like R. H. Thurston, President, Sibley College, Cornell University, and Octave Schanute, President of American Society of Civil Engineers, Chicago.
—Letter to the Secretary of the Navy from Theodore Roosevelt, Assistant Secretary of the Navy, March 25, 1898.

The Tom Terrifics of all military forces are found in the tactical fighter wings. These are the dogfighters. Swordsmen of the skies. Artists of the afterburner. Swivel-necked, eagle-eyed fusileers in their Phantoms, Mirages, MiGs. All the way back to Rickenbacker and von Richtofen. When they engage the enemy, it is for all the chips. There is no such thing as finishing second. They lose, and they don't go home. A special breed of cat. As the bomber pilots and the missileers jokingly put it, the fighter pilots are great guys to have around in the clutch, but you wouldn't necessarily want your sister to marry one. Free spirits. Lots of ego. Cocky. Get their kicks playing tag with missiles and shells.

During the Korean War, U.S. fighter pilots, flying mainly the F-86 Sabre, shot down Chinese and North Korean Soviet-built MiG-15s almost at will. But when American and enemy fighters tangled again, nearly a decade and a half later, it was a much different story. The two hottest fighters on both sides, an F-4 Phantom and a MiG-21, locked into combat for the first time over Vietnam in early 1966. The Phantom won it. U.S. air tacticians hoped that this outcome would be the forerunner of foregone conclusions in the clouds. It did not quite work out that way. The superiority of the American fighters slipped from the piece-of-cake twelve-to-one "kill ratio" of Korea to only two-to-one in Vietnam. During an especially discouraging period, in fact, as North Vietnam deployed better ground radar for vectoring the MiGs to interceptions, the Americans' margin disappeared altogether. One-to-one. For months on end. Bad news. Altogether, looking back, the Phantom can be said to have held its own, but that's about all. It handled the MiG-17s and MiG-19s handily. But the MiG-21 was something else again. As the war went on, many Phantom pilots, without actually putting the knock on their fighter, expressed the wish that they had a lighter, quicker-turning, less cumbrously weaponed warplane under their sticks and fire-control switches.

A droop-nosed, hulking airplane (its configuration has been likened to that of a big rat), the twin-engine Phantom was designed by McDonnell Douglas in 1959 primarily as an interceptor and attack bomber, not as a fighter. Its main job would be to protect the fleet against enemy bombers. For this, it would need range, speed and lots of missiles. But not all that much maneuverability. It was a Navy plane. The civilian leaders of the Department of Defense forced the Air Force, against its better judgment, to buy the Phantom as its first-line fighter. Fighter pilots, most especially, draw a clear distinction between a fighter and an interceptor. A fighter is for going up

against other fighters, head to head at close range. An interceptor can serve as a fighter, but usually gives away too much in
manueverability. Many fighter pilots will tell you that the last
"pure" U.S. fighter planes were the F-86 Sabre and the F-100
Supersabre. Later aircraft, such as the F-102, F-104, F-106, F-4
and F-8, only masqueraded as fighters. They were designed as
interceptors.

In Vietnam, the F-4 with its Mach-2 speed could outpace the
MiG-21 slightly and outclimb it, too. But the smaller, suppler
MiG could make tighter turns, terribly disconcerting—if not
fatal—to the other guy, in a dogfight of dervishes. The MiG,
lighter of airframe, fuel, engines, electronics and weapons,
lacked the Phantom's range, but did not need it. The MiG was
designed to stay home and fight, as an "air-superiority" fighter,
and its 30-millimeter cannon and small, heat-seeking missiles
would do quite nicely for that mission.

The Air Force Phantom was equipped with a 20-millimeter
cannon, radar-directed, long-range Sparrow missiles and heat-
seeking Sidewinders for close-in work, under three miles'
range. The Navy and Marine versions of the Phantom had
Sparrows and Sidewinders but—to the deep regret of its pilots
—no gun at all. Once it had unloaded its missiles, all it had left
was its speed, to flee the fracas. The problem was compounded,
early in the air war, by the dismayingly high percentage of
Sparrows which failed to find their targets. A Pentagon-industry team was rushed to Vietnam to find out what was wrong.
They later succeeded in making the Sparrow effective most of
the time, but it was touch and go for a while. The Sparrow,
after all, was supposed to be the Phantom's chief compensation
for the extra shot of quicksilver in the MiG-21, giving the Phantom's pilot and weapons-control radar officer, in the rear seat,
the first-shot advantage in any engagement. The MiG, theoreti-
cally, would never get close enough for the fancy maneuvering
that might be fatal to the F-4. The F-4 would pick up the MiG
on radar, well beyond visual range, and unleash a Sparrow,
which would blast off and blow the MiG asunder with its
60-pound proximity-fuse warhead. The trouble was, the MiG's
skinny silhouette made radar detection difficult until it had
approached within the fighting range of its own choosing.
Moreover, those planes out there, showing up on the Phantom's radar screen, were not always MiGs. There was a lot of

U.S. cargo and passenger traffic in the air over Vietnam, and the Phantom crews could seldom be certain. Nothing was said about it at the Pentagon, but there were at least three instances of Phantoms shooting down other Phantoms, with Sparrows, before the rules were changed. "Visual identification" of a bogey was required of the Phantom crews before they could fire their missiles. This played right into the guns of the MiGs. As a result, other planes were used as "scouts" for the Phantoms. F-104 Starfighters would fly out ahead of the Phantoms and verify, visually, that those blips on the Phantoms' radars were indeed bogeys. Then the Starfighters would veer off and dart clear, and the Phantom would fire its Sparrows. Awkward arrangement. On top of this, the Sidewinders, early in the war, also were unreliable. Clouds buffaloed their infrared homing-guidance systems. The MiGs, catching onto this, knew where to zag.

In the autumn of 1968, Major General Marion Carl, then the commander of the Second Marine Air Wing, declared: "We gave up the guns too soon. Visual identification is required before beginning an attack. It takes five seconds to get a missile off. Five seconds is too damn much when you are in a hassle." At the same symposium on fighter aircraft, in El Segundo, California, Admiral John S. Thach, father of the "Thach Weave" fighter tactic which dated back to World War II, said: "The pilot never gets what he wants. He needs guns whether he has missiles or not. Missiles are a fine weapon against bomber formations. Against enemy fighters, traditional fighter tactics must be employed, and the pilots need guns."

The Phantom has passed through many models, each embodying improvements of electronics or aerodynamics. The latest—of a long line of more than forty-five hundred F-4s which have been produced for United States and foreign air forces—is the F-4E, featuring slats fitted to the leading edges of its wings. This was done to correct the tendency of the Phantom to slip sidewise at very high speeds. The leading-edge slats helped, but did not overcome the problem. It was not a fatal flaw for a fighter in any case. From pilot after pilot came the word that in dogfights dash speed did not count for all that much. Rarely were they required to power up to anywhere near the 1,400 miles per hour that they could attain. Most of the dogfighting was done at much less than the speed of sound, down low, where the ability to turn inside the enemy meant nearly everything. And only rarely were there air duels in dirty weather, which meant that some of the electronics aboard the Phantom turned out to be extra baggage when it went up against a MiG.

As it became obvious that the Phantom would never over-match the MiG-21, the Russians threatened to make matters worse. They rolled out several new models of fighter planes at their Domodedovo Air Show near Moscow in 1967. Most ominous of these was the swing-wing MiG-23, capable of Mach 3 in dashes, and, even more portentously, of an acceleration on afterburner that came close to matching flying saucers for streaking out of sight. The MiG-23 first was called, by NATO code-namers, the "Foxbat." This name later was transferred to the MiG-25, when it came along, and the MiG-23 was redesignated the "Flogger." Floggers were never introduced to the skies over Vietnam. Lucky they weren't. The United States had nothing to come anywhere near matching them. They easily could have checked the bombing of the north, and delayed the withdrawal of U.S. forces. Or worse.

Over Vietnam, the Ling-Temco-Vought F-8 Crusader was considered the Navy's second-line fighter. But the Crusader, used more sparingly than the Phantom, accounted for eighteen of the fifty-five MiGs which Navy and Marine jets shot down throughout the war. The Crusader's kill-per-engagement ratio turned out to be three times better than that of the Phantom. What did the Crusader have that the Navy and Marine Phantom did not have? A 20-millimeter cannon. Like the F-4. It also had Sidewinders. But no Sparrows. One Crusader victory over a MiG-7, twenty-two miles southwest of Hanoi on May 23, 1972, was actually a forfeit, and thus not counted among the official "kills." The MiG pilot spotted two F-8s from the carrier *Hancock* coming at him and bailed out.

The F-4 pilots learned from necessity that they could make their plane do things it never was designed to do. Such as pull eight G's (eight times the force of gravity) in turns, without the wings falling off. Six and a half G's were supposed to be the most it could withstand. The pilots did well with what they had. The publication *Armed Forces Journal* told of how Navy Lieutenants Randy Cunningham and William Driscoll shot down three MiGs in one day, and then had to punch out over the Gulf of Tonkin, on their way back to the carrier *Constella-*

tion, when their F-4J took a hit from a surface-to-air missile. Both were rescued. Lieutenant Commander Ronald McKeown and his weapons officer, Lieutenant Commander Jack C. Ensch, shot down three MiGs thirteen days later, on May 23, 1972. According to the *Journal*, McKeown spotted a couple of MiGs, and called Ensch on the intercom: "Tally ho on the ridgeline, about five miles." "Let's get 'em," Ensch replied. "I'm right behind you." McKeown: "This is business. Quit screwing around." As McKeown related the encounter to the *Journal*: "It looked like there were only two MiGs and we thought, 'Man, they're really in over their heads.' But after we made that first turn, it started raining MiGs on us. Four MiG-17s. Two MiG-19s. And the two of us. Suddenly we were surrounded. . . . In the whole hassle, I don't think we ever flew above five thousand feet. Our wing man, Mike Rabb, got one guy off his tail, shooting at him, by flying between some trees."

By mid-1974, McKeown was the commanding officer, and Cunningham, Driscoll and Ensch were among the thirteen combat-tested instructors of an intensive fighter-pilot training program which the Navy had set up at Miramar Naval Air Station, California, in 1968, during the especially suspenseful months over Vietnam. The Air Force had instituted a comparable program called "Aggressor," at Nellis Air Force Base, Nevada. Ironically, the Navy program was called "Top Gun."

In the spring of 1974, the Tactical Air Power Subcommittee of the Senate Armed Services Committee held a "MiG Killer Briefing." The witnesses were Air Force and Navy fighter pilots who had distinguished themselves over Vietnam. Air Force Major Steve Ritchie, an ace who had shot down five MiG-21s, all with Sparrow missiles, spun a spellbinding account for the subcommittee. As he told it:

The average MiG battle took place between 5,000 and 20,000 feet in subsonic flight. The MiG-21—compared to the F-4—is about half the size, it leaves very little smoke, it is very hard to see, it has a lower wing loading, and it can turn tighter than we can, and that is very important in an air battle. The F-4 in comparison is large, bulky, leaves two big smoke trails, easy to see. It does not turn as well, but has a little more power, and a lot better speed and acceleration— particularly at low altitude—and better weapons.

The average MiG tactic was to hit and run. He liked to

take off, stay low, get behind, sneak up behind and fire his heat-seeking missiles and dive away. He was normally very closely controlled by his ground radar controller, who was also a pilot. He was told when to jettison his external fuel tanks, when to go full afterburner, when to arm his missiles, and where to break off and where to land. In other words, he was not trained to think for himself very much, and I think this is one area where we have always had the advantage over our adversaries. He seemed to have very little appreciation for vertical maneuvering and mutual support. Often he was not very aggressive. However, there were certain exceptions to this, and I would just like to briefly tell you about my most exciting engagement, which took place on the 8th of July in 1972. It was a definite exception to this general nonaggressiveness of the MiG pilot.

I was leading the egress flight, which means I was the last F-4 flight in. Our job was to be there to protect the rest of the force as they came out. Well, most of the action was normally at the beginning of the mission, so I thought it would be a pretty dull, routine day. I am coming inbound listening to the MiG CAP frequency, and sure enough, the MiGs are up, and one of the [radar-jammer] chaff escorts—Brenda Zero One—has been hit in the left engine by a missile from a MiG. He is headed out, his left engine is out, fire light on, bleeding fuel and hydraulic fluid, announcing position, heading and altitude on GUARD—the emergency frequency.

Well, about this time one of the MiG airplanes—Dallas Zero Four—has a fire light. He is headed out, announcing position, heading and altitude.

Historically, the North Vietnamese ground radar controllers would vector other MiGs against our people that were in trouble. So I changed my course and headed in the direction of these two guys who were in trouble, dropped down to low altitude—about 5,000 feet—and began to receive good information from Red Crown and Disco. Red Crown is the Navy ship off the coast which provides radar and intelligence information on the mission. And Disco, of course, is the Air Force EC-121 orbiting over Laos and providing that same service.

After about five or six 90-degree turns in tactical patrol

formation, I was in the vicinity of Banana Valley about thirty miles southwest of Hanoi. I had just made a turn from a heading of south to a heading of east when I received a key call from Disco. Disco said, "There are two MiGs north of you." I rolled left to a heading of north and picked up a lead MiG-21 coming in at ten o'clock. I called, "I got a MiG-21 left at ten o'clock level, two miles closing." I rolled left and blew off the external fuel tanks and went full afterburner. We passed canopy to canopy about 1,000 feet from each other. He was a spit-polished silver MiG-21 with bright red stars painted on him. Every other MiG that I had seen—a total of sixteen MiGs—were a dingy silver. This one was highly spit-polished.

I did not see the Number Two MiG, and from studying their recent tactics, which was one of the most important things we did during our training, I knew that if I did not see Number Two in a fairly close fighting wing formation —what they called a bearing-of-aircraft formation—that it would be somewhere in trail. Of course, what they wanted us to do was turn on the first MiG, and the Number Two MiG would then come in and shoot us down.

I did not see the Number Two, so I rolled out and headed for the ground in full power, unloaded the airplane, and waited. That was a little hard to do, because the shiny MiG was either getting away or he was turning to get in behind me.

Sure enough, here came the Number Two MiG about 10,000 feet in trail. I am down below him now. And as he passed, I went into a left 135-degree-bank, nose-down, slicing turn, about six and a half G's. It turns out to be just about the right amount of turn in terms of energy maneuverability —in other words, trying to get around the turn and yet maintain energy to fight with.

About halfway through my turn I picked up the Number Two MiG in a right turn, level and high. As I completed the turn I noticed a large angle-off developing—or what we call a large track-crossing angle. To reduce this angle I barrel-rolled to the left, put the MiG in the gun sight. I have the radar in boresight, which means it is looking through my gun sight. What I did was to put the MiG in the gun sight and lock on the radar with a switch on my left throttle called the auto-acquisition switch. It was a good lock-on. Now I have got to wait [deleted] seconds to fire the Sparrow radar missile. I waited, squeezed the trigger twice—they are always launched in pairs for better probability of kill—and it is another [deleted] until the missile comes off the airplane —that is [deleted] seconds, if you do everything right. And that is a long time in an air battle.

The MiG-21 can generate a lot of turn in [deleted] seconds. So he saw me, and started to turn down into me. I got the lock-on at about zero-degree to 10-degrees angle-off, and about 6,000 feet. About the time the first missile came off the airplane, the MiG had turned into me about 5 degrees, and he was 45 degrees past my nose, about 4,000 feet. I am pulling about [deleted] G's, which is very close to the limit of the capability of the missile.

The first missile came off the airplane and went through the center of his fuselage. The second missile went through the fireball.

The MiG broke into two big pieces—a big fireball and a lot of debris. I kept turning, rolled out and flew over the top of the left corner of the fireball and took a small piece of debris through the leading edge of my left wing. At that time I would have disengaged, thinking the other MiG would also disengage, because every other time that I saw two MiGs, and one MiG came anywhere near getting into trouble, the other MiG would split. In other words, they did not seem to appreciate mutual support.

But now, the first MiG, the shiny guy, hung right in the fight and tried to shoot down my Number Four man. My Number Four man called and said, "Steve, I have got one on me."

So I started another dive for the ground to pick up additional air speed and energy which I had lost in the first turn. This time I came hard to the right, a 135-degree bank, a nose-down, slicing turn, about six and a half G's. I came out of that turn in a very similar position on the shiny guy that I had on his wingman just a few seconds earlier. And by the way, from canopy to canopy on the first pass until the first missile impacted on the wingman, it was forty-seven seconds. Here is the shiny MiG, and here is my Number Four man, and he is getting into a good position to shoot at him —the MiG against my Number Four man. I came across the circle, rolled up, put the MiG in the gun sight and hit the auto-acquisition switch. It was a good lock. I waited [deleted] seconds and squeezed the trigger. I had time to get one missile off the airplane.

The MiG saw me, forgot about the Number Four man, and started a hard turn down into me. He was a little better than his wingman. By the time the missile came off my airplane, he had closed to 3,000 feet and was almost 60 degrees past my nose. I was pulling [deleted] G's, which is at or beyond the capability of the missile. I was reaching down for my master arm switch which turns on the gun, in the hope of getting a shot at him as he passed by. The missile came off the airplane, headed straight, appeared to do a 90-degree right turn, and smashed dead center into the fuselage. The MiG broke into two pieces, a lot of debris, and a big fireball.

At that time, there was another flight of MiG-21s being vectored by the North Vietnamese toward the fight. We had gotten this information from Red Crown and Disco. When I called, "Splash," which was our code word for a MiG kill, the North Vietnamese vectored the other flight of MiGs back to Hanoi. So we got out of the area, hit the post-mission refueling tanker, and returned to Udorn.

Within weeks after he testified on Capitol Hill, Major Ritchie retired from the Air Force and returned to North Carolina to run unsuccessfully for Congress.

Paradoxically, Ritchie, whose F-4 had a gun, never used it in making his kills, while Commander F.S. Teague, a Navy pilot whose F-4 did not have a gun, wished it had. At the Senate hearing, after recounting his own MiG kills, Teague had this to say:

I think it should be mentioned that the Air Force, in their F-4, has an internal cannon, and a very good one, the Vulcan. The Navy F-4 fighter does not have an internal cannon. As a consequence, we found ourselves in the battlefield with Sidewinders and Sparrows. The Sidewinder, of course, is independent of the radar system in the airplane, whereas the Sparrow requires that not only the missile and all its links be "up," but the radar must be "up" as well.

I was in a fight at Quan Lang Air Base in March where

I found myself alone, thinking I was good, with four MiG-17s. I felt very comfortable, until all of a sudden the circle kept getting smaller and smaller. I knew I could leave anytime just by throwing on the afterburners and running. But once you see a MiG you want one badly. So I stuck around. In that fight I had two perfect gun opportunities when the MiG had just stopped going straight up in front of me, where you fly right through them, and I could have hit him with a basketball, but I had nothing to shoot. I finally did get a missile off in that fight which exploded on the MiG. My wingman thought I had hit him. But a bunch of junk came off of him, and I only got credit for damaging him.

Why did the Air Force F-4 have a gun and the Navy F-4 not have a gun? Simple. For its longer-ranging fleet-defense mission, the Navy Phantom was fitted with extensive radar equipment that took up all the space in the nose of the plane. When, in the mid-Sixties, the Air Force realized it would need a gun, the F-4 was redesigned. By shifting the radar gear—a very expensive undertaking—McDonnell Douglas opened up enough space to stick the cannon in the noses of the F-4s produced for the Air Force. The Navy decided to leave the radar alone and do without the gun. In any case, the addition of the gun would have made the Navy F-4 heavier than desirable for carrier landings.

In November 1966, I spent some time aboard the new aircraft carrier *America*, which was undergoing sea trials in the Atlantic. The *America* shortly would head for Vietnam station. Its squadrons of Phantoms and A-6 Intruders practiced "cat shots" (catapulted takeoffs) and landings all the day long. Some of the pilots were checking out a new, all-weather automatic carrier landing system (ACLS) that would save many a plane and crew later on. Extending far beyond the conventional concept of instrument landings, in which the pilot himself must land the plane as it breaks out of the weather, ACLS made it possible for the planes to land deck-center, nose wheel smack on the yellow line, without the pilots needing to see the deck, touch the stick or "walk" the rudder controls. In ACLS, the automatic pilot on the aircraft, responding to signals sent from the carrier's big computer to a cockpit converter, did it all. It steered the aircraft on a path that was always true to the plane of the deck, no matter how the deck itself might be moving in accordance with the carrier's pitches, rolls, heaves or yaws. ACLS also compensated for air turbulence around the airplane.

In my fascination with this wonder of electronics, it never occurred to me that these same Phantoms, headed for combat, would ever need a cannon. It had never occurred to the admirals, either. The Navy F-4 did not carry a gun because its main mission was to be the defense of the fleets, of the carrier task forces, beating off enemy bombers with missiles. No one had dreamed that the Phantoms would be called upon to shoot it out with cannonaders in MiGs, in an air corral over a little land mass in Southeast Asia.

This did not, however, explain the absence of cannon in the F-4s of the Flying Leathernecks. The traditional role of the fighter plane in the Marine wings has been one of clearing and controlling the air over beachheads and salients. This means dogfights. Like those between the Zeros and the Hellcats of World War II, the Sabres and MiGs of Korea. What the answer comes down to is that the Marine Corps jolly well buys whatever first-line fighter plane the Navy brass tells it to buy. And in the case of the F-4, it was not the Air Force version, but the Navy version, which had begun coming off the production lines first. The Navy likes the Marine Corps to share the research and development costs of its fighters, and help pay the price of their procurement, off the same production line. Bigger production volume means lower unit prices, better public relations and Congressional relations, and lower-looking budgets for the Navy. This Navy tactic of force-feeding fighters into the Marine squadrons was to show up again, as we shall see later on, in the stormy developments of the two fighters which were chosen to replace the Navy and Air Force Phantoms in the late 1970s: the Grumman F-14 Tomcat and the McDonnell Douglas F-15 Eagle. Their development, with its twists and turns, is an outstanding example of the services' politicking and parochialism, under the same Pentagon roof, all carried out under the banner of a strong national defense. But it is possible that defense actually suffers in the final accounting. The setting is, of course, the Pentagon . . .

Your back is to the Potomac River lagoon, to the Columbia Island marina across the way. You are standing under tower-

ing flagpoles at the top of a flight of concrete steps sloping
down to the lagoon. You are facing, one hundred yards away,
the River Entrance of the Pentagon building, the closely
guarded, colonnaded portal of the top brass, civilian and military, of the defense establishment of the United States of
America. Within a walk or an escalator ride of a minute or less
from this entrance are the offices of all the men who make the
weighty decisions. Secretary of Defense. Deputy Secretary of
Defense. Joint Chiefs of Staff. Secretaries of the Army, Navy,
Air Force. Director of Defense Research and Engineering.
Comptroller. Assistant secretaries of defense for procurement,
construction, intelligence, communications, logistics and public relations and manpower affairs. Each has a commodious,
comfortably carpeted, individually appointed suite of offices
with a multi-windowed view of the lagoon, the Potomac, the
Jefferson Memorial and, off to the northeast, jutting above all
of Washington, the Capitol Dome. These panjandrums of the
Pentagon more often than not are at work in their suites early
enough each morning to see that dome glinting pink in the
sunrise, late enough in the evening to see it shine under the
floodlights. Which may help explain why the men of the military usually stay a jump or two ahead of Congress and why
they rarely fail to get their way, when all is said and done, on
Capitol Hill.

If the Pentagon chieftains feel trapped in their offices, sometimes jaded by the politicking and infighting that they must
wage, they can stand at their windows and watch the white-
gloved honor guards of soldiers, sailors, marines and airmen
come snick-snack to "Present Arms" at the military ceremo-
nies near the River Entrance, to remind themselves of what it
is all about. (Indeed, buttering up the brass is called, at the
Pentagon, "hanging around the flagpole.") Or they can walk to
the far side of the building, the side overlooking the helipad,
and gaze at the row upon row of white headstones on an Arlington Cemetery hillock, a quarter-mile away.

The Pentagon, appropriately, was controversial of conception and a cost overrun upon completion. Just as the F-III was
dubbed "McNamara's folly," so the Pentagon was called
"Somerville's folly." Brigadier General Brehon Somerville
was the chief of engineers who, as construction was begun four
months before Pearl Harbor, estimated that the new "War

Department Building" would cost $31 million. (Actually, the Corps of Engineers had calculated a cost of $35 million, but President Roosevelt, in a ploy which critics of defense spending would be quick to recognize today, ordered the corps to shave the estimate to an amount he thought Congress would swallow.) By the time the Pentagon was completed, it had cost $83 billion. Hardly anyone minded. For one thing, the speed of construction had been impressive. Only sixteen months to put up the largest office building in the world, almost like magic, from an excavation broad enough to contain two Washington Monuments and half of a third. Besides, the bugler had blown "Reveille" for the United States during those sixteen months. As the Pentagon opened for business, Rommel had just been routed in North Africa, the Russians were standing heroically at Stalingrad, and the United States Marines, at that very moment in January 1943 were slugging the Japanese off Guadalcanal. The military was not to be criticized, and the Pentagon stood then, as it does today, as the symbol of the military. Of the bad, now, as well as the good.

The Pentagon was built on swamps and auto junkyards, in a Potomac bottomland section of Arlington County, Virginia, known as "Hell's Bottom." Into this wasteland the engineers poured 5.5 million cubic yards of earth, and hammered 41,492 concrete piles. Atop this mound, they molded into the form of the building 435,000 cubic yards of concrete, processed from 680,000 tons of sand and gravel which they had dredged from the Potomac. The Pentagon was to accommodate 30,000 office workers, and that is what is does. By contrast, New York City's Pan American Building holds only 17,000. But the Pentagon is nowhere near big enough for the defense establishment of Washington and environs. The area abounds in other military installations and newer office buildings, large and small, which contain the overflow.

Take a tour. Don't begin at the River Entrance or at the Mall Entrance of the adjoining side. Instead, get off the bus from Washington, in one of the three bus lanes which slice under one side of the building. Mount the twenty-seven steps to the Pentagon concourse, an arcade long enough to contain five basketball courts, end to end. The concourse features a commercial bookstore; a government bookstore; a bank; medical and dental clinics; post office; barber shop; clothing stores for men and women; a laundry and dry cleaning establishment; ticket offices for travel, the theater and sporting events; bakery, drugstore, candy store; baggage lockers; photography shop; newsstand; jewelry store; university education information center; television consoles, tuned to the news. Along the length of the concourse, on any given day, are easel-mounted posters proclaiming a reunion of the Red River Valley Fighter Pilots Association, of the Eighth Tactical Fighter Wing, of a company of the Green Berets. At lunchtime, now and then, the "Singing Sergeants" of the Air Force or some other military music group will set up one end of the concourse to entertain the strolling secretaries and their bosses. Billy Graham has sermonized in this shopping area. In warm weather, the noontime entertainment moves outdoors to the center court, a vast greensward, laced with walkways, nestled amid the Pentagon's inner walls. Here, the brown-baggers bring lunches from home or from one of the nine snack bars inside the building. Or they patronize the luncheon bar, sporting carnival colors, at the hub of the courtyard. Pleasant. Lunch in the park. But not quite. Pentagonians, with gallows humor, call the center court "Ground Zero."

Just inside the walls which rim the center court is the building's "A Ring," one of five concentric rings which take you clear around the building. Piercing the five sides of the building, spoke-like, from the "A Ring" through to the "E Ring," are ten corridors. The rings and the corridors, laid end to end, would stretch more than seventeen miles. A walk all the way around the outermost E ring is a walk of a mile. By using the corridors and rings in the most efficient manner, it should take no longer than eight minutes to walk between any two offices of maximum distance apart. Unless you pause to inspect the paintings and photographs of weapons and combat scenes, or the glass-encased models of ships, planes, missiles and armor, or the real-life displays of small arms. The top-brass Army, Navy and Air Force areas on the second, third and fourth floors, E Ring, River Entrance side, resemble art galleries and museums. Pork Chop Hill is before you; the Coral Sea, just down the hall.

The Department of Defense has almost as many employees —4.5 million—as the thirty largest U.S. industrial corporations combined. Greater assets—$200 billion—than the seventy-five largest together. It deals with more than one hundred thousand prime contractors and subcontractors, and operates branch offices in all fifty states, and in more than one hundred foreign countries. It spends over $90 billion a year, half of this on research, development, testing, production and maintenance of weapons systems and other hardware and equipment. The man usually in charge of the business side of the Pentagon is not the Secretary of Defense but the Deputy Secretary of Defense. He is the systems man, the hardware man. Save for McNamara, the Secretaries have stuck to high policy and have left the nitty-gritty to their deputies. This division of duties was especially striking in the first Nixon administration, when Secretary of Defense Melvin Laird concentrated on getting out of Vietnam, pressing the flesh on Capitol Hill, reassuring our NATO allies, and working up the beginnings of the Volunteer Army. He delegated the thorny task of coordinating the services and their contractors to his deputy, David Packard, the "Mr. Inside" of the two. Packard would show how a man who could co-found and develop a giant West Coast electronics company like Hewlett-Packard, and make $300 million for himself while at it, could also square away the Pentagon. An intelligent man, Packard. Board of Trustees at Stanford University, where he lettered in football and basketball in the 1930s. A big man. Six-four. Two-fifty. Towered over the admirals and generals, most of whom had experienced no difficulty in meeting the height limitations of West Point and Annapolis. (General MacArthur, for example, was only five-ten. Flattering camera angles.)

Packard tried to do two things which turned out to be mutually incompatible: reform the services' practices of procuring weapons systems and, at the same time, give the services more leeway and responsibility in the procurement; impose on them, much less than McNamara had, the decisions of the civilians. His reforms were highly publicized. Although it will take many years to determine whether they actually are successful, at least Packard's rationale for them was sound. He introduced the concepts of "competitive prototyping," "fly before buy," and "design to cost." Taken altogether, these boiled down, at a time of severe budgetary constraints, to forcing the services and their contractors to think ahead more about the cost of a weapon in relation to its performance; to build and test prototypes of weapons, such as airplanes, before the Defense Department would approve their production; and, in general, to quit adding gimmicks and gadgets to weaponry just because some engineer thought it would be dandy to do so. But for all his good intentions, Packard failed to go far enough. He gave the services too much rope, and they hanged him. The denouement was the development of the new fighter planes. Shortly after he took office, Packard said:

> To be brutally frank about this situation, the services need to be organized so that the development and production of new weapons systems is managed by people who are experts in that business. This is not the practice in the services. Instead, the weapons management job is performed under a system in which too much responsibility is given to officers whose special expertise is not development and procurement. Most of the services are structured so that the project manager, even if he is selected as someone who has expertise and capability, is supervised and can be overridden by generals and flag officers who, although they may be the finest of men and highly competent in military affairs, often know little or nothing about development and production. I conclude, therefore, that it is going to require a major change in the organizational structure of all three services to straighten out the management of new weapons programs.

Fine. Soon, admirals and generals, instead of the customary captains and colonels, were taking charge of the individual weapons programs. This was great for protecting the programs against the second-guessing of other admirals and generals who might not have known what they were talking about. But it also gave the weapons programs themselves more political steam, and made for more powerful, more autonomous program managers, who were in better position to resist not only their uniformed peers in and across the services, but, ironically, Packard himself, and any civilian boss who followed him. For Packard also went about decentralizing the authority of the Department of Defense over the services which McNamara had tried to husband for himself and for an inner circle of his civilian colleagues, the "Whiz Kids" of the Office of Systems Analysis. In the eyes of the services, these civilians were bean counters with computers, perpetrators of paralysis by analysis. Laird and Packard promptly downgraded their judgmental role in the conception and development of weapons.

"What we're trying to do," Packard said, "is give these professional military people—and the service secretaries—a larger say in the decisions that have to be made. I feel very strongly that decisions must be made as close as possible to the point of execution. It is difficult for anyone to carry out a decision which has been imposed from above. The F-III is an example. The Navy was never very enthusiastic about the F-III. It wasn't a Navy decision."

In the Navy's lack of enthusiasm for the F-III—and in the Air Force's resentment, too, at having the Navy F-4 forced upon it by McNamara—lay the seeds of The Great Fighter Plane Battle of the early and middle 1970s. Among the wounded were to be Packard, William P. Clements, Jr., who became Deputy Secretary of Defense in the second Nixon administration, a whole raft of admirals and generals—and the citizenry at large. Let us begin . . .

The Navy, unable to unhorse McNamara, played along with him on the development of the bi-service F-III until Hughes Aircraft Corp. had enough of the Pentagon's money in pocket to complete design and development of the Phoenix missile. The extra-long-range, uncannily guided Phoenix had been conceived specifically as a weapon for the F-III in one of its roles—never to be realized—as a Navy interceptor. All the while, the Navy had in mind putting the Phoenix aboard another plane, being designed even then, and forsaking the F-III. McNamara would not be around forever. Sure enough, victory often comes to those who wait. McNamara had gone. Clark Clifford was in his final month as McNamara's successor. Richard Nixon had won the election, and in the next month would introduce a whole new team to the E Ring civilian offices of the Pentagon. The civilian leaders now in those offices were packing their things. The Navy struck. It signed a contract with Grumman Corp., which tidily enough had been chief subcontractor for General Dynamics on the F-III, to build the F-14 Tomcat as the end-all air defender of the fleet for as far into the future as the tacticians could see. Before Packard ever set foot in the Pentagon, the Tomcat contract had him by the tail.

Packard had the option, of course, of ordering the Navy to renege. He approved the contract because it would have been sticky not to do so, and because the Tomcat did promise to be a marvelous plane. But he was not happy with the terms. The contract locked the Navy into ordering, by a fixed date, no fewer than forty-eight production models of the F-14 beyond the original twelve development models and the first production lot of twenty-six. That was a big commitment for production before the first plane had ever flown. If the Navy were to back away from this commitment, the contract automatically would be broken, and Grumman might even be in position to sue. Thus, full-scale production was a foregone conclusion, even before the development and testing process—finding out whether the plane will do what it is supposed to do—had been completed. All Packard could do was hope that Grumman would have no major problems with the plane. Muffling his misgivings, Packard followed through, in the case of the F-14 program, on his theory that the services should be unfettered in their management of weapons programs. He made clear that he was giving the Navy its head. Two years later, he was in a mood to *band* the Navy its head. What happened in the meantime was ample evidence of the natal agonies of a weapon system when its wonders-to-be warp the judgment of what it will cost, or of what it will do.

The twin-jet F-14 is indeed some airplane. It was designed to range farther, fly faster, climb higher and pack more wallop than any interceptor ever built. While it possesses some of the features of a fighter, fighter pilots certainly would prefer to call it an interceptor. Its long suit is its fire control system and its missiles. With his AWG-9 radar and infrared-sensor-computer system, the backseat Missile Control Officer (MCO) of the Tomcat can track twenty-four separate targets, from sea level to one hundred thousand feet, up to one hundred miles distant. The silicon chips in the Tomcat's "little black boxes" of electronics are synaptic with six Phoenix missiles, which separately can seek out enemy planes or missiles coming at the fleet from different directions, altitudes and ranges, and with Sparrows and Sidewinders. Plus a 20-millimeter cannon. The Navy's response to the argument that a MiG-23 or a MiG-25 would overmatch the Tomcat in a dogfight is simply (does it ring a bell?) that neither would ever get close enough to turn

on the Tomcat's tail, and even then might find the Tomcat too
much to handle. The Tomcat's infrared search-and-track system can be used along with its radar, or independently. Unlike
the radar, the infrared system can detect and track targets
without transmitting, which means that it does not break radio
silence and resists jamming by enemy electronic countermeasures. The infrared system also can count and pinpoint clusters
of targets which may show up on conventional radar as mere
blobs. Against air-launched and ship-launched missiles, the infrared sensing range exceeds that of the radar. Could not this
Mandrakian masterwork of sensors be installed on some
fighter already in service? Here is what the Navy, in its self-
serving "Fact Sheet on the F-14," had to say about that:

> The sensors are controlled by an MCO through a unique
> set of controls and displays assisted by the most advanced
> and reliable airborne digital computer yet designed. Navy
> studies show that the F-14 AWG-9-Missiles-Gun combina-
> tion provides an air superiority increment equal to at least
> three conventional fighters. The weapon control system
> must be matched to an aircraft design of comparable aerody-
> namic performance in order to exploit its full capability. The
> F-14 is that aircraft. It is equally capable on combat air patrol,
> on escort, or in a dogfight. This versatility is possible only
> because of recent innovations, including its fan engine, the
> swing wing, maneuvering flaps and light alloys. This air-
> craft design has been evolving since 1959. It has benefited
> from all the mistakes and all the progress made since that
> time. Navy fighter pilots have been among the most impor-
> tant participants in this evolution, and they have the most to
> gain or lose by its success or failure. To install the AWG-9
> and Phoenix missile on an aircraft of lesser performance
> would be equivalent to putting Willie Shoemaker on a mule
> in the Kentucky Derby.

Nothing the Navy could have said about the Tomcat would
be so persuasive as the spy case which showed how intrigued
the Soviets were with the plane. A Soviet translator at the
United Nations contacted a Grumman engineer, who had
helped design the Tomcat, about handing over its blueprints.
The engineer told the FBI about the contact. When he met

with the Russian and handed over the blueprints, FBI agents swooped in for the arrest.

A few months after this affair, the Navy pitted the F-14 against the F-4 in eight air duels over Long Island Sound. Each time, the "dogfight" began with the F-4 already in the six-o'clock position, behind the F-14, all set to score an electronic "hit." And each time, the F-14 pilot wracked into a tight turn, out of trouble, and swiftly reversed the advantage. The Navy and Grumman publicized these trials to the hilt. But some fighter pilots remained skeptical. They said they would like to see the F-14 fly up against a MiG, or a plane more closely resembling a MiG. In their opinion, beating an F-4 proved little, for the F-4 was not a pure fighter.

The F-14 program began to come apart. Production fell behind schedule after a failure of titanium hydraulic lines caused the first F-14 prototype to crash, in its second test flight, off Long Island. The production lag and other problems caused costs to climb alarmingly. Four months later, Grumman told the Navy that it would be "commercially impracticable" to build any more than thirty-eight Tomcats unless the contract were torn up and a new one written which would provide Grumman with an added two to three billion dollars. Critics took note that the price increase almost exactly matched the amount by which Grumman had underbid McDonnell Douglas for the F-14 contract in the first place.

When the Navy broke the bad news to Packard, he blew up. First, he was angry with Grumman for not having given advance warning of big trouble ahead. Then he learned that Grumman had been trying to tell the brass in the Navy F-14 program offices, for almost a whole year, of the turbulence that lay ahead for the Tomcat program. Packard called a meeting of the Defense Systems Acquisition Review Council (DSARC) and let the Navy have it. When he had finished chewing out the admirals, he stormed from the meeting room in his E Ring suite, roaring, "You're fired," at all of them, most notably Navy Secretary John Chafee and Vice-Admiral Thomas F. Connolly, deputy chief of staff for Naval air operations. The next day, Packard called the DSARC back into session, but pointedly omitted the Navy. He apologized to the others for his outburst. He said he was drafting a memo ordering the Navy to take a second look—a hard one—at the F-14 program.

The participants at that meeting reported that Packard seemed not only subdued but, for the first time in their experience with him, a shade dispirited. The word began to spread that he was sick of the Pentagon, and was longing to return to his opulent California home, secluded in fifty acres of apricot trees, back near San Francisco. Six months later, he was gone. So was Chafee. So was Admiral Connolly. But Packard had left the Navy something to think about.

He had instructed the admirals, as part of their reexamination of the F-14 program, to find out whether the McDonnell Douglas F-15 Eagle, a fighter newly in development for the Air Force, could be adapted to the fleet-defense mission. Chuckles of satisfaction could be heard throughout the Air Force suites and in the board room of McDonnell Douglas. This could mean sweet revenge against the Navy for having foisted off the F-4 on the Air Force. The situation was ominous for the Navy and for Grumman. The F-15 program, which had counted Packard among its enthusiastic inceptors, was riding high.

The F-15 was designed to make fighter jocks wave their white silk scarves and show their perfect teeth in exultation. It was their kind of bird. An honest-to-goodness fighter which, unlike any plane ever before, could effectively double as an interceptor and as a long-range escort of bombers. It would pull so many G's in a turn that its pilots might even need pressure suits to keep their blood from rushing downward too quickly. It would climb like a rocket, accelerate like a missile. It would not be armed with Phoenix missiles, and could afford to disdain them. But it would bristle with Sparrows and Sidewinders at no sacrifice of speed or maneuverability. And a rapid-fire, 25-millimeter cannon. Its "heads-up" radar display would permit the pilot to "see through" the display and still be able to scan the sky around him. He would need no Missile Control Officer. He would have it all to himself, the way fighter pilots like it. The Eagle's twin engines, generating more than forty thousand pounds of thrust, would make it the first fighter ever with more thrust than weight. (Well, not quite. The F-104 had more thrust than weight, but the advantage wasn't worth much. At top thrust, a red light would come on in the cockpit of the F-104 which told the pilot that he had better either slow down or punch out, his fuselage and wings were about to melt. Not so the F-15. Titanium and composite-metal surfaces. Practically friction-heatproof.) And best of all, the Air Force–McDonnell Douglas F-15 development program was staying right on target, both as to performance and costs of the airplane. The Air Force planned to buy more than seven hundred of them, and there was nothing to indicate that this plan might be upset. Moreover, it now seemed that the Navy might wind up being dragged into the market for F-15s as well, which would double the market and drastically cut the price of each plane.

Meanwhile, Congress had forced a ceiling price on the Navy and Grumman for the F-14. Grumman said it would go bankrupt under the terms, and flatly told the Navy that it would no longer honor the contract. Frantic negotiations became the order of the day, for months on end, between the Navy and Grumman. These dragged on, as the F-14 program foundered, until a new Deputy Secretary of Defense charged into the Pentagon at the beginning of the second Nixon term, in 1973, confident that he could find a way to keep the F-14 flying.

William P. Clements, Jr., came to Washington from Dallas with a reputation as a hawk and a half. A multimillionaire with a hard-bitten look about him, Clements spoke his piece in accents less mellifluous than those of, say, his fellow Texan, John Connally, and in utter disregard of subtleties. He had worked hard for—and contributed to—Nixon's reelection campaign in Texas, and had been tapped for the Pentagon job by Nixon himself, giving him a little extra political clout vis-à-vis his bosses—Elliot Richardson and then, later, James Schlesinger. Clements reported for duty as a little-known government outsider. But where national security and defense procurement policies were concerned, he was said to be better prepared for the job than any of his predecessors. He had been counted as the most diligent of the fourteen members of the Blue Ribbon Panel, a group of highly placed civilians which Nixon had empaneled in 1969 to study Pentagon practices and organization. Shortly after the panel had issued its massive report in 1970, Clements and six other members published a supplemental report in which they cracked Congress on the knuckles for its efforts to cut the weapons budget. "The road to peace has never been through appeasement, unilateral disarmament or negotiation from weakness," they wrote. "The entire recorded history of mankind is precisely to the contrary. Among the great nations, only the strong survive."

Clements had come on even more strongly in an article he

wrote for the Dallas *Times Herald.* "America," he declared, "is in greater danger today than in 1940, before World War II. Does this shock you?" Comparing U.S. and Soviet strengths, Clements wrote: "Our defense posture has deteriorated significantly in the last ten years, and if this trend continues, America will become a second-class power. McNamara's policies started us on this decline." He warned against the United States becoming "a castrated giant." And although he faintly acknowledged the need of social reform, he asserted that "our top priority has to be our national security." He expressed impatience with the pace of development of the Trident submarine-missile system and of the B-1 bomber, in the face of the Soviet threat as he direly discerned it. "It is a disgrace," he wrote, "that the last major weapon system developed by the United States was the Polaris submarine, which now is being upgraded to the Poseidon system and is the single most important deterrent to Russia. The more advanced Trident system will require several billion dollars [he was low by more than half] and eight years of concentrated effort. We need an advanced, heavy type bomber as proposed in the B-1 program, but again, this represents a major weapon system and will take eight to ten years." The services fairly chortled at the prospect of Clements' coming.

The superficial similarities between Clements and Packard were striking. Both were self-made multimillionaires. Clements had founded Southeastern Drilling Company as a wildcat operation in 1947 and nursed it, later as SEDCO Inc., into a worldwide oil-drilling concern. Like Packard, he had never served in the military, had played football (guard) in college— at Southern Methodist University—and was blunt. His penchant for the pungent was illustrated at a Pentagon luncheon in honor of General François Louis Maurin, chief of staff of the French armed forces. Clements accosted Maurin, demanding to know why the French had sold Mirage fighter planes to Egypt in contradiction of the announced French policy of not supplying weapons to any nation which had been involved in the Arab-Israeli Six Day War of 1967. Maurin said he knew nothing of any such sale. "Why don't you know?" Clements asked. "Here they are." And he plopped onto Maurin's place at the table intelligence reports and aerial photographs of Mirages on Egyptian soil.

The press perceived in Clements much promise of good

copy, and began speculating on how long it would take him to put his foot inextricably into his mouth. Reporters began interviewing his former associates back home in Dallas to learn more about him. One of these, Dallas computer tycoon H. Ross Perot, was quoted as saying: "If you ever decide to run over him, kill him, don't leave him unconscious. He's as tough as anyone you'll ever meet, and I mean that as a compliment. . . . Bill Clements could handle anything he wanted to do. There are basically two kinds of people—workhorses and showhorses. Bill is a workhorse."

On becoming a full-time Pentagonian, Clements quickly was brought down from the cosmos of strategic policy. It could even be said that he was shot down. By the fighter-plane problem programs. Congress was applying pressure to get the F-14 issue resolved. Grumman was trying to cut corporate overhead it had been charging off to the Navy. The Navy was trying to figure out how to cut weight from the F-14. Weight is money. Clements took charge. He trekked to Grumman's headquarters at Bethpage, Long Island, to see for himself what was going on. The Grumman people did a little dance after he had departed. He had seemed, according to one of them, "a quick study, a businessman who understands our problems." When he got back to the Pentagon, Clements took another look at the Navy study of the F-15, which Packard had ordered. It said, naturally, that the F-15 would not really suffice. Its landing gear would need to be strengthened, for slamming into carrier decks, and its tail section would have to be equipped with a hook. These additions would mean much more weight. And the F-15 could never, of course, match the F-14 in the range or the firepower that would be needed to combat the anticipated Soviet tactic of saturating fleet defenses with coordinated aircraft and antiship missile attacks. The Navy needed a long-range interceptor which could take on many attackers all at once. So you seem to be stuck, Mr. Clements, with the F-14.

Now, Clements really mixed things up. He prevailed upon Dr. Alexander Flax, former assistant secretary of the Air Force for research and development, now president of the Institute for Defense Analyses, a defense think tank. He instructed Flax to supervise a crash study of the likelihood of using the F-15 on carriers and/or adapting the F-14 to the Air Force mission which had been plotted for the F-15. The Air Force promptly joined the Navy in the sweatbox. Puff sheets on both planes poured out of the services' publicity shops. Someone from the Air Force slipped into the Navy F-14 program offices a bunch of blown-up, color photographs of an F-15 with a tail hook and the marking "F-15N"—for "F-15Navy." The Navy people did not think this was very funny. Sanford McDonnell, Jr., president of McDonnell Douglas, flew to Washington from the company's St. Louis headquarters to brief Clements on the projected costs and performance of a Navy F-15. All this confusion (it began to resemble a schoolroom full of paper airplanes) was making a 1969 report of a Wall Street investment analyst firm—Bear, Stearns & Co.—look awfully prophetic. It had been published at a time when both the F-14, then called the VFX, and the F-15, then called the FX, were still in the experimental stage. Under the heading, "Pentagon Rivalries," the report had said:

How well a new airplane could do against a prospective Russian fighter is probably not really the battle which now matters the most. A much more important and basic consideration is the "Eternal War"; that is, the Navy against the Air Force and the Army, all within the Defense Department. It would appear that the Navy created the VFX [F-14] partly from a self-preservation instinct to escape subjugation by the Air Force–administered F-111 program. In some measure, the VFX also reflects the vanity of some of the Navy officials who thought that they could make a mutually satisfactory, variable-sweep-wing airplane where the Air Force had presumably failed. Some trade publications have boldly speculated that the Navy VFX might be good enough —and early enough—to be forced upon the Air Force in a budget-crunch situation, and emerge as another universal airplane for all services. The Air Force, on the other hand, has been quite embarrassed in the last few years when circumstances have dictated that it adopt tactical aircraft developed by the Navy. The thought of a Navy-developed VFX now being added to the Tactical Air Command, which is already dominated by the Navy's F-4s and A-7s, could be almost too much for the Air Force staff to bear. It appears, however, that the Navy's choice of the VFX-concept leaves considerable room for improvement, and an Air Force FX could now emerge with significantly better air superiority performance. . . . Logic would seem to lead to the conclusion that the Air Force FX could be expected to prevail over the Navy plane in any conflict for funds because of significantly better performance and of the larger and more urgent needs of what has become a service [the Air Force] deprived of [weapons] developments. The FX also may be adaptable for use by the Navy.

A clear-cut choice between the F-14 and the F-15, cutting out one of those two huge defense contractors, was not to be. Both had become imbedded in the fabric of fighter plans. Clements looked at the studies, heard out the admirals, generals, service secretaries and corporate executives involved, and went before the Tactical Air Power Subcommittee of the Senate Armed Services Committee with a plan-on-top-of-plans which left the subcommittee incredulous. He proposed a three-plane proto-type competition, with the winner to become the Navy's new fighter: a stripped-down F-14 sans Phoenix missiles and fire-control system; an F-15 reconfigured for carrier duty, and a modernized F-4. Clements said this program, replete with "flyoffs" among the three contestants, would cost about $250 million, but would settle the issue once and for all. The Navy immediately end-ran Clements and leaked its own cost esti-mate to the subcommittee: $475 million. Whatever the cost, the subcommittee asked Clements, why do you need "prototypes" of planes which already, in effect, exist? Where do you think you're going to get the money? Clements said he would answer the first question in detail at a later date. He said he hadn't figured out the answer to the second question. A couple of weeks later, Clements told the House Armed Services Commit-tee that his prototype-competition program would cost only $150 million because he had decided to eliminate the F-4 from consideration. He said he would get the money for the F-14-versus-F-15 remodelings and flyoff by slowing the Navy's con-version of two ships and transferring the funds from one place to another in the Navy budget. The House panel seized on this with great fervor. It not only denied approval of the prototype program but also cut from the Navy budget the $187 million which had been requested for development of the ships.

During this period, Clements was in charge of the Defense

Department. Schlesinger had been appointed Secretary of Defense but was awaiting Senate confirmation. Reporters, ever watchful for power struggles in a department where they abound, sought some answers from Clements. "Some people," said one at a press conference, "might think that since you are in an 'acting' position, you would clear things with him [Schlesinger] before you make decisions. I gather, from what you are saying, that you have not."

Clements replied: "That is correct. And the responsibility that I carry as the deputy involves the same responsibility that the secretary has, whether we have a secretary or whether we don't. This is the way the building works. . . . I have all the authority that I need to make these policy decisions. You also have to realize that we have some great talents here in the building who act as advisors and counselors, and participate in these decision-making processes. These are the same processes that this building has used through the years. These decisions are not made off in a closet somewhere by somebody thinking, 'I will make this decision,' with strong emphasis on the personal pronoun. This is not the way it is done. . . . The plan is to have these planes [prototypes] available for flying, hopefully, in July of 1975. . . . This is going to be a well-coordinated team between the Navy and the Air Force and . . . the Department of Defense."

Exactly one week later, a Grumman public relations executive telephoned a public relations executive at Raytheon Corp., Lexington, Massachusetts, which makes the Sparrow and Sidewinder missiles. Worrying about the F-14 had long since become their shared pastime. "Don't tell me," said the Raytheon man jocularly, on picking up the phone, "that a Sidewinder has shot down an F-14." Long silence at the other end and reflections on ESP. "No," said the Grumman man, "it was a Sparrow."

High over the Pacific off California, an F-14 had practice-fired a Sparrow. Instead of dropping the ten to twelve feet that it should have before its rocket motor fired, the Sparrow gyrated back upward and mashed the fuselage. The F-14 pitched up, caught fire, and plummeted into the sea. Fortunately, the Sparrow had been unarmed. The pilot and radar officer were rescued. No one held this mishap against the plane itself. But by now, the cost of each plane in a projected production run of more than three hundred had soared to more than $20 million, and the Navy publicity mill whirred furiously in behalf of the F-14.

Just in case Clements were to follow through with his scheme to strip the Tomcat of its Phoenix system, the Navy thought it politic, now, to begin emphasizing the plane's other virtues. "The F-14 fighter," said a puff sheet, "is not being purchased simply because it can carry the Phoenix missile. This aircraft has many other features not currently available in Navy fighters but which are vitally needed to accomplish the Navy mission. Its air superiority armament load is flexible. . . ."

The Navy also dragooned the Marine Corps, which had planned to renovate its squadrons with F-4Js. Secretary of the Navy John W. Warner and Chief of Naval Operations Elmo B. Zumwalt began pressuring Marine Commandant Robert E. Cushman to buy F-14s instead. Cushman balked. All three were called to testify before a House committee. Cushman insisted that he wanted F-4Js. Zumwalt chimed in that Cushman had made "a bad decision." Warner tried to keep the controversy from flaring any further in public, saying that the issue was still open and that he would make the final decision. Stubbornly, Zumwalt, who had become a zealot for the Tomcat, again referred to Cushman's "bad decision." A few weeks later, before a Senate committee, Cushman testified that the Marines now planned to buy F-14s. He was asked why he had changed his mind. "My mission has been changed," he said somewhat sheepishly. Simple. The Navy brass arbitrarily had decided that Marine fighter planes would take on the extra duty of helping Navy fighter planes defend the fleet. To do this, they would have to be F-14s. Senator Stuart K. Symington, at the time the acting chairman of the Armed Services Committee, accused Warner of "shoving the F-14 down the throats of the Marines." Warner flashed anger in his quick denial. It did not ring true. Neither, for that matter, did Symington's dudgeon. He represented Missouri, home of McDonnell Douglas, maker of the F-4 and the F-15. His concern with resolving the fighter issue was something less than pure.

Now, the battle got very rough indeed. Dispensing with the superficial niceties of interservice rivalries, the Navy fired directly at the F-15, aiming for the Eagle's experimental engine then under development by Pratt & Whitney. A "fact sheet" bearing the headline, "The F-15 Is Inherently a High Risk Design," was circulated in Congress and in the offices of the Defense Department. It went, including the italics, as follows:

Of the thirty-four major manned fighter-bomber weapon systems developed by the Air Force and Navy since the Korean War, only *three* with *simultaneous* development of *new engines, new airframes* and *new avionics* [a perfect description of the F-15] reached full production without major developmental problems. These aircraft were the B-47 and B-52, Air Force bombers, and the F-105, an Air Force fighter-bomber. Among those aircraft which were cancelled or limited in production due to *simultaneous* development were the YF-12, XB-70, F3H-1, F-111B, F-111A, SR-71, B-58 and A-5A. All other aircraft which reached production successfully had only one or two components developed at the same time. *The F-14 uses proven engines and avionics, combined with a new airframe. It minimizes risk.*

Like magic, the F-15 engine began acting up in tests. In the first ten months of 1973, it broke down several times, causing fires and explosions. By the middle of the year, vigorous Ben Bellis was in hot water at the Pentagon.

Major General Benjamin N. Bellis, USAF, one of the new breed of techno-managerial generals. His mission: direct the development of the F-15 and shepherd it into production. Background: U.S. Military Academy, 1946. Degree in military engineering, wings of a pilot. Master of Science in Aeronautical Engineering, University of Michigan. Master of Science in Business Administration, George Washington University. Graduate of the Executive Program, Graduate School of Business, University of California. Service with the Strategic Air Command; Air Force Systems Command; Special Weapons Projects Office; Air Research and Development Command; Air Command and Staff College, Wright-Patterson AFB; Industrial College of the Armed Forces, Fort McNair, Washington; Reconnaissance and Electronic Warfare, Aeronautical Systems Division; Legion of Merit with Oak Leaf Cluster; Air Force Commendation Medal with Oak Leaf Cluster; Command Pilot; Master Missileman Badge.

Watching General Bellis get into the cockpit of an F-15 was like watching Cinderella dance with the prince. Bellis would have done anything to bring off the F-15 program. He did one thing which he probably should not have done, in terms of furthering his own career, but which, as it turned out, may have been the best thing, at the time, for his program. He relaxed the performance requirements of the F-15 super-engine just before it was put to final testing in the air. The Defense Department and the Air Force had specified that those requirements—unrelaxed—were to be met or exceeded before the engine could be committed to production. Bellis had the authority to make his decision (remember Packard's dictate about giving program managers more authority and more responsibility?). But he made the mistake of not immediately telling his Air Force or Defense Department superiors what he had done. He just told them that the engine had passed its air tests. They then released $38 million to Pratt & Whitney to get the engine production started.

This might have gone unremarked had not the engine subsequently encountered severe problems during its 150-hour endurance testing. Run up to maximum thrust for long periods of time in a ground chamber which simulated high-altitude atmospheric conditions, the engine's turbine blades kept breaking off. Over one stretch, more than half of the sixty-four blades had to be replaced and their cooling tubes strengthened. They were overheating badly. The Air Force felt faint about it. The original deadline for the testing passed, with the engine still partially disassembled in the aftermath of the latest of the fiery failures. Finally, the engine passed the test. But the Air Force, already committed to its production and staking the whole future of the F-15 on its performance, was forced to spend more millions on what the service described, in characteristically dispassionate terms, as "engine component improvement." A big, black cloud had settled over the F-15. Maybe the engine would pan out and maybe it wouldn't.

One morning at the Pentagon, having flown in from his headquarters at Wright-Patterson, Bellis recalled his decision to ease the engine's air-test structures. It had been justified, he said, because the test pilots had found that the F-15 airframe induced less drag than its designers had anticipated. This meant that the engine could be checked out at lesser power, and the combined performance of the airframe and the engine (the aircraft as an entirety) still would surpass the standards.

"No other engine ever built could have passed that modified test," Bellis snorted, "and, still, I have to walk into Washington with my tail between my legs."

Not long after all this, Bellis was told that he would be reassigned as commander of the Air Force Systems Command's Electronic System Division at Hanscom AFB, Massachusetts. This appeared to be a natural progression in his career. He had seen the F-15 through development and into production. Despite the trouble with the ground-chamber testing of the F-15's engine, the power plants of the Eagles already in the air were performing superbly. So the reassignment probably was no knock on Bellis. Still, some in the Pentagon said that Bellis would have preferred to stay with his first love, the F-15, because it was not yet fully out of the flak. They said his move could be assessed as a boost upward or a shove sideways only later, when his promotion fell due. A buddy of Bellis', a fellow major general, discussed the situation briefly over cocktails at the Air Force Association dinner dance in Washington late in 1974. "Sure it was a leg up for Ben," he said. "Hanscom is a command, isn't it? But I'll say this: Hanscom may be unmanageable. It's got little pockets of scientists all over the place trying to do whatever they please. Good luck to Bellis. Some people in the Pentagon may have been irritated by him, but he gets high marks in the Air Force. I wish we had had him on the B-1 program back when it was getting into trouble."

While in charge of the F-15 program, Bellis figured in two incidents which showed how passionate, even puerile, the rivalry between the Air Force and the Navy over the fighter planes had become. Addressing a convention of aerospace writers at Edwards AFB, California, the F-15 flight-test center, Bellis extolled the F-15 as *the* fighter capable of "gaining and maintaining air superiority for the United States through air-to-air combat, using non-nuclear weapons, in the post-1975 period." When Bellis had finished praising the fighter's "firsts," a Navy F-14 pilot in the audience challenged, in all seriousness, the Air Force to a duel between the Tomcat and the Eagle, using live ammunition. To the relief of the dumbstruck audience, Bellis struck a blow for maturity by not responding in kind. Privately, he must have seethed.

The other incident was an air show of the new Navy and Air

Force fighters at Andrews AFB near Washington. Shah Mohammed Reza Pahlevi of Iran had come to the United States
to see President Nixon and shop for some more American
weapons. The year before, he had committed $2.5 billion of his
kingdom's oil treasury to buy more than two hundred attack
and heavy-duty helicopters, one hundred F-4s and a wide assortment of other weaponry. Iran already was on its way to
possessing the finest air force in the Middle East. But the Shah,
himself a pilot, was not content. Soviet Foxbats, more heavily
armed and longer-ranging than their pure-fighter predecessors
in the long line of MiGs, had been casing the kingdom from
altitudes up to 80,000 feet. The Shah wanted a plane which
could go up there, if need be, or at least fire up there, and get
them. He had his eye on the F-14 and the F-15. The Pentagon
showed them off for him.

The F-15 pilot demonstrated the Eagle's near-vertical takeoff,
rate of climb, slow approach, fast approach, acceleration and
landing, keeping it simple and straightforward. But the F-14
pilot did all that and more: Immelman turns, fancy rolls, up-
side down passes. That night at the Pentagon, several Air
Force officers groused about what had happened at Andrews.
"We had agreed with the Navy," said one, "that the demonstra-
tions would be limited to specific maneuvers. The Navy turned
it into a stunt show, hot-dogging."

Bellis, who had been there, brushed it off. He had briefed the
Shah on the F-15 on three occasions prior to the Andrews air
show, once in Teheran, and was satisfied that the Shah, if he
had any sense, would favor the F-15 in the end. Bellis speculated
that even the Shah would balk at the cost of the F-14. But the
Shah fooled him.

Early in 1974, His Highness signed up for thirty F-14s at
about $900 million. The Air Force offered to sell the Shah
fifty-three F-15s to go along with the F-14s, and was led to
believe, by Defense Department officials, that the sale probably
would go through. Sales to Iran of both fighters would have
been an enormous break for the services and their contractors,
Grumman and McDonnell Douglas. It would have assured
production runs of both planes well through the remainder of
the 1970s, and it would have meant Iran absorbing a big dollop
of the total cost of research, development, testing and production of the planes. But hold on.

In March 1974, Schlesinger told the Senate Appropriations Committee that he had ordered the Air Force to stretch out its production of F-15s partly because he believed that a slower rate would help induce orders from foreign nations—would give them more time to make their buying decisions and to work their orders into the McDonnell Douglas production schedules. Besides Iran, other nations interested in the F-15 were Israel, Japan, Australia and England. Air Force Secretary John L. McLucas estimated that an Iranian order of fifty-three F-15s would save the Air Force $150 million. Then, whoops. The Shah turned down the Air Force offer and signed up, instead, for another lot of fifty F-14s, at a price—over and above the $900 million already committed for thirty of the planes— of about $1 billion. The Air Force generals were livid. Stories spread like wildfire in the Pentagon. One of them suggested that the Defense Department had juggled figures to make the F-14 less costly to the Shah than it really should have been, and to make the F-15 more costly than it really was. Why? To go along with the Navy in trying to save Grumman's solvency and to make sure that the F-14 program did not meet an untimely death for insufficiency of F-14 funding by the Navy alone. Another story had it that overseas salesmen of McDonnell Douglas had pushed the Shah too hard to buy F-15s, and that he had reacted petulantly by buying more F-14s. Still another version, the most logical, was that the Shah had decided to buy only one type of fighter in order to simplify the logistics —the spare parts, ground-support equipment, training and the like—and that he was looking forward to augmenting the F-14 not with the F-15 but with one of the newer, lightweight fighters coming along. Whatever, the Air Force was down, the Navy, up. But not for long.

Moments later, it seemed, Grumman came knocking on the Navy's door, like a panhandler from the past, demanding another multimillion-dollar escalation of funding, and threatening once again to shut down F-14 production unless its contract was revised. The Navy pleaded with Congress to go along, and Congress grumpily agreed. The contract was "restructured" in a fashion to permit Grumman to start making a good profit on its F-14 sales to the Navy, starting in April 1975. The issue subsided for a while—until Grumman came back to the Pentagon, only a few months afterward. The company had been

unable to get bank loans to tide it over until April 1975. It was
in the nasty predicament of not having enough cash to keep on
meeting payrolls. The Navy had been "advancing" (Pentagon
code word for "lending") Grumman money at a rate of interest
that was so far below the prevailing commercial rate as to be
laughable. These advance payments had amounted to about $54
million. Now, Grumman wanted another $45 million or so,
and the Navy, in asking Congress for permission, had to reveal
publicly the scope and interest rates of the advances already
outstanding. Wham. Even though the Navy agreed to increase
the interest rate on the next loan to a level more like reality,
the Senate voted overwhelmingly and angrily to tell the Navy
and Grumman to hell with the whole thing. Let Grumman get
its next loan from commercial banks, like everyone else had to
do, or pay the consequences. Even F-14 buff Barry Goldwater
took this position. He also suggested sternly that maybe Grumman could shake up its management, do anything, but quit
asking for government bailouts. Goldwater's reaching the fed-
up phase in the F-14 fuss was decisive in the Senate vote. He
took many senators along with him in his vote against the
Navy loan, and left the admirals and Grumman executives
aghast at his turnabout. Things did indeed look bad for the
Navy and Grumman. But there was always the feeling that
they would, somehow or other, make do. For one thing, Grumman could go to U.S. and foreign banks and show the Shah's
letters of intent to buy a big bunch of the Tomcats. If the
Shah's collateral isn't as good as gold, whose is? For another,
the Shah himself could come through with an accelerated
schedule of advance payments on his future procurement of
the fighters. U.S. defense officials made nicely clucking noises
about taking too much money ahead of time from a foreign
nation to salvage what is basically (or is it?) a U.S. aircraft
program, but it was a safe bet that the rustle of the Shah's bills
would soon soothe the momentary moralists.

In September 1974, a consortium of U.S. banks and Mel-
liBank of Iran solved the problem for the time being by lending
Grumman $200 million. This enabled Grumman to pay back
the money which the Navy had advanced; maintain its cash
flow; meet its payroll; continue F-14 production at the pace the
Navy desired; and prepare to tool up for eventual production
of eighty of the Tomcats for the air arm of the Imperial Iranian

Armed Forces, starting in 1976. Irony laced the lightening of Grumman's load, however. As we shall note in the final chapter, in another context, relations between the new administration of President Gerald R. Ford and the cartel of Arab and non-Arab oil-producing nations, including Iran, were deteriorating. There was much talk in Washington, talk that was put down officially, but propagated privately, at the Pentagon, that the United States might have to resort to military action in the Middle East. Was it possible, then, that U.S. pilots might someday have to fight *against* F-14s over the Persian Gulf? This was only speculation, dangerous speculation at that. What was certain, at the moment, was that an Iranian bank, despite its, Grumman's and the Navy's disclaimers, had managed to get a piece of the Grumman action, and the foreign foothold in the American defense industry had become firmer.

In all the back and forth about the relative merits of the F-14 and the F-15, no one had gone to the pilots who were flying, or had flown, either fighter, to hear their versions of how a duel of the Eagle and the Tomcat would come out. So I went.

Air Force Colonel Frank Bloomcamp and Navy Commander René ("call me Sam") Leeds agreed on one thing only: the F-4 Phantom, which both had flown in combat over Vietnam, left an awful lot to be desired as a dogfighter. Bloomcamp, with a big grin, called the F-4 "dog meat" in comparison to the fighter he now was flying with the Tactical Air Command. Leeds, less assertive, noted that he'd had trouble seeing to the rear in the F-4, that the MiGs had been especially troublesome at "close quarters, in pop-up situations," and that adapting the F-4 to fighter tactics had been "like trying to make a Cadillac into a small sports car." So much for the F-4. But the issue, now, was the Air Force F-15, Bloomcamp's baby, versus the F-14, Leeds' new love. Which would win if the two superfighters, subjects of so much bitter controversy between the services, were to go at it missiles to missiles, gun to gun, speed to speed, turn to turn? Bloomcamp and Leeds disagreed, of course, on the outcome.

I interviewed Bloomcamp one clear blue day at Andrews Air Force Base near Washington, just before he settled into the sky-blue F-15, taxied out, released the brakes and, within thirty seconds, literally flew the fighter out of sight in a near-vertical climb. The blue of the sky and the blue of the plane blended perfectly, which is what the F-15's paint job was all about. Only the glint of the sun off the wings, as Bloomcamp rolled the fighter over sharply, showed you that he had reached the top of his climb. How would he do battle with the F-14? Would he win?

Sure, I'll be glad to talk about it, Bloomcamp said. Yes, I could take him, especially if he wants to come into me and try to turn with me. If he got the six-o'clock position on me, I'd use the turn performance I've got in this airplane and make him overshoot. My airplane lets me exploit classical tactics to the maximum. At long range, maybe we'd both be shot down early in the fight. He's got the Phoenix. But I've got the Sparrow, and it's a lot better bird than it used to be. It could go out and get him. Just give me one chance to find him and lock on with it. That's all I should need. I'd proba- bly see him better, too. I've got the best cockpit visibility any fighter has ever had. I think my radar is better than his. I've got the good look-down radar.

If we both miss with the radar missiles, I keep coming. I keep pressing the attack. Everything I do is aimed at accom- plishing one thing: getting around behind him, where he can't see me. As I come in, I shoot the IR [infrared Side- winder] missiles. If he's not dead by then, I go on in and get him with the gun. I'd go from maximum-detection range right up to his tailpipe.

By the time I interviewed Leeds, he was deskbound at the Pentagon, as the Navy's F-14 Program Coordinator. He had commanded the first F-14 training squadron at Miramar Naval Air Station, California. The carrier had just gone operational aboard the carrier *Enterprise*. "I wish I were back with them," said Leeds. "I'm eager to see us explore the tactics. We don't know yet just how much this airplane can actually do, and I'm sure it will do a lot more, even, than we might expect." Could he defeat the F-15? Leeds nodded. But he said he pre- ferred to discuss the relative merits of the F-14 and the plane it was replacing in the fleet, the F-4, and leave the F-15 out of the discussion. On being told of Bloomcamp's confidence of victory in the F-15, Leeds smiled and said: "I'd rather not play that game.

"The best thing in any air-to-air combat," he said, "is to get the quick kill. The longer you stay in the fight, the more risk you run—with any airplane—that somebody will get in behind you. The quick kill is the key to the F-14. It has the Phoenix and the Sparrow and a radar-fire control system that gives you a God's-eye view; continual, automatic mapping and lock-on; the *whole* picture out there. You can preempt six targets all at once with the Phoenix at very long ranges. It makes no difference whether you are up against missiles or a numerically superior fighter threat. The F-14 gives you selective, intelligent engagement. The radar not only spots all your targets at once, but even points out which one you should shoot at first. And not only at long range. The first MiGs to face us would get missiles shot at them at very close quarters, something they'd never seen before."

But what would happen if the F-15 penetrated the F-14's picket of missiles and the fight came down to cannon in the clinches?

"It would be very interesting," Leeds said. "It would be a two-man aircrew against one man, and the F-14 turns well too. We've pitted the F-14 against the T-38 and the F-86, which is probably the best-turning aircraft ever developed up to now, and we've been beating both of them in the dogfight."

About a month after the Bloomcamp and Leeds interviews, an intriguing story began to surface at the Pentagon. Chief of Naval Operations Elmo Zumwalt, prior to his retirement, had challenged Air Force Chief of Staff George S. Brown, prior to Brown's ascendancy to the chairmanship of the JCS, to a "flyoff" of the two fighters. Brown accepted. The planes did not actually go up against each other; rather, their performances were measured by data-processing devices, mounted on the fighters, which computed such dogfighter life-signs as sustained G-force, maximum G-force, turn rate, turn radius and thrust. In each category, according to the charts, and at all altitudes, the F-15 was the clear winner. The results, in keeping with Pentagon custom, were kept classified.

Then Senator Thomas F. Eagleton (D-Miss.) criticized the Pentagon for "covering up the test results showing the F-14 to be an inferior aircraft in order to preserve the pride of the

Navy." Eagleton's motives were brought into question at the Pentagon; McDonnell Douglas, maker of the F-15, is his constituent. But Eagleton had gained access to the flyoff charts, and was firing at the F-14 from six o'clock. "I am especially concerned," he said, "that the U.S. government may have given erroneous information about the two planes to the government of Iran in order to bail out Grumman. The F-14 may have been adequate in the air combat role if the F-401 engine it was designed to take had worked out. But with the twelve-year-old TF-30 engine, it is nothing more than a 'Tom Turkey,' the name assigned to it by Navy and Air Force pilots alike."

You'll never catch Commander Leeds calling it that. Or Bloomcamp either, at least not in public. Both services had long since agreed to lay off the fighter-plane rivalry, now that both their planes were in production. Besides, pilots tend to stick together in the end. They all like to talk with their hands, and they like best of all to talk to each other. Besides, the "Great Fighter Plane Battle" had wrung out both the F-15 and F-14 programs, and both services too. Neither fighter, it now seemed, would be produced in anywhere near the quantities which the Air Force and the Navy had counted on in the beginning of their development programs. The Eagle and the Tomcat would be augmented in the U.S. air arms by greater numbers of a new breed of bird—much lighter, less costly, less sophisticated in electronics and weaponry, but superior to even the F-15 as a clear-weather dogfighter.

In 1972, the Air Force awarded General Dynamics Corp. and Northrop Corp. contracts to begin developing prototypes of a new generation of quick-turning, superswift-accelerating, low-cost air-superiority aircraft. Neither company had good reason to anticipate an eventual production contract. The prototypes were to be built only to demonstrate and test advanced aerospace technologies. The ruling circles of the Air Force did not, in fact, want the fighters ever to come into being. They might constitute a threat to the full production of the F-15. But Packard, in one of his final moves, had insisted that the Air Force start developing them. He was worried that the high costs of the F-14 and the F-15 would preclude producing enough of the superfighters to fill out Air Force and Navy fighter forces, leaving only skeleton squadrons of modern fighters. Schlesinger picked up where Packard had left off. "We cannot afford and we do not need," he told Congress, "an all high-capability fighter force [meaning F-14s and F-15s] in the Navy and Air Force. We believe that development of a new, low-cost, high-performance fighter which can perform tactical air missions under visual flight conditions is entirely practical and should be vigorously pursued."

This is exactly what the fighter pilots had been waiting to hear. The new fighters would maneuver more vigorously and adroitly. They would not be loaded down with missiles, fuel and electronics. This did not mean, however, that they would lack enough range or be deficient in electronics. Advances of technology now made it possible to put cut-rate electronics aboard fighters at no sacrifice of performance. In fact, said Dr. Malcolm R. Currie, the new director of defense research and engineering, the radar being developed for the General Dynamics and Northrop prototypes by Westinghouse, Hughes, Rockwell International and others would be a "whole generation beyond the fantastic radar in the F-15." And it was Currie's opinion that the new planes would be able to "take the F-15 in a dogfight."

If the dogfighting demands of the Vietnam War had induced the development of these new fighters (and, for that matter, of the F-15), the dogfighting results of the Mideast war of 1973 just about clinched their eventual mass production in the late 1970s. Israeli fighter planes achieved a phenomenal, unprecedented, fifty-five-to-one kill ratio in that war, nearly tripling its twenty-to-one ratio of the war of 1967. Israeli pilots shot down 330 MiGs, many of them MiG-21s, in the air-to-air combat, and lost only six fighters. For dogfighting, they flew the French Mirage and Israeli Barak fighters, both of them light and highly maneuverable, armed only with cannon and heat-seeking missiles, including the Sidewinder. The Israelis used the American F-4 mostly as an attack plane, not as a dogfighter. They had judged it inferior to the MiG-21 for the clear-sky, canopy-to-canopy shootouts just east and west of Suez. But the Israelis lost more than a hundred attack planes to ground fire, including twenty-seven F-4s and fifty-two American-built A-4 Skyhawks. In only a few weeks, the war destroyed hundreds of millions of dollars worth of airplanes. This gave pause to the Pentagon as it shaped and sized its own air wings of the future. The heavy attrition of equipment in any modern war alone is enough to militate against forming air forces exclusively of airplanes costing $15 million to $20 million, or more, apiece. One F-15 might be as good as three lightweights, but when it has been shot down, there is nothing left.

So Schlesinger pushed the Air Force toward selection and production of a lightweight fighter. Part of his push—strange as it may seem to anyone unfamiliar with the military Id—was to change the designation of the planes from "Lightweight Fighter" to "Air Combat Fighter." This made the Air Force feel better. Now it sounded like a hot weapon, not a cheap piece of junk, not a copout from the F-15, not a "lightweight." It sounded like it might be able to shoot something down, not just dart around looking like a fly amid a swarm of wasps. "Why did the Air Force change the name?," I naïvely asked a senior Defense Department civilian. "To sell the plane to Congress?" He gave me a patient look. "*We* changed the name," he said dryly, "to sell the plane to the Air Force."

In the summer of 1974, the first prototypes of the Air Combat Fighters—the General Dynamics YF-16 and the Northrop YF-17—zipped into the air at Edwards Air Force Base, California, to begin undergoing tests, leading to an Air Force choice of one or the other in early 1975. The Air Force was still not wild about putting the plane into production. But then, events elsewhere in the world clinched matters for the Air Force.

For many years, the Lockheed F-104 Starfighter had been the main fighter of a number of European countries, and it had long since become obsolete. Belgium, the Netherlands, Denmark and Norway formed a consortium to seek out together —and eventually procure—a replacement fighter. France quickly offered its latest, lightest, hottest Mirage; Sweden, its Saab-Viggen. Northrop already had been trying to sell these countries, and others, its Cobra. In fact, the Northrop entry in the U.S. Air Force Air Combat Fighter competition, the YF-17, was a modified Cobra, tailored more to Air Force specifications but basically the same plane. As Northrop's competitor in the U.S. bidding, General Dynamics could not afford to ignore the interrelated European market. After all, if the Europeans decided to buy the Cobra, this might influence the U.S. Air Force to buy the Northrop Air Combat Fighter instead of the General Dynamics YF-16. Or vice versa. The winner of the USAF competition probably would have an edge with the Europeans. A lot depended on who bought first—the Europeans or the USAF. The situation could shake down in several directions, and the competing American, French and Swedish contractors had to cover all possible bases. So General Dynamics marketers began covering the territory across the Atlantic, bird-dogging their Northrop competitor-counterparts.

In June, representatives of the consortium visited Edwards AFB, with top Defense Department and Air Force officials in solicitous tow, to watch the YF-16 and YF-17 perform. The U.S. officials desperately wanted the Europeans to buy one or the other of the U.S. planes. This would cut the price to the Air Force, and it would be a bonanza for the U.S. balance of payments. It also would enhance considerably the standardization of NATO–U.S. fighters, long a goal of the U.S. But the French were perhaps even more desperate to make sales of their Mirage throughout Europe. They claimed to their fighter-shopping European neighbors that, indeed, the French aerospace industry might go down the drain if the four countries did not buy the Mirage. And that, said the French, would be bad news for all of Europe, so interdependent are the economies of all its nations.

Michael Getler of the *Washington Post* told it in a front-page piece of August 5, 1974. He wrote in part:

A Pentagon project involving development of a new lightweight fighter plane is the focus of one of the most titanic battles for a defense contract in history. Possibly $10 billion to $15 billion in business over the next several years is at stake for companies that could wind up building 2,000 or more of these relatively low-cost but highly maneuverable jets. The battle is international in scope and bitterness. Aside from the planned U.S. Air Force purchase of the plane, several European members of NATO must decide whether to buy the American aircraft or the newest French Mirage jet. The Paris newspaper *Le Monde* calls it "the weapons contract of the century." Top aides to French President Valery Giscard d'Estaing are calling on European governments personally to persuade them to buy the French plane. With both France and the United States aggressively pursuing overseas sales of military hardware as one way to offset rising oil import prices, the decision of the Europeans—no matter how it comes out—is certain to put new strains on U.S.–French, U.S.–NATO or French–NATO nations. . . . In this country, interest and stakes in the project heightened even further Thursday when the powerful House Appropriations Committee strongly recommended that the Navy buy a modified version of the Air Force plane rather than design still another craft. Just a few weeks earlier, oil-rich Iran—which ordered an unprecedented $3.5 billion worth of U.S. military hardware during the past fiscal year—also expressed interest in buying 250 of the planes.

As Getler's piece suggested, the Swedes by now were out of the competition. It had come down to the United States versus France in the intercontinental competition, and to General Dynamics and Northrop back home. Then two things happened. The Air Force announced that it would choose between the YF-16 and YF-17 several months earlier than it had planned, at no sacrifice of the thoroughness of the testing, in order to accommodate its timetable to the European consortium's own deadline for a procurement decision. Schlesinger fired off an invitation to the defense ministers of the four countries to come see him at the Pentagon, and go on out to Edwards to take a good look at the sleek, swift, super Air Combat Fighter prototypes for themselves. This, a month later, they did. But not before they had stopped off in Paris for a session with French Defense Minister Jacques Soufflet. Schlesinger had an offer ready for the Europeans as an inducement for them to buy whichever U.S. plane the USAF eventually would choose. He said the Europeans could help the USAF define the new fighter's mission (and thus dictate, to some extent, the scope of its electronics) so that it would satisfy their own mission needs; they could include their own industrial teams in the planning of the final configuration of the plane, and they could share in its production by manufacturing, in Europe, much of the airframes and spare parts of those Air Combat Fighters which would be assigned to their squadrons. The defense ministers thanked Schlesinger for a nice visit, strolled noncommittally through the River Entrance, got into Defense Department limousines, went to Dulles Airport, and flew back home, leaving Schlesinger the arms salesman to sweat it out. Later on, it became apparent that the European nations did indeed favor the American Air Combat Fighter which the U.S. Air Force decided upon, and there were glad tidings, at Christmastime, 1974, beside the Potomac. In January 1975, the Air Force chose General Dynamics to build at least 650 F-16s. And then the Pentagon nervously waited for the final word from the Europeans.

The Air Force, which in the beginning would have preferred to build an Air Combat Fighter strictly to suit its own purposes, began to feel like a wallflower amid all this Defense Department dancing for Eurodollars. Now, it became the Navy's turn up against the wall. At the urging of Congress, Schlesinger and his deputy, Clements, began leaning on the admirals not only to plan on buying an Air Combat Fighter for the fleet but also—the ignominy of it all—to plan on buying a variation of the *Air Force* Air Combat Fighter. The Navy was getting tired of this. First, it had been forced to fend off the bi-service F-111, then the F-15; and now, behold, a bi-service Air Combat Fighter, the newest of the threats to all-out production of the F-14. It was the same old story, only with different airplanes, and, by now, more of them, in a stew which had long since been overcooked at the Pentagon.

Through it all, McDonnell Douglas did not stand idle. Its Eagle had been caught in the middle. The F-15 had become too high-priced for the European countries, now in line for the Air Combat Fighter. The Shah also had passed it by for the F-14, and now indicated that he, too, would buy the Air Combat Fighter in the future. Still, McDonnell Douglas pushed its F-15 sales pitch in Teheran and in the European capitals. And the company did something else which the Pentagon brass thought was in bad taste: It made the Pentagon an offer: buy one thousand or more of our F-15s and fill out the Air Force with them instead of mixing the F-15s with Air Combat Fighters. This, said McDonnell Douglas, would give the Air Force a more versatile, more lethal, *all-weather* fighter which, because of the increased quantity in the purchase, would cost little more than the combination of F-15s and Air Combat Fighters then being contemplated. Moreover, said the company, think what the Pentagon would save on maintenance and spare parts by having only one kind of fighter in the Air Force inventory. This proposition embarrassed the Air Force, which tried to keep it quiet. The Air Combat Fighter was where the action abided, now, and McDonnell Douglas, its F-15 so recently the most favored fighter, was mucking up the new scenario. It was truly amazing how Air Force officers, who only a few months previously had sworn by the F-15 as the end-all, now were proclaiming the Air Combat Fighter as the plane of planes.

Deep down, the military is most comfortable with a potpourri of planes, if not for combat and logistical efficiency, then for perpetuating the military-industrial-Congressional complex. The Pentagon likes to feed as many aerospace companies as it possibly can. If it were to buy all planes of any one type—fighters, close-support, fighter-bombers, you name it—from only one company, other companies undoubtedly would die. In dealing with an aircraft industry which operates, in its best years, at a grossly inefficient 60 percent of capacity, the Pentagon's approach is to hand out as much money as it can to as many companies as it can, rather than concentrate its aircraft procurement on just a few of the best and force the marginal ones either to adjust to the commercial market or go out of business. Having a lot of companies compete for an increasing number of airplane contracts may seem the epitome of free enterprise. But it really isn't; it isn't truly competition. Whenever a company languishes, it seems the Pentagon can always come up with a new mission which will require a new airplane which the languishing company can provide. Oddly enough, that company wins the contract. The competition is regulated and so—indirectly—is the aircraft industry. By the Pentagon. This goes a long way toward explaining the never-ending swirl of new types of planes in the skies, and why there will always be a superfighter of tomorrow to supersede the superfighter of today. The tyranny of technology has, of course, a lot to do with it, too.

In the very same year that F-14s and F-15s began forming up in Navy and Air Force operational squadrons and that the Air Combat Fighter came into its own, the Air Force pushed forward with a brand new "Advanced Fighter Technology Integration" (AFTI) program. This was the research and development of new control techniques for sharper maneuverability, and of new airframe technology—embodying composite materials and streamlining fighter configurations. Many innovations, some of which had been tested tentatively in the

Air Combat Fighter R&D, were on the drawing boards. The Defense Department insisted that the new programs were only "technology demonstration" pursuits, and were not intended to be cartwheeled into production of an actual plane. But the Air Combat Fighter was in the air, and, surely, that could not be the end. As they say at the Pentagon: "If it has already flown, it is already obsolete." Something new must be the successor.

Among the innovations studied in the advanced-technology programs was the incorporation of titanium and of boron and graphite composites to a far greater extent than these had been built into the skins of the F-14, F-15 and Air Combat Fighters. The goal: add strength and cut friction and weight. Some aerospace scientists were foreseeing airplanes of the future built mostly of thread—because graphite composite comes in threadlike form. It is made by converting threads of acrylic fiber into graphite, under intense heat, and then bonding the fibers with supertough industrial glues. Layers of this material are stacked, then subjected to terrific heat and pressure. The product is much, much tougher than aluminum, and can be machined and cut just like ordinary metal.

The new-new class of fighters in embryonic development in the mid-1970s also featured semireclining seats for the pilots, enabling them to withstand the crushing G forces which they generate as they wheel about the skies. But perhaps the most intriguing embodiments in test planes and in the new F-16 were control systems called "Fly-by-wire," another of those unfelicitous descriptive phrases of the military wordsmiths which manage to give exactly the wrong connotation, a connotation of Rube Goldberg at his wires and pulleys. Fly-by-wire is precisely the opposite. What it means is that the intricate control systems of the planes will be actuated by electronic signals, not by mechanical links, thus giving the pilots a tremendous advantage.

The mechanical control systems of modern aircraft—mazes of cranks, rods, pulleys, cables, hydraulic lines and pumps, stretching all the way through the wings and along the entire length of the fuselage—have become increasingly costly, complex and difficult to maintain in the seven decades since powered flight began. If any one element fails, the plane goes out of control. The new electronic system will weigh less, cost less over its life in service, take up relatively little space, and be easier to install and maintain. If one signal path fails, control can be shifted quickly to one of several backup channels. To a fighter plane and its pilot, this stands for survival. (It would mean survival to a commercial airliner too, of course.) Small, redundant computers are dispersed throughout the plane. Their circuits, each capable of overriding and taking over from the others, run to each control-surface actuator. These actuators still must use hydraulic power to move the fins, ailerons, elevators and trim tabs. But they are snuggled close to the control surfaces which they operate. This cuts drastically the risk of hydraulic failure from gunfire or mechanical malfunction. Gone are the hydraulic lines which now are interlaced throughout a plane, from pumps on the engines to all actuators.

Ever since the days of the Gemini earth-orbiting flights, the National Aeronautics and Space Administration has been using this type of control system in its spacecraft. But the NASA type was too expensive and too fragile to be installed in fighters destined for rugged duty. Advances in semiconductor microcircuits now have engendered electronic units small, sturdy and inexpensive enough to put into fighters or any other plane.

The impact of fly-by-wire through the next decade and beyond will be a profound one for the entire field of aerodynamics. As the system fine-tunes flight controls, planes no longer will need wings and horizontal stabilizers of the size now required to keep them on keel. Some aerospace engineers foresee planes of missile-like silhouette which will fly laterally or vertically without changing the axis of the fuselage, and without pitching, rolling or yawing. Much of the technology of the future will have been gained the hard way, in arenas such as that of the Great Fighter Plane Battle of the Pentagon. And the men who made the decisions, good and bad, contend that there is no substitute for trial and error. Perhaps.

Shortly after he became Secretary of Defense, Schlesinger, reviewing all the fuming over fighters, hinted that the services would have to pull together better in their trying and erring. "We want," he said, "the beneficial effects of interservice competition while avoiding the nefarious effects of interservice rivalry." What he had in mind, he said, "was the tendency of each of the services to build into itself those capabilities that will permit it to be independent of the other services, so that it doesn't have to rely, as it were, on external sources of support. I don't think we can afford that. I think each of the services is obligated to think in terms of a common national defense, rather than in terms of the separate interests of the individual service." Only the future would show whether Schlesinger could persuade the uniformed fiefdoms of the Pentagon of the merit of his philosophy. It promised to be difficult. The military had begun making a comeback, after Vietnam, in national esteem, and the last thing Schlesinger wanted to do was to put its psyche through another period of disrepair. He could crack down a little on the services to shape up their fighter programs. But the Joint Chiefs of Staff would have no quarrel with his cheerleadership of their comeback, especially where strategic policy and strategic weapons—the big stuff, the stuff of Schlesinger's own career—were concerned. He was with them all the way on that.

3

The
War Rooms

A few years back, I flew east from Helsinki in a small plane with another American and two Finns to relax for a day in the snowy countryside near the Soviet border. The pilot gave us the grand tour. Banking slightly south over the coast of the Gulf of Finland, we flew near a new nuclear power station which the Russians were helping the Finns build. Heading back northeast, our starboard wingtip pointed toward the smoke of the mills of Svetogorsk, on the Soviet side of the border, in Karelia, a former Finnish province which the Russians had overrun and occupied in the war of 1939-40. The day was clear. We could see to the horizon. It was March, and the Baltic ice was beginning to show cracks. Blue skies. Flat, forested landscape. Peaceful. In Helsinki, emissaries of the United States and the Soviet Union were preparing together for the second round of Strategic Arms Limitation Talks (SALT II). Things were looking up. We landed. A half hour later, our Finnish hosts were in a dither. The Soviets had complained to the foreign ministry in Helsinki that our plane had violated Soviet air space. The Finnish ministry, which treads softly in its dealings with the Soviets, had telephoned, in turn, to chastise our hosts. It would seem to have been much to do about nothing, until you become aware that the air space at issue is the hunting preserve of MiGs. They patrol in profusion around there because nests of Soviet intercontinental nuclear missiles are strung out from Lake Ladoga, near Svetogorsk, all the way north to the White Sea. "It is a wonder," said one of our hosts, "that we were not forced down. It has happened before."

There are some corridors in the Pentagon you can't just amble into. Without a pass. To penetrate one of these areas, of about 30,000 square feet, encompassing a score or more of rooms, you need a very special pass. With your picture on it. Evidence that you've never harbored so much as a fleeting subversive fantasy. "Restricted Area. Joint Chiefs of Staff." Off the ninth corridor, "The Bradley Corridor," just a few steps to your right as you come into the building on its second floor, River Entrance. This compound is where the Chairman of the Joint Chiefs of Staff; the Chief of Staff, Army; the Chief of Staff, Air Force; the Chief of Naval Operations and the Commandant of the Marine Corps conduct their urgent business in concert. It is where they literally keep an eye on everything that happens, every second, in every military command around the world. From the Sixth Fleet in the Mediterranean, the Seventh Fleet in the Pacific, the Strategic Air Command headquartered in Nebraska, to the point battalion on the Elbe, the National Security Agency's electronic listening post in far off Asmara, Ethiopia, the Navy station in Keflavik, Iceland, which monitors the passage of Soviet missile submarines southward into the North Atlantic and beyond, to their undersea posts off our East Coast.

The chiefs assemble for two, three, four hours at fourteen-thirty every Monday, Wednesday and Friday in Room 2E294, which is still called "the Tank," a carryover from the days when the only way to get into it was by descending a spiral staircase from above. Now, it also is called "the Gold Room," after the color of the thick pile carpet and the heavy drapes. The Tank does not have the countdown aura of military command and control. More like the board room of a corporation. Sixteen-foot hexagonal walnut table, eight feet wide in the middle, seven at the ends. A yellow pad, five black pencils, two red pencils, an ashtray and a bowl of hard candy at the place of each chief. Formica top, impervious to cigarette charring. On one wall, hidden from view behind sliding wooden panels, is the steel case containing maps of those parts of the world under discussion on this day. On another wall is a chart showing nothing more commonplace than the vacation schedules of the chiefs and their top deputies. On the floor near the chairman's leather chair is a facsimile machine. He uses it to send messages and orders to aides waiting in the anteroom beyond the locked doors. A red light glows over the door when the chiefs are top-secreting, *in camera*. Within reach of the chairman are several telephones of different colors. Secure lines. One to the White House. One to the Secretary of Defense. One to NATO commanders. And so on. Speak into the red one, and your message is automatically encrypted on a "scrambler" system.

A dozen steps from the Tank is another, much larger room, where the chiefs meet on operational matters. Gulf of Tonkin. Bay of Pigs. Cuban missile crisis. Berlin airlift. Bombing of Hanoi. Berlin wall. Soviet invasion of Czechoslovakia. Wars in the Middle East. Soviet missile test. It is called, simply, "the Conference Room," or, although this is now considered poor public relations, "the War Room." Here, the huge table can seat sixteen or so. Another forty can be accommodated on tiers of seats, arranged bleacher fashion, along one wall. The War Room is more like it. More like the movies, with all the accoutrements of command in the electronic age. Maps that light up, television displays, batteries of telephones, computer consoles linked to the Ballistic Missile Early Warning System (BMEWS), showing "minutes to next impact," "predicted impact," "actual impact" of enemy missiles. "Call up CINCPAC [Commander-in-Chief, Pacific] and ask him what the hell is going on out there." In seconds, CINCPAC is on the line.

Right next door is a much larger room, a workaday room with a cork floor, called the National Military Command Center, the cynosure of all military communications. Its more than 25 million miles of circuits link all commands, the White House, the Pentagon, the State Department, the Central Intelligence Agency, the National Security Agency, the Defense Nuclear Agency, the Defense Intelligence Agency. It is under the command of a general or flag officer every second. Its shirt-sleeved officers and noncoms keep track of the whereabouts of the President and of all cabinet officers, just in case. A chart on the wall shows the Secretary of State in Cairo, the Secretary of Defense in Brussels, the Secretary of Transportation in the Virgin Islands. Now at breakfast. Now back in his hotel room. Now gone off to make his speech. Now . . .

At one end of this big room is a smaller one called "Molink." It contains the White House–Kremlin hot line, two teletype-writers tapping their messages through a transatlantic cable which runs through the British Isles. Two teleprinters, made in East Germany and furnished by the Russians, receive, in Cyrillic, the messages from Moscow. Five teams of Russian-linguist JCS staffers man Molink all the time. If anything should go wrong on the circuits, there is a high-frequency radio backup. Cable messages go out in cipher, to be decrypted at the other end. Radio messages are plaintext, "in the clear." The Americans send on the even hours; the Russians, on the odd. Their ground rules forbid messages about politics, military matters or religion. Never, never propaganda. The Russians have just sent a description of the beauty of a scene in the Urals, a short story by Pushkin. Earlier this night, the Americans sent a poem by Robert Frost. Now they are preparing to send Mark Twain's "Life on the Mississippi." Listen to the officer in charge, a tall, cool WAC colonel who learned her Russian at the Army Language School, Monterey, California:

> Our test messages are either language challenges or information that we think they might find interesting, enjoyable. We do not exchange translations of test messages. And we do not play games. We do not consider that professional. We are mindful of our major mission: to translate into Russian any governmental message for the President and transmit it to the Soviet Union. We enjoy our work. Russian is an expressive language.

Like the rest of the Pentagon, the National Military Command Center is a "soft target." If those missile-monitoring consoles in the War Room ever flash the minutes-to-impact message (unlike Moscow, Washington has no antimissile-missile defense), battle-ready command centers at sea or in the air, all the time, would take over. One key element in this is called "Looking Glass"—a post-attack command and control system

made up of nine aircraft, on an ultra-high-frequency link with
the National Command Authority. One at a time, these planes,
Boeing 707s, have been airborne continuously since 1961. They
fly at random over a territory of about 80,000 square miles, out
of Offutt Air Force Base, Nebraska, the headquarters of the
Strategic Air Command. The "Looking Glass" planes that are
not airborne at any particular time remain on ground alert at
air bases dispersed in the Midwest. There is a special plane at
Andrews AFB, just outside Washington, for the President, if
he needs to use it, and for the defense and military chiefs. It
would take the President fifteen minutes to fly by helicopter
from the White House to Andrews, and be airborne in his
command post. Or he could head by helicopter toward his
Camp David retreat in the Catoctin Mountains of Maryland,
about seventy miles north of the White House, veer off and
land, instead, at the nearby Alternate National Command Center. Called "the Rock," it nestles behind and under hundreds
of feet of mountainside granite. Two tunnels lead into it. They
could be plugged in minutes, sealing off three thousand inhabi-
tants, who could survive without surfacing for a solid month.

All these trappings exist to support the President, who is
Commander-in-Chief of the armed forces, and the Secretary of
Defense, his civilian executive officer. But its nexus is the
Tank, or the War Room, or wherever the chiefs, jointly or
singly, hang their gold-braided caps. The chiefs are the embodiment of the military in American society. They are restricted by law in the influence they can wield over that
society. They are bidden to give direction to the armed forces
and advice to the President and the Secretary of Defense. They
cannot make defense policy, have final say on weapons or manpower budgets, peremptorily order the development or production of weapons systems, or even issue commands to the
troops in the field without first getting civilian approval. The
law is set up that way because Americans always have worried
about military control. Long memories of European militarism
and "the man on horseback." Never any single chief of staff.
Never any evolution of the generals and admirals into a Prus-
sian-style General Staff. Still, the chiefs can take advantage of
great latitude within the law. What it comes down to is that the
chiefs have as little, or as much, power as the Secretary of
Defense, who derives his own power from the President,

chooses to let them have. They have the ear of the President, however, and are free to testify in opposition to the Secretary of Defense on Capitol Hill. The chairman sits on the National Security Council.

The chiefs always have been prudent in public, if sometimes profanely plainspoken in private, in expressing such opposition. They would have too much to lose, personally, were it otherwise. It is at their level, in the Tank, that the services work out accommodations with one another and with the civilian overseers. These accommodations are the synapses of defense and foreign policy. They are crucial to the functioning of a democracy. In the quarter-century following World War II, the power of the country's four-star fraternity steadily waned, becoming weakest under McNamara. Then came the Nixon administration, and more power to the chiefs. Their comeback was a steady one, perceptible only if you look back for perspective.

World War II. All for one and one for all. Franklin Roosevelt was the Commander-in-Chief, no question. He made the final decisions. But the military actually ran the war, and the public was glad of it. General George C. Marshall, Chief of Staff of the Army. General Henry ("Hap") Arnold, Chief of the Army Air Corps. Admiral Ernest King, Chief of Naval Operations. Admiral William Leahy, working side by side with Roosevelt at the White House, perhaps the most influential of all. Roosevelt did not have, and did not need, a Secretary of Defense. He had Secretaries of War and Navy, but they pretty much rubber-stamped the admirals and generals. In matters of war, Roosevelt all but ignored his Secretary of State, Cordell Hull. Hull later was to write in his memoirs that he was left out of war councils and pointedly not invited to the Roosevelt-Churchill meetings at Casablanca, Cairo and Teheran. Hull did not even know that the American military was developing an atomic bomb. Vice-President Harry Truman didn't know it, either.

After the war, rivalries between and inside the services, long simmering, began to surface. President Truman wondered if it might not be a good idea to put everyone into the same uniform as a first step toward stopping the bickering. There was considerable support of this concept in Congress, but not enough. The services had clout on Capitol Hill. (They still do.)

The compromise was the National Security Act of 1947, which created the Department of Defense and the Office of the Secretary of Defense, the Department of the Air Force (separate from the Army) and the Joint Chiefs of Staff—along with the Joint Staff, an organization of no more than one hundred top officers working in support of the JCS. In 1949, the Act was amended to create the Office of the Chairman of the Joint Chiefs of Staff. On August 16, of that year, General of the Army Omar N. Bradley was sworn in as the first chairman. The size of the Joint Staff also was increased to 210 officers.

In 1952, Truman, in pique at the Marine Corps, advocated its abolition. Congress rode him down, and then stomped on him. It gave the commandant of the Corps co-equal status with members of the JCS on "matters that directly concern the Marine Corps." Later, a story went around the Pentagon that one of the first Marine commandants to take part in JCS sessions was castigated by an Air Force chief for having expressed misgivings about Air Force plans to develop a new bomber. "This has nothing to do with the Marines," snapped the Air Force general, "so why are you getting into it?" "Because I am an American citizen, goddamnit," retorted the Marine.

In his first term, Truman turned to the soldier-statesmen of World War II to help him put across his foreign policies. Marshall served as both Secretary of Defense and as Secretary of State. The Marshall Plan. Lucius Clay governed the American sector of Berlin and ran the Berlin airlift. James Van Fleet led the American mission against a Communist takeover in Greece. The Truman Doctrine. Then along came the Korean War and the first head-to-head test of military versus civilian authority. Douglas MacArthur precipitated it with his "no substitute for victory" approach in the face of Truman's decision to keep the conflict confined to the Korean peninsula, and was fired. From that day forward, the military declined in power.

Dwight D. Eisenhower's own stature as a military hero far overshadowed that of the generals and admirals who served him. Ike constantly skirmished with the Joint Chiefs of Staff over the magnitude of the defense budget during his eight years in office, and invariably had his way. Eisenhower issued a directive in 1958 which made plain that the JCS was "not a command body" but "an advisory group," responsible for formulating strategic plans but not for directing the operations to carry them out. And his parting shot against the potential mischief of the "military-industrial complex" has shown up in nearly every antimilitary speech ever since.

During Eisenhower's Presidency, Congress, at his urging, passed the Defense Reorganization Act of 1958, which further strengthened the authority of the Secretary of Defense over the military. The Act also permitted the chiefs to beef up the Joint Staff to a maximum 400 officers, but sternly specified that the Joint Staff "shall not operate or be organized as an overall armed forces general staff, and shall have no executive authority" in support of the JCS. Over the years since then, however, the chiefs have managed to build up a much larger supporting cast. Another 700 officers, 400 enlisted men and women, and 400 civilians work for various agencies grouped under the special designation, "Organization of the Joint Staff." Notable among these are the Joint Reconnaissance Center, which oversees surveillance by satellites and spy planes (remember the U-2?); the Studies, Analysis and Gaming Agency (once called, it was decided too blatantly, the Joint War Games Agency); the Joint Command and Control Requirements Group and the Office for Strategic Mobility.

Three years following passage of the Defense Reorganization Act, along came pedantic, precise, painstaking Robert McNamara to take advantage of it. He mustered all the power which had been accruing to the Office of the Secretary of Defense for fifteen years, under a succession of statutes, and applied it to put down the JCS. It had been Truman's defense policy, Eisenhower's defense policy, Truman against the chiefs, Eisenhower against the chiefs. You may remember Charles E. ("Engine Charlie") Wilson, who served under Eisenhower, for something he said about the good of General Motors and the good of the country. What else do you remember about him? But you will remember McNamara for a long time. Columnist Joseph Alsop compared McNamara, toward the end of his seven years as secretary, to "Alexander the Great's hunchbacked cousin, Harpalus, who literally invented the profession of Defense Minister (at any rate, in the West, for they had defense ministers in China long before). . . . Technological development has now accelerated to an almost frightening degree, and this acceleration in turn continuously demands new defense choices of life-and-death importance and truly staggering cost. From the time of Harpalus until the time of McNamara, however, there had been hardly any change in the old way of making defense choices."

So it was McNamara's defense policy; McNamara, against the chiefs and their ingrained service rivalries; McNamara, up against the vastness, the unmanageability of the Department of Defense. Not Kennedy. Not Johnson. McNamara. Until a whole war later.

It has been recorded that McNamara was hard on the chiefs because he never got over his resentment of their advice, which he took in making his first tactical decision, to assault the Bay of Pigs. This was not the whole truth. For one thing, the Bay was the brainflop mostly of the Central Intelligence Agency. But the ready acquiescence of the JCS did engender McNamara's distrust of their military judgments. Within a year of that misadventure on the Cuban beach, all the chiefs except Marine Commandant David Shoup had retired. General Maxwell Taylor came aboard as Chairman of the JCS, after having served as Kennedy's special military advisor in the White House. Even handpicked Taylor was to have his troubles with McNamara, albeit in a relationship of mutual respect.

McNamara warred with the chiefs over the entire spectrum of issues—budgets, weapons, strategy, force structures, even tactics. During the naval blockade of Cuba in the missile crisis of 1962, he set himself up in the Navy's sacrosanct command center, the Flag Plot, and talked with the captains at sea. This infuriated Admiral George W. Anderson, the Chief of Naval Operations. Anderson later bucked McNamara in resisting the F-III for the Navy. Too much. He was relieved of duty and appointed ambassador to Portugal.

The chiefs bitterly resented the Johnson-McNamara decision not to mobilize the reserves, as they had recommended, during the burgeoning buildup and deployment of American troops to Vietnam, starting in 1965. They told their civilian bosses to go to hell, in effect, by dragging out their drafting of the plan for Vietnam mobilization which McNamara had instructed them to devise. In the end, they never did present a plan to McNamara. Instead, his systems analysts had come up with one.

Throughout the war, the chiefs battled with the office of the

Assistant Secretary of Defense for Systems Analysis, created by McNamara to make some integrated sense of the weapons programs and the missions which the separate services had been in the habit of pursuing in isolation. The F-111 decision emanated in that office. So did the decision to use the M-16 rifle, originally an Air Force weapon, for all services, over the objections of the Army, which had plans for another shoulder piece. The systems men were behind McNamara's thumbing down the chiefs' plans for a new bomber, a "thick" antiballistic missile defense system, a nuclear navy. But it wasn't merely a case of the computer and cost effectiveness versus the chiefs' "wish lists" of weaponry. In Vietnam, as in the blockade of Cuba, McNamara usurped command and control. He reluctantly went along with the chiefs when they advised bombing selected targets in North Vietnam following the attack against U.S. destroyers in the Gulf of Tonkin. But he insisted on running the raiding. He dictated how many and what kinds of planes were used. He edited and sometimes changed the targets which the chiefs had chosen. He even prescribed, on occasion, the altitude at which the fighter-bombers would fly. God help us, said the military, the next thing will be McNamara on the line to infantry platoon leaders, keeping track of their combat controls on computer printouts, telling them how to spread out their riflemen. On Capitol Hill, powerful hawks, chafing at the no-win nature of the war, invited the chiefs to come up and get it off their chests, to unload on their civilian boss. They never really did. They expressed their opinions, but kept it civil. McNamara took no chances, however. He sent his aides to take notes of the chiefs' testimony in closed sessions. He combed through their speeches and the transcripts of their testimony, looking for mutinous mutterings.

There is nothing like common adversity to unite political factions, especially in the smoke-filled Tank. So the chiefs decided that if McNamara wanted to play the game of civilian versus military, they would keep their interservice feuds to themselves, do a little more compromising of their differences of opinion, and confront the secretary with a flying wedge.

When the chiefs cannot agree on an issue, the paper which they present to the secretary, containing disparate decisions, is called a "split." They had learned that McNamara was a master of divide and conquer. In his early years, the more than one thousand major papers which the chiefs average annually had included as many as forty-five "splits," and McNamara invariably leaped into the vacuum. By the time he left, the number of splits had dwindled to only five or six a year. Unwittingly, McNamara had spawned, in the Tank, a "military mind," in a corporate sense. Military men always had scoffed at, and taken exception to, the notion that there is such a thing as a military mind. But during the McNamara period, JCS Chairman Taylor acknowledged its existence, in "so what?" terms.

"It is a matter of gratification," he said, "to belong to a profession whose possession of a mind of some sort is a generally recognized attribute. Personally, I've never been overly exercised by the charge of possessing a military mind. We soldiers, sailors and airmen regard a military mind as something to be sought and developed—an indispensable professional asset which can only be acquired after years of training in reflecting and acting on military and related problems. We hope that such a mind, when properly matured, will prove itself analytical, accurate and decisive in time of crisis because history has shown that neither the battlefield nor the national council table is the place for conjecture, vagueness or obscurity of thought."

Taylor also declared, with perhaps too much weight on the letter of the law, that, "As Chairman of the Joint Chiefs of Staff, I command nobody except the personal aides outside my office door."

Like his fellow commanders, Taylor was at pains not to criticize McNamara in public, to be correct of demeanor. In fact, top military men of the day frequently praised McNamara, if not for his military insights, at least for his qualities of decisiveness and strength of character. In private, however, they fumed at the popular notion that he was the restraining influence and that they were a clique of warmongers, sitting around the Pentagon trying to think of ways of making, or widening, wars. They pointed out, circumspectly, that civilians, not generals, had shoved the nation into the war in Vietnam, overriding the advice of many military men who had warned of the woe ahead in Asia. And now, the civilians would not let the military fight its way out. Tired of being tagged with the catchy Clemenceau judgment that "war is too important to be left to the generals," the generals came up with a line of their own: "Peace is too important to be left to the civilians." They had a point. The standing battle between the military and the civilians is never pitched on a plane so simplistic as the military, wanting to go to war, versus the civilians, wanting to keep the peace. The battle centers on how to keep the peace, and on how, once in a war, to fight it. Not until the latter days of the first Nixon administration did the chiefs and the civilians finally have a meeting of the minds, on both counts. This didn't just happen overnight. It had been coming, as part of the comeback of the military.

The Vietnam years marked a much-overlooked change in the military makeups of the men in the Tank. It may have had something to do with McNamara's ability to dominate them. Gruff, tough Air Force Chief of Staff Curtis LeMay, the last of a long line of swashbuckling, legendary combat commanders of World War II and Korea, had retired. (LeMay always had been meticulous about keeping his archconservative political views separate from his public pronouncements on defense policy. In his heart, he harbored the notion that the bastards should be nuked if they got out of line. Kennedy, to whom those views were anathema, once said that if he were going to ride in the lead bomber, he would want LeMay in the left seat.) Paratrooper Taylor also retired, and was made ambassador to South Vietnam. Arleigh Burke, Arthur Radford and the rest of their seadog breed had long since become memories in military circles. Occupying their big leather chairs in the Tank were men good and true, but lacking in luster. All had seen combat, but not from the high perches of the Pattons and the Patches. The Army chief, who had sat out World War II in a Japanese prison camp, having been captured on Bataan, was most renowned for having directed a study of tactical nuclear weapons. The Navy chief's combat experience had been limited to a year as executive officer of a World War II carrier. The Air Force chief had been deputy commander in Europe and vice-commander of SAC. The career of the Marine commandant had been studded with staff and planning duties. At their head sat General of the Army Earle G. (Bus) Wheeler, an intelligent, mild-looking sort. He had commanded an infantry division in World War II, but was best known for having briefed Kennedy on military matters during the Presidential campaign of 1960 and for having served as director of the Joint Staff and then as Chief of Staff, Army.

So unspectacular were the chiefs in this period of the middle

1960s that many in the services feared their top officers had lost clout outside as well as inside the Pentagon. Then, as Vietnam turned into a full-scale war with hundreds of thousands of American troops, the situation changed. President Johnson, risking, and then reaping, political downfall, began heeding Ambassador Taylor, General William Westmoreland, the field commander in Vietnam, and the JCS. McNamara's days were numbered. *Army* magazine, early in 1968, summed it up as follows:

> Even before Mr. McNamara's announced intention to leave the Pentagon, news reports began to allege that he was on the decline and the Joint Chiefs were on the rise; his transfer to the World Bank presidency was attributed in some quarters to threats by the Chiefs that they would quit if he stayed. A television network commentator said that the military was already dominating Vietnam and other policy now that Mr. McNamara was leaving. A columnist said that the defense secretary was compelled by the White House to reverse his opposition to the Nike-X antiballistic missile defense system and approve the anti-Red China Sentinel system which the Joint Chiefs supported as the first step toward a full-scale ABM defense. And a national magazine, reiterating previous rumors that President Johnson had overruled Mr. McNamara on bombing targets in North Vietnam, noted, over the past few months, the embarrassing spectacle of McNamara publicly opposing tactics that later became official military policy.

The article made the point that if the President supports his Defense Secretary, the chiefs are rendered impotent in their opposition. But once the President starts listening to the chiefs, the Defense Secretary's powers shrivel.

McNamara did not crack, as James Forrestal had in another time, another world, twenty years earlier. But he showed the weariness and the pressure. In public, there were times when tears would come to his eyes and his voice would falter. "I hope you can do something," he would beseech civilian chieftains whom he sent off to Vietnam on increasingly quixotic missions. What really rocked him was the night in the summer of 1967 when Johnson summoned him to the White House to account for his testimony to a Congressional committee that the bombing of military targets in North Vietnam had been a waste. Johnson raged at him for that. A McNamara friend described the scene as "like something out of a Kafka novel, frightening." He was getting fire from the top, the front, the flanks and the rear. His theory that efficient management and steady pressure could win the war had been blown. Now, the charges crashed upon him that not even his management had been worth much. The F-III. Cost overruns on the C-5 and the Minuteman II missile. On and on. Maybe the worst wound, though, was inflicted by his former friends and intellectual peers of the Kennedy years. Richard Goodwin. John Kenneth Galbraith. Marcus Raskin. Twisting the knife into McNamara, they wrote:

The Kennedy administration took office in 1961 with the avowed aim of establishing greater civilian control over the military. Yet the harsh fact is that military considerations today play a greater role in determining American policy than at any time in our national history. In the name of efficiency we unified the operations of the armed services, introduced the techniques of computer management and encouraged closer interactions between the military and industry. As a result, power once checked by rivalries and inefficiency is now wielded as a single force, defying effective democratic control. . . . We should be clear on one point: It is not the uniformed military which has created the present situation, but the civilian leadership and the institutions they have created to centralize and expand the performance of national security functions.

The chiefs thought this was a lot of thumbsucking. All they knew was that McNamara had sat on them. Hard. They were relieved that Clark Clifford was coming across the Potomac. He knew what the hell it was all about over there on the Asian rimlands, and he would knock off the civilian poaching, nitpicking and nutcracking. They took him at face value.

Clark Clifford, the ultra-rich, urbane, tall, handsome, smooth, droll, brainy Washington lawyer who had given Johnson hawkish counsel from his catbird seat in the "kitchen cabinet," succeeded McNamara on March 1, 1968. Clifford had been to Vietnam three times on Presidential missions. He had advised Johnson, in 1965, against the thirty-seven-day pause in the bombing of selected targets in North Vietnam, on grounds that the pause would not persuade the enemy, as McNamara had hoped, to relent. Clifford had been right; McNamara, wrong. It had been the pause that only refreshed the enemy. Still, Clifford was a Democrat. Could a Democrat really be a heartfelt hawk? Or would he turn out, as so many of them had, to be a dove in disguise? "I am not conscious," said he, on taking charge, "of falling under either of those ornithological divisions."

Some year, 1968. The Tet offensive. Johnson announcing that he would not run for reelection. Martin Luther King assassinated. Washington and many other cities burned and looted. Racial strife everywhere. Robert Kennedy assassinated. Soviets crushing the rebellious regime in Czechoslovakia. Through it all, who noticed the remarkable reversal of the route which Clifford himself had mapped out for the nation, way back in 1947, in the "Truman Doctrine" speech which he had written for the President? It promised U.S. support of all peoples "resisting attempted subjugation by armed minorities or by outside pressures." Now, twenty-one years later, Clifford became convinced that Vietnam did not apply. With Johnson a lame-duck Vietnam casualty, Clifford firmly enforced his own policy of "non-escalation" on the chiefs, and pressed for the soldiers of Saigon to begin fighting their own battles as soon as possible. In his methodical way, Clifford began creating the political and military climate for disengagement, for "Vietnamization" of the war. The concept had not originated with Clifford. But he was first to set it in motion. Nixon and Laird later would claim it as their own, but by the time they occupied the White House and the Pentagon, in January 1969, Clifford already had marked it high on his list of policies to be passed on to the Republicans. After he returned to his law offices, he wrote of his transformation in the ten months of his secretaryship:

> I became convinced that the military course we were pursuing was not only endless, but hopeless. A further substantial increase in American forces could only increase the devastation and the Americanization of the war, and thus

leave us even further from our goal of a peace that would
permit the people of South Vietnam to fashion their own
political and economic institutions. Hereafter, I was convinced, our primary goal should be to level off our involvement, and to work toward gradual disengagement.

So be it, said the chiefs. If we were allowed to blister Hanoi
and Haiphong we could win this godforsaken war. But we
aren't allowed to. Clifford calls the shots, in the political context, and we must go along. But he sure did turn flaccid on us.
Four years later, they got their way, after all, with Hanoi and
Haiphong. Not to "win" the war but to get out of it. They had
come a long distance back under Nixon and Laird, from the
oppressive days of Mac the Knife and Clark the Cooer. Let it
never happen again. As late as the winter of 1974, the new
magazine *Strategic Review*, its editors and contributors made up
of high-ranking, retired military officers (an interesting development in itself, in the publishing field), harked back and
harped again on civilian policy. "Many scholars," said *Strategic
Review*, "are moving on from the question of 'Who won?' to the
question of 'What happened?' They are drawing lessons from
the experience. It is a cause for dismay that the passions
aroused by this conflict can lead to such erroneous conclusions
about its significance. . . . The failure of decisively superior
U.S. forces to repel the North Vietnamese aggression is vari-
ously viewed by critics as evidence of the futility of sophisticated weaponry, of superior fighting spirit on the North
Vietnamese side, of the inconstancy of U.S. public support, of
weakness of the South Vietnamese army or body politic, of the
superiority of guerrilla warfare. It is none of these things. It
is rather the predictable consequence of war-policy decisions
made by America's top leadership. . . . The disaster of Vietnam
was wrought by national leaders who thought they could abro-
gate the inexorable laws of war."
Melvin Laird forswore the old McNamara policy of icily
excluding the chiefs from his deliberations. He let them spread
their influence from the Tank into his own third-floor suite
directly above that of the JCS chairman, and into the offices of
the civilian service secretaries as well. He called this technique
"participatory decision-making." He also decentralized weapons development and procurement, thus freeing the chiefs to

resume the interservice sniping and snarling which had characterized the pre-McNamara years; to testify with greater abandon on Capitol Hill, on grounds that they were being left to devise their own hardware and, so, had the right to explain and defend their own decisions; to "wing it" in their public speeches. To the chiefs, McNamara had been an Indian-giver. He encouraged them to draft their separate budgets without considering fiscal restraints. And then, when the crunch came, in the final weeks of the year, when the whole defense budget had to be pieced together for presentation to Congress, McNamara and his civilian systems men and assistant secretaries would do major surgery on the Army, Navy, Air Force and Marines. Laird, conversely, told each service what its own budget ceiling would be, and let each shape its forces and weapons within the limit. The chiefs regarded this policy affectionately for its realism and for the added responsibility it gave them. For Laird, and his civilian subordinates, it meant freedom from the onerous need to hack and prune, displease and discourage the services. It also gave Laird more time to prowl his old haunts on Capitol Hill, dining on the House side, discussing on the Senate side. The whole thing put together is probably why he was able to brag, as he departed, that he had never lost a major weapon-buying battle to Congressional budget-cutters in his entire four years. That, together with cutting military manpower, a political consideration of great importance on Capitol Hill. Did the chiefs not resent losing men? No, indeed. Not when they were given greater power to command the men they had, plus a widening array of weaponry.

What endeared Laird to the chiefs more than anything else was his compatibility with their view that we were heeding too little the Soviet threat, his willingness to speak out about it, and his approval of accelerating the development of modern weapons. He only went so far, however. They understood. President Nixon was pushing for détente, and could not be undermined. The sentiment in the Tank was for turning away from the McNamara policy of "assured destruction," toward a policy of "counterforce." This would have meant, when you got down to it, precision targeting of our Minuteman missiles on Russian military installations, less emphasis on threatening Russian population centers, and more explosive power and accuracy for our warheads. Laird agreed with them, in private, that U.S. nuclear strategy should be stated, at the very least, in sterner terms. But he disagreed that now was the time to do it. He had managed to get Congress to approve the installation of multiple independently targeted reentry vehicles (MIRVs) on Minuteman. That in itself had lengthened the arms-race stride of the United States. MIRVs had been tested during the Johnson years—in fact, during Clifford's months as Secretary of Defense—but their deployment had begun under Nixon and Laird. Since then, détente had become the order of the day. So the chiefs would have to make do with MIRVs, for now. But Counterforce was coming . . .

Laird denied that the exercising of raw airpower over Hanoi and Haiphong in the last days of his stewardship was an example of the military running amok. The bombings, he and other Nixon administration officials insisted, represented the use of military power in accordance with political—not military—strategy, to achieve political—not military—aims. The military still was doing what it was told, never mind what it was doing. But there was more to it than that. It set a tone in the Tank which would carry over, and forward, to bigger things. It marked, for the chiefs, their first chance, finally, to punch the enemy in the face after seven years of jabbing at his limbs. For them, there was a very significant difference. The civilians had let the leash develop some slack. Letting 'er rip over the enemy's capital and principal port restored a large measure of confidence and ebullience in the Tank and in the commands, and began changing the stance of the military from one of subjugation to civilian policy to one of compatibility with civilian policy. Nixon was two men. One pursuing détente. The other, a warrior, underneath, like them. Like Nixon, the chiefs wanted out of the Asian war. And like him, they did not share the national nay-saying over the way it was done. The means were, for them, a redemption of sorts, a beginning of the return to national awareness of what armed might, however hateful its consequences, can accomplish. For our country. And we had it to use, by thunder. We hadn't seen its like since World War II. A comeback for the chiefs. A psychological catapult. Now, gentlemen, let's see about this giveaway strategic arms policy of ours. What are those people in the striped pants up to these days?

Indeed, what had the military itself been up to? Not until Laird left office was it discovered that Air Force Brigadier General John Lavelle had taken it upon himself to order the bombing of targets in North Vietnam which had been ruled off base by the Pentagon. Moreover, from March 17, 1969, to April 30, 1970, the date that American ground troops thrust into Cambodia, the Seventh Air Force had flown more than 3,500 sorties into Cambodia, dropping more than 100,000 bombs, at a cost of nearly $150 million.

Congress had never known about it. Neither, so he testified, had civilian Air Force Secretary Robert Seamans. Not even the entire Air Force command hierarchy had known about it. Senator Harold Hughes (D.-Iowa), a member of the investigating Senate Armed Services Committee, said the missions—and the omissions—raised "very serious questions, not only of civilian control of the military but of the military's control of the military itself." General George Brown had been in charge of the Seventh Air Force when it happened. He became Chairman of the Joint Chiefs of Staff in 1974, after a year as Air Force Chief of Staff. At a private Pentagon reception in celebration of his passage into the Tank, Brown was asked why the bombings had happened. "We followed orders," he said simply.

News of these events was breaking at the same time as news about Watergate. The government was rocking a little. It would rock a whole lot more violently later. Those who tended to worry that a military takeover "can happen here" had more reason, now, to wonder. Those who thought the military had taken a beating from civilians all along, who had no fears about the chiefs and their brethren ever resorting to, or agreeing to, a coup, said it was baloney. Most people were somewhere in between.

Other odd things had been happening, too. Admiral Thomas Hinman Moorer, naval air hero of World War II in the Pacific, was Chief of Naval Operations and then Chairman of the Joint Chiefs of Staff during the seven years of Vietnam troop buildup and withdrawal. Throughout, he never took his eye off the Russians. Or the Chinese. Moorer's own military posture statements, as Chairman of the JCS under Laird, rang out to the Armed Services committees with Praetorian passages about the need to become stronger, to watch closely what the Soviets did, not what the Soviets said. Ever the courtly, gentlemanly Alabaman—stocky of physique, steely of eye, stentorian of drawl—Moorer never once suggested that his civilian superiors should not pursue détente, or that they might be guilty of letting down their guard while at it. And yet, for many months, Navy personnel attached to the White House had copied National Security Council papers dealing with Russia, China, India and Pakistan, and passed them to Moorer. He later told Defense Secretary James Schlesinger and Congress that he had neither requested nor condoned these actions, had had no need or use for the papers, and had, in any event, found them uninstructive. His defenders noted that Moorer, as JCS chairman, sat on the NSC and had every right of access to every doodle of its deliberations. Everything that Henry Kissinger did, this side of dalliance, Moorer should know about. Otherwise, how could the JCS do its job? In his ordeal, Moorer was supported strongly by Deputy Defense Secretary Clements, less strongly by Schlesinger.

Seapower, a magazine published by the Navy League, turned its guns on critics who would denigrate the admiral after such a meritorious career as his. *Seapower* noted that the Joint Chiefs' billet on the NSC dated clear back to 1950, and had been created to keep the chiefs up to date on—and part of—the making of foreign policy. "We believe," the magazine editorialized, "that if we all aren't willing to support Americans who give their country the best they can for almost two-thirds of the estimated life span of man within this Republic, in the future there won't be nearly as many Americans who will be willing to stay on the firing line as long as Thomas Moorer has."

Questions of Moorer's culpability or lack of prudence aside, the "Pentagon spying case" pointed up the military's concern over the pathways of foreign policy. Agatha Christie fans would have been offended by the blatancy of the clues which the men with the stars on their shoulders had strewn about, leading up to this denouement.

Ever since the Soviet Union exploded its first nuclear bomb and emplaced its first intercontinental missile, the single, overpowering, contrapuntal concern of U.S. policy has been that of staying strong enough to survive a nuclear attack and then retaliate, but not strong enough—or at least *apparently* not strong enough—to risk striking first. Be tough but don't bang around like a bully. Orchestrating the trumpets of the Tank into this fugue of frustration, so the trumpets didn't drown out the woodwinds of the Arms Control and Disarmament Agency, had been the main reason, over the years, for the inexorable gravitation of power away from the JCS. Political goals over military goals. Military strength not an absolute moral evil. But not an absolute moral imperative, either. Centralization of defense decisions on budgets, strategies, choice of weapons, command and control. Until this decade, at least, this balance between bombs and olive branches kept us out of nuclear war. But things began to change in the countries of Nixon and Brezhnev, even as they strove together for harmony. Nuclear parity came unstuck. Warlocks loose among the warheads, turning them into multiples, incanting of Armageddon.

In April 1970, the United States and the Soviet Union sat down to the first round of Strategic Arms Limitation Talks (SALT) in Vienna, Austria. The strategic stability which had prevailed for two decades was being shaken by more accurate missiles (on our side) carrying multiple warheads; by warheads of mammoth megatonnage (on theirs); and by antiballistic missile systems (on both) which neither side could afford to let the other develop fully. Surprise. Two years later, SALT I worked out. Nixon went to Moscow to sign the five-year interim agreement limiting missile launchers. Both sides seemed satisfied. But there were frowns in the Tank. Nixon may have given too much away.

The late Army Chief of Staff General Creighton Abrams broke the silence of the military about détente in October 1973, during the Mideast war. He had been top commander in Vietnam and was highly respected. Schlesinger called him "a superb soldier, just a hell of a man." He was not given to speechmaking. A man of action, not words. When he spoke, he spoke for the JCS. This time he had some things to say: "The word 'détente' for some people evidently colors everything rose and turns their perceptions away from even obvious threats. . . . Détente is expressed by some as a fact; it is applauded by still others as a policy; saluted by still others as a new era; and it provides the basis—at least the semantic basis —for some who would reduce military capabilities to what I believe would be a dangerous level."

Abrams made a round of speeches on the same theme before

such sympathetic groups as the Pikes Peak and Fort Dix chapters of the Association of the U.S. Army. "We must insure that our nation survives," thundered the craggy combat commander, "but we cannot be satisfied merely with survival. We are a global nation. Our well-being as a nation depends upon our freedom of action. We are not self-sufficient now, and we could not become self-sufficient in the lifetime of any one of us here. And even if we as a nation could arrange our lives and interests to survive by ourselves, what kind of nation would we be? A weakened, shriveled and mean land at best. So we need to be concerned about our well-being around the globe. The major military challenge to our global interests is the Soviet Union. It is the only other truly global military power. And so we must gauge our ability to maintain freedom of action in terms of the Soviet Union, and in terms of the challenges that Soviet global interests and actions pose for us.

"This is not saber rattling. This is not warmongering. This is not some kind of idle scare tactic. It is the most reasoned, responsible position I know for having our military strength up to par."

By this time, in the early and middle months of 1974, Moorer, Abrams and other military spokesmen had recent events on their side, and they could well afford to swing away. The Russians have an uncanny way of vindicating the U.S. military's "worst case" predictions of what they will do (in the incessant back-and-forth of the arms race, the Russians probably could say the same thing about the Americans vindicating their own "worst-casing"), and now they had done it again. A pall pervaded SALT II talks just resuming in Geneva, Switzerland. The chiefs were saying we told you so. Wipe out SALT I, they said. It means little, now, if anything. The United States had accepted, in that interim agreement to last through 1977, a numerical inferiority of land-based and submarine-launched intercontinental missiles—1,758 to the Russians' 2,300—because the U.S. missiles were being armed with MIRVs and the Soviets' were not. The United States also had more long-range bombers, and, although the Soviets were catching up, more ballistic-missile submarines. In their giant SS-9 Scarp and their SS-11 Savage single-warhead missiles, the Soviets had the advantage of megatonnage, by something like fifteen to one. But the U.S. missiles, even then, were more accurate. Stalemate.

Perhaps, said the chiefs, but it's more like Checkmate, and it's our king that's in the corner. They had added everything up and concluded that what the United States had done in SALT I was agree to fall behind fearsomely in propulsion and payloads—together called "throw weight," which makes the big bangs that obliterate. The United States had a technological advantage. The Soviets had a throw-weight advantage. Throw-weight is scarier than technology. Or is it?

In July 1973, less than a month after Nixon and Brezhnev had conferred cheerfully in Washington, a U.S. spy satellite snapped pictures, in the red band of the spectrum, of a plume of fire and a rocket reaching for space from the Soviet launching site at Tyuratam, near the Aral Sea, in Kazakhstan. The Soviets had been test-launching ICBMs for years and years. But U.S. monitoring stations perceived something different, something ominous, about that shot onto the Kamchatka peninsula. The Soviets obviously had developed an onboard computer, and they finally, inevitably, were testing MIRVs, which the computer had made possible.

In mid-August, Schlesinger announced that the Soviets were testing, overland, four new ICBMs—the SS-X-16, a solid-propellant missile probably slated to replace the solid-fuel SS-13, possibly to be land-mobile as well; the SS-X-17 and SS-X-19, liquid-fuel missiles believed to be in competition to replace the SS-11 (which is comparable to the U.S. Minuteman); and the SS-X-18, the burliest of the bunch and the heir apparent to the SS-9. All but the first were fitted with MIRVs. On top of all this, earlier in the year, the Soviets had begun deploying a new class of ballistic-missile submarine, of the NATO code name "Delta," armed with twelve SS-N-8 missiles of 4,000-mile range. Previously, only the Soviet "Yankee" subs, with their 1,300-mile missiles, had been a strategic threat to the United States.

In September, hawkish Ira C. Eaker, a retired Air Force general turned columnist, wrote:

> The recent Soviet MIRV tests have completely altered the rationale for our defense posture. No event since the revelation that the Russians had the hydrogen bomb has so drastically and dramatically changed the "balance of terror." Any claim of weapons parity between the United States and the

Soviets [has] lost validity. Ever since 1945, whenever the U.S. was on the verge of unilateral disarmament, the Kremlin leaders invariably warned us by some blatant aggression. The savage attack on Hungary, the Berlin blockade, the Cuban missile crisis, the brutal invasion of Czechoslovakia, each halted unilateral and irreparable reduction of U.S. defenses. U.S. defenses planners had almost despaired that the Russians would come to our aid in the present disarmament crisis. . . . Now the euphoric climate of détente is completely shattered. The Kremlin's error in testing the MIRV at this time was a cruel blow to their apologists and sympathizers in this country. The "doves" in Congress and the liberal-left wingers have assured us that the Russians would gladly follow suit if we led the way and unilaterally disarmed. These visionaries have now been completely discredited.

Eaker hadn't seen anything yet. Less than a month after his column appeared, the bloody, vicious Arab-Israeli War pitted American equipment and moral support against Russian equipment and moral support, sending a chill across the land. Not the chill which resulted from the ensuing Arab embargo of oil. Another kind of chill. A graveyard kind of chill. The war on the banks of the Suez and in the Golan Heights had been a testing ground for the most modern Russian and American military hardware and electronics. And it had come out discouragingly close to a draw. The implications, however, went beyond the mere kinesis of the combat. The visceral and ideological sympathies of American intellectuals lay with Israel, and the Russians were on the other side. Détente came out of it badly damaged. This disaffection of U.S. intellectuals with the Soviets was nurtured even more by the tribulations of dissident writer Alexander Solzhenitsyn, who had taken his government to task for its oppressiveness, and by the message of his fellow writer, Andrei Sakharov, who shortly before the Mideast war had written:

For decades the Soviet Union has been developing under conditions of an intolerable isolation, bringing with it the ugliest consequences. Even a partial preservation of those conditions will be highly perilous for all mankind, for international confidence and détente. . . . The world is only just entering on a new course of détente, and it is therefore essential that the proper direction be followed from the outset.

Not to be overlooked, however, were two plus factors. Without the measure of détente which had been achieved prior to the Mideast war—based in large measure, by the way, on the Russians' need to import Western technology—it is entirely possible that the war would have expanded into a global firestorm. Moreover, in bygone days, there would have been no outspoken Solzhenitsyn, and if there had been, he likely would have been shot or imprisoned, not deported, as it turned out.

On November 8, with the Mideast cauldron no longer spilling over, but still bubbling hot, the Kremlin chose once again to stir up the U.S. strategic analysts. The avant-garde attractions of the military parade in Moscow celebrating the fifty-sixth anniversary of the Bolshevik revolution were two of the new ICBMs, the sleekness of their seventy-foot length obvious even inside their green jacketing, only their tapered red noses fully exposed to view. TASS, the Soviet news agency, reported enthusiastically of their "unique power and accuracy" and hailed them as "the latest achievements of Soviet science and technology." In the Tank, the interpretation was clear: multiple warheads and much-refined guidance systems.

Meanwhile, intelligence reports were filtering into the Tank of the possibility that the Soviets had actually landed one of their latest, swing-wing Backfire bombers in Syria. The French government magazine *Défense Nationale* reported in the week prior to the Moscow parade that the Russians had built twelve Backfire prototypes capable of two and a half times the speed of sound, and designed, like the still-unbuilt U.S. B-1, for low-altitude penetration at top speed under enemy radar.

In mid-January 1974, the Soviet Union blasted two SS-X-19s —probable successor to the SS-11 Savage—into space from the Tyuratam rocket research center 4,500 miles downrange into the Pacific, 850 miles northwest of Midway Island. It was the first full-flight, reentry trial of the SS-X-19. U.S. intelligence took no time at all, in examining flight and impact data, to conclude that the missile had multiple warheads, and probably was more sophisticated than any missile in the U.S. arsenal. Intelligence also estimated that the Soviets could deploy the SS-X-19 by 1976.

SALT II had recessed in the autumn of 1973—had nearly aborted right then, in fact—when the Russians gave a flat "nyet" to the U.S. position that the talks should lead to numerical equality of ICBMs. Senator Henry Jackson (D.Wash.), who always takes a dim view of any détente too tasteful to the Kremlin, characterized the Russian position as "a classic case of what's mine is mine, what's yours is negotiable." SALT II was scheduled to be resumed in Geneva on February 19, 1974. The day before, the Soviets, through TASS, warned all ships and planes to stay clear of a missile-impact area in the Pacific, an area larger than any they had ever sealed off. Radius, 130 nautical miles. Centered at coordinates 34 degrees, 49 minutes north latitude and 177 degrees, 14 minutes west longitude, several hundred miles north of Midway, about 1,500 miles northwest of Honolulu, 5,000 miles to the bull's-eye, from Tyuratam. The tests, said TASS, would continue through March 10. Shrieking through the atmosphere came one, then two, SS-X-18s. Only one warhead on each, even though U.S. missile watchers were convinced that this probable successor to the SS-9 Scarp could carry multiples. Even with one, the megatonnage of the SS-X-18 would be one-third again as much as the Scarp's twenty-five. But why only one warhead in the tests? U.S. missilemen said there could be several reasons. Testing decoy devices. Or one MIRV at a time, and then building up to several. Or maybe the Soviets had yet to decide whether to stay with one, or put more on the new giant.

In the first three months of 1974, the Soviets test-fired every single one of their new missiles into the Pacific. There was a suggestion of frenzy about this flurry, of slaughter, SALT notwithstanding. The Pentagon drew no comfort from its long-time knowledge that Russian MIRVs would have to happen sooner or later. Schlesinger remarked on the "astonishing depth and breadth" of Soviet research and development in ICBMs which the intensive tests had revealed. "I think it is fair to say," the secretary told reporters, "that many people, particularly people in the arms-control community, have been surprised by the strength of those programs. The SS-X-19 and the SS-X-18 in particular appear to be programs that are far advanced. What we were unprepared for was the enormous expansion of Soviet throw weight represented by the SS-X-19."

On the other hand, argued some, what were the Russians supposed to do? Back in 1970, when the United States began

MIRVing its Minuteman III, the *Bulletin of Atomic Scientists* sounded an alarm for all who pleaded the cause of disarmament. Headlined, "MIRV—Gorgon Medusa of the Nuclear Age," the article said:

> The irresistible urge to behold Medusa has its counterpart in the nuclear age: the Pentagon asks for more weapons of mass destruction, more ways of delivery, and more warheads for each intercontinental missile (ICBM). By placing several warheads on each ICBM, "more bang for the buck" is provided. But such a development has serious implications not directly measurable in immediate effects. Proliferation of MIRV expands the race by an order-of-magnitude. The result can be an ever-decreasing level of national security, arising from two ugly consequences of MIRV: the revival of first-strike concerns, and increased hazards to the civilian population from accidental launch. . . . It is possible that the Strategic Arms Limitations Talks can fulfill the aspirations of peace-minded nations by immediate cessation of MIRV development, accompanied by a combination of satellite reconnaissance and occasional, non-intrusive, on-site inspection.

A vain hope. In Congress, after the Soviet tests of 1973-74 and Schlesinger's quick reaction to them, a few senators suggested somewhat limply that maybe we should wait and see whether the Soviets actually deployed any of the new missiles. Among them, Senator William Proxmire (D.-Wis.), called for "a year-by-year cutback in land-based strategic missiles—the most destabilizing element of nuclear deterrence—as a prime aim of the SALT II negotiations." The Soviet tests, and their evidence of onrushing Soviet missile technology "should not be taken lightly," said Proxmire, "but neither should we jump to unwarranted assumptions." Maybe the Soviets were like us, he suggested. Maybe they had sunk so many billions into the research and development of the new family of ICBMs that they felt they owed themselves the testing, to see if the weapons actually worked. After all, the Soviets had said that they would pursue every strategic program which SALT I had not explicitly forbade. Including these new missiles. Perhaps, Proxmire suggested, the Soviet R&D community was locked

into following through on the testing of their designs and
could not buck, as the U.S. R&D community cannot buck,
their institutional and bureaucratic imperatives. Moreover,
said Proxmire, the Soviets were still five years behind us in
MIRV technology, and had a long, tough road ahead to perfect-
ing it. Furthermore, he said: "Soviet MIRV tests have come
nearly five years after the Defense Department first claimed
they would. As early as 1969, defense officials claimed that the
USSR had tested a MIRV. This is a time for prudent evaluation and cool thinking on our part. Let us proceed with caution, rationally measuring Soviet technology but not
deliberately forgetting our own substantial capabilities."

The plaints of Proxmire and a like-minded, minority cadre
on Capitol Hill were brushed aside in the Tank. The Joint
Chiefs of Staff had rationally measured Soviet technology and
throw weight against U.S. technology and throw weight, and
had concluded that the United States, before too many years
had gone by, would be at a serious strategic disadvantage.
Standing squarely with them in this was Schlesinger, who
even then, after six months in office, was drafting his first
defense budget and posture statement for presentation to Congress. These documents promised, as the Brookings Institution
wrote of them months later, to "turn out to be the most far-
reaching changes in U.S. defense policy and military strategy
since 1961, when the new Kennedy administration sought to
reformulate defense goals and restructure forces." Somewhat
surprisingly, the writers from Brookings, a nonpartisan research organization which had not found much to cheer about
in the Nixon administrations, tended to agree with Schlesinger's thesis that the time had come to power up, to show the
Soviets that the United States was prepared to proceed with
SALT II, or with cold war II, whichever they preferred.

4

The
Hardliners

As the Psalmist tells us: "Where there is no vision, the people perish."
      —Secretary of Defense James R. Schlesinger, March 4, 1974.

Soviet actions during the October 1973 Middle East War show that détente is not the only—and in certain circumstances, not the primary—policy of the USSR.
                          —Schlesinger, March 4, 1974.

The Soviet Union now has the capability in its missile forces to undertake selective attacks against targets other than cities. This poses for us an obligation, if we are to ensure the credibility of our strategic deterrent, to be certain that we have a comparable capability in our strategic systems and in our targeting doctrine. And to be certain that the USSR has no misunderstanding on this point.
                          —Schlesinger, March 4, 1974.

It is not helpful to us to talk ourselves into a state of mind in which we are strategically inferior.
      —Secretary of State Henry M. Kissinger, April 26, 1974.

Only six months after James Rodney Schlesinger became Secretary of Defense at the age of forty-four, it was clear that even if he were to leave the next day, his impression on U.S. defense and foreign policy would remain indelible. The Mideast war and the Soviet missile-menacing had taken place during those six months. In their aftermath, Schlesinger laid out for Congress and the nation a reshaping of nuclear strategy which can fairly be described as revolutionary. A Secretary of Defense of lesser intellectual reputation might not have confronted Congress quite so cockily with it as Schlesinger did. He said, right off the bat, that he had "no apologies to offer" for the size of the $93 billion budget, or for what it portended. He was to say the same thing a year later, in February 1975, about a $104.7 billion defense budget. Congress made it relatively painless for him, despite some mutterings about his donnish demeanor. He seemed to have mesmerized Capitol Hill and the Washington press corps. The *Washington Post* summed up the feeling of the press in general, calling Schlesinger "the Pentagon's most articulate warrior-spokesman in many years."

Until Schlesinger came along, the Pentagon's missile-and-bomber men had been forced by their civilian overseers to constrain their strategic plotting within the confines of a script which had played the stage for nearly a quarter of a century. The scenario was the one of the half-hour nuclear war. Two spasms and it would be all over. The Soviets would launch a fleet of ICBMs. Crushing explosions and blinding bursts of light would engulf our cities. Our buildings would be blown to bits; our people, to shreds. As their missiles approached, however, we would launch our own, and demolish every city and industrial complex worth the trouble, from Leningrad to Vladivostok. The hundreds of millions who died in the blasts soon would be joined by other hundreds of millions, from Montreal to Macao, who died of leukemia or some other form of radiation-caused cancer. Or starve. Or kill one another for food. The strategy was called "assured destruction," or "city busting." It had worked, as it were. Not since Hiroshima and Nagasaki had a nuclear weapon been detonated in anger. But technological advances in computer guidance systems, warheads and rocket propulsion inevitably combined with man's urge to defend himself—or with his itch to quit being teased by the technology and test it out, or with nothing more complicated than his aggressive instincts—into the evolution of a theory of nuclear warfare as sophisticated and threatening as the technology itself. In the United States, this theory germinated in the conclusion of our leaders that the Soviets were about to attain a state of strategic nuclear parity. This stability of opposing strategic forces would provide the Soviets with an umbrella. Under it, they might be tempted to pursue some military ventures around the world—most especially in Europe—designed to expand their political, military and economic influence, and to erode the influence of the United States. When the Soviets muscled up behind the Arabs in the Mideast war, U.S. strategists regarded the move as a case in point. Another piece of evidence was the Soviet buildup of troops and equipment in Eastern Europe. Despite their dabbling in détente, they seemed clearly in an expansionist frame of mind. This, as much as their testing of new strategic missiles, lay behind Schlesinger's decision to go public with Counterforce.

We should have seen it coming. In the spring of 1973, when the White House staff still was wondering what kind of vodka to order for Brezhnev's visit to Washington that summer, President Nixon spelled it out in a foreign-policy message.

"An aggressor," he said, "might choose to employ nuclear weapons selectively and in limited numbers for limited objectives. . . . No president should ever be in the position where his only option in meeting such aggression is all-out nuclear response. [This] could tempt an aggressor to use nuclear weapons in a limited way in a crisis. If the United States has the ability to use its forces in a controlled way, the likelihood of nuclear response would be more credible, thereby making deterrence more effective and the initial use of nuclear weapons by an opponent less likely."

The idea of counterforce was not brand new. Off and on, the U.S. military had been trying, since the "massive retaliation" mystique of the Eisenhower years, to sell it to Presidents and to Secretaries of Defense. No luck. The United States would stick to "assured destruction" as a deterrent ("Mutual Assured Destruction" was the preferred description; it put the onus on both sides. Unfortunately, its acronym was "MAD.") But Nixon had been toying with Counterforce, and in Schlesinger, he found a Secretary of Defense who believed in the policy, sold the President on it, and put it over, now that Vietnam lay in the past.

Schlesinger had been a constant in an administration noted for its musical chairs, its upheavals, of cabinet officers and other top officials. Not far into his second term, Nixon had run through more of them than any other President, ever. Some, like Hickel at Interior, Nixon found nettlesome and nudged out. Others, like Richardson, at State, HEW, Defense and then Justice, finally found Nixon unpalatable, and quit. Some, like Shultz at Labor, the Office of Management and Budget and then Treasury, got sick of the grind. More, like Haldeman, Ehrlichman at the White House, Mitchell at Justice, fell under Watergate. The shortest-termed of all had been Robert Mayo, Nixon's first budget director, who returned to banking in Chicago almost before he had unpacked, saying he could not get Nixon's ear. Mayo's number-two man at the Bureau of the Budget, back then, was James R. Schlesinger, who preferred a top job at the Pentagon but could wait. Let us go back . . .

Harvard bachelor's degree, 1950. Classmate of Henry Kissinger. Both Summa Cum Laude. Harvard master's degree, 1952. Harvard doctorate in economics, 1956. Taught at Harvard as an instructor. Atmosphere too liberal there. Off to the University of Virginia as an associate professor of economics, 1956. Atmosphere too confining there. In 1960, wrote a book: *The Political Economy of National Security*. In 1963, joined the RAND Corporation, an Air Force Think Tank in Santa Monica, California, later rising to the position of Director of Strategic Studies. A systems analyst all the way. Led a RAND study on nuclear proliferation. A strategic thinker, but lacking in leverage.

In 1965, with McNamara still riding high at the Pentagon, Schlesinger, at RAND, wrote a paper: "The Changing Environment for Systems Analysis." In it, he advocated for the Pentagon "a wide-ranging, austerely conducted research and development program in which it is fully recognized that many successful developments will not lead to procurement. . . . A major problem with this strategy, of course, is that the willingness to cut off a successful program goes against the grain of both the technologist and the organizations responsible for its development. . . . As a general rule, one may observe, it is easier to cancel commitments made by earlier decision-makers than it is to cancel one's own." He was beginning to sound as if he might be cocking an eye to a future in the Department of Defense. But this would have to wait for a

Republican administration. Schlesinger had been consistently a Republican. Until he became known in his own right, he had to suffer from association-by-surname with that other decidedly un-Republican Schlesinger, Arthur, whose liberal approaches to history and to current events he regarded with undisguised distaste.

At RAND, Schlesinger had been the author of another paper, "Defense Planning and Budgeting." It contained this passage: "In recent years I have become less sanguine regarding the efficacy of the interservice rivalry and criticisms . . . in flushing out new alternatives or criticizing obsolescent activities. Large hierarchical organizations tend to be remarkably efficient mechanisms for the suppression of new ideas and alternatives." At his first Pentagon press conference, a half decade having passed, Schlesinger bore down on what he called "service parochialism," on the tendency of each service to try to be self-sufficient. "I don't think we can afford that," he said. His remarks sent a shudder through the military departments, for by this time James Schlesinger had made his mark in government as a lightning lopper of heads. It had taken him awhile to get into that E Ring suite, and he could hardly wait to get to work. He might have made it there earlier, had it not been for his penchant for speaking his mind back at RAND, at a time that systems analysis was riding high at the Pentagon. Congress was exploring the likelihood and desirability of spreading through the rest of government this technique of feeding data into a computer and retrieving, clickety-click, models for cost effectiveness. Schlesinger was invited to come east and testify before the National Security Subcommittee of the Senate Government Operations Committee. Schlesinger said that systems analysis was a handy tool for programmers but should not be regarded as a be-all, end-all. In the wry way of speaking which later would distinguish him on the daises of Washington, Schlesinger told the senators: "I have two and a half cheers for systems analysis. There is little doubt that analysis has been oversold . . . analyses vary substantially in quality. Each should be taken with a grain of salt. . . . The volume of government resources that may be lavished on the care and feeding of white elephants is simply staggering." Too bad.

Three weeks before the Nixon administration took office, Melvin Laird and David Packard secluded themselves in a suite

at the Sheraton Carlton Hotel on K Street, with the White
House in view to the south across Lafayette Square, and began
assembling the team that would serve them at the Pentagon in
the forthcoming first administration of Richard Nixon. Schlesinger was among those whom they considered as Assistant
Secretary of Defense for Systems Analysis. Even though Laird
later would downgrade systems analysis, he heeded the professional recommendations of the men at the Pentagon who practiced it, when it came to picking their leader-to-be. These men
saw trouble in Schlesinger's halfhearted huzzahs for his craft
and theirs. He had been semifaithful. They advised against
him. When Laird and Packard greeted their new crew, Schlesinger was not on hand. But the smoke from his omnipresent
pipe was wreathing a color portrait of Richard Nixon in an
office only paces away from the one to which the President
himself repaired when he wanted to be alone (which was often)
—in the Executive Office Building, next door to the White
House on Pennsylvania Avenue. James R. Schlesinger had
been appointed assistant director of the Bureau of the Budget,
chiefly responsible for dealing with the Pentagon. How sweet
it was.

Right off, Schlesinger got into it with Laird. Displaying
qualities of accessibility and candor in dealing with reporters,
Schlesinger soon had the word around town that he thought
defense budgets were too fat. He took a jaundiced view of the
Air Force's Manned Orbiting Laboratory project, and was in-
strumental in killing it. He upset Laird and the Navy by questioning their plan to develop and begin deploying, in eight
years, ten or more huge Trident ballistic-missile submarines at
the enormous cost (if everything went just right, which was
laughable) of $13 billion. Schlesinger was smacked down on
that one, but he had spoken his piece. Who the hell is this
character from RAND anyway? A tinkerer. A messer. Upsets
the admirals' applecarts. That smart aleck Harvard hotshot
with the New York City accent. Look what he did? He
managed to take $6 billion out of the first defense budget he
ever got his hands on.

Much later, after he became Secretary of Defense, Schlesinger sat down to a private off-the-record lunch in Washington
and spoke freely, a life-style of which he had always been fond
but which he seldom, anymore, felt free to indulge.

"When you left the Budget Bureau," said one of his companions, "there was a story around Washington that Secretary Laird had urged your removal because you tamped down the defense budget."

Schlesinger: "It could have been true. I don't think it was the reason for my departure. I suspect Mel was irritated with me on occasion, as I would have been if I had been in his shoes. But I think the point you are getting at is that we have been cutting down in terms of defense capabilities, and . . . it is time to stop the cutting process."

This was four years later, and damned if Secretary of Defense James R. Schlesinger was going to put up with the Office of Management and Budget cutting *his* Pentagon budget. With Mayo having departed in 1970, Schlesinger, as acting director, presided over the transformation of the Bureau of the Budget into the much more powerful, more pervasive Office of Management and Budget. And then, off to the Atomic Energy Commission. He served as AEC chairman for sixteen months, and one of his most significant speeches during that period told you more about where he really wanted to be, more about the change coming over him, than it did about where he was and what he was doing.

"I am firmly persuaded," he said, "that the time has come, if it has not already passed, to call a halt to the self-defeating game of cutting defense outlays. . . . It is an illusion to believe that we can maintain defense forces adequate for our treaty obligations to, say, NATO and Japan, with sharp curtailment in defense expenditures supposedly directed only to waste and duplication."

At the AEC, Schlesinger continued his education in nuclear weapons and in what their technology promised for their proliferation. More importantly, for the moment, he established himself—the professor-planner drawing upon latent talent—as an administrator. The AEC was bedraggled. The Nixon administration had proposed to create a new Department of Natural Resources and assign to it, mercifully, some of the AEC's functions. Environmentalists and utilities were whacking away at one another, and the AEC's nuclear plant-licensing policies were taking shocks from both sides. Glenn Seaborg, an eminent scientist, had run the place on a "papa knows best" basis for many years, and had been content to make speeches about the benefits of nuclear power to mankind while letting

the agency go to pot in an everyday way. Schlesinger over-
hauled both the regulatory and promotional branches of the
AEC, streamlined departments and appointed new department heads, and, to the delight of reporters, introduced an
"open agency" policy. One of the old-timers at the AEC, agape
at all this, said Schlesinger "seems to be that amazing combination, an intellectual man of action." At a meeting with leaders
of the power industry, Schlesinger said that the days of the
AEC's near-incestuous relationship with them were over.
When they complained that he was sounding a bit too tough,
he snapped: "Gentlemen, I'm not here to protect your Triple-
A bond ratings." The happening which really popped him into
public notice, however, was Amchitka. The AEC had planned
an underground test of a high-powered nuclear explosive at
that site in the Aleutians, and environmentalists were vocifer-
ous in their objections. Schlesinger allowed that the test would
hurt nothing and no one. He packed his wife, Rachel, and two
of their eight children off to Amchitka to stand by his side, as
proof. Until then, hardly anyone had regarded the size of
Schlesinger's family. Afterward, he tired of people alluding to
it, drawing assumptions. When a new acquaintance brought it
up, or so the story goes, Schlesinger said, "No, I'm not Catho-
lic, I just happen to like kids." Schlesinger, Brooklyn-born of
Jewish parents, spent his Sunday mornings at Lutheran services, and his Sunday afternoons on the towpath along the
Potomac River, or on the river's Theodore Roosevelt Island
wildlife refuge, watching birds, just like Richardson. Odd how
the human touch of a man attracts reporters, most of whom,
in Washington, were somewhere to the left of Schlesinger's
politics. He got high marks from them for introducing wine to
the executive dining room of the AEC, and for permitting
alcohol to be served at AEC receptions, proving that not all
blasts need be nuclear. Correspondent Llewellyn King, maybe
the best chronicler of the now-defunct AEC in all Washington,
wrote of Schlesinger:

"At an AEC reception recently, as several stragglers approached the bar for another round, the bartender replied po-
litely that the party was over. 'The hell it is,' said the chairman
of the AEC, extending his glass for a refill. Those who know
him believe that the CIA is in for a shot of change, and they
feel pretty good about it."

Indeed it was. Next stop: Central Intelligence Agency. The

CIA, according to its critics (notably Nixon and Kissinger) badly needed shaking, too. What better man than Schlesinger, who had accomplished so much in a miraculously short time at the AEC? Besides, to the awareness of practically no one, none other than James R. Schlesinger had drafted a systems-type study of the entire intelligence community in 1971, just before he became AEC chairman. In transferring to the CIA, he would be following a trail of his own blazing.

The United States spends upwards of $6 billion a year on a sprawling intelligence system which is compartmentalized into the CIA, the Defense Intelligence Agency (a McNamara creation), the National Security Agency, the State Department's Office of Intelligence & Research, the Federal Bureau of Investigation and numerous other odds and ends. This global network is not nearly so heavily populated, as myth would have you believe, with James Bond-type espionage operatives. Most of the intelligence consists of simple fact-gathering from "open" sources, such as foreign language broadcasts and publications, and from mechanical spying via satellites, spy planes (like the U-2 and the SR-71) and spy ships (like the *Pueblo*) equipped with photographic, electronic, infrared and other types of sensors. The capstone of all this, since the early 1950s, has been the National Intelligence Estimate, a super-secret document. One of the most important in all of government. The degree of its accuracy is critical. So are the outcomes of the behind-the-scenes debates over its accuracy. These debates occur in and are resolved by the National Security Council, the "Forty Committee," and by the President. There have been some monumental debates over how to interpret intelligence assessments. Bomber gaps. Missile gaps. Antiballistic missile gaps. Our reactions to foreign crises, to Russian and Chinese weapons developments and troop deployments, to the thrusts of international terrorists, to drug traffic, can be traced to the National Intelligence Estimate. Presidents and Secretaries of Defense are prisoners, in effect, of this intelligence system. Reports from it flow to them throughout the day, every day. The system's goofs can send the nation to the brink of war, cause it acute embarrassment or lead it to vastly overspend to meet a miscalculated threat. The Bay of Pigs. The U-2 incident. The exaggerated "missile gap" of the late 1950s. Underestimates of the enemy in Vietnam. Prime examples. The military had always groused about the tendency of the CIA to interpret the Soviet missile threat as less scary than military intelligence would have led the brass to believe. In 1969, military intelligence told Laird, through the DIA, that the Soviets had begun putting MIRVs on their missiles. The CIA disputed this, saying there was no hard evidence. The Soviets had begun to test MRVs, multiple warheads but without independent guidance, so the reality had lain somewhere between the military and the civilian intelligence. The CIA also told the military—and the White House, of course—that the Vietcong were far stronger and more influential in South Vietnam than the military command at Saigon was willing to believe. Among other things, the CIA discerned that the farmer of South Vietnam was getting a bum deal from the Saigon government on prices of his products, that his sons were being forced to fight for a government of corruption and of princely life-style which held him in economic servitude, and that this farmer's loyalties were, at best, mixed. In light of this, said the CIA, "pacification" of the South Vietnam countryside was a dubious proposition. Nor did the CIA also believe that Air Force interdiction of supply lines in Laos and Cambodia would make much difference in the end. And the agency cautioned against backing Pakistan against India in 1971. Meanwhile, of course, the CIA was running its own little war in Laos, and was not, itself, above suspicion of bias in its interpretations of the proclivities of the Pentagon and the State Department.

At any rate, the military and the White House became very much annoyed with CIA advice cutting so often across the grain of military predilections. They began shutting out the agency. CIA was not asked for an opinion of the DIA plan to send an airborne commando force to the Son Tay prisoner of war camp in North Vietnam, to free the Americans confined there. When the raiders dropped in, Son Tay was empty. The CIA was not brought into the planning of the administration's invasion of Cambodia in 1970, aimed at finding and destroying COSVN, the mobile communications command headquarters of the North Vietnamese. (COSVN never was tracked down.) Nor was the CIA asked to assess the soundness of an attack by the South Vietnamese regulars into Laos, in 1971, to cut off the Ho Chi Minh Trail. The attack was thrust back, with heavy losses. The CIA clearly had come to be regarded by the Pentagon—and by Kissinger, still at the White House—as a messenger of bad news.

The entire intelligence community, not just the CIA, was in for a rousting. The Defense Intelligence Agency, military focal point of the intelligence matchups with the CIA, had turned soggy. DIA was created in 1962 by McNamara. He wanted the intelligence branches of the separate services to speak with one voice. By 1970, this centralized agency had outgrown its civilian counterpart, and alone accounted for some $4 billion of the total $6 billion price tag for all U.S. intelligence. In the military, an intelligence billet always had been regarded as a temporary tangent in a career officer's climb to the top. Officers on intelligence duty naturally did not want to jeopardize their chances of getting off that tangent and back into the mainstream by purveying analyses of enemy strength which ran counter to the pet schemes of the JCS for more combat troops, better weapons. The intelligence officers also tended, despite the tri-service format of DIA, to bear in mind the distinctive color of their uniforms, and not to communicate very well with their DIA colleagues from the other services. Notable failures of U.S. intelligence, resulting in the loss of the *Pueblo* spy ship, the downing of a reconnaissance plane over North Korea, the Son Tay raid, the Tet offensive of 1968, the North Vietnamese invasion of Cambodia in 1970 and of South Vietnam in 1972 could be traced at least partly to DIA inefficiency. Both the military and civilian intelligence services had been caught napping, incidentally, by the Russian invasion of Czechoslovakia. President Johnson learned about it from Soviet Ambassador Anatoly Dobrynin, and he was most unhappy with his spymasters.

DIA had been fashioned from three service-intelligence bureaucracies; their agglutination into a larger bureaucracy came out just about as you would expect. But the CIA had started out, far back in the days of the Office of Strategic Services, as a lean and hungry outfit. Now, it, too, had become puffy around the eyes. Its network of "old boys"—blue-chip agents and analysts of yore, long past their prime of the World War II and postwar eras—had begun to ossify. The older men seemed to draw apart from the younger, many of whom decided to take their talents elsewhere. The immediate scapegoat for this was Richard Helms, a cool CIA careerist and onetime agent of distinction, who had been the agency's director since 1965. Henry Kissinger made no secret of his disaffection with Helms. From his crow's nest at the National Security Council, Presidential counselor Kissinger had come to regard the CIA's analyses as fudgy, fatuous and faulty in their bias, which too often, for Kissinger's tastes, reflected the thinking then prevalent in academe. (Academe had changed since Kissinger's day. Since Schlesinger's, too, for that matter.) Helms also stood accused of not having followed through on Nixon's instructions of 1971: take charge of the entire intelligence community, as was his prerogative as Director of Central Intelligence, and get it all together. In fact, the need to widen the authority and responsibility of the man in charge of CIA had been emphasized as long overdue in the very plan which Schlesinger had devised, for Nixon, to synchronize the spies. Helms ignored the plan as so much muck. His friends said it was a Kissinger trap, in any case, to flush him out of his director's digs at CIA and plunge him into interagency controversies which would embarrass him publicly. (He was to be embarrassed publicly in any event, in 1975, amid the storm over the CIA's role in spying on Americans inside the U.S. during his directorship.) So the White House, seizing on Helms' dilatoriness, told him he had to go—to Iran, as ambassador, just a few years shy of retirement. Into the shops of the surreptitious strode Schlesinger, turning cloaks into gunnysacks, daggers into trowels.

Schlesinger immediately bore down on the agency's clandestine operations. They soaked up about half of the CIA's $600-million budget and subsumed close to half of its sixteen thousand employees. Couching it only a bit more circumspectly, he told Congress, at his confirmation hearing, that the CIA had a surfeit of spooks who had become superannuated at their craft. "The trouble with this place," he said on another occasion, "is that it is run like a gentleman's club. And I'm no gentleman." In his short but snappy term as director, Schlesinger purged more than one thousand men and women, mostly by forcing their retirement. Thomas Karamessines, the veteran Deputy Director of Plans (DDP), the covert, espionage, coup-planning side of the CIA, was among those who took retirement. He insisted that he had been planning to retire for two years. But Schlesinger's arrival and Karamessines' departure were too sequential to have been coincidental. Schlesinger replaced the deputy with William E. Colby, a former CIA operative who had headed, for a time, the U.S. pacification effort in Vietnam, and who had worked closely there with the military. To the extreme discomfort of the CIA traditionalists, Schlesinger also brought over from the Pentagon Army Major General Daniel O. Graham and Air Force Major General Lewis Allen, both of whom had held top jobs in military intelligence, including DIA, and who had known Schlesinger since his days at RAND. He posted them on the newly formed Intelligence Resource Advisory Committee, and it was clear that someone up there thought the CIA bore watching from inside. Graham later became director of DIA; Allen, of NSA.

Again, following the same, old pattern, Schlesinger endeared himself to the press by abolishing many of CIA's Mickey Mouse trappings. He instructed secretaries to quit answering phones by coyly reciting their extension numbers, as per tradition, and start saying, "China desk," or "Soviet desk," or whatever. He got rid of the roadside turn-off signs which identified the cozy CIA glade as a Bureau of Public Roads reservation, and had new signs posted which proclaimed, "Central Intelligence Agency, Langley, Va." CIA's satraps did not mind this. They too had grown weary of silly, self-perpetuating rules which forbade them to tell acquaintances—or even old friends—where they worked. But they judged Schlesinger on graver grounds, for they regarded him as Nixon's and Kissinger's "hit man," come to transform the agency into a political tinkertoy. They predicted its downfall, and the nation's, too, if it were to become a wand of the White House, a plaything of the Pentagon. They resented Schlesinger's heavy-handed dismissal of so many operatives, so fast, so ruthlessly. In a few old hands, the resentment actually hardened into hatred.

Feelings ran high. The CIA guard force was beefed up. Some said this was done to protect the director. Others said more guards were needed in the building only because Schlesinger worked such long hours. Two incidents in the CIA cafeteria pointed up both his own style and the depth of the disregard for his leadership. Early on, Schlesinger plopped down at a lunch table and asked the man seated there how things were going. "What do you do here?" he asked one. Flippantly came the reply: "As little as I can." Within two weeks, or so the story goes, the man was gone. Another time, a veteran CIA career officer, his indignation welling into his craw, stalked over, confronted Schlesinger at table and told the new director, in very certain terms, what he thought of developments. Nothing happened to this man. Schlesinger had made it clear, early in his term at the AEC, that he did not believe in reprisals against underlings who disagreed with him or who talked to the press about it, so long as they did their jobs. He followed through on this at the CIA. Watching him practice what he preached, his critics began to soften somewhat. But not completely. They agreed that he did the right thing by coming clean with the Senate about the CIA's involvement in the White House-orchestrated burglary of the office of the psychiatrist of Daniel Ellsberg of "Pentagon Papers" notoriety. No special credit accrued to Schlesinger for this, however. With Watergate having burst open, coverups clearly were no longer the fashion of the times. Schlesinger's critics also carefully and disdainfully took note that in his testimony, he had reminded the Senate committee three times that the burglary boffo had taken place before he had taken over the CIA. These critics were, of course, Helms' men.

Withal, Schlesinger won a reputation for playing it straight. Rough but straight. Only five months after he had transferred from the AEC to the CIA, came time for a new Secretary of Defense. Richardson, packing up at the Pentagon, recommended Schlesinger as his successor. Schlesinger's honesty-integrity-straightforwardness reputation had a lot to do with Richardson's selection. David Packard, too, voted aye. Melvin Laird, yet to join the White House staff as a last-of-the-ninth pinch-hitter for the departed Watergaters, was not consulted, back in private life, on the Schlesinger appointment. For Schlesinger, maybe it was just as well.

The day his appointment was announced, I sat beside a swimming pool in surburban Virginia with an acquaintance who worked for the CIA. "What kind of Defense Secretary will he make?" I asked. "Remember McNamara?" he replied. "Well, if you thought McNamara was a boss, this guy is a boss, boss, boss. He makes things happen. Good or bad, he makes things happen."

Schlesinger arrived at the Pentagon puffing on his pipe and waxing philosophical. At his welcoming ceremony, he used the expression "nihilistic individualism" in referring to a trend which he said was becoming evident in American society. At his first press conference, a few days later, he was asked to elaborate on this. "I was not referring at that time," he said, "to draft evasion or anything of that sort. I think it's a broader spirit in the land. The notion that the individual can decide for himself whether something is inconvenient or unpleasant, and that there are no restrictions placed upon him by being part of the body politic. My observations were in these more general and philosophical realms, rather than associations with particular groups. We all understand, I think, that we have a balance in any society between liberty and authority, and that the maintenance of liberty depends upon the respect individuals have for authority, and that the greater is this built-in respect for the limits of individualism, the greater is the amount of liberty a society can maintain. It's those kinds of issues I was referring to." In that same session with Pentagon reporters, most of whom were encountering him face up for the first time, Schlesinger discussed his hope that the Cambodian government would marshal the resources to compensate for the recent cutoff of American bombing, in its behalf, of the invading North Vietnamese troops. "Dr. Johnson," he said, "once observed that nothing collects a man's mind better than the knowledge that he might be hung." That one sent the reporters scrambling to their reference books, to find that Schlesinger had taken some license with Dr. Samuel Johnson, the eighteenth-century English lexicographer, whose exact words had been: "Depend on it, sir, when a man knows he is to be hanged in a fortnight, it concentrates his mind wonderfully."

This was heady stuff from a Secretary of Defense. The Chicago *Tribune*'s Fred Farrar wrote of that press conference: "There was the feeling that one should pay attention because the speaker might later give a test on what he said. He came into the room, this rumpled, rough-cut former professor, plucked the worn pipe from his jaw, and for the first time in modern memory, introduced quotations from such people as Henry David Thoreau and Dr. Samuel Johnson into a Defense Secretary's press conference. . . . The name of Thoreau, a nineteenth-century writer and philosopher and early advocate of civil disobedience, came up when Schlesinger was asked what he meant by 'nihilistic individualism.' He quoted Thoreau as telling Ralph Waldo Emerson, when Emerson asked him what he was doing in jail after an act of civil disobedience: 'Ralph, what are you doing out there?' Schlesinger went on to say that Thoreau expected to be punished and believed he should be. But, he added, many of today's dissenters do not, and the delicate balance between liberty and authority is being threatened."

A few months later, Schlesinger, in prose again professorial, styled one of his first major speeches as Secretary of Defense in Spenglerian-modern.

The question that we face in the United States and in the other western Democracies is the stamina—I repeat, the stamina—of these countries in the current period, and whether they have the moral conviction to survive. Because ultimately, the ability of these countries to withstand the pressures that will be exerted against them, in a variety of circumstances, will depend on moral conviction. We live at a time in which, for a variety of reasons, the morale of the western societies is at a lower ebb than it has been in the past. And it must be revived. These are the important issues. The underpinnings. The morale. The support of populations, in a democracy. They are more important than weapon systems. No foreign policy has ever been based upon anything other than the support of the public. In a democracy. One can have a vividly rhetorical foreign policy. One can pile up weapons systems. But unless there is the public support and the appropriate national character to support the foreign policy, any nation will be in trouble. We live in a peculiar period of withdrawal symptoms; withdrawal from Southeast Asia. It was a conflict that engendered a high degree of divisiveness within the American society. Some of that is understandable. But the important thing to recognize is that there is no alternative in the present world to American leadership and strength. In the absence of that strength the Soviet Union will dominate all of the Eastern Hemisphere, at least, and, to some extent, the Western Hemisphere. This is why we must maintain our military power. Not because we will necessarily use that military power. A military establishment is most important when it is not used. It is important in order to deter, in order to provide the political basis

for negotiations. And if we lack an adequate military establishment, we will be hard put to play the leadership role that
we must play in the world.

Lofty. When he struck the same theme, at his first appearance as featured speaker before the National Press Club,
Schlesinger was asked how, if he placed such a premium on
moral values, he could be comfortable as a cabinet officer of the
post-Watergate Nixon administration. He said he would continue to serve at the President's pleasure. But he did not answer the question. Only days before, Vice-President Gerald
Ford had let it be known that he probably would not, should
he succeed to the Presidency, retain Schlesinger as Secretary
of Defense. Ford's reason was that Schlesinger had been inef-
fective in failing to prevent Congress from slashing military
aid to South Vietnam. There may have been more to it than
that. For one thing, Ford and Laird were longtime friends, and
had worked together closely in the House of Representatives
for a good many years. More likely, though, Ford may have
seen, in the Vietnam aid issue, the beginnings of a Congressional resistance to Schlesinger's attitude and approach. Members of the House and Senate had almost uniformly described
his maiden performances before their committees as "brilliant." But brilliance is not a quality that wears well in Congress. As in the example of McNamara, it sooner or later incurs
suspicion, and then is described, instead, as superciliousness,
arrogance, condescension.

Brilliance and articulateness do, however, tend to captivate
the press. Schlesinger had become stereotyped as a hawk for
his stance on strategic matters. Most reporters, even Pentagon
reporters, are definitely not hawks. Still, Schlesinger had won
them, for the time. Llewellyn King, who had introduced
Schlesinger at the Press Club affair, expressed the ambivalence.
"You know," said King, "Schlesinger is too conservative for
me, a little too much of a hawk. And yet, he's the only officer
in this administration I'd go to work for." It seemed that a
sharp mind, straight talk and the appearance of honesty could
take a man a long way, regardless of his views, in the Washington of Watergate, dismally lacking in towering figures. By 1975,
Schlesinger had come a long way with Ford, who had a potful
of problems in his new Presidency and who needed a plain
talker, not a shoulder slapper, at the Pentagon.

Schlesinger had bruised sensibilities on Capitol Hill with his remarks around town of the "postwar follies" of Congress in its attacks on the defense budget. In another striking example of his disdain for the diplomatic, he remarked sardonically on how doves in Congress on the issue of Vietnam had turned hawk (either sincerely so or because of pressure from constituencies notably lacking in voters of Arabic origin) on the issue of supplying weapons to Israel. He had come on quite strenuously, in fact, at the very time he first set foot in the Pentagon. With Brezhnev in Washington in 1973, Schlesinger had asserted: "I strongly believe that we must continue to have during this period of détente the capabilities that fulfill U.S. foreign policy. I am ready, willing and eager to spread that message."

Syndicated columnist Richard Wilson, mostly conservative, wrote: "One after another, presidents and secretaries of defense succeed each other in the White House and the Pentagon and they all come to the same conclusion. From time to time the military confrontation with the Soviet Union varies in intensity but it remains as a real and incontrovertible fact of life. Now and again, a Secretary of Defense is able to articulate the problem with clarity. That is the case today, and makes James Schlesinger worth listening to. He is more like some of the earlier intellectualizing secretaries of defense, James Forrestal and Robert Lovett, and less the human computer like Robert McNamara. . . ." And columnist Nick Thimmesch wrote: "We have an unusual defense secretary in the Pentagon. Besides being one of the worst-groomed men around, he is also brilliant, hard-headed, testy and determined to rebuild our defense establishment at a time when seeming détente with the Soviet Union would suggest the contrary. James Rodney Schlesinger inherited a department run down by the Vietnamese war, picked on by Congress and wondering what its future role would be. Melvin R. Laird used all his political skills to keep the Pentagon healthy and safe from Congressional ire, and extricate the military from Vietnam. Mr. Schlesinger is the first defense chief to preside without a war on his hands since 1963. Consequently, he must refocus on the nation's strategic needs—namely, nuclear missiles and the positioning of our military forces around the world. He tells associates that it is a myth to believe the cold war is now a myth, that the United States needs at least specimens of new, advanced weapons to serve as 'bargaining chips' with Moscow. It might seem ironic that an American would have to remind Europe that it better shape up its NATO defenses, but that's what Mr. Schlesinger has done repeatedly since taking office. Hardly a disciple of the Dale Carnegie method, Mr. Schlesinger ruffled some feelings on the Continent in his first encounters, but was somewhat conciliatory in his Brussels meetings last week."

Wilson also wrote: "Schlesinger is different as secretary of defense because he is pulling no punches. He is not romancing Congress, like Melvin Laird, or trying to outwit it, like Robert McNamara, but is laying it on the line that the Russians are going ahead toward military superiority without any apologies and this country needs to be fairly warned."

There was, of course, the contrary view, as expressed by Washington *Star-News* columnist Frank Getlein. He described Schlesinger as "an ideal Secretary of Defense from the point of view of the Pentagon," and went on: "In times of peace and friendship with the Russians and Chinese, we must pour ever-increasing amounts of money into fantasy arms because that's the only way we can keep them friendly. In times of unfriendliness on the part of either the Russians or the Chinese, on the other hand, we must pour ever-increasing amounts of money into fantasy arms because that's the only way we can keep them from attacking us tomorrow. In times that are neither friendly nor unfriendly we must pour ever-increasing amounts of money into fantasy arms so as to be prepared for either eventuality. In a changing world, one thing alone is constant: more money for arms. . . . What the Pentagon needs at the top is a mind capable of saying: Once we can kill every Russian and Chinese twenty times—or two hundred times—that is enough; we don't need to kill them more times than that. For Schlesinger, as for his generals and their hired think-tankers, that is the real unthinkable thought."

Getlein, in toting up the abysmal numbers of kill and over-kill, had it all wrong. By Pentagon reasoning. The name of the new game was to respond to the Russian missile-testing with some movement in the research and development outer reaches of our own missile technologies; but even beyond this, as a matter of strategy, to refine our nuclear arsenal so that it would not necessarily wipe out half the face of the earth if it were indeed put to use. Guide the warheads so they will strike only military targets, if that is the President's decision. Give him the option of making that decision, of not being forced to blow whole cities into smithereens. Widely overlooked in this scenario was the psychological effect which it had of blurring the long and fiercely held distinction between strategic weapons and tactical weapons. By working up a frame of mind in which nuclear warheads could be perceived as "limited-strike" weapons, those warheads might eventually be reduced from the awesome to the commonplace in the psyches and in the contemplations of the strategic planners. From orbit to ordinary. It had been the very awesomeness of the nuclear weapons which had kept them at bay. A tactical weapon is something which one military force shoots at another military force. A strategic weapon is something with which one nation blows up another. A nuke is a nuke. In the never-never land of computer planners, it might even be possible to conceive of a "tactical" nuclear war so "clean," of such targeting virtuosity, that the civilian populations need only cower in their cities, themselves untouched, while the international gunslingers shot it out.

Schlesinger first hinted at the hard line he later would take, in public, at an off-the-record session in September 1973, only three months after he had become Secretary of Defense. He was asked by his companions at a private luncheon to assess the Jackson amendment—by Senator Henry Jackson (D.-Wash.)—which the Senate had imposed on the Nixon administration. In ratifying Nixon's SALT I interim agreement with the Soviets, which dealt mainly with limiting antiballistic missiles, the Senate gave the President permission to sign a SALT II treaty only if that treaty "would not limit the United States to levels of intercontinental strategic forces inferior to the limits provided for the Soviet Union." Schlesinger was all for it. He perceived in it, in fact, a commitment of sorts by the Senate to go along with the strategy of "Essential Equivalence" which he later would enunciate as broad policy. "Essential Equivalence" would mean, in short, not letting the Soviets catch up in the strategic arena. Its main elements were to be Counterforce, improving the existing U.S. missiles so they would be sure to strike Soviet military targets, and "Flexible Response," widening the array of future U.S. strategic weapons. Here is what Schlesinger had to say, months before he made his new policy public, to his luncheon companions, about the Jackson amendment: "I think the Jackson amendment is not a mere happenstance or a sop to the right wing, or what have you, but is really an integral part of the U.S. defense posture which the administration did not include in SALT I, but is necessary. In SALT I you have a clear balance, a clearly perceived balance. You have got these qualitative advantages of the U.S. forces—technical advantages, MIRVs, greater guidance, much greater guidance, and warhead technology that the Soviets didn't have. Which meant that with much fewer number of launches and much less throw weight, that we had a hell of a lot of RVs."

QUESTION: "A lot of what?"

SCHLESINGER: "Reentry vehicles. We outnumbered them two to one, and we had greater accuracy in the rest of them. The Soviets might reasonably say that under those circumstances, for balance—given the fact that you have got those technical advantages—that we have got to have something to compensate for it, and we will take that in numerical advantage. We have a greater number of launchers, and although our missiles are big and clumsy, they have got more throw weight. And we said, fine. That is a kind of a square deal for the two sides, on an interim basis. But all of our advantages or relative advantages are waning advantages, and as the Soviets acquire these technologies—given their throw weight and numbers—they can outclass us and have a strategic advantage.

"So my judgment would be that, by God, the Soviets have got to be told at the outset of SALT II that there is going to be a rough equality, and that as they build up in terms of the numbers of RVs and improve the quality of their forces, they have got to come down in terms of numbers and throw weights to the U.S. level. Unless they are willing to do that, we have got to be very tough and say there just can't be an agreement. And we have got to be prepared to resume our deployments of our weapons systems that we would not otherwise have to do. Now, my own feeling is that if we are tough enough with the Soviets, that they will say, yes, it was implicit in SALT I that as we obtain your qualitative and technical advantages, that there would have to be a rough equality."

QUESTION: "How, then, would we respond if they said, well, screw you?"

Schlesinger replied that the Soviets already were showing signs, in their first MIRV tests, of saying just that, as he had pointed out in a press conference on the Soviet testing a month previously. Referring to the tests and his announcement of them, Schlesinger continued the conversation:

"Oh, hell, I have been very careful to understate the numerical values. It is a milestone, inevitable [MIRVing]. The Soviets have to cross it. . . . But I very carefully tried to understate it because I think the [Defense] Department has gotten into trouble in the past by grabbing every little bit of evidence on the thing [Soviet missile development] and rushing it on. I don't think it should disturb us in the immediate future. I think, by and large, on the strategic front we have got enough money. I worry more about the general purpose forces. Now, three years out or four years out, if the Soviets don't come around and they begin to pull the SS-9 out of the holes and put in SS-18s, or one-megaton RVs, and so on, we would have to look at those circumstances. But I would certainly consider deploying more submarines, deploying the Trident in addition to the Polaris, or whatever submarines we want to deploy. And I don't think the Soviets want to resume the arms race. I think that each time that we have been fairly tough in negotiations with them, they have been willing to accommodate themselves. The change in Soviet society has been much greater than the change in ours. When they agreed that there was going to be no antiballistic missile [except around Moscow], by God, they were saying something. The Soviet motherland is defenseless against attack, and that was a greater risk for the Soviet military than it was for our own."

Less than a month after this discussion, the Mideast war erupted. President Nixon put U.S. forces worldwide on the alert at a signal that the Soviets, having been rejected in their proposal that the United States and USSR intervene bilaterally, were getting ready to go it alone and dispatch airborne troops. Many U.S. commentators, in and out of government, wondered aloud if the President had not needed a trumped-up triumph in a showdown with a Soviet straw man, and had overreacted. Nixon called it our touchiest confrontation with the Soviet Union since the Cuban missile crisis. How about that? Schlesinger was asked. Had not the U.S. reaction been, perhaps, a bit "over-quick"?

SCHLESINGER: "I would say that our reaction was timely, that it was not extra quick. . . . It was necessary to go on alert because of the possibility of the movement of forces in a certain region of the world. The alert also had the function of demonstrating the strong belief of the United States government that the movement that was being speculated on would be disadvantageous to world peace. Consequently, to the extent that that message was conveyed, I think that this has been a success."

QUESTION: "So the reading here was that the Soviets might be putting themselves in a position to move troops into the Middle East and you wanted to warn them not to do it. Is that correct?"

SCHLESINGER: "I think the first part of the question is the correct reading. The second part is your inference and you're welcome to it. I wouldn't confirm that."

The war, the near-confrontation with the Soviets, the abrupt realization of the breadth of their missile development, all these combined to reinvigorate the Pentagon. Feet seemed suddenly to quicken, shoulders to straighten, faces to show purpose. The snap, missing for a long, long time, was back in the building. Now it had a boss who could, and did, define the job to be done, utterly in keeping with what the military advocated, and lead the way. Schlesinger was at the top of his form, indifferent to the trappings of power but enamored of its exercise. He still moseyed around his suite and elsewhere in the building with his shirttail half out, trousers slightly baggy, skinny necktie akimbo, socks sagging. He still casually propped his feet on his desk. He still puffed away serenely at his pipe and managed the feat of continuing to talk without removing it. He still drew his innocent-looking countenance frequently into those smiles so unusual for their semicircular symmetry. He still didn't bother to curb the cowlick tendencies of his medium-cropped, prematurely white hair. He still, to the wonderment of official Washington, declined invitations to White House dinners and other haute affairs (don't have the time; big family, other pursuits). He still drove his beatup 1964 Plymouth (it having replaced a 1960 Falcon which he donated to the CIA to be used in target practice). He still whiled away, home in Arlington, at his guitar and harmonica. But he was hardening, for all that. You noticed it if you watched the signs. Less inclined to the arcane discourse, the wit for its own sake, the ambience of the lecture hall. He marshaled his musings, got

to the point faster, put dedication to his policies—*his* policies
—less hesitantly on display. He had something going, and it
was hurrying him along.

Michael Getler of the Washington *Post* wrote a piece during
this period, toward the end of 1973, which was headlined:
"Things Stir in Pentagon Under Unconventional Schlesinger." Getler told of how Schlesinger had relaxed, following
a two-day NATO meeting in Brussels, by spotting birds in the
Belgian coastal marshlands, of how he had boarded the home-
bound Air Force jet "wet-footed, red-eared . . . wrapped in
tattered old corduroys and sweater." "For Schlesinger," wrote
Getler, "birdwatching is an old hobby. But for military men,
civilian bureaucrats, NATO ministers and Kremlin planners,
Schlesinger-watching has become increasingly interesting and
important."

On a rainy, dismal day in January 1974, Schlesinger, hatless
as usual, was delivered by limousine across the Potomac to a
charcoal-hued building at the corner of Eighteenth and K
Streets, Northwest, Washington, the home of the Overseas
Press Club. He was taking time off from his on-deadline drafting of the Pentagon budget for the fiscal year which would
begin the following July. It was to be the first budget of his
own devising, and it would contain the money to begin implementing the strategic policy which he now prepared to start
sketching out for the press. At the luncheon was a broader-
gauged press than he had been accustomed to addressing: the
State Department regulars as well as the Pentagon regulars. A
perfect forum. For what Schlesinger did that day was to signal
a new defense policy that would dig deeply into foreign policy
as well. Henry Kissinger was in town, for a change, but all of
"his" reporters were off covering Schlesinger. The Secretary
of Defense announced that the Air Force would begin retargeting Minuteman missiles on Soviet military targets. He emphasized that some of the missiles already were programmed to
strike silos, airfields and tank parts, for example, but more
needed to be. He also emphasized that this retargeting would
not require new hardware, and should not, for heaven's sake,
be construed as an inclination of the Pentagon to power up for
a "first strike." His tone, if not his meaning, was altogether
mild. But as the *Wall Street Journal* reported it later: "By dropping a few codewords at a press luncheon, Defense Secretary

James R. Schlesinger has sparked quite a debate in the esoteric circles that worry about the philosophy of nuclear weapons. For in effect he announced that the Pentagon has started to modify the philosophy that has dominated strategic thinking since the McNamara era."

A few days later, Schlesinger called a Pentagon press conference to pin his new policy more firmly onto the public consciousness. And then, in his budget and in his "Posture Statement," which he dispatched to Congress in early February, he laid it all out. Counterforce. There is not much point in targeting many more Minuteman missiles on Soviet silos unless steps also are taken to make sure that the warheads will actually strike those targets. And so the Pentagon would need some research and development money to bring the accuracy of the missiles up to the exigencies of their new mission. He hammered at the point that he was by no means turning his back on the philosophy that the overriding purpose of deploying nuclear weapons is to ensure that they never have to be used, and that they obviously cannot be brandished indiscriminately—to forestall each and every action anywhere in the world that might be considered inimical to the interests of the United States. But for all that, he said, the Soviets now were forcing the United States to face the hard fact of life that nuclear weapons, by their very existence, should be regarded as the means of deterring not only nuclear attacks on the American mainland, but also, perhaps, nuclear—*or non-nuclear* —attacks on our allies in Europe, Asia or the Middle East. The wide range of R&D which he proposed on missiles, including the genesis of new types, also was based on the increasing danger (the Mideast war was a reminder) that we might need to use nukes to beat off—or retaliate against—a Russian invasion of Europe. Under the policy which Schlesinger set forth, the President, on learning of such an invasion, could decide to launch our precisely targeted ICBMs or our cruise missiles (more later on these) against Russian military targets. Maybe with just a modest launching at first, just to show what we could do. Like at Hiroshima and then, because the Japanese thought Hiroshima was a fluke, at Nagasaki. If the Russians struck back at our cities, then, of course, we would feel morally free to strike back at theirs. What good would it do to strike Soviet missile silos from which the missiles already had been launched? Well, the Soviets would be unlikely to launch all of their ICBMs at once, so we would destroy those that were left. And besides, the Soviets were developing a "cold-launch" technique which involves pushing the ICBMs to the surface and then blasting them off, enabling the silos to accommodate another round of missiles fed in from underground tunnels. It was called "magazine loading." Like rounds in a rifle clip. The United States, too, would be researching this technique. Schlesinger did not state the scenario this baldly or graphically. But his meaning was clear enough.

Schlesinger invited a great debate on his strategy. Congress took stock of it tamely. Congress was, as Schlesinger knew, still rattled by the Mideast war. But there was another factor, too, one which largely escaped attention. Washington was just not in a frame of mind for any more fights. The biggest fight ever was building up and would become ever fiercer—that between Nixon and Congress and the courts over impeachment. More trouble, in a capital which had known nothing but trouble for many, many years. An emotionally enervated capital. It seemed, in fact, that both the Pentagon and Congress had seized on the menacing moves of the Russians with a sort of perverse relief. At least the Russians were living up to form, giving us something in common, for a change, to combat. We could find brotherhood in national defense, if in nothing else. And it was comforting to lean on our technology. Technology gave us no arguments, and was the product of Yankee ingenuity which seemed to be lacking in other spheres, such as government. Moreover, Schlesinger, whatever else he was, was obviously a leader, so let's follow him, at least for a time. If he lacked a political base, at least he had a well-founded political sense, as exemplified by his obvious passion for such English political philosophers as Burke, Hazlitt, Carlyle, Pitts. Some, in fact, perceived in him the influence of the Continental philosophers.

The American Security Council, a lobby in behalf of a burly defense establishment, was among the gratified. Said ASC's "Washington Report": "The new Secretary of Defense, James R. Schlesinger, must have studied Voltaire. Among the philosopher's memorable lines is the one: 'Define your terms if you wish to debate with me.' In his first Posture Statement to the Congress [Schlesinger] has redefined the terms for this year's debate on national defense policy. And that is quite an undertaking for a man who has only been in office for nine months. . . . This year's Posture Statement has style, almost flair. It is very long but it is not tedious. . . ."

In excruciating detail, Schlesinger recounted for Congress the evidence of the USSR's "vigorous strategic R&D program," and explored the gamut of Kremlin gamesmanship. "The changes we are making in our strategic planning this year," he said, "are specifically intended to shore up deterrence across the entire spectrum of risk. We believe . . . that we will reduce to an even lower point the probability of nuclear clash between ourselves and other major powers." Adroitly, he injected a dash of bipartisanship. "During the early 1960s," he told Congress, "it was stated quite clearly by President Kennedy—and also by a large majority of Americans in both parties—that the United States needed alternatives other than suicide or surrender, that it needed options which did not imply immediate escalation to *major* [italics mine] nuclear war. If anything, the need for options other than suicide or surrender, and other than escalation to all-out nuclear war, is more important for us today than it was in 1960, because of the growth of the capabilities possessed by other powers. These additional options do not include the option of a disarming first strike. Neither the USSR nor the U.S. has, or can hope to have, a capability to launch a disarming first strike against the other, since each of us possesses, and will possess for the foreseeable future, a devastating second-strike capability against the other. This almost certainly will deter the deliberate initiation of a nuclear attack against cities, for it would bring inevitable retaliatory destruction to the initiator. Thus, this basic deterrent remains intact."

The *New York Times* put a different construction on this rationale. In an article headlined, "Is Another Variety of Missile War Desirable?" the *Times* reasoned that one side or the other might now be tempted to start a limited nuclear—not a limited conventional—war by striking the other's missile silos and bomber bases. The need to develop a Counterforce capability must have occurred to the Soviets, too, said the *Times*, as they watched the United States "build up its arsenal of ever more numerous, ever more accurate missile warheads—first with the independently targeted MIRV warheads and now with the MARV warheads that can be manuevered onto a target." Finally, said the newspaper: "Those who have reached the conclusion that nuclear war is thinkable have somehow skipped over and never satisfactorily answered the question of why a nation would think it could conduct a counterforce strike and not have its cities destroyed in retaliation. The question remains to be debated, therefore, of whether the past strategy of mutual destruction does not continue to make any form of nuclear war unthinkable."

Dr. Herbert Scoville, Jr., formerly deputy director of the CIA for science and technology under Eisenhower and Kennedy, and then assistant director of the Arms Control and Disarmament Agency for science and technology under Johnson, also broadsided the Secretary of Defense: "Schlesinger has said that 'we must not contribute to any failures of deterrency by making the strategic forces a tempting target for attack.' Yet his proposed improvements only *add* [Scoville's italics] to the attractiveness of ICBMs as targets, and to the other side's incentive to strike first. Much is said of the gains that can be made in accuracy through advanced technology—lasers or TV for guiding smart bombs to their destination. An objective of all such refinements is to make the use of nuclear weapons more acceptable by minimizing unintended collateral damage. But a safe nuclear war is a mirage. Reducing the aiming error from a quarter to an eighth of a mile is inconsequential when the weapons involved will kill at distances of several miles. Furthermore, Schlesinger has undermined his own objective by seeking ever higher yields for his nuclear warheads, which are already three to ten times as powerful as the bomb that destroyed Hiroshima and killed 100,000 people. 'Smart' bombs may have some value with conventional explosives, but we are kidding ourselves if we think they will make nuclear weapons tolerable."

The Federation of American Scientists also pounced on the new nuclear strategy. Fearing its escalatory effect, the FAS called upon both the United States and the USSR to agree to destroy all land-based missiles because they "will look more and more vulnerable to attack if MIRV and increases in accuracy cannot be prevented. Without determined efforts to control these developments, each land-based force will, in time, be able to largely annihilate the other depending only upon who strikes first." The statement was signed by the FAS executive committee, composed of Scoville; Dr. Herbert F. York, director of defense research and engineering under Eisenhower; Dr. Morton H. Halperin, formerly deputy assistant secretary of defense for arms control planning under Johnson and senior staff member of the National Security Council under Nixon-Kissinger; Dr. George W. Rathjens, formerly deputy director of the Defense Advanced Research Projects Agency (DARPA) and director of the Weapons Systems Evaluation Division of the Institute for Defense Analyses; and Vice-Admiral John M. Lee, USN (Ret.), former assistant director of the Arms Control and Disarmament Agency.

Not a ripple from the ACDA. It had changed, too, since the days of Scoville and Admiral Lee. Now it was under the directorship of Fred C. Ikle, who agreed with Schlesinger that the United States should fashion more accurate missiles and target them on Soviet military sites, for "selective" response. Ikle did not subscribe to the conventional wisdom that nuclear attacks, because they would cause so much damage, so much overkill, could never happen. He pointed out that the United States and the USSR missile forces had been positioned against one another for only a little more than a decade, and that there was no justification for extrapolating the non-war of that relatively brief time span into a non-war forevermore. The confrontation, he said, "is more fragile than we are in the habit of thinking." In fact, he said, the more time that passes, the more chance of a nuclear attack, either accidental or deliberate— contrary to the notion that if it hasn't happened yet, it won't happen ever. Therefore, in a speech at a Harvard-MIT joint seminar on arms control, Ikle, the man chiefly in charge of American disarmament efforts, came down on the side of Schlesinger's Counterforce concept: "Doesn't it make sense to introduce a last chance—should something go wrong—to prevent the utmost catastrophe . . . to make crises more easily reversible?"

Schlesinger, too, was obdurate. He had spread his strategy carefully before Congress and the public. (*Air Force* magazine called it "the most persuasive, best-articulated presentation of its kind in the annals of the Defense Department.") The time had passed for blue-penciling, short of a breakthrough at SALT II. "I am proposing," he told Congress, "a number of research and development programs which would enable us to respond in kind—in order to maintain the delicate balance of deterrence—should the Soviets decide to deploy a more efficient counterforce capability than they now deploy. We would prefer, of course, that neither side take this step. [But] we are determined to preserve an essential strategic equilibrium with the USSR both in capabilities and in targeting options. . . . We must," said this Secretary of Defense, who had trained his binoculars on a different breed of bird, "continue to build our peace structure on the hard facts of the international environment rather than on the gossamer hopes for the imminent perfectability of mankind." One month later, on Good Friday, April 12, 1974, Secretary of State Henry M. Kissinger concluded a breakfast meeting with Soviet Foreign Minister Andrei Gromyko and announced that, the way the discussions had been going, it was obvious that the United States and the USSR could not hope to sign a permanent arms control treaty in 1974, as they once had hoped to do. No one was aware of it at the time, but Kissinger had been "counterforced." By Schlesinger, who had come a long way from RAND, and who now, obviously, had supplanted Kissinger as "director of strategic studies" in the Nixon administration.

Four months later, there no longer was a Nixon administration. Shortly after Gerald R. Ford became President, he sat down with Leonid I. Brezhnev at Vladivostok in an attempt to get the nuclear arms talks back on track. For a few breathless days following their meeting, it appeared that Ford might have worked wonders, where Nixon had failed the year before. Ford announced a tentative agreement which would, he proclaimed, "put a cap on the arms race." True, he said, the accord still needed to be worked out in detail, ratified and signed, and he hoped that all this could be accomplished by the time Brezhnev came to Washington the following summer, the summer of 1975. It all sounded so melodic at first, and then it turned mostly to noise. The cap turned out to be not a cap for now but a cap for later. Ford and Brezhnev had agreed to work out an agreement "limiting" both sides to far more delivery systems—missiles and bombers—than either possessed at the moment. This would permit both sides—perhaps even encourage them—to push ahead with the deployment and the research and development of bigger and better missiles, until they attained—and thus, ironically, lived up to—the new limits. Moreover, the limits were only half the illusion. They applied to the number of warhead carriers, but not to the number of warheads, meaning that MIRVing would know no bounds. And so, while it probably was the best that Ford could do right out of the box, and while he at least appeared to be trying, the Vladivostok agreement augured more, not fewer, nuclear arms. It even may have augured an advantage to the Soviets, who only now had begun to MIRV their missiles, with only the sky as their limit.

5

Missiles in
Wonderland

Does a proposed innovation help us control the rate and direction of a subsequent advance? Or does it tend to accelerate a host of processes over which we have no control? How does it affect the level of transcience, the novelty ratio, and the diversity of choice? Until we systematically probe these questions, our attempts to harness technology to social ends —and to gain control of the accelerative thrust in general— will prove feeble and futile. Here, then, is a pressing intellectual agenda for the social and physical sciences. We have taught ourselves to create and combine the most powerful of technologies. We have not taken pains to learn about their consequences. Today these consequences threaten to destroy us. We must learn, and learn fast.
                            —Alvin Toffler, *Future Shock.*

The sobering (some think, appalling) thing about weapons— especially nuclear weapons—is that they have a life of their own, quite independent of the downs and ups of cold-war diplomacy. They just keep growing. Their technologies, once set in motion, become tyrannical. The men who conceive these technologies of aerodynamics, propulsion, guidance and explosive power become their servants. A common expression at the Pentagon is, "We have the technology, we might as well use it." In military argot, having technology in hand is having it "on the shelf," to be plucked down when needed—or when *thought* to be needed. The technology itself is father to that thought. "On the shelf" connotes gathering dust. Not so. Those technologies pulsate on those shelves, demanding nourishment, ready to burst forth as the components, subsystems and systems of prototypes of new weapons. Translation for "on the shelf": the technology has been designed, developed and tested, and awaits only the word from the White House, from the Secretary of Defense, from Congress (although there are all kinds of ways of *not* needing or not heeding the word from Congress) to go into service. The military-industrial complex (a better word is "team," in military-industrial circles) does not propagate technologies out of a desire to use them to make war, or even, down deep, out of a desire to use them to keep the peace. It propagates them mostly because it is trapped, pure and simple, into doing so. Pentagon officials are forever emphasizing their attentiveness to "return on investment," a phrase to capture the approbation of every citizen who has ever bought a car, a house or a share of stock. We won't spend money on researching and developing a weapon, or a component of a weapon, unless we're reasonably sure that the weapon will be used, that the money won't be wasted. The other side of this coin, however, is that all the while the R&D money is spent, the chances of the weapon being produced and deployed become better and better. Who ever heard of designing a computer that will guide a missile to within a few feet of its target, an entire ocean and a whole continent distant, and then abandoning the project short of perfection? A target is there to be hit. We must improve the computer so that we can strike that target. Bull's-eye. Edison would not have settled for half a filament, after all, or the Manhattan Project scientists for half a fission. As governments change, as Secretaries of Defense and Presidents, Premiers and Politburos, come and go, as Congress drones on and on, the men who designed that missile computer just keep on working through the years to perfect it. Justifiably, they take pride in their work. They get paid for it. They get prestige from it. They support their families by it. No one tells them to quit working just because of some transitory trend toward arms control. They finally come up with that refined computer, capable of steering the several separate warheads of a Minuteman missile straight out of space to dead center. Silo to silo. And now, that computer—the promise of what that computer could accomplish as the nerve center of a new generation of ICBMs—changes the whole world, all by itself. "General, we have this new computer . . ." "Mr. Secretary, we have this new computer . . ." "Mr. President, we have this new computer . . ." Keep in mind how President Truman's options broadened, as the military might have said it, after he received the message, while attending the Potsdam Conference, that the atomic bomb really worked. And when you hear or read of how lasers on spacecraft can shoot down ICBMs, what options then? For now, the ICBMs are enough to ponder.

The advance of technology is never checked, even on the rare occasion that either the Defense Department, Congress or the White House makes a decision not to deploy or only partially to deploy the particular weapon system for which the technology was devised. For example, consider the Safeguard antiballistic missile system. The SALT I interim agreement limited both sides to just two ABM sites. The United States decided to complete its Safeguard installation at Grand Forks, North Dakota, already well under construction, but deferred construction of the second Safeguard site planned for Washington, D.C. The scaling down of Safeguard was a setback for hundreds of companies which had been involved in the planning of buildings, radars and missile hardware, electronics and propulsion for several Safeguard installations, originally conceived as a "wide-area" network defense of the continental United States against enemy ICBMs. But did the development of antiballistic missile technology stop with the curtailment of Safeguard? It did not. The technology immediately was applied to a new, "thin" antiballistic missile system which the Pentagon dubbed "Site Defense of Minuteman," or SDM. Congress howled about it, and cut some of the funds which the Army requested to begin developing SDM, but the project marched forward relentlessly nonetheless. The prototype SDM—radars, computers, missiles—will be tested in the late 1970s at the Kwajalein Missile Range, where Safeguard had first shown life in the middle 1960s.

Other examples of technology fathering weapons, which in turn father strategy, tactics and force structures, are abundant. But the relationship of the computer to the intercontinental missile may be the most striking. Research on integrated circuits for computers, utilizing the micro-tiny silicon "chips" and "wafers" (which make the argot of the electronics industry sound something like plans for a cookie sale) was an outgrowth of work on transistors in the early 1950s. The Pentagon stimulated this research later on by awarding research and development contracts for the Minuteman missile computer. But the inventions which made it possible had come out of laboratories at Texas Instruments and Fairchild, whose scientists and engineers had been looking ahead at least as much to the commercial application—and sales—as they had been to defense contracts. In turn, the large-scale integrated circuit (LSI) in Minuteman led to the development of metal oxide semiconductor circuits now being used for analog and digital signal processing in military electro-optical and infrared sensor systems. These semiconductors, so small that you practically have to peer to spot one in the palm of your hand, so efficient that they need only the puniest of electrical pulses, were marketed first in commercial products. Pocket calculators, for instance. The orientation of these semiconductors to the electronics systems of missiles (and of aircraft) was obvious, but there was a problem. They had to be "hardened" against radiation. So the Defense Nuclear Agency, probably the least-publicized of all defense agencies in relation to its importance, was assigned the task. DNA's mission is to test and analyze U.S. nuclear weapons to make sure they inflict the damage they are supposed to inflict, in keeping with plans for their targeting and prospective delivery, and to analyze the impact of the nuclear weapons of potential enemies on U.S. forces. The Atomic Energy Commission develops U.S. nuclear weapons. DNA determines their effects.

DNA's scientists and engineers never let up, either, regardless of the waxings and wanings of the cold war. Air Force Lieutenant General Warren D. Johnson, DNA director, summed it up:

> Our job is to fight the technical side of a nuclear war in the laboratory, in the computer and—when possible—in underground nuclear tests, to help insure that all of our systems and our plans for using those systems are as good as they need to be. Our work supports the continual efforts of the services to ensure that their forces can do the job. Their

efforts range from basic research to intensive testing of new weapons systems. DNA plays its part at each step of the way. We have to keep emphasizing nuclear effects because new systems present novel and more complex problems, and because advances in nuclear weapons provide new opportunities that our forces can exploit and that other countries can use against us. It is particularly difficult to insure weapon-system effectiveness because we have not had atmospheric nuclear tests in nearly twelve years, and probably will never have them again.

I must emphasize that there has never been—and there never will be—an actual test of nuclear engagements involving the sophisticated weapons systems of the 1970s and 1980s. Unless we actually go to war. At the time of our last atmospheric tests, solid-fuel missiles were just being deployed in silos and submarines. Considerations of nuclear antiballistic missile systems were in their infancy. In the early sixties we foresaw the need for real-time, automated command and control systems. But we had only a glimmer of the possible effects of a nuclear attack, such as a wide-scale blackout of communications or the damaging effects of high-energy electromagnetic pulses on communications circuits and computers. The modern microelectronic devices had not yet been invented. So now it is necessary for us to handle the modern problems of force effectiveness through elaborate theoretical analysis—including some of the most complex computer codes; through simulation techniques, often involving massive laboratory facilities or field expeditions. And, of course, underground nuclear tests. We are dealing with phenomena and events totally removed from ordinary experience. So we must spend some considerable effort to make sure that we have thought of all the problems. We not only work on new systems and new weapons, but we are constantly uncovering new phenomena of military importance.

One of these was a phenomenon of Mother Nature. You might, if your mind works that way, look on it as her repayment to the bomb testers for having ceased to pollute her atmosphere. For years, the testers had recognized that the electronics of command-communications systems on the ground and in the control systems of airborne missiles were thrown out of kilter by Electromagnetic Pulse, the high-intensity radiation pulse which a nuclear explosion generates. Exploding nuclear bombs in the upper atmosphere was believed to be the only way to test out, and develop the means to counteract, this radiation threat to our offensive and defensive missile systems. Then DNA discovered that the Aurora Borealis exudes, as General Johnson expressed it, "some low levels of phenomena which are close to the radar blackout and infrared effects of high-altitude nuclear detonations. We are obtaining extremely useful data on this by launching instrumented rockets from Alaska." In concert with such research, DNA tackled the problem of hardening metal oxide semiconductors against radiation to permit their usage in the electronics systems of missiles. Several possible solutions, all highly classified, came to light, and the agency prepared to put them to test, for the first time, in 1976. Tidy timing. For just about then, the research and development of the guts of Secretary of Defense Schlesinger's new Counterforce strategic policy would be settling into stride. So would the R&D on the other part of Schlesinger's strategic policy; the part called "Flexible Response." This would bring into being a new generation of missiles, going well beyond the present force, presaging a thunderous tympani of hydrogen bombs over the Soviet Union, should it ever have to come to that. To appreciate the significance of Schlesinger's plans for the sons—and the sisters and brothers—of Minuteman, and to understand how he finessed Henry Kissinger, Congress, and even, maybe, President Nixon, it is necessary to start at the beginning.

Back in the late 1950s and early 1960s, 120 liquid-fueled Convair Atlas missiles, in "soft" sites aboveground and in hardened silos, made up the U.S. ICBM arsenal. In the drive to close the "missile gap" (a mostly mythological Presidential campaign issue in 1960), the Pentagon rushed the development of liquid-fueled Titan III missiles and the solid-propellant Minuteman. By the turn of the next decade, the prairies and mountains of the North American midcontinent were dotted with the silos and the launch-control centers of 1,054 ICBMs—54 Titans and 1,000 Minuteman I and Minuteman II models. All these ferried but one warhead. A monster five-megaton bomb on the Titans. A warhead of one-to-two megatons on the Minutemen. Technology on top of technology. On February

1, 1961, the very first Minuteman blasted off its pad at Cape Canaveral, Florida, and speared into space as a black speck over the South Atlantic. Success. But already, obsolescence had begun setting in. The scientists and engineers were working feverishly on developing MIRVs for Minuteman. Only seven and a half years after the first Minuteman test—on August 16, 1968, Minuteman III lanced skyward with multiple warheads. On that same day, the Navy's new Poseidon missile, successor to the Polaris, emerged from a tube of a ballistic-missile submarine, broke the surface and streaked into space—with MIRVs. Five days later, the Soviet Union invaded Czechoslovakia. The invasion had nothing to do with the U.S. testing of MIRVs. But *The Economist* of London, expressing shock at the Soviet move, wrote that it "almost certainly swept away the last doubts" that the U.S. would eventually deploy the MIRV-carrying Minuteman III, in reaction to the renewed evidence of Soviet military repression. More likely, the United States deployed Minuteman III simply because it was there, now, to deploy. Ralph E. Lapp, author of *The Weapons Culture*, wrote of MIRV in 1969:

Like the H-bomb, when it became technologically "sweet," it became ineluctable. How did MIRV come about? It is generally assumed that MIRV was a development "hedge" against the possibility that some day the Soviets might deploy an ABM system. That is, each U.S. missile such as Minuteman or Polaris could be fitted with multiple warheads in order to penetrate a ballistic-missile defense. But last summer Senator Mike Mansfield asked the Pentagon's research chief, John S. Foster, Jr., the following question.

"Is it not true that the U.S. response to the discovery that the Soviets had made an initial deployment of an ABM system around Moscow, and possibly elsewhere, was to develop the MIRV system for Minuteman and Polaris?"

Answer: "Not entirely. The MIRV concept was originally generated to increase our targeting capability rather than to penetrate ABM defenses. In 1961-62 planning for targeting the Minuteman force, it was found that the total number of aim points [targets] exceeded the number of Minuteman missiles."

"This response," wrote Lapp, "is a pure shaft of candor illuminating dimly lit rooms in the Pentagon. A Soviet planner would surely interpret this answer as meaning that the United States was beefing up its strategic deterrent so as to have a first-strike capability."

That was back in 1969. Now, in 1974, the argument had transcended itself, like the technology which had given rise to it. Or was it *because* the technology had transcended itself? Largely ignored in the debates over MIRVing, in the first place, and then overrefining the MIRVs, in the second, was a reason that had little to do with strategic postures, offensive and defensive forces, possible Soviet expansionism. Perhaps the best reason. The old one. Research and development of a weapon, if carried out long enough, at ever-growing expense of money and scientific and technical manpower, just about decrees that the weapon finally be fashioned and holstered, whether on the hip or deep in the earth.

Minuteman II, suspended in its silo above the blast space, has a nasty-looking, needle-nosed upper stage. Inside this cone is the hydrogen warhead. Around its outside is the heat shield, enabling the "reentry vehicle" to withstand the friction of speeds up to 15,000 miles an hour and temperatures of more than 12,000 degrees Fahrenheit as it nibs into the atmosphere and hurtles to its target. The nose cone of Minuteman III is a bullet-shaped shroud of more benign configuration, rounder, longer, fatter. But capable of dealing death more widely, more selectively, across the atmosphere and the earth. Inside are three warheads, MIRVs.

The air-conditioning hums in the silo, seventy-five feet deep, structured of superhardened steel and several feet of concrete. The temperature is a steady sixty degrees, just right for the well-being of the solid fuel that powers the rocket's three stages. A single, small light bulb faintly illumines the silo. The Minuteman III is gleaming white, with Air Force markings, fifty-nine feet, ten inches, from nozzle to nose. Six feet-plus in diameter at the "interstage" juncture of the first and second stages, where it is thickest. Nothing moves.

The only men who see Minuteman are the Combat Missile Crews in the underground control capsules of the Launch

Control Centers. Two men at a time. Eight-hour shifts. Around the clock. They don't know where the warheads will explode over the Soviet Union if they are ever called upon to "smoke a bird," as they put it, and they don't particularly care to know. Only the President and the top brass in SAC and the Pentagon know. Let them live with it. It is tough enough just staying acutely alert, waiting for the four or five test alerts which are staged every month, or for EWO (Emergency War Orders) training. Or for the real thing. But it is not wholly bad duty. Eight hours of sleep in an above-ground billet, and eight hours off, every day. Three days a week completely rid of the Doomsday duty.

The crew takes an elevator down a sixty-five-foot shaft and enters the capsule through a three-foot-thick, concrete-and-steel "blast door." The capsule is forty feet long, twenty feet wide, twenty feet high, ranged with racks of computers and communications equipment and air-conditioning units. Wires and tubes running overhead connect the capsule to each of the ten missiles in the silos of Alpha Flight, or Bravo Flight, or whichever flight the capsule controls. One capsule serves as the command center for fifty missiles, a full squadron.

There are no buttons to smoke the birds. There are keys. The command of the President to send Minuteman to war is received at SAC headquarters, Offutt AFB, Nebraska, or at March AFB, California. It is deciphered and authenticated. SAC relays it to the appropriate Combat Missile Crews. The crew commanders immediately confer over supersecure telephones and set the exact second that the "votes" will be taken. Each capsule has a vote. A capsule's vote is registered when each of the two men in the capsule inserts his individual key in his individual control lock, and turns the key clockwise to the position marked, "Launch." At least two of the five capsules must register a vote to launch. Three of the five could refuse, and the missiles still would go. All this takes only a few minutes.

In the decade and a half since the first flight of a Minuteman, the Air Force has never waited until one model was in place to begin building a more devastating one. Why wait, when the electronics permit haste? Air Force development of Minuteman III was begun as far back as the spring of 1966, even as Minuteman II was coming off the production line and being snuggled into silos, and less than a year after the emplacement of Minuteman I had been completed. Indeed, only a little over three years had elapsed since the first two "flights" of 40 Minuteman I's were declared operational at Malmstrom Air Force Base, Montana. In December 1962, on the heels of the Cuban missile crisis. By July 1963, Malmstrom stood fully stocked with three squadrons of Minuteman I—150 missiles in all. By June 1965, Malmstrom had been joined by Ellsworth AFB, South Dakota; Minot AFB, North Dakota; Whiteman AFB, Missouri; and Warren AFB, Wyoming, as the marshaling yards of Minuteman I. Five full wings. Eight hundred missiles. Meanwhile, Minuteman II had sprouted. Contracts for this second-generation Minuteman were let, well before its precursor had been fully deployed, to reduce the weight and increase the range of the rocket carrier, beef up the megatonnage of its warheads and, above all, render them more accurate. Sharpening the accuracy of the Minuteman reentry vehicle was not the controversial issue back then that it was to become two missile generations later, in 1974. Computerized Guidance and Control (G&C) technology had force-marched forward, but not far enough to conceive of steering a Minuteman II warhead out of space to explode directly above—or dead on—its target. SAC's missileers define accuracy in terms of "CEP." Circle of Error Probable. If they state the CEP as a half mile, they mean that the warhead has maybe a little better than a fifty-fifty chance of exploding within a half-mile radius of the target. The CEP for Minuteman I was well over a half mile. SAC wanted a half-mile CEP for Minuteman II. Closer would have been better, but the technology was not yet at hand to achieve it. A half mile cut it pretty fine, but still not fine enough.

The D37, a new digital computer that did its sums super-swiftly, made Minuteman II possible. It was the heart of the missile's G&C system. The culmination of inventions in miniaturization, the D37 was only one-fourth the size of its predecessor in Minuteman I, one-half its weight, and needed only half its electric power. Other goodies from the electronics and aerospace industries for Minuteman II were a new gyro compass assembly; equipment which kept the missile's electronic controls and regulators more precisely in tune, and a complex, new navigation device called PIGA—for Pendulous Integrating Gyroscope Accelerometer. The significant shedding of weight and upgrading of reliability of Minuteman II was attributable also to a new guidance platform made of beryllium.

Even with all its refinements, Minuteman II was a heavyweight with only one punch. Inefficient, considering its cost and upkeep. MIRVs would make all the difference.

In the action-reaction pattern of the arms race, both the United States and the Soviet Union began adding clout to their strategic missiles after each had harnessed the technologies of antiballistic missile (ABM) systems in the mid-sixties. A classic example of intercontinental tic-tac-toe. Each adversary trying feverishly to mark the decisive square. Death to the loser. By aspiring to ICBMs which could overwhelm, deceive, confuse or nullify whatever defenses the other might deploy, the superpowers refined their offensive weapons to the point that these weapons destabilized the structure of "mutual deterrence" to a far greater degree than the ABMs had threatened to do. In the United States, this work had its focus in Air Force program 627A. The "Penetration Aids" program. Directed by the Air Force Systems Command's Space and Missile Systems Organization (SAMSO). Its most spectacular achievement, at an expense of $2 billion over eight years, starting in 1962, was the development of MIRV. The culmination was Boeing's Minuteman III, specially designed to carry three MIRVs, and Lockheed's submarine-launched Poseidon missile, successor to the Polaris, designed to carry up to fourteen MIRVs. In February 1969, the Navy berthed its U.S.S. *James Madison* Polaris sub at General Dynamics Corporation's yard at Groton, Connecticut, for conversion to Poseidon. In May, the U.S.S. *Daniel Boone* followed suit at the yard of the Newport News Shipbuilding & Drydock Company. They were the first of thirty-one Polaris subs now converted to Poseidon—all but ten of the total Polaris fleet.

The Russians, too, were working on multiple warheads. They test-fired their SS-9 Scarp carrying three. But these were not MIRVs. They were MRVs. The difference was that the MRVs were not independently targeted. They fell away from the Scarp in a cluster, buckshot style, presumably far less accurate. But U.S. intelligence passed on some information about the "footprints" of the Scarp which worried the Pentagon and the White House. The Scarp's dummy warheads had just happened to plop into the Pacific in a pattern which would have bracketed U.S. Minuteman silos had they landed in Montana instead. Armed. This was in 1969. It probably was a coincidence. If the Minuteman-bracketing footprints had been planned by the Soviets, then the test shot should have been scored a rousing success in Moscow. If this were so, then why did the Soviets give up on MRVs and stay with a single warhead on the Scarp? Perhaps the reason was that their R&D of MIRVs already was proceeding so well that deploying MRVs, as an interim move, would have been a waste of money. Whatever, the MRVs on the Scarp shook up the Pentagon. Each was believed to pack five megatons. A fully deployed Scarp missile force could have shattered more than eight hundred of the Minuteman silos in one blast of hellfire. So it was full speed ahead for the U.S. MIRV program, which would triple the number of Minuteman and submarine Poseidon warheads to about eight thousand by the mid-1970s.

A bird is smoked. A Minuteman III-C. Vaulting out of its silo, boring through the clouds, the atmosphere, into Space. A javelin of the gods of war. Heading 8,000 miles out, over the crown of the globe, toward the Carpathians. First-stage burnout. Telemetry tracking. Second-stage burnout, 125 miles downrange. Climbing, climbing. Third-stage burnout, 350 miles high. The protective-shroud nose cone falls away. All that is left, on trajectory, is the platform and its mounted warheads, a space shuttler with payloads for passengers. Now, apogee. Coming over the top. Flattening out. Descending. Target One, a silo which a Russian crew at that moment is reloading with a monster Scarp. Ahead and below. The first of the 200-kiloton warheads drops off the bus. It follows the orbital plane which the guidance system of the bus had selected for it. Pyrotechnics at the edge of, and into, the atmosphere, as the warhead plummets earthward. Now the computer of the space bus issues a command. The small attitude-control motors receive the command and fire short bursts. The bus assumes a different attitude, a new trajectory, now on course to Target Two. Another hundred miles. Nothing down there. Second warhead gone. But it isn't a warhead. A reentry vehicle, but not a warhead. The RV rides out fury of atmospheric friction, then triggers not a bomb, but a whirlwind of chaff, of metal balloons shaped like warheads, showing up on Soviet radar as an entire wing of warheads, spreading through the sky, drawing defensive fire. The thrusters of the space bus by now have fired again. Still another, slightly different trajectory. Two hundred more miles. Third warhead gone. Bearing on a Soviet missile command and control center. No more need of the bus. Down it goes, becoming another fiery decoy for the Soviets to shoot at. A "penetration aid," in Pentagonese.

Something is missing from this schematic for sledgehammering Soviet silos. It is called "terminal guidance"—giving the warhead a guidance system of its own, to take it right down the pipe, no Kentucky windage, no chance of error induced by atmospheric variations. Terminal guidance is the technological end-all in the world of ballistic missiles. Bombs of smaller size and bigger bang are being combined with miniaturized guidance systems and thriftier propulsion systems in reentry vehicles which are lean enough to ride the bus in ever-larger groupings. But the poser for the engineers lies in figuring how to tell the warhead how to "recognize" the target. Research on this involves various methods and their combinations. For example, stellar navigation as dictated by satellites. Or having the reentry vehicle scan the terrain by radar or some other sensing device, and then match up what it "sees" with the contours of a terrain map which its onboard computer has memorized. As a result, mapmaking has become more than a routine endeavor in the military.

By the mid-1970s, MIRVed Minuteman III missiles were well along in replacing 550 of the Minuteman II—at Minot AFB, Warren AFB and the newest site of the expanding missile network, Grand Forks AFB, North Dakota. Malmstrom, Ellsworth and Whiteman would continue as bases for the remaining 450 Minuteman IIs. The deployment of Minuteman III was far from finished, however, when Schlesinger came along—proposing a new generation of Minuteman and a few new branches on the missile family tree—to continue the same, old pattern of planned obsolescence in the omnibuses of ballistic land.

The Counterforce heart of his defense R&D budget for fiscal 1975 was a paltry but portentous $77 million to bring Minuteman's electronic brains and bombing brawn up to the snuff that the Schlesinger strategy required.

"The principal impact of the new emphasis on other strategic options," he spelled it out for Congress in his Posture Statement, "is on the Minuteman program, particularly Minuteman III. This missile, with its capacity for three RVs, relatively good accuracy, rapid retargeting capabilities, and relatively secure and reliable communications links to the National Command Authorities, is clearly a most versatile and cost-effective weapon. Even without any additional R&D funding, we believe that the CEP of the Minuteman III will gradually improve with continual testing. Beyond that point, further improvements in the counter-military capabilities of our ICBM force would require the deployment of more than the currently planned 550 Minuteman III missiles, larger-yield warheads, an improved or new guidance system, terminally guided manuevering RVs (MARVs) or the development and deployment of an entirely new ICBM. In view of the ongoing SALT talks, we propose in the fiscal year 1975 budget to take only those first few steps which are necessary to keep open these options. No decisions have been made to deploy any of these improved systems. . . .

"We propose to develop the option for some additional refinements in the existing Minuteman guidance system, mostly in the [computer] software program, which should further reduce the CEP. . . .

"We propose to proceed with engineering development of a new, higher-yield warhead for Minuteman III. The new warhead plus the more advanced [i.e., miniaturized] arming and fusing mechanism would be incorporated in a new center section, which could be retrofitted into the existing Minuteman III Mark 12 RV without any changes in its weight, balance or other flight characteristics. . . .

"We plan to initiate advanced development of a terminally guided MARV for possible retrofit into both ICBMs and SLBMs [Submarine Launched Ballistic Missiles]. This MARV could give the Minuteman III a very high accuracy. . . .

"We plan to flight test a Minuteman III with a larger number of smaller RVs. This payload would give us the option to expand the target coverage of the Minuteman force without any increase in the number of missiles deployed."

The Minuteman III CEP in Schlesinger's and SAC's future books figured out to about 700 feet, about one-eighth of a mile, half of the present CEP for the missile. The payloads in those future books were classified, but believed perhaps to double the 200-kiloton warheads of the three Mark 12 reentry vehicles now nestled in the business end of the rocket. Combine the guidance and the payload, and not even a supersuperhard Soviet silo could withstand the shock. Add MARV, and the Air Force could pick and choose sites for instant excavation all over the Soviet Union. The MARV development program involved the Mark 500 reentry system by General Electric for the Navy's future Trident ICBM, and a version which McDonnell Douglas had devised as part of SAMSO's Advanced Ballistic Reentry Systems (ABRES) program. GE's MARV, dating back in its research to the mid-sixties, is a dandy. As it approaches a target, it can pull up, turn and dive back down again. The McDonnell Douglas MARV, fired downward from ballistic trajectory, glides down through the atmosphere, straightens its path, and approaches the target at an altitude low enough to avoid radar detection.

As a fillip, Schlesinger also proposed a new program called "Pave Pepper" to fabricate small, low-yield warheads that might be ferried by Minuteman, or fitted into the nose cones of tactical missiles and the new breed of strategic cruise missiles, which he also drew from his satchel. Schlesinger's program was altogether startling. But Congress, clearing its hoppers in record time in anticipation of a long summer of impeachment proceedings, stabbed limply at the Counterforce R&D package which the Secretary of Defense sent sailing through its committee rooms and chambers in the early months of 1974. The House Armed Services Committee quickly approved, and hardly even analyzed, the nuclear R&D. In the Senate, the Research and Development Subcommittee of the Armed Services Committee tried an arm tackle, but was swept aside. The subcommittee voted to deny authorization of the payload-guidance R&D money for missiles. But a week later, the full Armed Services Committee resoundingly rejected the recommendation of the subcommittee and authorized everything Schlesinger wanted. Senator John Stennis (D.-Miss.), the committee chairman, was asked why he had become an advocate of enhancing the explosive power and accuracy of Minuteman, when for many years he had opposed such a move. "Because I think that now, this may be where our deterrent lies," Stennis said.

Senator Thomas H. McIntyre (D.-N.H.), chairman of the R&D subcommittee, was among the handful in Congress who did not subscribe to the Schlesinger-Stennis thesis. The year before, McIntyre had fought with some small success against the Navy's plan to swiften the pace of development of the Trident submarine. Now, he was in for an even tougher battle, with fewer allies on Capitol Hill. "His problem," said one of his staff men, "is that the money Schlesinger wants for this Counterforce R&D is such a chicken-shit amount. Not even $100 million. The Trident program—all those billions—is something a senator or a congressman can hack at. But this. Who cares? Besides, a lot of the people on the Hill agree with Schlesinger that the Russians have been behaving badly, and that they have taken a more threatening posture. And these people think, what the hell, it's only research and development. If the Russians cooperate at SALT, we won't ever need to deploy these systems."

McIntyre had been around too long, had watched the endless leap-frogging of defense technology, to buy that notion. He and a few others were afraid that Counterforce would only spur the Soviets to mark still another square, and that Counterforce was not necessary to preserve the security of the United States. Too bellicose, they said. In trying to convince others of his case against Counterforce R&D, McIntyre wove it into the whole fabric of his frustration.

My work on the Research and Development Subcommittee [he said], has consumed more of my time and effort than any other responsibility I have had in the Senate. The size and complexity of our military R&D exceeds one's grasp. The Pentagon wants $9.3 billion for R&D spread over three thousand individual programs and projects. My subcommittee has the responsibility of reviewing all of them. I feel sometimes as if we are wrestling with a greased octopus. But I've spent six years as chairman of the subcommittee and ten years on the full Armed Services Committee. Even a country lawyer like me should have learned something in that time. By osmosis, if nothing else. Technology's importance to our military security was evident to me when I became chairman, and my experience since then has only intensified my appreciation. The axiom that superior military technology can give a nation a decisive advantage over its adversaries was true in the fourteenth century when the English long bow made the armored knight obsolete. It is true today with electronic countermeasure technology and smart bombs. And it will be true tomorrow whenever a nation can harness a laser to its military purposes. So to insure a technological edge, my subcommittee will have recommended during these six years more money for military R&D than was spent during any previous six-year period in the history of our Republic. [But] we must learn to exercise greater selectivity in our military R&D. This is necessary because a program, once initiated, becomes most difficult to stop or substantially alter. It picks up momentum with each step in the R&D cycle. A service, or elements within a service, develop vested interests in programs, deriving from R&D beginnings. In the realities of Washington politics, decisions are often forfeited to willful advocates who organize their every day for the purpose of perpetuating their program. So R&D programs, even in their early stages, acquire force and power unrelated to the programs' merits. This bureaucratic momentum moves them into the more expensive stages of the development cycle—perhaps even to procurement. For example, the Defense Department's request for a third of a billion dollars this year for ballistic-missile defense is in part due to the potency of $5 billion of R&D investment in the Safeguard (ABM) program—a potency which makes the decision to complete the ABM deployment at the Grand Forks site irresistible whatever its military justification. . . .

This year we are once again facing the same issue in the set of R&D requests for silo-kill accuracy. R&D programs gain momentum because each step in the R&D progression flows indistinguishably into the next, so that clear decisions are avoided. When the Defense Department identifies a possible application of a technology and recommends moving it to advanced development, we are told that such a step is only "tentative," "exploratory" and "inexpensive." When the programs move to engineering development, we are told that laboratory development has reached its limits, and we must now find out whether in practice it is possible to integrate the component technology into a system. We are assured we are only trying to develop an option but not making a commitment to production. When the program moves toward production we are told that we should protect the schedule for deployment, in case such a decision is made, and that we must, therefore, fund the long-lead money—and sometimes, expensive preproduction models.

As a practical matter, by the time we come to the decision on whether to deploy, that decision has already become an accomplished fact. We are told that we have now invested millions, perhaps hundreds of millions, in the program. Great sums which the taxpayer would lose if we cancelled out.

This year's request for silo-kill accuracy and development of higher-yield warheads is in the same class because it would—even in R&D—drastically alter longstanding strategic policy. We cannot say, "It's only R&D." President Eisenhower warned us in his farewell address of the "danger that policy could by itself become the captive of a scientific, technological elite." Such would be the case if we let basic policy be set by forfeit.

It was like flinging a frisbee into a windstorm. After the Senate Armed Services Committee and the full House of Representatives had approved Counterforce, a few senators, led by McIntyre and Minnesota's Walter Mondale, tried to capitalize on the rift between Schlesinger and Secretary of State Henry Kissinger over the accuracy-payload policy, and enlist Kissinger's backing of their last-ditch drive against the policy during the Senate's consideration of it on the floor. They knew that Schlesinger had pulled a power play on Kissinger, and they hoped that Kissinger might take advantage of the letter which they wrote him asking him to go on the record with his views on Counterforce, as a way of checking the momentum which Schlesinger had built up for it. Their hopes were dim. For Kissinger to speak out, at that late date, however much he may have wished to do so, would have meant dividing the already beleaguered Nixon administration in eyes of the Soviets, thus perhaps weakening the hand of the United States at SALT and undermining the Moscow summit which Nixon was preparing to attend later that summer.

For several weeks, reports had circulated in Washington that the Secretaries of Defense and of State had fallen out over Counterforce. But specifics were lacking. Top aides of both men were at pains to put down the reports, insisting that the two former Harvard classmates shared a kinship of the intellect unsurpassed in the entire government, that they met and conferred amiably, when both were in town, at least twice a week, over breakfast or lunch, and that even though Kissinger might seem to take a softer line on strategic policy, make no mistake, their goals were the same: peace through strength. There were those who remarked on the other hand, that comity may not always be the correct catchword to describe a relationship of philosopher-kings, whose careers had been seeded in scholasticism. Faculty dons, warned these Schlesinger-Kissinger watchers, have a way of falling out. And it was happening on Counterforce.

Kissinger had been faked out. He had left his sentry post as Nixon's strategic counselor in the White House to become Secretary of State. Tel Aviv, Cairo, Damascus, Moscow, 'round and 'round again. He was not paying attention as Schlesinger simply preempted his role as Mister Strategic Policy, ramrodding Counterforce with the strong backing of powerful White House Chief of Staff (and former Army Vice-Chief of Staff) Alexander M. Haig, Jr. Indeed, there were reports that Schlesinger brashly went ahead and articulated his new policy to the press at the Overseas Writers Club even before Nixon—but not Haig—had formally approved. When Kissinger realized what had happened, he confronted Schlesinger in some acrimony. But Counterforce was out of the bag.

In its report authorizing items of military procurement for Fiscal 1975, the Senate Armed Services Committee sounded more like Schlesinger than Schlesinger himself. Noting that the tougher stance of the Secretary of Defense might persuade the Soviets to back up a bit at SALT, the Committee reported:

> Given the growth and development of Soviet strategic forces, a deterrent posture based principally on the threat to retaliate against Soviet civilians, knowing that such a strike would almost certainly lead to the destruction of millions of American civilians, is less and less credible. Development of the technology required for a range of more discriminating —and more credible—responses, is . . . simple prudence. A

purposeful failure to improve the accuracy and yield of our strategic warheads would be a gratuitous self-constraint. Since the growth of Soviet strategic forces, especially that reported to the committee by Secretary Schlesinger, appears to be accelerating, such a unilateral constraint on our part would give the Soviets the strategic initiative. Several members [of the committee] emphasized that the development of these yield and accuracy improvements would not be a commitment to deployment. At a relatively modest cost, these developments provide an important hedge against future as well as developing Soviet programs, in addition to preserving flexibility. . . . The committee would like to stress that these improvements are not intended to provide the United States with a first-strike capability.

There was no disagreement between Schlesinger and Kissinger—and virtually no opposition from Congress—with respect to the remainder of the strategic section of the Schlesinger R&D budget request. It foreshadowed an arsenal of weapons which the Air Force and Navy had been researching for several years but never had formally funded, as a matter of public policy. The scope of this arsenal-to-be was spectacular. It was regarded mildly by Congress as being primarily for defense, for survival, without the overtones of the offensive which Counterforce carried. Proving again that nearly anything can be rationalized.

With the refinements contemplated for Minuteman III, the appellation "Minuteman IV" already was catching on in the Pentagon. How about Minuteman V, this one airborne, the culmination of the Air Force dream of "Missile System X" or, simply, "MX," the missile system of the future? New post-launch guidance techniques make it possible. Still in the picture, too, was the possibility of an ICBM of limited mobility on land, although the Air Force preferred the airborne version. An air-launched ICBM would be more difficult of technology but much less vulnerable to a Soviet strike. But much of the technology already was on the shelf. With each new graft of guidance in the land-based Minuteman, its air-launched cousin of the future had moved closer to realization. General Samuel

C. Phillips, who took over the Air Force Systems Command in 1973, expressed the command's confidence in coping with MX. "A common trait of all major options is that fact that we are in position technologically to proceed at any time to build whatever is required," he said. "Depending on the urgency with which such a system might be required, and the level of effort we therefore would be expected to expend, we could demonstrate hardware feasibility conclusively within one or two years from program go-ahead, and come up with operational equipment within three to four years." He was talking about 1978 or 1979. Already available was the equipment to give the MX missiles precise post-boost correctional guidance through stellar navigation, and terminal guidance through a terrain-contour-matching system (TERCOM). Destined for a future starring role in the saga of missile guidance is NAV-STAR, a system of twenty-four communications satellites in three sets of eight, each set in a separate orbital plane. NAV-STAR satellites should be able to correct and maintain the courses of air-launched and land-launched ICBMs with pinpoint precision. The Pentagon emphasizes the utility of these satellites in the future navigation of ships and aircraft, commercial as well as military, and plays down their connection with intercontinental missiles. The first of them should be orbiting by 1978. All will be in space by 1984.

Well in advance of the Pentagon's decision to go ahead with MX, Boeing and Lockheed had drafted proposals to convert their respective 747 commercial and C-5 military jumbo transports into Minuteman-carrying aircraft. B. T. Plymale, vice-president and general manager of Boeing's Space and Ballistic Missiles Group, said the company could convert a 747 to ferry four 100,000-pound ICBMs or eight of half that weight.

"If an ICBM is carried aloft and launched facing forward," said Boeing's "Mister Minuteman," "a 20 percent range gain is achieved, due primarily to the initial velocity from the moving platform." He said new and future technology would have a "dramatic effect" on the performance of both land and air ICBMs. "The relative throw weight of Minuteman is far below —only 57 percent—the throw weight for a new missile of the same launch weight. Or, viewed differently, a 47,000-pound new missile will deliver as much on target as the 78,000-pound Minuteman." Plymale even proposed that the Pentagon consider, next time around, a massive missile-bearing amphibian aircraft which could lurk anywhere "in over thirty-million square miles of ocean." He had it all figured out. The plane would have four engines mounted atop its wings to avoid ingestion of sea water; a wing span the length of a football field; a gross takeoff weight from land of 1.2 million pounds, from sea, 875,000 pounds, and a 200,000-pound load of missiles aboard. The missiles would be "ejected laterally in flight from missile bays in the fuselage above the waterline." He had it figured even down to the R&D cost: $1.37 billion. The Pentagon did not scoff. But for now, at least, it had other plans for a huge, new airplane that might double as a tanker and missile carrier.

Fortuitously for the fast deployment of flexible-response weapons, the technology for maybe the most wondrous of all —the cruise missiles—had already been perfected. In the Air Force development of the Subsonic Cruise Armed Decoy (SCAD), a program which was abandoned in 1973. SCADs were designed to be released in droves of twenty by B-52 bombers and, later on, by the supersonic B-1, still in development. With their wings retracted, these decoys—fourteen feet long, a foot in diameter, weighing about 1,700 pounds—could be ferried under the wings of a bomber or on rotary racks inside the fuselage. They had engines and could manuever. Ranging up to one thousand miles, they would baffle enemy radar, giving the bombers a better chance of penetrating the defenses by showing up on radar screens as unsingularized objects. Somewhere along the track of SCAD development, however, it became obvious that they also could be armed with warheads, thus augmenting the striking power of the bombers which carried them. But the Air Force mightily resisted doing anything about arming the SCADs. Giving the B-52 such a potent "standoff" weapon, the generals reasoned, would extend the life and the range of the aging bomber and cause the Defense Department and Congress to think again about going ahead with the B-1. To the Air Force, the B-1 is an article of faith. If the B-1 program were to be shut down, the manned bomber might disappear forever from the strategic arsenal. The bomber, insisted the Air Force, is the only one of the "Triad" of strategic weapons—along with land and submarine missiles —to have been tested in combat. It is the only one which can be relied upon to strike the target it is supposed to strike—the only proven "hard-target killer."

At Mach 2 to 3, the B-1 would get to the perimeter of enemy defenses twice as fast as the B-52. Then it would cut back to subsonic speed, drop to the deck, go in under the radar. It would be armed with a short-range attack missile (SRAM), a bomber defense missile (BDM), and penetration aids, such as SCAD. It would be able to shift and adapt its range, altitude, speed and payload for a wide variety of missions and tactics beyond the capacity of the unversatile missiles. About the size of a 707 jetliner, the B-1 also could operate from many more bases than the bigger, heavier B-52. It would be more secure from attack. Or so said the Air Force.

Apart from the threats to it from other strategic systems, the B-1 program had begun to show symptoms of illness that might prove fatal. Costs were skyrocketing, and the builders at Rockwell International were having trouble assembling the first prototype. It also was becoming apparent that the intercontinental range—and then some—which the Air Force had advertised for the B-1 had been misleading. The B-1 would gobble fuel down low, and probably would need, despite previous Air Force disclaimers, the in-flight services of a tanker to reach targets in Russia. Moreover, the bomber's weight had risen 35,000 pounds above the originally estimated 360,000 pounds.

Schlesinger and Dr. Malcolm R. Currie, director of defense research and engineering, decided to order the Air Force to slow down on B-1 development, take more time at integrating its systems, subsystems and components. Stretching the program would add to its costs, but the Air Force was courting technological disaster in its headlong rush to get the bomber into production.

Even before the stretchout, the cost of the program had gone up from $9.4 billion in 1970 to $15 billion in 1974—an overrun of $5.6 billion before the first prototype had taken off. The projected cost of each B-1 stood at $80 million, approximately triple the original estimate, making it the most expensive weapon system the world had ever known. Add armament and support costs, and each bomber would average out to at least $140 million. An awful lot of investment to be shot down by a $50,000 Soviet surface-to-air missile before the target is bombed.

Schlesinger and Currie tried to convince the Air Force that they had not lost faith in the bomber as a weapon of the future. Both went to bat for the B-1 in their Posture Statements to

Congress. They emphasized the need of a bomber—the B-1—
for all the reasons stated by the Air Force for years and years
and years, plus, now, for its future role as a weapons platform
for the cruise missiles. Ah, said the Air Force generals to one
another, nice of them. But what do they really have in the
backs of their minds? Maybe those civilians in the E Ring,
those conjurers of the cruise missile, would just as soon stick
with the B-52. Or adapt the missile to the bomber version of the
F-111, which can range 3,300 miles without refueling. Or to
cargo planes or tankers. Or, in the end, as technology allows
for smaller but still-powerful nuclear missiles, even to fighter-
bombers and attack planes flying off carriers. At any rate, some
of the B-1's foremost champions in Congress, while continuing
to vote approval of the $700 million-plus each year for B-1 R&D,
acknowledged that the program was sick. It seemed that about
all the Air Force had on its side, really, was the more than $2
billion which the nation already had sunk into B-1 development. Damn tough to just call it off and throw all that money
away. (Remember the McIntyre thesis?)

For a time, the civilian chiefs at Defense had toyed with the
idea of building a tanker aircraft which would double as a
launcher of cruise missiles. They broached this idea in the
department's budget message for Fiscal 1975, without first having told the Air Force of the plan. Minds blew at SAC and in
the Air Force suites at the Pentagon. The Air Force could see
the logic for a new tanker, obviously, because the B-1 would
need one. But combining it with cruise missiles presaged an
ominous pattern: B-1 costs would keep going up; B-1 performance would keep going down; someone would get the bright
idea (an idea perhaps extant already) to transform that huge,
new airplane into a combination ICBM-cruise missile carrier,
or a cargo-cruise missile carrier, forget the tanker part of it.
And the B-1's death would be sealed. Only six months earlier,
the Air Force had felt compelled to beat off a proposal by Elliot
Richardson, just before he left the department, that it study the
possible conversion of wide-bodied commercial jets into missile carriers. Now, the Air Force was confronted by another
threat to the B-1.

An incident took place in Currie's office which showed, he
said, how very upset the Air Force was with the Defense Department's tanker-cruise missile concept, and at not having

been warned of it. A SAC general approached Currie and requested permission to speak his piece. He rose from his seat to talk, his lips moved, but no words came out. So passionate was his opposition to anything which might impinge on the ultimate success of the B-1 program that it had done temporary violence to his vocal cords.

The plan was dropped, at least for now. A month later, in their separate Posture Statements, neither Schlesinger nor Currie mentioned putting cruise missiles on tankers. Instead, they presented a plan for a "strategic tanker," doubling as a cargo plane. They put the cruise missiles on the B-1. The Air Force was willing to go along. The generals grudgingly had become convinced that the cruise missiles might, in fact, be the weapons the B-1 needed, if not to strike the enemy, at least to gain approval for production. You do the best you can with what you have.

The cruise missiles, showing stubby wings and tailfins, will resemble airplanes more than they will their bulletlike ICBM counterparts. They will contain their own guidance systems and air-breathing jet turbofan engines only two feet long, a foot wide, and about 100 pounds, with enough power to take the missiles 1,500 to 2,000 miles. With the Air Force version expected to be an outgrowth of SCAD, Boeing had the technological edge in early competition for the contract. The Navy, on the other hand, chose LTV Aerospace Corporation and General Dynamics to construct competitive cruise-missile prototypes for submarines. Both the airplane and submarine missiles will be less than twenty feet long and less than two feet thick.

The Navy's potential for preeminence in the strategic field was another cause of Air Force consternation at the advent of the cruise-missile program. What the missiles mean for the Navy is that every submarine in the fleet, numbering a hundred or more by the end of this decade, could become a strategic weapon. Not only the Polaris-Poseidon and Trident boats. Attack submarines, too. For the Navy cruise missiles are being designed to be fired from the torpedo tubes of those submarines. Just the right size. They will not require the vertical launching of the Polaris, Poseidon and Trident ICBMs.

The cruise missiles, once free of the tubes, will be propelled to the surface and into the air by solid-fuel boosters. Once airborne, they will shed sections of metal skin. Aerodynamic control surfaces—wings and tailfins—will pop out. Air inlet ducts for the engines also will be exposed. At about two hundred feet, the missiles will level off and their engines will take over, driving them far down range toward land or sea targets. Once over land, they will rely on terrain-following computer-mapped guidance to clear—but still hug—hills and mountains, coming in under enemy radar guidance feature. This will be crucial, for their speed will be subsonic (about 600 miles an hour), making them vulnerable to the radar tracking of air and ground missilery if they home in too high. The entire flight of the missile, from a preselected firing position to preselected target, will be programmed into its guidance system. The only basic difference between the air-launched and sub-launched cruise missiles will be the addition of the solid-fuel booster to the Navy model. The Air Force missile presumably will have somewhat greater range, since it will have the speed of the plane going for it at the time of its launching. The Pentagon's plans for these missiles are not limited to bombers and submarines. LTV has built a model of an A-7 fighter-bomber brandishing four of them under its wings. The day almost certainly will come when smaller planes—even smaller submarines—are equipped with them. If so, good-bye bomber.

When the Defense Department decided to go "crash" on cruise missiles, it set up a joint program office for their development. To the irritation of the Air Force, the Navy was chosen to run the office, chiefly because of its experience in development of Harpoon, a tactical cruise missile just now coming along for submarines and surface ships. The Army, too, is involved. Nothing much was said about them, but plans were afoot for a cruise missile which the Army, someday not too far off, will be launching from land vehicles.

The cruise missile will be a "hard-target killer," capable of figuratively (literally?) hitting a dime fifteen hundred miles down-range. What its development will accomplish, the way the Pentagon views such matters, is to force the Soviets to spend massive amounts of money and manpower in learning how to defend against it. Because the cruise missiles will come in low, from every which way, by air and by sea, the Soviets would need thousands of super-refined radars to cover all possible approaches. The technological problem will be extremely hard to solve; the expenditure, enormous. So the missiles may divert substantial Soviet monetary and intellectual resources from the development of offensive strategic weapons or, best of all, persuade the Soviets to say enough's enough, let's call it off. But one side's development of what it thinks is enough has always induced the other side to decide that it has not yet developed enough, and so long as the technology is handy, who's to stop?

There was no reflecting at the Pentagon, amid the fervid preparations for deployment of cruise missiles by 1976, on how their development by both sides (the Russians are developing them, too) and the companion upgrading of ICBMs by both sides was making a mockery of the ABM treaty which had been signed at SALT I. Meaningless. Sit down at the table with the other guy, and talk about the road to peace, and get ready to blow his ass off the face of the earth. You just can't trust the bastard. As Schlesinger put it: "Now that the Soviet Union is catching up with us in reentry technology, we must renew our efforts to stay ahead in this critical aspect of the strategic balance."

When you get right down to it, it doesn't make an awful lot of difference whether or not Congress approves the Defense Department's request for authorization and appropriation of funds to carry out R&D of strategic weapons. The R&D goes on anyway, inexorably, and sooner or later, it will turn into a system, regardless. In May 1974, the plans for Missile System X and the request for the hundreds of millions of dollars to get MX into the works were still being analyzed by House and Senate Armed Services committees. The committees would have to authorize the R&D, and the two houses then would have to vote approval. Then the Appropriations committees would have to approve the money for it, and the two houses would have to vote aye to the funding. Suddenly the Air Force announced its award of two contracts. One of $19.6 million to Aerojet Solid Propulsion Company, which already had built more than 3,000 Minuteman motors, to design and build a propulsion system for the second stage of Minuteman that could be applied—the Air Force proudly proclaimed—to "the MX upper-stage program." The work would include development of an advanced, high-energy propellant, an advanced thruster nozzle, a thrust-vector control system. The other, a

$4.6 million contract, went to United Aircraft Corporation's United Technology Center to develop and demonstrate a high-deflection, low-torque, movable nozzle system for the MX booster stage, using a newly developed carbon-composite material. These contract awards were legitimate, said the Air Force, because the money to be expended had already been appropriated by Congress as part of the continuing develop-ment of the existing Minuteman. Everyone knows there is a lot of "commonality" between Minuteman R&D and MX R&D. Don't split hairs. A staff member of the Senate Armed Services Committee acknowledged that the Air Force had a debating point. It was awfully difficult to draw distinctions in R&D funding, hard to follow or control the allocations of money to specific programs—some of them approved, some of them pending—within broader programs already sanctioned. But the Air Force, this staffer noted, could have been tactful enough not to make such a big thing about the money being applicable to MX. Or the Air Force could have had the decency to hold off for a couple of months, considering that Congres-sional approval was a foregone conclusion. Unseemly haste. Oh, well. Nothing anyone can do about it.

Two days after these contracts were announced, Lt. General Kenneth W. Shultz, commander of SAMSO, told an Air Force Association symposium at Vandenberg AFB, California, that the United States now had the technology for—and should start developing—a prototype of an entirely new interconti-nental missile, embodying all that was beautiful, which could be launched from silos, aircraft or all-purpose huge trucks. He emphasized that he was speaking for himself, not for SAMSO, for the Air Force at large or, certainly, for the Department of Defense. The new missile, said the general, would contain a far-out inertial-reference guidance system being fashioned by the Charles Stark Draper Labs at the Massachusetts Institute of Technology. The Pentagon had no comment on the gener-al's proposal. But keep an eye out. It will come up again.

If anyone ever believed that the Air Force really needed Congressional approval of a heap of money to put more punch into its missile warheads, Colonel John Hepfer, deputy direc-tor of the Minuteman program, unwittingly set them straight. Addressing a seminar of the American Institute of Aeronautics and Astronautics in Washington, Colonel Hepfer asserted that "basic development has been completed to allow the rapid deployment of larger reentry vehicles, if this should prove necessary." He also noted that, without any more R&D, "the present Minuteman III system can carry a larger number of reentry vehicles than [the three] we now employ."

All kinds of exotic research had been going on for a long time, in a plethora of programs: At the Air Force Special Weapons Center at Kirtland AFB, New Mexico, on "the effects of nuclear detonations at and below the surface of the earth"; at Sandia Corporation, on bombs which penetrate the earth to depths of fifteen to one hundred feet; at DNA, and elsewhere on superhardened Minuteman silos; at the Defense Advanced Research Projects Agency (ARPA) (years before MARV surfaced in the ABRES program), on manuevering reentry vehicles, using jet interaction to control the warheads' flight attitudes; at Air Force and Navy labs, and at those of such companies as Avco, General Electric, McDonnell Douglas, on reducing the "visibility" of warheads by shaping them and "posing" them so that they return as few echoes as possible to radar scanners. Also, research on quenching the ion-loaded "wakes" of the warheads which act as reflectors for the enemy scanners. Also, noise devices to jam radars.

The ultimate warhead may turn out to be the one that homes on the signals of enemy radar and dives into its antennas. When this is developed, as it has been for the tactical missiles, both sides will no doubt feel compelled to replace their radars with new detect-and-track systems.

Air Force missile research has concentrated heavily in the past decade on offsetting the fear that the land-based missile would become outmoded—vulnerable—by the end of the 1970s. Companion to studies of putting Minuteman into an airplane were others on shielding them more securely below ground, or on moving them around on the surface. Aerospace Corporation, under Air Force contract, investigated several concepts, among them: "Janus," a multipurpose missile, named for the two-faced Roman god of doorways, which would serve as both an ICBM and an ABM; "Nemesis," an ICBM positioned deep under water (Many years before, the Air Force had dabbled with the idea of an underwater missile to be called Orca, after the killer whale.); "Vulcan," to be launched from superhardened silos 1,000 to 3,000 feet underground, in abandoned brimstone mines connected by caverns and tunnels; "Ranger," a missile to be moved around by trucks or railroad cars. The Air Force picked up some valuable technological tips from the studies, but wrote off these concepts and their offshoots—for now, anyway. A plan to drill silos into mountain granite fell, literally, between the cracks. Tests showed that unforeseen fracture lines in hard-rock sites rendered them much less resistant to blast than the Air Force had anticipated. Underwater was too expensive, too difficult. With Safeguard ABM in the works, there was no need of the technologically taxing endeavor of converting Minuteman into an ABM. The land-mobile idea was a political hornet's nest in any case. One variation of this was the wagon-wheel concept, with roadways leading to five possible firing sites, each about a mile from the central cluster of Minuteman missiles. On warning of attack, the missiles would be wheeled by truck or rail to these positions, far enough away from the aim point of the incoming ICBMs to insure survival. This plan continues to figure in the Pentagon's pondering. Moving the missiles greater distances, on the surfaces, though, would certainly evoke outrage. Following the cue of McNamara before him, Laird put down that land-mobile plan in 1970, in testimony before the Senate Appropriations Committee. "We have had enough trouble," he said, "moving some mustard gas. I think if we had a few ICBMs rolling around on our railroad cars today, or if we had them on highways on trucks, I can tell you what would happen in the United States. It just would not work out too well right now. Although I think the system has some real merit, I am afraid we would have trouble moving them around the country."

The Air Force is gravely concerned that the monumental gains of guidance and control technology in recent years will culminate, down the road, in the Pentagon putting its chips on the ballistic-missile and cruise-missile submarines as the main-line strategic weapons. At the mid-1970s, the Poseidon missile and the Trident I missile, still in development, were regarded solely as city-busters. But manueverable warheads were coming along for the new Trident missile, and their development suggested the terminal guidance electronics which would transform the sub, too, into a silo-killer some future day. Neither the U.S. nor the Soviet Union antisubmarine warfare specialists seemed to have much hope of detecting the other's deep-running, almost spectrally silent ballistic-missile boats. But they were working feverishly on the problem, and whichever side solved it first would control the seesawing of strategic arsenals.

6

The
Sea Monsters

Poseidon, in Greek mythology, god of the sea and of water generally. . . . Homer tells the myth that he was a son of Cronus and Rhea and brother of Zeus and Hades. When the three brothers deposed their father, the kingdom of the sea fell by lot to Poseidon, whom Homer represents as dwelling in a palace in the depths of the Aegean. His weapon was the Trident, which he used to raise storms and split rocks. . . .

—*Encyclopedia Britannica*

Poseidon, god of the seas and rivers, had the second-largest throne. It was of grey-green white-streaked marble, ornamented with coral, gold and mother-of-pearl. The arms were carved in the shape of sea beasts, and Poseidon sat on a sealskin. . . . Zeus had married him to Amphitrite, the former Sea-goddess, and allowed him to take over all her titles. Though Poseidon hated to be less important than his younger brother, and always went about scowling, he feared Zeus's thunderbolt. His only weapon was a trident, with which he could stir up the sea and so wreck ships; but Zeus never travelled by ship. . . .

—Robert Graves, *Greek Gods and Heroes*

The year is 1979. It is late autumn. Midnight, Pacific Standard Time. Chill rain pelts Puget Sound. The wind whips. The

Straits of Juan de Fuca, leading from the sound to the sea, are flecked with white. There is movement at a promontory on the Hood Canal, in this inland waterway. Quietly, a black-hulled monster of a submarine, darker than the night, casts off from her berth near Bangor, Washington, and slides into the straits. She is almost as long as two football fields. She is—as several members of Congress gasped on first hearing of her planned dimensions and technological triumphs—"incredible." She has the same blimplike body of the smaller craft which antedated her in the generations of United States Fleet Ballistic Missile (FBM) submarines. But it distorts the imagination to call her a boat, as all submarines traditionally have been called. She is too huge for that. Nearly twice the hulk, overall, of any which came before. Her hull looms, a forbidding silhouette in the night, like that of a dreadnaught. The Polaris-Poseidon submarines of the previous generations weighed more—displaced more tonnage—than a World War II destroyer. This new FBM submarine dwarfs them. She displaces more than 18,700 tons, twice as much as the next-biggest boat and five times as much as the Nautilus, the first of the nuclear submarines. Three-fourths as much tonnage, in fact, as a World War II aircraft carrier.

Atop her hull, just forward of amidships, stands her dorsal fin, her "sail," two stories high, containing her periscope and radio and radar antennas. The wing-size planes of the sail just straight out. The whole sail assembly looks like the "T" tail of a jet plane, and serves much the same purpose. The sailplanes stabilize the submarine, keep her even of keel, permit her to "fly" in the depths. Fore and aft of the sail, her deck is studded with the hatch covers of twenty-four vertical firing tubes, each suspending, in her deadly belly, a MIRVed intercontinental missile of 4,000-mile-plus outreach. In a few years, these new missiles will be carried only by the smaller FBM submarines. This new queen of the FBM fleet will then be armed with missiles, still in development in 1979, which can span 6,000 to 7,000 miles. She was designed for these monster missiles. With them, she will be able to strike the Soviet heartland without ever leaving her berth on the Hood Canal. But this, she was not meant to do. This would reduce her to the equivalent of an immobile, closely packed cluster of Minuteman missiles. And so, on this night, she is heading to sea to carry out her mission.

Not to join the fleet. She is a loner. She will lurk somewhere out there in the deep range, and wait. Her "Blue" crew is manning her on this mission. When she returns, months and months from now, her "Gold" crew, standing by on shore duty, will take over.

Quickly the Trident slips beneath the whitecaps. Five years earlier, back in 1974, when the Navy chose this West Coast homeport of the ten Tridents then being planned, critics of the Trident program pounced on the possibility that the Navy had made a big mistake. Would not the inland port be too confining, rendering the Tridents vulnerable to detection, missile targeting and mining? Were the straits commodious enough to permit the Tridents to submerge to sneak through depth well before they actually put to sea? To manuever laterally in case they found this necessary? Would it not have been prudent to base the Tridents on the East Coast—at Charleston, South Carolina, where the Polaris-Poseidon boats are berthed, at the St. Mary's River in Georgia, or at Mosquito Lagoon in Florida? The Navy responded to the querulous as follows:

> The effective mining of the Straits of Juan de Fuca is far more difficult than accomplishing this task in places such as Charleston, St. Mary's or Cape Kennedy. Not only are these areas shallower and narrower than the Straits of Juan de Fuca, but any Atlantic port is significantly more vulnerable to mining efforts from advanced bases such as Cuba than are the Straits of Juan de Fuca. Even if we consider mining the straits as a threat that our military forces could not thwart, only a small portion of our Trident force would be in port and bottled up. Those forces at sea could return to port for provisioning and would be able to operate in this manner for extended periods of time. It seems unreasonable to assume that any potential enemy could plant and *maintain* a mine-field in the Straits of Juan de Fuca from bases thousands of miles away against our forces capable of either destroying the mineplanting platforms [meaning Soviet submarines] or sweeping the mines.

Rear Admiral Robert Y. Kaufman, a flinty submariner who had been in charge of the Trident program since the beginning (his title: Director, Strategic Submarine Division and Trident

Program Coordinator, Office of the Chief of Naval Operations), discussed the homeporting rationale with Congressional committees, always in executive session. The record of one such hearing, with the usual deletions in accordance with security, went like this:

ADMIRAL KAUFMAN: "We have got three hundred feet of water in that [Hood] canal, in that channel. We can, if we choose, dive all the way out from up here at the [deleted]. So that is one avenue open to us right now. And this is not a narrow strait. It is a deep strait and it is over fifteen miles wide. That is 'operating area' size to the submariners. . . . The Soviet ships could be out here in the same manner they are now out there in each of our SSBN [ballistic-missile submarine] ports. They are intelligence ships. We can get out without his knowing when we are coming because we do not need to be on the surface to give him that signal. And we can be [deleted] until we are well out in the international waters and can go different ways. Our mining people have looked at this and they say mining is not a severe threat here compared to the coastal shelf on the east coast where you have to run on the surface until you are well out in international waters. This is a tremendous advantage. . . . In some of our studies where we have examined attack submarines similar to our own best, against the Trident with its planned noise specifications, it would take a rotating force of about [deleted] of all the Tridents going out."

Admiral Kaufman then trained his testimony on the need for the Trident. "Trident," he said, "is the most survivable component of our very effective mix of Air Force and Navy strategic systems. It builds survivability into the twenty-first century. It provides assurance that neither expected Soviet antisubmarine warfare advances, dramatic antisubmarine warfare breakthroughs, nor age and obsolescence of today's very capable submarines will be cause for any diminishing of confidence in our deterrent. The name of the game in Trident is survivability. . . ."

Now submerged, this billion-dollar FBM submarine, named after the three-pronged spear of Poseidon, traverses the waterway that separates the mainland of the continental United States from Vancouver Island, Canada. She penetrates the Pacific, heading west-southwest. At the mouth of the strait, two smaller shapes mate with her course, one to her stern, the other to her starboard and slightly ahead. These are the American hunter-killers, the attack submarines. Speedsters of 35 knots or so (there is no military information more highly classified or closely held than the actual speeds and collapse depths of submarines). The hunter-killers screen the Trident out to sea. Suddenly their sonars ping. Another metallic shape has joined the set. A Soviet attack submarine, intent not on killing (this time) but on stalking the Trident to her station, on finding out where she—the first of her much-feared kind—will set up to launch. The Soviet skipper was lucky. Or smart. The Trident runs too quietly for his noise-finders to have sensed her coming out. But the skipper had known that she had finished with her shakedown, and should be about ready to go on duty in the deep, and he had been prowling off the mouth of Juan de Fuca. Waiting. Listening. When the two American attack subs had shown up earlier this day, the skipper knew why they were there. It was an old American tactic—hunter-killers escorting Polaris-Poseidon boats clear of the continental shelves off their harbors at Charleston, South Carolina; Rota, Spain; Holy Loch, Scotland; Guam. They might be wiser, mused the Soviet captain, to let the Trident free lance. If she is as stealthy as they claim, I would have small chance of picking her up. And if she is as fast—some say 40 knots—she could outrun me, in any case. Her sonar is supposed to be superior to mine, so she probably could have avoided me. He eases his boat in closer, thanking fortune, but not for long.

The American subs start manuevering. First one, then the other, intersects the course of the Soviet sharksub, trying to confuse her sonarmen. They keep this up, diving and ascending, crisscrossing and curling. The Trident, down gently by the bow in a shallow dive over the shelf, forges onward. Finally, an hour later, far out to sea, the American subs "wipe off" the interceptor. The Soviet skipper has been forced to change course randomly once too often in this deadly game of blind man's bluff. He has lost the Trident. She is free to rove the Pacific unchallenged, unmolested, gone forever from detection, save by miraculous chance. The Soviet skipper is all at sea. For nearly twenty years, his scopes of operation had been the circumscribed preserves of the Arctic, Atlantic and Mediterranean waters where the Polaris-Poseidon boats had been confined by the range of their missiles. They and the few

Poseidons in the Pacific had presented a major problem of detection, of course, but nothing like this one. This Trident would be able to bombard Russia from practically anywhere. A fleet of ten could hide in 60 million square miles of ocean and cover all possible targets in the Soviet Union and the People's Republic of China. The forty-one-boat Polaris-Poseidon fleet was limited to about one-tenth of that square mileage. Now, the Soviet skipper and his admiralty had a whopper to work out, that of patrolling the Pacific in all its breadth and much of its depth, made imperative by the imperial Trident.

With their enormous leeway to breast the latitudes, the Tridents will be able to pick parts of the Pacific where prevailing storms defy the dowsing of ASW planes and surface ships; where the ocean's own inmates swirl in abundance, keeping up a cacophony of "biological noise" to baffle hydrophones and sonobuoys.

The Tridents need their giant hulls to house not only their giant missiles of the 1980s but also for a superpowerful power-plant, the most advanced ever, providing the energy of the ultra-quiet turbine-electric system; for the sea-spearing sonar and its companion electronics gear; for the big horizontal tubes with their wire-guided Mark 48 torpedoes and Harpoon anti-ship tactical cruise missiles. The Trident will be to the fleet what the battleship used to be, and much more. She should be able to fight off her enemies, but before it comes to that, she should be able to steer clear of them. "The greater detection range of the new sonar alone will provide a giant step in surviv-ability," said Admiral Kaufman. "It will permit Trident to evade adversaries long before she herself becomes detectable."

President Truman authorized construction of the first atom-ic-powered submarine in 1950. "The *Nautilus*," he told an in-credulous nation, "will be able to move under the water at a speed of more than twenty knots. A few pounds of uranium will give ample fuel to travel thousands of miles at top speed. She will be able to stay under water indefinitely. Her atomic engine will permit her to be completely free of the earth's atmosphere. She will not even require a breathing tube to the surface." On January 21, 1954, the *Nautilus* splashed into the Thames River at New London, Connecticut, and immediately revolutionized undersea warfare. Her records for endurance and speed soon were outclassed by her hunter-killer sisters of succeeding generations—*Skate, Seawolf, Skipjack*, which was the first, upon commissioning in 1959, to feature the blimp-shaped hull. In 1958, the *Nautilus* made history by passing under Arctic ice from the Pacific to the Atlantic. That same year, the *Skate* accomplished a "first" which nudged the supernations significantly closer to possible strategic showdown. In the dead of winter, after having traversed more than three thousand miles of the Arctic range, *Skate* stuck her sail up through the ice and surfaced, proving that a ballistic-missile submarine could disappear under that vast, white polar wasteland, come up through its capping, and vent her vertical tubes.

Until Trident, the world's largest submarine was *Triton*, designed as a radar-picket boat, the first to be powered by twin nuclear reactors. On February 16, 1960, *Triton* set out from New London on her shakedown cruise, submerged off Montauk Point, Long Island, and did not come fully to the surface again until May 10, eighty-four days and a trip around the world—and more—behind her. Leaving Long Island, the 447-foot, 7,700-ton *Triton* (large as a light cruiser) headed almost directly southeast to Saint Paul Rocks off the northeastern shoulder of South America. This was the reference point for a course of circumnavigation which Ferdinand Magellan had followed four hundred years before. *Triton* rounded Cape Horn, set course for Easter Island, passed about 1,200 miles off Hawaii. Then on to Guam, pausing to hold memorial services as her track passed about a hundred miles from the spot where the first U.S.S. *Triton* was sunk on March 15, 1943, by a Japanese depth charge. Once past Guam, *Triton* passed near Magellan Bay on Macton Island, cleared the Philippines, turned south to the Indonesian Archipelago, and then west-southwest to the Cape of Good Hope. She rounded the tip of Africa on April 17 and returned to Saint Paul Rocks on April 25, completing her circumnavigation. For frosting, she continued submerged to a point off Cadiz, Spain, broached the surface briefly, and then cut back westward across the Atlantic to the U.S. mainland. *Triton*'s crew and passenger scientists had collected a lode of information about human endurance, atmospheric control and habitability of a submarine, and had made hydrographic, oceanographic, magnetic and gravitational surveys as well. In the final paragraphs of his log, *Triton* Captain Edward L. Beach wrote that the 41,500-mile voyage "has accomplished something of value to our country. The sea may yet hold the key to the salvation of man and his civilization." Or it could go the other way.

Six months later, almost to the day, the first Fleet Ballistic Missile Submarine invaded the inner space of planet Earth. On November 15, 1960, the U.S.S. *George Washington* (SSBN 598) deployed on Atlantic patrol with a full load of sixteen missiles named after Polaris, the North Star, the heavenly beacon of man since the time he first ventured beyond sight of his shoreline. The first five Polaris boats are called the *George Washington* class; the second set of five, the *Ethan Allen* class. The third set of thirty-one, those eventually converted to the proliferant Poseidon missile of 2,880-mile range, are called the *Lafayette* class, after the first of their line. The twelfth of these, the U.S.S. *Daniel Boone*, became the first FBM submarine to put out on patrol in the Pacific, on Christmas Day, 1964. Prayers of thanks were offered that day, wherever submariners worshipped together, for the submarine having become, as the Navy put it, "truly a global deterrent." The last *Lafayette*-class boat, the U.S.S. *Will Rogers*, was commissioned in 1967.

On August 3, 1970, the U.S.S. *James Madison*, the first of the *Lafayette*-class Polaris boats to be converted to the MIRVed missiles, test-fired a Poseidon for the first time under water, off the Florida coast. In a damn-the-torpedoes manuever, a Russian ship moved in to try to collect Poseidon debris from the surface. It narrowly missed colliding with a U.S. ship on *Madison* escort.

Apart from its arsenal of Poseidons, the *Lafayette*-class boat differed most markedly from the *George Washington* and *Ethan Allen* classes in its upgraded navigation system, which enabled it to receive position fixes from orbiting "Transit" satellites once every four hours. The Tridents' vastly expanded ranges and patrol areas will require them to possess an inertial navigation system of proportionally finer precision. If a strategic submarine is improperly positioned on station, its missiles are in arrears on accuracy from the moment they broach. The improbability of parking a Polaris-Poseidon boat hull perfect on a launching benchmark has been the main reason for the Pentagon's reluctance to rely on their missiles as smashers of small-scale military targets, such as missile silos or underground aircraft shelters. The NAVSTAR communications satellites being planned for the 1980s should change all this dramatically. Drawing on signals from twenty-four of them in equatorial, polar and diagonal orbits, the submarine skippers will know exactly where they are, at all times, within a matter of feet. The position of each satellite will be an always-established fact. A beep from a ground station will be relayed from satellites to submarines (or airplanes, or surface vessels) as a time-reference signal. The submarines' computers will show the time difference between the signals, and fix the subs' positions with respect to the positions of the satellites. Those positions also will be transmitted continuously, concurrently. In the control rooms of the submarines, the computers, toting up in a twinkling the altitudes, speeds and positions of the satellites in relation to the depths and speeds of the boats, will show the skippers their latitudes and longitudes dead on the mark. This terra-go-round of transmissions also, of course, will be necessary to the accuracy of missiles launched from airplanes on the move.

A big drawback of the Polaris-Poseidon boats is the uncertainty of their communications with shore while submerged. To assure the Tridents—and the older boats—of a reliable radio link, the Navy devoted fifteen years of research, at a cost of $75 million by the mid-1970s, on "Project Sanguine," The heart of this extra-low-frequency system would be a huge underground antenna, buried in rock, to transmit and receive signals through the earth, to and from submarines submerged at depths down to about two hundred feet (the basic operating depth of a sub all set to launch). Sanguine also would consist of more than one thousand square miles of grids, cables and generators. The system works. Signals from the Sanguine test facility in Wisconsin have been picked up clearly by submarines in the eastern Atlantic. But there was a big hitch in bringing the system to flower. When the Navy proposed Sanguine's construction for keeps in Wisconsin, environmentalists rose up to propound the likely bad effects of its electronic emissions on humans, plants and animals. The Navy then turned to Texas. Ditto. To Michigan. More of the same. Of no avail was a report by the National Academy of Sciences which said that Sanguine's emanations would harm nothing and no one. Critics also noted that Sanguine's powerful magnetic field, only six feet underground, might interfere with radio and television signals. Still another reason for the opposition was that the Sanguine grid would, naturally, be a prime target in the event of nuclear war. A doomsday grid. In counterclaim, the Navy contended that Sanguine's sharpening of our seagoing deterrent force would render nuclear war all the more unlikely. But in its need to acknowledge publicly its dire need of Sanguine, the Navy played into the hands of the Air Force, which had been bucking the trend toward near-total dependence, eventually, on the subs in the strategic schematic. The Air Force argument always had been that while the subs may be less vulnerable than land-based missiles or bombers, how potent are they, really, if they can't communicate when the chips are down? The sine qua non of the waging of war, said the Air Force, is, after all, command and control. Dr. Malcolm R. Currie, director of defense research and engineering, made the point, too. Imploring Congress to keep on funding Sanguine R&D, and to regard more sympathetically the Navy's problem of finding a Sanguine site, Currie declared: "The effective command and control of our SLBM [submarine-launched ballistic missile] force, the element of our strategic offensive forces which is the least vulnerable to sudden nuclear attack, is of major importance. At the present time, the communications links from the National Command Authority to the individual ballistic submarines are much less survivable than the submarines themselves. Reliable and survivable communications links must be maintained with these forces." But Sanguine's detractors had amassed widespread support in Congress, and in 1974 the Navy ran out of money, at least temporarily, for the project. Doggedly requesting another appropriation of $16 million for 1975, the Navy turned to examining thinly populated federal lands in the West as fallback sites.

Incidentally, the political poison of the times seeped into discussions of Sanguine. At Llano, Texas, the county seat of the area in which the Navy had proposed to build the Sanguine antenna, critics at a public hearing compared the Navy plan to Watergate. It seemed to them an attempt by the government to ride down individual rights. The Navy, its brass never noted for the conciliatory approach, didn't help matters. The Texans took exception to a crack Admiral Kaufman made in trying to defuse their nuclear-target fears. "The Russians might attack Washington," he was quoted as saying, "but I'll be damned if they'd be insane enough to attack Texas." Commented the publication *Aerospace Daily:* "If Texans have any higher loyalty than the United States, it is their state. And Pentagon officials wince when asked if Kaufman is quoted accurately in news accounts."

Sanguine and satellites should not be regarded as incidentals to the story of the buildup of U.S. ballistic missile submarines in the second half of the twentieth century. These communications projects are, in their fashion, the heart of that story. Futurists in the fleet and in the research shops of the Pentagon perceived, far back in the 1960s, what the advances of communications and space technologies—married to the advances of nuclear power and metals—could do to make the FBM submarine's role a superstellar one, of top billing on the ballistic marquee. The year the U.S.S. *Will Rogers* was commissioned as the last of the long line of *Lafayette*-class Polaris-Poseidon boats, a Defense Department think tank presented the results of a supersecret study, called "Strat X," to the Directorate of Research and Engineering. Strat X dealt with the likelihood that the Soviets sooner or later would test and deploy formidable ICBM's of counterforce capability, and it proposed ways of offsetting this in advance. One recommendation of the Strat X report was to harden our Minuteman silos in order to postpone, over the short term, the inevitable obsolescence-through-vulnerability of those immobile missiles. Another, and the most important, was to depend far more, over the long term, on missiles launched from the sea. This would mean, in the end, Trident.

The late 1960s and early 1970s were not the best of times for the dozen or so think tanks—Federal Contract Research Centers—which worked exclusively, or almost so, for the Department of Defense and the separate services. Military spending cutbacks, inflation and budgetary ceilings imposed by Congress had combined to curtail the growth which these FCRCs had experienced in their heydays of the previous decade. Student uprisings against the Vietnam War, the draft and all things military or quasi-military had strained and, in some cases, ruptured the ties of the think tanks with the nation's universities. They had depended on the universities for faculty guidance and participation, for facilities and for free-flowing intellectual exchange. The leak of the top-secret "Pentagon Papers" by RAND Corporation alumnus Daniel Ellsberg compounded the miseries of the think tanks' alliances with the military, which also had begun to erode beforehand. The Ellsberg case made the Pentagon very nervous indeed about the easy access of the think tankers to highly classified information. The Air Force clamped tough security restrictions on its creature RAND, where one James Schlesinger once had been the star strategic thinker. But the Ellsberg case only marked a deep declivity in what had been a steady decline of the think tanks at large. One of the sufferers had been the Institute for Defense Analyses, *the* think tank at the disposal of the Secretary of Defense himself, and of the Director of Defense Research and Engineering, working hand in glove with the Defense Department's Advanced Research Projects Agency, disdaining slavishness to the military services, dealing in big ideas, big plans, big think. IDA's specialty had been systems analysis, and systems analysis had gone out of style. There were signs in the mid-seventies, however, that it was making a bit of a comeback, and that IDA was, too. Even though IDA had lost its official claim on the consortium of twelve universities which had founded and fed it in years long gone by, it still was drawing on their resident brains in an unofficial, informal —even sub rosa—fashion. But nothing like the heady years of absorption in the most critical of national security affairs, such as Strat X.

IDA still has the same wide-ranging mandate of its salad days. Its scope is discernible in the language of IDA's contract with the Defense Department, which specifies that the institute provide ". . . personnel, facilities and material required for surveys and analyses of the effectiveness of various weapons systems; evaluation of new equipment in the light of military requirements; evaluation and analyses of military problems to predict the operational behavior of new material and equipment; development of new tactical doctrines to meet changing military requirements; studies and reports on the technical aspects of strategic planning; and analysis of combat reports, tactical and strategic plans, and field exercises in both the continental United States and elsewhere, with a view to determining how existing weapons and weapons systems could be more effectively employed."

Given all this, it should not be surprising that IDA's workings are highly classified. Security is stringent at the modern ten-story building which it occupies, complete with penthouse view of the Potomac panorama, just across the freeway from the Pentagon. Visitors make every step under escort. About five hundred people work there, half of them professionals in the scientific and engineering disciplines and in systems analysis. Consultants from universities often are teamed, in special projects, with consultants from pertinent parts of the defense industry, and the Strat X study was a case in point. The brain-trusters at IDA, then headed by General Maxwell Taylor, fresh back from his ambassadorship to Vietnam, told the Pentagon they would undertake Strat X if they could get a particularly qualified man like Fred Payne, a vice-president of Marquardt Corporation, to organize the project. Among other credentials, Payne had been deputy director of defense research of strategic weapons from 1961 to 1965, so Strat X was right up his alley. The Pentagon brass went to bat for IDA and landed Payne, persuading Marquardt to give him a leave of absence for the nine months that Strat X took.

Assembling the Strat X team posed, however, another problem. The study required a thorough knowledge of missile designs. While IDA had scientists and engineers who knew quite a bit about the design of missile propulsion and guidance-control subsystems, it had no one who could call himself an expert on the missiles as wholly embodied. So IDA turned to the missile-making companies, plucking off twenty designers of top talent to work with twenty of its own analyst-engineers.

IDA traces its history to the Weapons Systems Evaluation Group (WSEG) at the Pentagon, which was set up in 1949 on the order of James L. Forrestal, first Secretary of Defense. The group had both military officers and civil-servant scientists. Six years later, Defense Secretary Charles E. Wilson asked for organized university support to back up WSEG in weapons development. Five universities—MIT, California Institute of Technology, Stanford, Case Institute and Tulane—promptly set up IDA with the idea that they could, through cross-fertilization, serve themselves along with the defense establishment. In 1959, they were joined by Columbia, Penn State and Michigan; in 1961, by the University of Chicago; in 1962, by Princeton and Illinois; and in 1964, by California at Berkeley.

In the early days, IDA's weapons activities were confined

largely to studies of radioactive fallout, nuclear stockpiling and continental air defense. Over the years, the activities ranged into the broad areas of command and control, strategic offensive and defensive systems, antisubmarine warfare (although this is more especially the domain of the Center for Naval Analysis, a Navy-nourished think tank a five-minute ride up the parkway from IDA), tactical weapons systems, reconnaissance and surveillance. In 1966, IDA completed a study called "Pen X," which analyzed the ability of ICBMs to penetrate ballistic-missile defense networks expected in the Soviet Union in the latter twentieth century. A year later, Strat X was born.

In somewhat oversimplified terms, the Navy wound up the winner, the Air Force the loser, in Strat X. The study suggested the sea as the likely way to go. Ironically, Strat X had been ordered up by McNamara and his research chief, Dr. John S. Foster, Jr., at a time when the Air Force was pushing for its WS-120A weapon system as the future replacement of Minuteman. WS-120A missiles were to be perhaps twice as big as Minuteman. But the Defense Department major domos wanted to see which other strategic systems might be mixed into the works. The Navy came front and center with a couple of concepts, of course—one of missiles on surface ships, the other of missiles below, in a bigger, better Polaris-Poseidon designated ULMS (for Undersea Long-Range Missile System). Fired up by the encouragement of the Strat X study, the Navy's Office of Strategic Offensive and Defensive Systems dug into the designing of ULMS. Not long afterward, the Soviets began rapidly deploying their SS-9 missiles and their "Y"-class ballistic-missile submarines, comparable in size and missile range to Polaris. Trident was on its way. Actually, the name "Trident" would not be chosen until later. The appellation which had the early edge in the Navy's namestakes was "Perseus," the Greek god of the winged sandals and the helmet of invisibility. It was Perseus who slew the gorgon Medusa, whose face turned men to stone. It was Perseus, too, who saved the gorgeous Andromeda, along with her father's kingdom, from the sea monster Tiamat. The Navy never really said why it finally rejected "Perseus." Perhaps he had been too rampantly a destroyer, a first-striker. He also made a bit of a mess of things. As Robert Graves wrote of him in *Greek Gods and Heroes:*

Perseus, now wearing the helmet and sandals, flew unseen to Libya. Coming upon Medusa asleep, he looked at her reflexion [sic] in the polished shield and cut off her head with his sickle. The only unfortunate accident was that Medusa's blood trickling from the bag, in which the head lay, turned into poisonous snakes as it hit the earth. This made the land of Libya unsafe for ever afterwards.

A sickle? Hardly a proper symbol for the United States Navy. And snakes?

In January 1969, the new Nixon administration asked Congress for $20 million, small change by military standards, for advanced development of the new submarine-missile system called ULMS. Congress was not quite ready to be unreserved. Its committees examined the Pentagon's plans extant to put sixteen Poseidon missiles, each ferrying up to fourteen MIRVs, on thirty-one Polaris submarines, and it cut the ULMS funding to a token $5 million. To the Pentagon, however, a token means a toehold. The time to kill ULMS was right then, or never. Year by successive year, the ULMS-Trident development and development-production money just grew and grew, until, in the defense budget for 1976, it had attained the remarkable proportion of more than $2 billion. The Navy got its seed money for ULMS in 1969 mostly on the persuasiveness of Defense Secretary Melvin Laird's argument that he could not guarantee the security of the Polaris-Poseidon fleet much beyond the next five to seven years. The Russians, he said, might well be forging ahead faster than we knew with their antisubmarine warfare research. With benefit of hindsight, Laird's position (really the Navy's position) now can be passed off as so much whistling under water. But he knew what he was doing. His real worry—the same worry which had led to the Strat X study—was not the advancing Soviet ASW research but the increasing vulnerability of U.S. land-based missiles. Laird did not want to make a big thing of this in public. It was not to become the Pentagon's *cause célèbre*, in fact, until James Schlesinger took over the department four years later. Laird stuck with the position, which he rightly believed would be sufficient to convince Congress of the need for Trident, that the Polaris-Poseidon boats would start wearing out in the 1980s, no longer were all that secure, and, if you examined their deployment closely, might not really do a complete job of blanketing the Soviet Union with their missiles. The limited range of the missiles—2,880 miles—required them to nestle too close to the Eurasian land mass for comfort. To back Laird's play, the Navy trucked charts, graphs and maps to sessions of the Armed Services and Appropriations Committees (closed meetings, as usual, to keep the Russians from finding out and, not incidentally, to give the committee members that satisfying feeling of knowing something that no one else in Congress did and that they shouldn't—but would—talk about). A pertinent Navy map showed how three Tridents could do the work of six Polaris-Poseidons, and do it better. The map depicted one Polaris-Poseidon in the North Sea off the coast of Norway; three in Arctic waters, at the northern rim of the Kara Sea just off the island of Novaya Zemlya, in the Laptev Sea off the Taimyr Peninsula, and in the Arctic Ocean off New Siberian Islands; one in the Pacific off the southeast coast of the Japanese island of Kyushu, and one off the southern coast of Iran, where the Indian Ocean becomes the Gulf of Oman. Of all possible positionings of Polaris-Poseidon, the only one that had a chance of striking strategic nuclear installations at Lake Baikal in central Russia was the submarine off the Taimyr Peninsula. And this boat, the Navy noted, was one of three which lurked in waters frozen most of the year, making their task, should they be forced to perform it, all the dicier. Three Tridents could handle the same targeting with missile range and sea room to spare, said the Navy. All would be in deep, deep water —one in the Atlantic, one in the Pacific, one in the Indian Ocean. Adding a dip of whipped cream, the admirals proudly noted that if the technology of the Trident II missile for the 1980s were to live up to the dreams of its designers, a solitary Trident submarine slinging twenty-four MIRVed rockets 7,000 to 8,000 miles, would be able to enshroud all of Eurasia from a firing position 1,000 to 2,000 miles directly south of the tip of India. This goes a long way toward explaining why the Navy, in 1974, presented big plans for expanding its communications installations, improving its airfield and dredging a deep-draft harbor at Diego Garcia, a forlorn atoll in the middle of the Indian Ocean, at just about the spot where the Trident would lie. The idea is to provide air, surface and communications support for Trident, not base it at the atoll. For none of the supersubs will be based, as is a portion of the Polaris-Poseidon fleet, away from their homeland. And none will need venture into the Mediterranean, which has become, at its eastern end, south of Turkey, a Russian lake.

The ultimate need of the Trident was never an issue in Congress. The controversy which finally arose there was focused on the question of how quickly the Tridents should be deployed.

In 1970, a group of about one hundred senators and representatives calling themselves "Members of Congress for Peace Through Law" (MCPL) had issued a report strongly backing the Pentagon's rationale for the new submarine. It was needed, said MCPL, "to make a sea-based nuclear missile system the first line of deterrence." The new submarine, said the report, would be "the epitome of the blue-water option at a time when the probable obsolescence of fixed-based missiles has become clear in the ABM debate. When viewed as a successor to land-based missiles, and to their requisite defense systems, ULMS is cost-effective."

This was the kiss of life for the Trident program on Capitol Hill. For MCPL is the only Congressional group which ever attacks Pentagon plans in an organized way, and its rare support is pure bonus for those plans. In its opposition to defense programs, MCPL makes some good points—and now and then, an inroad—but is never wholly successful. The Armed Services and Appropriations Committees are stacked with pro-Pentagon members. And while these committees may nip off a million here or a billion there, they are loath to recommend killing major weapons programs outright. Arms debates in recent years have shown that there simply are not enough votes in either house to overturn the largely pro-weapons recommendations of the committees. In consequence, opponents of the weapons programs and of the committees' recommendations must mount their challenges on tangential matters such as production schedules and pace of research and development. This is precisely what MCPL did after the Navy, in 1972, proposed stepping up the development of Trident and blending the latter stages of its development with a much-quickened onset of production. Hastily, MCPL formed a bicameral committee, studied the situation and issued a "research paper" in 1973, saying, in effect, that the Navy should have left well enough alone.

The original Navy timetable had called for deployment of the first Trident submarine in 1980. Two old hands in the Polaris-Poseidon program, General Dynamics Electric Boat Division and General Electric Company, had been given contracts to develop the submarine and its nuclear reactor, respectively. Lockheed Missiles and Space Company, a subsidiary of Lockheed Aircraft Corporation, which had produced the Polaris and Poseidon missiles, became the contractor for the new missiles. There were to be two. The Trident I, of 4,000-to-4,500-mile range, and the Trident II, of 6,000-to-7,000-mile range. In the scenario, the Trident boats initially would be fitted with the Trident I, later, with the Trident II. Trident I was to be of a size compatible with the Poseidon tubes. Trident II would be too big for them. A lot of people in the Pentagon and Congress suggested putting the Trident I on the Polaris-Poseidon boats, but the Navy wanted none of that, for the very same reason that the Air Force later would resist fitting B-52 bombers with air-launched strategic cruise missiles. The new missile might militate against deployment of the ardently courted new weapons platforms—in the case of the Air Force, the B-1; in the case of the Navy, the Trident submarine. But the idea of putting Trident I missiles in Polaris-Poseidon boats was catching fancies all over the place, including that of Laird. So what the Navy did was push up the development of the Trident submarine and push back the development of the Trident I missile, so they would coincide in time. The Navy proposed getting the first submarine ready for champagne by the late fall of 1978, and sending it to sea fully armed with Trident I missiles. Not only that. The Navy also proposed (what the hell, as long as we're at it) a production rate of three Trident submarines every year following the shakedown of the first. Laird went along. Hold it, said MCPL.

"The Department of Defense," said its report, "has drastically accelerated the hull program, delayed the development of the Trident I missile, and bypassed the quicker and more cost-effective option of installing this missile in existing ballistic-missile submarine hulls. These alterations have been hypothecated on a possible sudden Soviet breakthrough in antisubmarine warfare technology and on inflated estimates of the growth of the Soviet submarine forces. This is not a convincing argument for an accelerated Trident program." Contending that the Polaris-Poseidon boats would "remain a highly survivable sea-based deterrent well into the 1980s," MCPL ticked off item after item in a lengthy bill of particulars against the Navy's compression of Trident development-production. Among them were:

—"Many of the advantages of the Trident program, including the Trident I missile and certain quiet-running features, can be incorporated in the existing Poseidon fleet, thus providing adequate safeguards against a greater-than-expected ASW threat but at a much lower price."

—"The Trident submarine system does not possess any advantages over present analagous submarines which are sufficient to justify the spending of four to five times as much per submarine, using conservative estimates, of the anticipated program costs."

—"The Trident program may represent an irreversible commitment to the wrong system or system components. Acceleration limits U.S. flexibility in meeting a wide range of possible threats, flexibility which may be repurchased only through expensive design changes at a later date."

—"The Trident system has a major flaw in comparison to the present deterrent force; it involves the concentration of more missiles in fewer platforms, thus making it more vulnerable from a purely numerical standpoint."

And then, touching on the reverse twist of the services' avidity for the bigger and better, MCPL noted:

"If, as seems probable, the cost of each Trident submarine makes procurement of a large fleet prohibitively expensive, then the United States could be aiding a potential enemy by offering a smaller number of targets for strategic ASW forces."

This angle had not passed unnoticed by the U.S. Air Force in its attempts to stave off the strategic supremacy of the Navy. *Air Force* magazine had published the following piece of wishful thinking in 1971:

Most Air Force planners agree with the majority of other defense analysts and support the Triad concept. They support eventual development of the Navy's advanced-technology ULMS. But there is considerable doubt, on technical grounds, that such a force could long survive if it were the sole U.S. strategic deterrent. Numerous possibilities can be postulated. One is the possibility of improved ASW technology, permitting the enemy to stealthily eliminate U.S. submarines, one by one. Another is the idea of a massive enemy ICBM bombardment of the ocean quadrants where the Polaris-Poseidon fleet must operate because of the range limitations of its missiles. The range argument, of course, is cited in favor of ULMS by its advocates. But, on the basis of information made available to this magazine, yet another technique looms as a potential threat to any submarine-launched missile force. Operating areas of the U.S. submarine fleet could be seeded with air-dropped sonobuoys, possibly just prior to an attack. Sonobuoys have an effective detection range of about twenty miles in radius. Suppose a network of buoys could establish the location of individual submarines with an error factor seven miles in radius. It can also be assumed that the one-to-two megaton warhead of the Soviet SS-11 missiles, detonated underwater, would destroy any submarine located within its lethal range of three and a half miles. Simple mathematics establishes that only four SS-11s need be expended to destroy one submarine. Because each submarine carries sixteen missiles, this is a pretty favorable ratio. Even doubling the margin for error to fourteen miles would mean only sixteen SS-11s to trade off against a like number of Polaris-Poseidon missiles. One for one is a good trade in the strategic missile business and, with each ULMS-type sub projected to cost more than $1 billion, sheer numbers cannot be the answer. The obvious conclusion is that an enemy could reasonably expect to be able to launch a successful attack on the U.S. submarine fleet and still maintain a strong re-strike capability against the U.S. proper as insurance against failure. More than any other strategic system, the Air Force ICBMs are geared toward deterrence of nuclear war. While an attack on submarines, if detected, can be viewed with a degree of ambiguity, an attack on the land-based ICBM force constitutes an unequivocal act of war.

Whew.

Putting his chips on the Navy's hyped-up Trident program, Laird asked Congress in 1972 for $977 million, in contrast to the $508 million which would have been required to sustain the program at its originally planned pace. Immediately, the acceleration drew fire from the feisty Research and Development

Subcommittee of the Senate Armed Services Committee. The subcommittee voted unanimously to deny Laird and the Navy the increase which would press down the pedal on Trident. Then, by the closest possible margin, a tie vote, the full committee overturned the subcommittee and restored the money. Senator John Stennis, the committee chairman, provided the Trident-favorable swing vote at the last minute. It was a surprise. He had complained privately about the Trident acceleration, and was believed all set to vote against it. But he got a telephone call from President Nixon at the eleventh hour, and it swung him. The antiacceleration forces were not finished, however. On the Senate floor, Lloyd Bentsen of Texas, a member of the R&D Subcommittee, tried to make the case that the tie vote of the committee really had been tantamount to a "hung jury," to no verdict at all. He introduced an amendment to the military procurement bill which would have implemented the R&D Subcommittee's cut of Trident funds. The Senate beat it back. But the relatively close vote of 47 to 39 left the losers calling for a rematch the following year, and they got one.

In 1973, the Navy and new Secretary of Defense Elliot Richardson asked Congress for $1.7 billion to continue accelerating Trident, a dizzying doubling of the budget request of the year before. By now, Senator Bentsen had forsaken the Armed Services Committee and its R&D Subcommittee for a seat on the Senate Finance Committee. Senator Thomas J. McIntyre of New Hampshire, the subcommittee chairman, assumed Bentsen's antiacceleration leadership mantle. The subcommittee followed its script of the previous year, voting unanimously to cut the Navy funding by $885 million, or a little more than half. This would have moderated production of Trident and put off its deployment to 1980. The cut would not have affected R&D on either the sub or the missiles. But it would have prevented the Navy from contracting for production of hulls on the first few submarines. Succeeding scenes in the Senate drama spread premature panic in the Pentagon and left nonparticipants at sixes and sevens.

The vote of the full Armed Services Committee on Trident was announced as eight to seven upholding the subcommittee. Stennis was not involved. He had been seriously wounded by a street mugger earlier in the year and was still convalescing. The Navy nearly went over the side. But hold on. It turned out that Senator Barry Goldwater of Arizona had been counted erroneously, in absentia, as having voted against Trident. Goldwater had instructed Senator Strom Thurmond of South Carolina to cast his proxy vote in the Navy's *favor*, but Thurmond got the signals switched. So the committee reassembled, took another vote, and the Trident acceleration was salvaged. It was only natural that Thurmond had become confused as to where Goldwater stood on the issue. As a member of the R&D Subcommittee, Goldwater had voted two years in a row against the Trident acceleration. But this time, Goldwater said he had received last-minute information from the Navy brass, notably from nuclear-propulsion boss Admiral Hyman G. Rickover, which induced him to change his stance. The Navy's blitz of swing man Goldwater greatly irritated the foes of Trident hightailing, but they hadn't seen anything yet. The issue still had to be resolved on the Senate floor, and the Navy had hardly begun to do battle.

During the August recess of Congress, with the Trident vote anticipated hard upon the Senate's reconvening in September, the Navy engaged in what may well have been the most intensive, most uncommon lobbying campaign in the annals of arm-twisting. The admirals already had dazzled—or disturbed—individual senators with their do-or-die dramatics. Now they turned to the senators' staffs, in the notion that many senators were fence-sitters on the Trident issue, and that the best-paved pathway to their persuasion was through the men and women—chiefly legislative assistants—who did the spade-work for them on the big issues. Admiral Elmo K. Zumwalt, then the Chief of Naval Operations, launched a series of break-fast and luncheon briefings of key staffers of all one hundred senators and of every committee germane, however remotely, to the coming call of the roll. One top aide of an anti-Trident senator told me after his breakfast at the Pentagon: "I certainly have never been lobbied like this. I don't see anything wrong with it. The Navy is entitled to try everything it can. There's a lot of back and forth of ideas, and we felt free to raise objections to the Navy's line." Another breakfast-session staffer of less impressionable inclination complained that Zumwalt had conveyed "the idea that a vote against Trident is a vote for the Russians. I didn't like that." Others, however, denied that Zumwalt had put it so baldly, at least to them.

Through it all, Schlesinger, only two months into his secretaryship, kept his distance. This would be recalled later in the year. At the time, he was taking a stern look at the disturbingly high failure rate of test-fired Poseidon missiles, by then in the tubes of nineteen converted *Lafayette*-class Polaris subs. Schlesinger said the failures didn't particularly worry him; after all, the Navy had experienced a lot of problems in the early days of the Polaris missile, too. But he obviously wasn't very happy about it, either. Some admirals began getting the wind up. They had been skeptical of Schlesinger ever since his high-handed days at the Bureau of the Budget, when he showed an unsporting resistance to the onset of Trident. Remember? He had been incubated as a strategic planner at RAND, which rallied around its client, the Air Force. Would he play the Navy's game?

The Senate came back into session in September and voted 49 to 47 to let the Trident program proceed at flank speed. It was the closest vote on a major weapons project since the Safeguard squeaker—when Vice-President Spiro T. Agnew broke a tie vote to save the ABM system—four years earlier. Trident's champion in the Senate had been Henry M. Jackson, whose home state the Navy subsequently chose as Trident's homeport. This sort of tit-for-tat is common in the interplay of Pentagon-Capitol Hill porkbarreling. But while there was no suspicion of Jackson's sincerity in espousing the Trident cause, there will remain considerable concern about the possible bottling of the submarines in the Straits of Juan de Fuca, and of the wisdom of, and the motives behind, that choice.

Congress was not, however, done with Trident. The House Appropriations Committee sprang a surprise on the Navy by nicking a little over $240 million from the nearly $2 billion which both houses already had authorized. Subsequently, both the House and the Senate, inconsistent with their previous actions, sustained the House committee's cut. The cut would have slowed Trident production somewhat, and was remarkable for that. But what happened next was even more remarkable, or—if you were the Chief of Naval Operations—regrettable. A pithy summing up was provided in the 1974 report of the Senate Armed Services Committee, to wit:

The Secretary of Defense has restructured the [Trident] program, consistent with the actions of Congress, but has gone even further. He has adopted the recommendations made by the Research and Development Subcommittee last year [1973] to slow the pace of submarine construction from three to two per year, and has approved the backfit of Poseidon submarines with the C-4 [Trident I] missile, beginning in fiscal year 1979, now planned for ten submarines. Previously, this was approved only as an option for initiation in the early 1980s.

Schlesinger had made the Navy compromise. He had strung out the production and deployment schedules of all ten Tridents, but had approved, along with Congress, the christening of the first boat around mid-1979, not much later than the Navy had wanted. He did something else, however, which left the Trident program admirals sputtering. He budgeted $16 million for Fiscal 1975 to develop a smaller ballistic-missile submarine. He said that this was a message to the Soviets: cooperate at SALT II and the United States will deploy the smaller subs to augment a Trident fleet of no more than—perhaps even less than—ten submarines. Don't cooperate, and the United States will go full speed with Trident. The $16 million (reminiscent, in magnitude, of the first-year funding of ULMS five years earlier) was to be spent on a feasibility study by the Naval Ship Research and Development Center at Carderock, Maryland. The smaller FBM sub would contain either twelve or sixteen missile tubes. It would be powered by the S5G "natural circulation" reactor, which had been developed for the "quiet" *Narwhal*-class (SSN-671) attack subs, deployed starting in 1969. This reactor eliminated the noise generated by other classes of attack subs by dispensing with their large reactor coolant pumps and their attendant electrical and control equipment. Instead, it took advantage of natural convection currents to circulate the reactor coolant.

Schlesinger testified before the Senate Armed Services Committee that he had proposed a *Narwhal*-class FBM submarine "in connection with the Trident capability." If the Soviets showed restraint, the United States would not have to go ahead with the "vast and expensive" Trident program, he said. The committee, so imbued by now with the Navy notion of Trident's indispensability, seemed slow to catch on to Schlesinger's meaning. Chairman Stennis asked Schlesinger if he

actually meant that the smaller sub might be a replacement for
—not an addition to—Trident.

"Yes sir," Schlesinger replied.

STENNIS: "In other words, if we built that, we might not have
to build Trident?"

SCHLESINGER: "I think that is a possibility."

In the shops of the Navy purists, there was profound resentment of Schlesinger's roughshod demotion of Trident from its
pinnacle as the premier ballistic-missile submarine to the common level of a political bargaining chip with the Soviets. There
seemed little point in the admirals' getting all upset, however.
More than $4 billion already had been committed for Trident
R&D, and Congress, always enamored of the program, if not
always of its pace, would never stand for throwing all that
money into the ocean, so to speak. Moreover, Trident's port
had been picked. Once construction of the base near Bangor
got under way, tearing it up would be traumatic. Sure enough,
the Senate Armed Services Committee voted down Schlesinger's proposal to study the design of a smaller FBM *Narwhal*
submarine as having been "premature." The committee made
clear, furthermore, that any FBM sub should always be
planned to complement, never to supplant, the Tridents.

Taken all of a piece, the Navy faced tough years ahead. First,
of course, there was Air Force-oriented Schlesinger, who
openly disagreed not only with the admirals' claims for the
superurgency of Trident, but also with their hyperalarmist
views of the potency of the Soviet fleet. Then there was the
Navy's loss of leverage on the Joint Chiefs of Staff—Admiral
Thomas J. Moorer had retired as chairman and been replaced
by a Schlesinger favorite, Air Force General George S. Brown.
Admiral Zumwalt, who had been faulted by his peers for his
alleged relaxation of naval discipline but certainly not for his
exhortative leadership on behalf of top-priority weapons, was
replaced as CNO by Admiral James L. Holloway III, an
unknown quantity in that job. Finally, there were the monumental tasks ahead of modernizing a geriatric surface fleet, of
coordinating and sharpening antisubmarine warfare systems,
of coming up with tactical and strategic cruise missiles—all
within the constraints of a budget which the ballistic submarine and fighter aircraft programs for years had been bleeding
dry. The Navy could have used the cost overrun on the B-1

bomber. In the mid-1970s, that overrun computed out to almost exactly the cost of converting all thirty-one *Lafayette*-class FBM submarines from Polaris to Poseidon missiles. Looking at it in Air Force perspective, however, the billions already sunk into Trident would have bailed out the B-1. Altogether, the military establishment dared not expose too nakedly its internal funding over priorities among strategic weapons. It much preferred having them all, even if this were to mean the near-total immersion of the nation in the never-ending technological rites of Triad.

In February 1975, Schlesinger announced that he had elongated the production timetable of the ten Trident submarines even more. The timetable still called for putting the first Trident to sea in 1979, but the final Trident, not until 1984 or 1985. This production stretchout of at least two years did not, however, signify any disaffection on Schlesinger's part. To the contrary. The slowdown had been dictated by the worsening shortages and the steeply climbing costs of materials needed to build the submarines. It now seemed, indeed, that Schlesinger had begun to "go Navy" in the interservice battle for dominance in strategic weapons. He told Congress flatly: "The portion of the missile force at sea is still the least vulnerable element of our strategic Triad, and as far as we can see ahead, it is likely to remain so."

What a difference a year makes. Now, in 1975, Schlesinger had switched from discussing the possibility of not building all ten Tridents to the possibility of building even more. He said that more might be needed if the Soviets continued to beef up their own land and sea strategic missile forces to the outsized limits tentatively permitted by the yet-to-be-signed Ford-Brezhnev agreement at Vladivostok the previous autumn. This line of thought fed the growing suspicion that the Vladivostok affair had been more an inducement than an inhibitor of the arms race.

7

Jules Verne
Revisted

Nearly all the military people running the Navy are not experienced in what is required to carry out a major engineering development successfully, and are not experienced in the training required to operate complex equipment using modern technology. . . . We have a situation in the Navy today where there are basically three groups of officers. There are the aviators, the surface ship officers and the submariners. The aviators have the greatest influence. Next are the surface ship officers, and lowest on the totem pole are the submarine officers. This is largely because the submariners are so few in number. Submarine officers represent less than 4 percent of all the officers in the Navy. Decisions are generally made according to influence, and so the programs of the Navy mirror the relative influence of these three groups. Our entire submarine force today, including the strategic ballistic-missile Polaris submarines as well as the attack submarines, spend less than 20 percent of the Navy's budget. The attack submarine force spends less than 10 percent of the budget. Perhaps it is natural and in consonance with human nature that the decisions are made this way, but this does not mean that they are in the best interests of our country."

> —Admiral Hyman G. Rickover, Director, Division of Naval Reactors, U.S. Atomic Energy Commission, and Deputy Commander for Nuclear Propulsion, Naval Ships System Command.

In the defense establishment's myriad cockfights over carving up the budgets and settling on weapons and strategies, the pit inside the United States Navy may be the one where the feathers are strewn most furiously. It is a largely unpublicized fight. Of all the services, the Navy cares the most about the appearance of unison and propriety, goes below to settle family fights, and then masks the scars of the face which it shows the public back up on deck. This is why there was overweening rage among the admirals, captains, commanders and chiefs of the fleet when Elmo Zumwalt, at midpoint in his tenure as Chief of Naval Operations and at a time of much racial mutiny on capital ships and others of the line, spoke out for all to hear about the need to give blacks a better break. The admirals probably would have stomached Zumwalt's dictum had he confined it to the wardrooms. Instead, he addressed his peroration to a group of admirals who were on staff duty in Washington and whom he had assembled expressly to provide himself a forum, and then saw to it that his remarks were distributed to a press which his peers believed had already made too much of a pet of him. In the Navy, by all that's a tight ship, you don't do that sort of thing. Zumwalt made powerful enemies, and lost forever his chance, if he ever had one, of being appointed Chairman of the Joint Chiefs of Staff. His enemies regarded him as a minstrel of the misbegotten, and consigned his future to Davey Jones.

Admiral Rickover has pricked his fellow admirals in public forums for decades, but has gotten away with it. His shock value has abated over time, and inside the Navy, his ripostes have come to be regarded as routine. There is very little the top brass can do about it, in any case, except to keep putting off his promotions. This has never stopped the promotions from coming. Congress, which seizes with satisfaction on his soundings off, has seen to it—by statute—that Rickover has risen through the ranks of admirals, over the Navy's head, to four-star status. Even Rickover's harshest critics concede that it was he, and he alone, who persisted in propelling the Navy into nuclear power back in the 1950s, and who saved it from becoming second to the Soviet fleet by the skin of its stern. The Rickover technique no doubt would get a lesser officer court-martialed, but it has worked beautifully for him. His national prestige, his popularity with Congress and his two-hat duty with the AEC and the Navy has permitted him to have his own way, one way or another, nearly all the time. Rickover scored his first success in the late 1940s when the first nuclear subs, the *Nautilus* and the *Seawolf*, were just a vision. At the time, the Department of Defense was balking over the need for nuclear power. So Rickover and the Congressional Joint Committee on Atomic Energy teamed up to bypass the Pentagon chiefs, persuading the Atomic Energy Commission to develop and build the reactors and then turn them over to the Navy, which couldn't just store them somewhere after all that. Since the success of this venture, and the vindication of Rickover's insistence on nuclear-powered submarines, the Joint Committee on Atomic Energy has been his biggest fan and staunchest supporter. He has a legion of friends on the Armed Services and Appropriations committees, too, and he used them, in the late 1960s, to snooker the Defense Department once again. Rickover wanted authorization of a new class of attack submarines with speeds well beyond the estimated 25 knots of the then-latest *Permit* and *Sturgeon* classes. The Defense Department had not denied him this wish, but had delayed a decision pending further study, and had given him no evidence that his wish would come true. When the department failed to ask Congress to authorize funds for the "fast" class of boats, Rickover characteristically cut out of channels and sped straight to Congress on his own to seek the money. From the Armed Services Committees he secured as many millions as he needed to buy the long-lead items for the new nuclear-propulsion plant that the fast subs would require. From the Joint Committee on Atomic Energy he secured insurance money—several millions more for his naval reactors program than the AEC had requested. Those subs are in the fleet today, and Rickover still is not satisfied.

Biding their time until the salty septuagenarian retires or dies, the Navy brass barely tolerates the scathing way he often speaks of their strategies and their weapons programs, and puts up with his lesser scattershots, such as the one that the U.S. Naval Academy perpetuates juvenility and turns too many bright young men into Annapolis automatons who cannot cope with the rigors of independent thinking. Rickover has had many unkind things to say about the U.S. shipbuilding industry, too, and the captains of that industry have never been able to understand his complete indifference to their pleas that they must turn a pretty fair profit. He insists that it is their patriotic duty to build Navy ships and submarines and build them perfectly, profit or no. He is roughshod with them. In 1974, he bulldozed through the top levels of the Defense Department a ruling which denied Todd Shipyards Corporation priority, under the Defense Production Act, on deliveries of steel. Todd needed the steel to build merchant ships. Rickover was mad at Todd—and at other yards—for shifting their resources away from Navy ships to production of higher-profit crude-oil tankers and liquefied natural-gas carriers. Lacking the Pentagon's assurance of priority for steel, Todd was forced to ditch its plans for a $100-million shipyard in Galveston, Texas, where it had proposed to build such merchantmen. Even though every defense and industry official involved in the case attributed the blockage of Todd steel to Rickover, his own straight-faced response was: "I had nothing to do with it. How can I block a Defense Department priority?"

Rickover lets almost nothing pass. His scorn for systems analysts and for bureaucrats in and out of uniform is blistering. At one point, he took disdainful note of an effusive, multipage holiday greeting from the Chief of Naval Matériel which congratulated all hands on having done "a splendid job for the Navy" and which remarked on the progress in "clarifying and gaining acceptance of the organizational concepts under which the Naval Matériel Command operates," etc., etc. Wrote Rickover in reply: "Considering the problems the Navy has been encountering and the need for greater economy, I believe that the Chief of Naval Matériel's message of holiday cheer could be greatly reduced without diminution of substance. I, therefore, recommend the following succinct greeting: 'Happy New Year.'" But this sort of thing was mere byplay for the Navy's buzzsaw. When it came to what he lived for, wrote *Seapower* magazine: "One is tempted to predict that in [the year] 2000, H. G. Rickover, 100 years old and the Navy's first eight-star 'double' admiral, will still be urging Congress and the Secretary of Defense to build faster, quieter, deeper diving and better armed attack submarines."

Over the years, research and development of attack submarines had consumed a steady 7 percent or better of the Navy's R&D budget. But the five-year projection of that budget, the one that looked ahead to 1980, showed only about 4 percent per year for the hunter-killers. Rickover contended that this slippage of attack-submarine R&D already was resulting in work falling behind schedule or not being done at all on advanced sonars, electronic countermeasures, hydrodynamics, communications, silencing techniques and navigation. This was the upshot, he said, of "the hidden fight going on all the time against submarines."

"And you are," the admiral was asked at a Senate Armed Services session, "unable to persuade the Secretary of Defense and the Secretary of the Navy of the importance of this?"

RICKOVER: "Well, the real decisions are made by the Chief of Naval Operations, and you know that as well as I do. I can talk to you as a nice naval officer, or I can tell you the truth as I see it. Which do you prefer?"

The admirals of Navair and Navships only smile grimly when asked to comment on Rickover's runs on their money and their rectitude. The last thing they want is to engage him in a running battle of barbs. In the spring of each year, he gets it all off his chest before the Congressional committees (House Appropriations Chairman George Mahon of Texas once remarked that Rickover's appearance as a witness is "always one of the highlights of the year" in what is otherwise a leaden litany of milito-lingual witnesses for this and that weapon system. Rickover then proceeded to tell the bemused committee why the nation desperately needed tax reform). After his road shows on the Hill, Rickover retires to the business of his reactors, and things settle back into place. But in recent years, his harpoonings have been hitting the nonsubmariners where they hurt. For despite Rickover's protestations to the contrary, nuclear submarines have been soaking up enormous amounts of the Navy's annual budgets. Research and development of Trident, alone, accounted for more than 6 percent of the entire Navy budget of $28.9 billion for fiscal 1975 (including pay, maintenance, mothballing: *everything*) and for a dock-walloping two-thirds of the cost of all Navy research and development. Moreover, the estimated cost of all Trident procurement— probably to come out to around $15 billion in the unlikely event that all goes perfectly—would be enough to finance half the Navy budget of any one year. Add Polaris-Poseidon to this, and you begin to see why the other admirals regard Rickover as a self-serving insatiate. Then throw in the $500 million a year that the Navy has been spending on the fast *Los Angeles* class of submarines, and Rickover comes off as a caterwauler without a case. None of this is to suggest that Rickover is against all surface craft; only those which are diesel-powered. If he'd had his way, the entire fleet—not just submarines, three carriers and a frigate—would have been running on reactors long since. Following the Mideast war and during the oil embargo in 1974, Rickover lunged to the advantage in the Pentagon and on Capitol Hill. He pointed out that it was costing twenty-five dollars a barrel to buy and deliver oil to diesel-powered aircraft carriers. Using this as a base, he figured out that the cost of fueling nuclear task forces—a carrier and its four or more escort ships—would cost only a pittance more than the refueling of diesel task forces. This would go a long way toward justifying an all-nuclear Navy, he said, and Defense Secretary James Schlesinger seemed to be leaning his way. As usual, the House Armed Services Committee fell over itself following Rickover, and stuck into its military authorization bill a section which did indeed mandate nuclear power for all major ships of the line.

"They say," said Rickover speaking of his Pentagon bosses, "that if I can get money out of Congress, in addition to what is needed for all of the other things in the Naval budget, they will then build the nuclear ships. And that is where we stand. And yet, the lessons of naval warfare in the last fifty years are pretty plain. The Germans came pretty close to winning both world wars on account of submarines. . . . The value of submarines is forgotten now in a desire to have what is called a balanced Navy. The Navy's idea of balance is like a chicken-horseburger sandwich: one horse, one chicken. The Navy has many surface-ship officers who see promotion and command opportunity denied them if we get more nuclear submarines."

At the time of this Rickover blast, the Navy had eighty-five attack submarines at sea, sixty-one of them powered by his reactors and twenty-four by diesel engines. Fifteen more nuclear subs were under construction or contract, and Rickover had in hand enough money to award contracts for long-lead equipment for the powerplants and hulls of another dozen or so. What it all meant was that the Navy, in the mid-1970s, was committed to production of a fleet of at least ninety nuclear attack subs. Would that be all? Or would there be more? Eighteen of the submarines would be spanking-fast. This number, cried the critics, should be enough, in view of the dilapidated state of the surface fleet and of the need to diversify antisubmarine warfare forces through a wider array of speedier ships, helicopters, planes, and listening devices. There was simply too much overloading of the ASW forces with hunter-killer submarines, they said.

The mission of the submarine as a killer of other submarines is a relatively new one. In February 1945, the British submarine *Venturer* sank the German U-864 while both were submerged at periscope depth in the North Atlantic. While submerged submarines have sunk many surfaced submarines, the feat of the *Venturer* is the only recorded instance of two subs going at it in their mutual element. Now, however, the chief chore of whole schools of hunter-killers is to destroy enemy ballistic-missile and attack subs. They form undersea barriers by patrolling "choke points" through which their adversaries of the deep would have to pass to reach the open sea during wartime. But this tactic was becoming questionable. If the Soviets were preparing to start a war, said the questioners, they almost surely would disperse their submarine fleets to the open seas beforehand. The FBM boats, no doubt, were already there. Such dispersal, so the argument went, would place even greater urgency on developing surface ships, aircraft and listening devices which could find and track those subs with much greater efficiency than our submarines could do it. And although the U.S. attack submarines had demonstrated that they could indeed trail the Soviet FBM subs, how would it be possible to trail probably as many as sixty of those subs all at once? This would leave too few U.S. submarines to perform other missions, such as protecting U.S. fleets and stalking Soviet men-of-war. Moreover, the Soviet FBM submarines were credited with being able to launch their sixteen missiles, in series, in about four minutes, faster than the Polaris-Poseidon boats could do it. Would that be enough time for a U.S. attack-sub skipper to detect the first launch, and get his torpedoes to target before all the bombs had gone? There was another grating question, too. Navymen who resisted Rickover's incessant campaigning for ever more powerful reactors to squeeze a few extra knots out of his submarines contended that the added speed of the *Los Angeles*-class boats—which cost twice as much as those of the *Sturgeon* class and are 2,500 tons heavier—actually works to some disadvantage. Their noisier powerplants and the friction-furious rush of water around their hulls at top speed make it easier for enemy sonarmen to hear them, and harder for their sonarmen to hear the enemy. Besides, why all the speed, when they did not need it to stay with Soviet subs, and had in their tubes the new flash-fast Mark 48 torpedoes.

The Mark 48, a product of Ocean Systems Division of Gould, Inc., contains as much electronics, pound for pound, as the newest air-launched missile. An antiship and antisubmarine torpedo, with a guidance system that makes it more an underwater missile, it will by 1980 have replaced the obsolete and not very reliable Mark 37 torpedo in all submarines and in as many as one hundred surface ships—mainly destroyers and destroyer escorts. The Navy will pay out, during this period, $70 to $80 million a year for the Mark 48. It is designed to be the mainstay anti-submarine torpedo of the fleet until the twenty-first century, and the bits of information which are available about its performance indicate that it is indeed a technological marvel. It is played out by wire—some ten miles of wire. But its range is much greater. When the wire is gone a computer takes over for another (classified) number of miles, as the eighteen-foot, two-ton fish picks up to a speed of probably 40 knots or more, faster by far than any submarines likely to be found in the Soviet fleet. The Mark 48 is designed to explode when it gets within a few yards of its quarry, rupturing the pressure hull. It will explode underneath the hulls of surface vessels. It also may replace the Mark 46 torpedo, now deployed only on surface ships, in the Navy's plans for "Project Captor," an acoustical mine planted by planes, subs or ships, which in turn launches a torpedo on sensing the passage of vessels whose powerplants and other emissions are peculiar to those of the enemy.

Along with conventional torpedoes, a kill weapon used by submarines is SUBROC, a short-range torpedo-missile which is launched into the atmosphere. It then flies to the vicinity of its target, plunges back into the sea, homes on its prey and detonates a conventional or nuclear warhead in its nose. SUBROC is not to be confused with submarine-fired tactical or strategic cruise missiles, which are something else again in the wonderworld of weaponry. They are central to Department of

Defense plans—as we shall see later in this chapter—in which Admiral Rickover, for once, did not get his way.

The next war could just as easily be conflagrated at sea and, in the extreme likelihood of its escalation into nuclear Armageddon, be finished off with missiles from the sea. Among all the varieties of arms races in the worldwide technological track meet, the marathon of most immediate menace may be taking place on and under the oceans, in more oceans than ever before. A shooting match at sea, in the opinion of many U.S. naval strategists, is almost inevitable, sooner or later. The United States probably would win a strung-out slugging match because of its superior airpower and firepower. But this is by no means certain. The Russian fleet bristles with ship-to-ship and sub-to-ship guided missiles which far overmatch their U.S. counterparts in numbers. Withal, it probably is an academic exercise by now to indulge in the traditional sort of naval "war gaming." Shots at sea between opposing task forces, or between individual warships, would be only a preliminary to the main event, which quickly would degrade homelands into wastelands, leaving every ship and submarine to fend for herself on oceans befouled and no longer worth disputing. Still, neither the U.S. nor the Soviet naval tacticians can afford to concede to cataclysm and ignore the problems which they keep posing for one another.

The Soviets were building submarines and capital ships at white-water speed. They had sent to sea about forty-five *Yankee*-class FBM submarines of sixteen tubes apiece—boats comparable to Polaris-Poseidon—and at least three Delta-class FBM subs. The Deltas had only twelve tubes each, but those tubes contained Sawfly missiles of about 4,000-mile range, a monumental leap forward for the Soviets. It meant that the *Delta* boats need not pass southward from the Norwegian Sea through the U.S. barriers of submarines, ships and hydrophones to the east and west of Iceland. They could remain on station north of there, even just a short distance out in Kola Bay from their homeport at Murmansk, and still strike Washington. Even so, five or six or more Soviet FBM subs were ranging off the U.S. Atlantic, Pacific and Caribbean coasts at all times, and they, along with their smaller-sister hunter-killers, now were using Cuba as a stopover. Altogether, the Soviets had 250 diesel and more than 110 nuclear subs available for prowling, and the nuclear-powered hunter-killers were splashing down the ways at the steady rate of four a year. Their *Charlie*-class attack submarines brandished 200-mile tactical missiles, as did their guided-missile cruisers, coming off the line at the rate of one per annum. Until Rickover's *Los Angeles*-class attack subs began joining the fleet, the Soviet *Charlie*-class boats could run faster and dive deeper than any in U.S. service. In the opinion of our Navymen, these boats and their kin would be quite capable of shutting off the Persian Gulf, for one, to commercial shipping, and it would take only a short time after that for the economy of western Europe to grind down for lack of oil, with the economy of the United States not too far behind.

Representative Les Aspin (D.-Wisc.), a maverick member of the House Armed Services Committee and a former Defense Department systems analyst who delights in baiting the brass, was among those who believed that while there was reason to be concerned about the Soviet buildup, the U.S. Navy was being too alarmist about it, was overblowing it to get the money to modernize the U.S. fleet at flank speed. Writing in *Foreign Policy* magazine, Aspin said in part:

The Pentagon likes to have Congress play these comparison [of weapons and forces] games, even though such comparisons are usually irrelevant. The Russians often have different types of forces just because they have different geographical and strategic needs. Congress listens to briefings about how many more submarines the Russians have without once hearing the briefer explain that the Russians are building a large submarine fleet to interdict the U.S. naval supply lines in a time of war, and that the United States does not need so many submarines because the Russians do not have long naval supply lines. But the Pentagon does not explain comparisons, it only makes them. The Navy is probably better at this than anybody else in the Pentagon: when necessary, the Navy can come up with a whole new set of statistics to reinforce an otherwise questionable argument. . . .

Vice-Admiral W. J. Moran, Director of the Navy Office of Research and Development, Test and Evaluation, was no fan of Aspin's line. Moran was as attentive as the next blue-suiter to the Soviet buildup at sea. Yet he sat erectly at his Pentagon desk and put the buildup into a perspective not at all panicky.

"I think we're seeing," he said, "a growing need of all the navies of the world—our navy, the Soviet navy, everybody's navy—to use the oceans more in every sense. All navies are showing steady growth. What are the Soviets really doing? Go back in the history of the United States, back to the whaling ships and the clipper ships. We established our presence in all the ports of the world, and we built our Navy to protect our maritime commerce, just as the British had done. We set up a system which ended up with the dollar established as the standard of world commerce. This had very much to do with industrial growth in the United States. There is a remarkable similarity in what the Russians are doing. They are building beautiful merchant and navy ships, the most modern of our day. They have excellent, well-trained, well-disciplined crews." He paused. "We are," he said slowly, "seeing ourselves starting to share the world with our competitors, and we must have a modern Navy to permit us to compete."

Before a Congressional committee, as he sat amid Navy witnesses who had testified that the Russians were coming, Defense Secretary Schlesinger allowed as how their buildup was bad enough, but maybe not all that bad. The Navymen were discomfited. "The Soviet navy, contrary to some opinion," Schlesinger noted dryly in his Posture Statement, "is not presently growing in numbers. It is growing in capability. The Soviet navy has a vigorous shipbuilding program to replace older combatant ships with new, more capable types. By 1979, the Soviet Union could have several aircraft carriers of the *Kuril* class, the first of which is now approaching operational status. We expect their major surface combatants to continue for the next several years at a level of about 200 ships, nearly the same as the United States now has. We are seeing a decline in the overall size of the Soviet submarine force, as they retire older diesel ships at a greater than one-for-one rate as new nuclear submarines come into the fleet. Even so, we estimate that by the early 1980s the USSR will have approximately twice the planned United States submarine level. This relatively large Soviet submarine force will continue to pose the primary threat to our sea lanes throughout the decade. . . . In sum, as we look ahead, we see a Soviet navy that is becoming increasingly capable of overseas deployment, whose submarines could pose a significant threat to free world shipping, and whose surface combatants, with their considerable antiship cruise missile capability, could inflict serious damage on our naval forces in a surprise attack. . . ."

And then, Schlesinger got down to what navies are all about, in the context of the eternal war of economic and political systems: "We can and must become increasingly competitive with our potential adversaries in a more fundamental sense. We must not be forced out of the market—on land, at sea or in the air. Eli Whitney belongs to us, not to our competitors. He, rather than the medieval craftsmen of Mont St. Michel and Chartres—however magnificent and unique their art—must once more become our model."

The Soviets first showed in 1961 that they were dead serious about putting to sea. This may have been the result, nothing more, of a decision that their economic future demanded their becoming a maritime nation. Or it may have had something to do with the fact that U.S. Polaris submarines had begun setting up on stations all around Mother Russia. Whatever, the Soviet naval buildup picked up steam sharply the next year, after the Cuban missile crisis demonstrated to the Kremlin the military, diplomatic and political clout to be derived—as President Kennedy had derived it with his blockade of Soviet missile transporters—from seapower. In the next several years, the Russians dispersed many major elements of their burgeoning sea-strike force from the confined waters of the Mediterranean and the Baltic. They stationed a fleet of more than 150 submarines and about 50 surface ships in the Barents Sea, based at Severomorsk on the Kola Peninsula. They stationed another fleet of 120 submarines and about half that many surface ships in the Far East, out of Vladivostok and Petropavlovsk-Kamchatki. From the Barents, the Soviets deployed their forces through the Norwegian Sea and into the Atlantic, straddling the Great Circle commercial route to Europe and sweeping southward into an Atlantic once considered Anglo-American.

From their Pacific bases, they deployed to interdict, if need be, the North Pacific trade routes to Japan and China, and to show force in the Indian Ocean. Russian warships in the North Atlantic outnumbered all NATO craft in those waters by six to one. This alone shook an alliance of seafaring nations which already had lost France, was witnessing a Soviet army buildup east of the Elbe, had seen the Soviets crush Czechoslovakia and stir ominously during the Mideast war, and was, finally, made up of governments all the more precarious for their political and economic problems of the mid-seventies.

In the Mediterranean, by that time, Moscow's armada outnumbered, if not outgunned, the U.S. Sixth Fleet. The alarmist Admiral Zumwalt said that the Sixth Fleet could very well have lost a shootout during the Arab-Israeli war if air support from central Europe had not arrived in time to redress the Soviet punch at the opening bell. All this disturbed Italy, Turkey and Greece—and Yugoslavia, too. Through the years, the Kremlin's attempts to intervene in Yugoslavia's internal affairs and bring Marshal Tito back from revisionism had been based on one, big strategic goal: gaining access to Yugoslavia's Adriatic ports. No one doubted that if war came, or threatened to come, the Russians would sail in and take over those ports. Already ensconced in the Persian Gulf and Indian Ocean, the Soviets are expected to swarm into those waters once the Suez Canal is reopened in the latter half of the 1970s.

Although the submarines are the Soviets' front-line weapons at sea, they seldom are seen and therefore do not constitute a "show of force" which the U.S. Navy can reel out to sell skeptics. The Soviet surface fleet, now becoming studded with carriers of short-takeoff attack planes, is another matter. It is the visible entry in the flag-showing contest. In the summer of 1962, the Soviets conducted their major naval exercise of the year in the North Atlantic and the Norwegian Sea. It involved four surface warships, about twenty diesel submarines and a squadron or two of land-based patrol planes. It obviously was a demonstration of naval force designed to defend Soviet shores. In April 1970, they conducted another exercise, which they called "Okean," with about 150 surface ships, 50 submarines, most of them nuclear, and several hundred planes. The surface ships included two new guided-missile helicopter carriers and flotillas of new, fast, missile-equipped cruisers and destroyers. The Russians ran these exercises in the Baltic,

Norwegian, Barents, Black, Philippine and Mediterranean seas, the Sea of Japan, and the Atlantic, Pacific and Indian oceans. They had become a fleet for the attack. The strongest signal that this was so emanated from their new emphasis on carriers. Once, they had disdained carriers as floating coffins. No longer. Deploying far from home, they would need air power.

In his way, Sergei G. Gorshkov is the Rickover of the Russians, only more so. Bearer of the one-and-only rank of Admiral of the Fleet of the Soviet Union, Gorshkov led the Russian navy out of Black Sea bondage to sail the world. In *Morskoi Sbornik (Naval Almanac)* Admiral Gorshkov proudly wrote of how his navy had become a first-class "blue-water" strike force. His article, in part, went like this:

> In light of what has been said above, the old well-known formula—the battle of the first salvo—is taking on a special meaning in naval battle under present-day conditions—conditions including the possible employment of combat means of colossal power. Delay in the employment of weapons in a naval battle or operation inevitably will be fraught with the most serious and even fatal consequences, regardless of where the fleet is located. . . .

To the admirals of the United States Navy, this came through ominously like the filing of a hair trigger, and it prodded them to make haste. Some others, however, noted that if you were a Russian, and you had taken the time over the years to read U.S. Navy journals and the death-dealing testimony of all the admirals before Congress, you might have been justified in developing a full-blown paranoia yourself.

"It must be spring again," editorialized the Louisville *Courier-Journal*. "Not only are the birds and blossoms bursting out, but those pesky Soviet submarines are popping up off the Atlantic coast. They may well be cruising around there all year, but isn't it funny that the Defense Department only seems to get agitated in the spring—at budget time? There's nothing like raising a patrol of enemy warships within missile firing distance of Washington, D.C., to discourage Congress from quibbling too long over the Defense Department's appropriation. . . ."

And Senator McIntyre, he of the futile stand against

Schlesinger's Counterforce doctrine, was at it again, too. "Our Navy," he said, "habitually counts the Soviet diesel submarine as an important part of the formidable Russian submarine fleet, as if they somehow equate with ours. So this year I have been asking each Navy witness if they would like to have some diesel submarines in our own fleet. 'Oh, no,' they say. 'They're too noisy. They're old technology.' So let's not forget or discount the quality of our own military technology, a technology that has been richly funded and represents the premier product of American engineering, scientific and industrial talent. The Soviet subs are *not* as quiet. Their missiles are *not* as accurate. Their warheads are *not* as efficient. Their computers are *not* as advanced. Their antisubmarine warfare is *not* as effective. Their sub-launched missiles are *not* MIRVed. My point is simply that to assume in every case that the Soviets are better than us is as uncritical as to assume, as we once did, that American know how is in every case better. What we need to do is discriminate realistically, to identify real gaps or advantages, so we can allocate our R&D monies accordingly."

Pounding on the witness table over on the other side of Capitol Hill, Admiral Rickover slammed away. "I believe it is clear," he gritted, "that the Soviets must believe it is credible that there could be a United States-Soviet confrontation at sea, because the Soviets are pouring vast resources into a navy capable of challenging our Navy at sea. If they did not consider that to be credible, I can see no logical reason why they would be building the particular fleet they are building. There is no fleet other than ours in the world for the Soviets to challenge. If we are unable to provide naval support to overseas forces, then we are not able to conduct overseas operations of any kind —by the Army, Navy or Air Force. Practically, we have no other way than to send our supplies by sea."

In this rhetorical ramming, Rickover was making a point very special to him. "The Soviet navy," he said, "recognized the great potential for tactical cruise missile submarines many years ago. Their surface-launched submarine missile has been deployed for over ten years. The Soviet navy has progressed through five classes of tactical cruise missile-firing submarines, but I have not been able to get even one of these submarines approved by our Navy."

The Navy, backed by the Department of Defense, had

tacked into Rickover's teeth on that issue. He had dreamed of a giant attack submarine armed with tactical missiles of about 200-mile range to be launched against surface ships, as well as with torpedoes for underwater infighting. It was conceivable that such submarines could even displace carriers as the capital ships of the fleet. Now, however, the miniaturization of electronics and the compact packaging of their computers, altimeters, accelerometers and the like had made it possible to develop a tactical cruise missile, called Harpoon, small enough to be fired from the tubes of the *Los Angeles*-class attack subs for which Rickover had fought so furiously. Beyond that, the technology worked up by McDonnell Douglas and its subcontractors for Harpoon was marriageable with the strategic cruise missile of 1,500- to 2,000-mile range. That missile, too, would be fired from the tubes of subs already at sea, or under construction or contract ahead to 1980. Rickover's dreams of giant attack-missile subs seemed to have been dashed. They would have cost an estimated $300 million apiece, or about half again as much as a *Los Angeles*-class boat, and the Navy needed to do without them if it could. Rickover, however, was far from defeated. He viewed Harpoon, which had been designed originally for launching by planes and surface ships, as an interim missile at best, certainly far from proven as a submarine weapon. It would have to be launched from torpedo tubes in a buoyant capsule. The capsule would surface, and then Harpoon's engine would fire and away it would go, on low-level trajectory. But even if Harpoon did indeed prove unsuitable for submarine launch, the early indications were that its strategic-range cousin might be sufficiently versatile—in its ability to speed up and slow down, to pick and choose ranges—to double as a short-range tactical missile into the bargain. Even as Rickover dourly noted the omission in the 1975 Defense Department budget of R&D money for a submarine tailored to missiles, and the inclusion in that budget of much R&D money for missiles tailored to submarines, the strategic cruise missiles were well on their way to prototype testing. The program was being directed by Captain Walter E. Locke, USN, whose offices—significantly—were situated in Navair, not among the submariners. Locke, wistful about the way the big-brother ballistic-boat programs had "sucked up all the money all these years," told how the TERCOM guidance system of his cruise missiles already had been tested satisfactorily with "off the shelf" electronics which were actually inferior to the real thing to come.

TERCOM stands for Terrain Contour Matching, wherein the missile's map-memorizing computer matches up what the missile "sees" as it cruises along with what it is supposed to be seeing on course to target. The conventional U.S. Coast and Geodetic Survey maps were not detailed enough to be fed into TERCOM's missile computers. The missiles' maps had to come from the Defense Mapping Agency, headquartered at the U.S. Naval Observatory in Washington proper. To achieve the quintessential contour cartography demanded by the missile computers, DMA draws from the enormous stacks of practically on-scale closeups of the Soviet Union as photographed by U.S. spy satellites. Many in the Navy and the Defense Department were reluctant to discuss this aspect, but Captain Locke, a quiet-spoken officer, had no reservations. "What good are deterrents if no one knows we have them or what we can do with them?" he asked.

To test out TERCOM, the Navy put its guidance system into a pod affixed to the wing of an A-7 attack plane, and let the computer in the pod tell the pilot where to head. New England was chosen for testing because its terrain closely approximates that on the way to an appropriate target area in Russia. TERCOM must be sensitive, for example, to such nuances of nature, as seen from above, as the seasonal changes of foliage and waterways. Feed the missile's computer a picture of the terrain on the way to Tyuratam in May, and it will not steer the missile to Tyuratam in November.

The A-7 took off from the Patuxent River Naval Air Station, Maryland, flew to a point near Boston and then, on the electronic steering of TERCOM, doglegged over all the New England states and eastern New York State until—there it was, right underneath, the target, the Burlington, Vermont, airport.

Too bad TERCOM cannot help the Navy sense, chase, find and finish off enemy submarines. For this, the Navy had plans for a new kind of fleet through the remainder of the twentieth century, a guerrilla fleet, a superfast one—in the notion that the ultimate weapon against submarines and ships is not speed under the sea but speed on top.

"The Navy," wrote the Brookings Institution analysts in their report on the 1975 federal and defense budgets, "faces the worst modernization problem. The number of aircraft carriers will decline to 12 by around 1980, simply by virtue of the age of existing carriers and the long lead times necessary to build new ones. In order to maintain 12 carriers indefinitely, moreover, the Navy soon must begin to replace the seven vessels commissioned from 1955 through 1961. Because of fiscal constraints, these ships are not likely to be supercarriers like the *Nimitz*, joining the fleet in fiscal 1975, which cost more than $1 billion. According to Secretary Schlesinger, future carriers will be much smaller than the *Nimitz* and possibly not nuclear powered; they will cost about $600 million apiece."

The huge fleet of sleek new ships that the Navy built during and right after World War II had become doddering by the 1970s. Far more were being retired each year than were being built, and the new ones, embodying the most sophisticated technologies and trying to be all things for all purposes, cost so much that there was no way they could replace the retirees one for one. So the Navy came up against the dilemma common to all the services: what to do, ask for impossible budgets, cut forces, or build cheaper ships? For several years, the Navy tried to do the first, minimize doing the second, and reject doing the third. This eventuated in a reduction of vessels from the level of 976 in 1968 to a low of 508 by mid-1976. But the Navy's plans for a hit-and-run, hide-and-seek surface fleet began jelling, and it was possible, at the beginning of 1975, for new Chief of Naval Operations James L. Holloway III, a trained technologist and surface-fleet veteran (accent on aircraft carriers), to project a fleet of 600 or more vessels—with about 230 major combat ships—into 1980, and then a leveling off. In 1975, for the first time in recent memory, the Navy planned to send more new ships to sea than it retired. Picking up where Zumwalt had left off, and with the support of Schlesinger, Holloway drew the line at about 90 attack submarines, all told, instead of the 105 or more which the Navy once had ascribed as the minimum needed in the 1980s. Holloway also signed off on a plan to slow the production rate of the hunter-killers from five a year to five every two years. Rickover had seen it coming, sure enough.

The tendency of the Congressional committees to roll over

for Rickover undoubtedly had something to do with their reluctance, at first, to go along with the plans of the Navy brass and the Defense Department for a surface fleet that promised to revolutionize naval warfare in the last quarter of the twentieth century. Those plans probably were overdue, and seemed sound enough in view, again, of the advances of permissive technologies. But Capitol Hill's kingpins, evoking costs this time as a red herring for a submarine, hemmed, hawed and did all they could to hamstring.

It made no difference on the fourth-floor flag bridge in the E Ring corridor of the Pentagon. The sailors in supremacy there had in their sights a lean, mean fleet of ships remindful of John Paul Jones and his *Ranger*. It would taunt the enemy with its speed and destroy him with its firepower. It would be a "high-low mix" of supercarriers and pocket carriers to be called Sea Control Ships, too small to board conventional jets but with short decks accommodating helicopters and vertical and short-takeoff (V/STOL) aircraft, outgrowths of the British-built *Harrier* then in service with the U.S. Marines. The SCS would look something like, but be somewhat larger than, the Soviet pocket carriers *Moskva* and *Leningrad*, whose flight decks do not stretch stem to stern. The SCS ships would double as attack and antisubmarine warfare carriers. Ten or more would be built in the decade starting about 1978, and thus they would average out to less than twenty years of age by the year 2000. There was active speculation in the Navy that these ships might even turn out to be, before all were built, double-hulled catamarans (all design credit to the Polynesians). With conventional hulls, argued the catamaran enthusiasts, the small SCS ships—about 20,000 tons as compared with the 75,000 to 95,000 tons of the present-day giant attack carriers—would pitch too violently in heavy seas for the liking of their incoming pilots. We may yet see SCS ships with twin hulls and fins. But for now, the Navy believes that conventional hulls will suffice; vertical-lift planes and helicopters should not be bothered by heavy seas.

Along with the plans for Sea Control Ships, the Navy was putting into service in the mid-seventies new, much-faster destroyers, destroyer escorts and patrol frigates (half the size of oldtime destroyers), plus a new class of ship called DLGN, for destroyer leader armed with guided missiles. These were programmed to replace—and far outnumber, in the end—the nine cruisers still at sea but getting old. There also would be amphibious, helicopter-carrying warships of sufficient number to land an entire Marine or infantry division. Already at sea were the nuclear frigates *Bainbridge* and *Truxton,* and the nuclear cruiser *Long Beach.* The *Bainbridge,* in fact, replaced the aging carrier *Hancock* as the capital ship and chief show of U.S. force in the Indian Ocean during the latter stages of the Arab-Israeli War of 1973. And these ships were being joined by the first of the line of DLGNs—the *California* and the *South Carolina.*

All of this would seem futuristic enough for a service which had tended to resist charting courses on tangent to the traditional. But it was only the beginning, and the admirals had become peppy about what lay ahead. They foresaw a brand-new breed of ship, of pizzaz and punch never seen on the oceans of Earth. These would be big, 2,000-ton Surface Effects Ships (SES), capable of speeds of 50 and, someday, 80 to 100 knots as they streaked along on self-created air bubbles, their skirts skimming the wavetops. Complementing them would be other, smaller hydrofoils, of about 100 tons, also armed with missiles, for sentry duty and slashing attacks at close quarters. The bigger of these hydrofoils would attack with their own weapons and with the vertical-takeoff planes and helicopters which they would ferry. Of them, Zumwalt had said:

> They will give us a capability to make great end runs around the presence of missile-firing submarines and surface ships, the capability to rapidly reinforce naval forces with the surface-to-surface missile. And with that kind of speed, all the aircraft that we have in our modern inventory are in essence V/STOL [the "S" stands for "short"] because they could land and take off vertically as the ship makes 100 knots. So the SES has a tremendous capacity to change the whole nature of warfare. It could make as much of a breakthrough in the nature of war at sea as nuclear propulsion did when it first came along.

Ah, but where would that leave Rickover's reactors?

The smaller hydrofoils of 100 tons and up would form a "shadow fleet," stalking the warships which the Soviets sent out to stalk U.S. fleets. They would trail the trailers. They would hit hard and be hard to hit. And they would be ideal for antisubmarine warfare, overtaking submarines hither and yon and outsprinting not only the subs but their torpedoes. These ships, also, could carry helicopters or even a vertical-lift plane or two.

What it came down to was that every single ship in the Navy's future was being designed or dreamed of as a formidable combination of its own speed, searching ability and striking power and the speed, searching ability and striking power of the planes—fixed-wing, V/STOL, V/TOL or helicopter—that it would carry. In short, every ship of the line, by the turn of the century and perhaps well before, would launch some kind of aircraft. None of the ships would be large enough (although 10,000-ton hydrofoils were already on the drawing boards) to mount many squadrons of planes. But they would be fast enough to spread out at sea (an old infantry tactic) and then cluster at the scene of the fight.

"One can imagine," wrote L. Edgar Prina in *Seapower*, "what a 10,000-ton SES, armed with the latest mix of missiles and new rapid-fire bombardment guns which shoot extended-range shells [made deadlier by terminal guidance], and able to cross the Atlantic in little more than a day, will do to naval tactics, strategy and base structure."

Until surface speed becomes a transcendental factor in the fight against submarines, the Navy will continue to piece together the complex system of ships, helicopters, patrol planes, attack submarines and moored, suspended and towed arrays of hydrophones and sonobuoys which make up ASW in its abundant aggregate. If you include all the money for all the big ships, planes and attack subs which have at least a partial ASW mission, the ASW portion of the Navy budget comes out to about $7 billion, or about one-fourth, a year. But this tells more than the whole story. Those big weapons systems are used for other purposes, too, and cannot be counted as wholly ASW systems. There are, of course, exceptions, notably the land-based four-engine turboprop P-3C Orion (an electronics Electra) and the twin-engine, heavily armed, electronics-crammed, sonobuoy-sowing, carrier-based S-3A Viking jet just entering service in 1974. The Navy also was developing, in 1975, a tactic which many ASW officers thought would be the best seeker-spotter of all, called LAMPS (for Light Airborne Multi-Purpose System). It would be geared to new helicopters flying off the fantails of destroyers and frigates. But none of the air, sea or undersea ASW systems could be all-purpose. The ASW mission is too copious for that. It involves a multitude of much different activities, all of which have something to do, and some of which have more to do than others, with the spotting, fixing, tracking and killing missions of the ASW mosaic. What's more, there are two divergent ASW aims, each involving specialized tactics. One is to find and destroy ballistic-missile submarines; the other, to find and destroy attack submarines which threaten our military and commercial shipping. A largely unnoticed goal of some arms control advocates in recent years has been to get the government and the Navy to ease up in efforts to track Russian FBM submarines, to get the Russians to do likewise, and permit all FBMs to roam unchallenged. Nothing worries either side more than the ASW threat of the other. Therefore, say the advocates of ASW controls, if this worry were lifted through a permissible standoff of strategic subs, stability of a sort might be attained in the arms race.

In the antisubmarine offices at the Pentagon, and at the new complex of high-rises off U.S. Route One nearby, such an approach is regarded as heretical and downright dangerous. The counterargument of the officers who man these offices is that since ASW is so diversified and so hush-hush an oceanic art form (or formless art), how could either side ever be sure that the other has ceased perpetuating it? There seems to be no way ever to inspect ASW while ASW is inspecting—or not inspecting—submarines. And as a matter of unilateral urgency, the U.S. Navy would not think of relenting in its pursuit of a Soviet sub fleet expanding faster than our own.

So the Navy, in 1975, was spending about $4 billion on ASW, and preparing to increase this amount yearly through the remainder of the decade, at least. With all this money pouring out, and all those new systems coming in, the wide-eyed insisted that an ASW breakthrough simply had to be inevitable. No problem, they said, could withstand the penetration of all those wonderful ASW technologies which were being brought to bear. But wait. A closer examination of the budget showed that of the total $3 billion being spent on all types of Navy research and development, only about $200 million could be classified as funding for exploration of ASW technologies, scattered across dozens of programs, throughout the intricate welter of industry and Navy laboratories. Beefing up these R&D programs, and getting a clearer picture of them as they pertained to one another, quickly became one of the chief goals of Dr. Malcolm Currie, the new director of defense research and engineering. Meanwhile, the Navy Office of the Director of Antisubmarine Warfare, an arm of the Chief of Naval Operations, kept plugging along trying to make sense and order of the whole ASW operation.

"Making advances in ASW is a tedious, inch-by-inch process," said Vice-Admiral Harold E. Shear, the head of that office. Shear did not interview comfortably. He is a stern-faced admiral, not much for extraneous conversation. Besides, there isn't much that a strictly ASW admiral can talk about without butting up against superclassified information. In all the military, there is no topic more whisper-whetting than what's going on in ASW. Some of the work the Navy does not even admit even after its nature has sneaked into print. Officers directly involved in workaday ASW are not available to the press. They, even more than the submariners, have become the "silent service." Other officers, not directly but peripherally involved in ASW, turn mute at the mention of it. Admiral Shear did, however, emphasize the "big changes" in its nature.

"In World War II," he said, "ASW was confined to the escort ring of ships around convoys and task forces. Today, it takes in entire ocean basins. Tactical ASW [that aimed at spotting the attack submarines] takes in a 200-mile radius at the very minimum. If we can't detect, track and localize submarines within several hundred miles of the fleet, our first indication that one is out there will be a missile coming at us several feet above the surface. No one part of the ASW system can handle it alone; it takes a combination of all of them, and it probably always will. Of the three fundamentals—detecting, localizing and killing—the toughest is to detect."

Success at detection depends to a great extent on mastery of the technology of underwater acoustics. As submarines become quieter and cruise deeper, the dimensions of the detection problem expand exponentially. The ocean, with its varied and shifting thermal layers, salinity, pressures and noises, is the natural enemy. It muffles and muddles sounds. For all the research that the Navy has done on sonar, it concedes that its equipment is reliable for distances of only about fifteen miles, under the most favorable of underwater conditions. Those conditions may be favorable in one location one day, unfavorable there the next. But what the Navy disclaims for its sonars may not be the whole truth. In buffaloing the enemy, bending the truth sometimes can be as effective as buttoning it up—and certainly more diversionary. Still, Navy sources say that sonar is of almost no value, for example, in the Mediterranean—a fish pond compared to the Atlantic and Pacific—unless the Russian subs come within "kill" range, which they often, and easily, do.

Sonar is an "active" system. It transmits a signal in order to receive an acoustic reflection. When the Navy figured out how to make sonobuoys active, it named the new system that embodied them "Julie," after a Philadelphia stripteaser who had a reputation for turning passive boys into active boys. This is not to suggest that the Navy takes its sonobuoys and sonars lightly. They are the pulses of a potpourri of underwater systems, along with a myriad electronic devices aboard satellites and aircraft. Some of these employ infrared, in much the same way as an infrared missile homes on the engine heat of an enemy aircraft, to watch for changes in the temperature of the ocean surface which might be made by a submarine cruising underneath. Another airborne system has the acronym MAD, for Magnetic Anomaly Detector. This one spots the movements of submarines by reacting to the changes which they generate in the planet's magnetic field. While these systems search and spot—none all that successfully, yet—they seem less promising than the passive systems. These do not emit signals. They sit silently in the ocean, hundreds or thousands of feet down, cocked to the passage of submarines many miles away, alert to the sound "signatures" of the enemy engines.

The veteran among these systems is called SOSUS (Sound Surveillance System), a vast network of hydrophones which has been poised on the continental shelf off the U.S. Atlantic coast for several years. Outgrowths of SOSUS, all of them either experimental, still in the development stage, or yet to be turned into any kind of hardware, are the Moored Surveillance System (MSS), consisting of self-mooring hydrophone arrays dropped by aircraft, the Towed Array Surveillance System (TASS), arrays which trail behind U.S. ships and attack and FBM submarines, and the Suspended Array Surveillance System (SASS), the latest-comer and the mind-bender of the whole bunch. SASS was conceived as possibly a series of huge structures—hydrophone towers—scattered at depths down to 10,000 feet or more on abyssal plains near choke points through which Soviet submarines would have to pass. Another design mentioned for SASS (when it was mentioned at all, which was almost never) depicted giant-squid-like contrivances of hydrophone cables suspended upward from anchors thousands of feet into the depths. Why go so deep, when the submarines themselves cannot dive down there? Because sound travels extra-far and with special clarity in the deep ocean, below the thermocline. (The thermocline is a layer of ocean which separates the upper, warmer layers from those of the frigid lower depths. In the thermocline, temperature drops at least one degree centigrade with each meter increase of depth. A monster hydrophone array beneath the thermocline, where the water propagates sound practically to infinity, could monitor the movements of quiet, deep-running subs throughout the entire North Atlantic.)

SASS was so highly classified that when Schlesinger mentioned it in his statement accompanying the fiscal 1975 budget, the Navy was aghast. It was the very first time any defense official had so much as breathed of SASS in public. That Schlesinger had not elaborated on SASS was not at all mitigating, in the Navy's eyes. The mention was bad enough. "We took it out of his statement when we looked it over," one ASW official told me, "but he put it back in."

No listening device is worth a beep unless it can relay, on "real time," its signals to the shore stations and ships of a network called the ASW Centers Command and Control System. It would take a separate, too-technical chapter to describe the communications linkages involved. The key to the whole affair, as to all military systems technology nowadays, is the computer, storing messages, transmitting them to ships, planes and submarines, transcribing them from typewriter keyboards for display on tubes or tapes at the control stations of the hunter-killers of whatever description, calculating navigation and dead-reckoning positions of moving and stationary attackers and targets, computing for (and firing for) the full range of ASW weapons.

In the kaleidoscopic ASW picture at the Pentagon, SASS was competing for funding not only with the other surveillance systems, but with the air, space, submarine and surface systems as well. The admirals in these other bailiwicks were unenthusiastic about SASS. They pointed out, as part of their pressure against it, that it might be extremely vulnerable and outrageously cost-ineffective. Russian trawlers fish for more than fish in the open seas. Every now and then they cut—by accident, they say—a U.S. communications cable on the ocean floor. Imagine their satisfaction, said these U.S. admirals, on coming across a SASS data-link cable running shoreward across the bottom. SASS and the other passive systems had strong backing at the top levels of the Pentagon, however, and showed the added promise of compatibility with a fascinating signal-data-processing technique developed by the Defense Advanced Research Projects Agency (ARPA). It was named the "seismic array signal" technique because it was conceived and used to monitor underground nuclear explosions. The Naval Electronics Systems Command (NAVELEX) was given the job of assembling the data links and hardware which would be used to conduct "seismic array analysis" in detecting and locating submarines in such systems as SASS might turn out to be. Over the years, NAVELEX has been hampered—has been forced to claw for funds—by its position in the pecking order. Its commanding officer carries the rank of rear admiral. The CO's of all other ASW commands and of the research and development hierarchy as a whole, wear one star more. This, in view of the ascendancy of electronics in ASW and all things Navy, is due for a change.

ARPA had experimented with actually tracking submarines —not just detecting their presence—by processing, on real time, the signal-data outputs of several SOSUS arrays. ARPA researchers also had found, to the satisfaction of the SASS program officers, that low-frequency acoustic signals can propagate over enormous distances and remain coherent, relatively undiffused. Which meant that SASS might even become, someday, a Julie, too.

Created in the 1950s as part of the Directorate of Defense Research and Engineering, ARPA is a group of civilian and military scientists and engineers who oversee and coordinate the far-out research of think tanks, and military, industrial and university laboratories. At the mid-1970s, ARPA was devoting more than one-tenth of its $200-million annual budget to ASW research. In comparison, the agency's research of advanced weapons concepts—research which once had consumed the great bulk of its budgets—was accounting for about $25 million, or not much more than ASW. Dr. Stephen J. Lukasik, Director of ARPA, described its mission as basically one of "maintaining technological superiority" for the U. S. military. "Strategic deterrence is a major problem area," Dr. Lukasik said, "and the emphasis in ARPA is primarily on the undersea deterrent and the associated question of ASW. Our programs span a broad spectrum of technologies required for use by future advanced platforms and associated hardware. . . . Improved systems are required to address the threat which we postulate will be posed by quieter Soviet FBM submarines in the 1975-85 period."

Among Navy laboratories, the Naval Undersea Center (NUC) at San Diego emerged only lately as the one chiefly responsible for development of underwater array systems. NUC and other labs had engaged in undersea surveillance research for years, but such research did not have a home base until NUC was selected in 1972. Then, it became the one lab which NAVELEX could hold accountable for the advancement of research on developing the technologies perhaps the hardest of all to fathom. When a House subcommittee expressed bewilderment in trying to sort out the respective missions of NUC and of the Naval Underwater Systems Center (NUSC) at Newport, Rhode Island, the Navy supplied the following explanation, of value mostly in the range of work which it revealed.

The primary mission of the NUC is to be the principal Navy R,D,T&E center for underseas surveillance, ocean technology and advanced undersea weapons systems. NUC maintains in-house research and development capability for: undersea surveillance, undersea/surface weapons and fire-control systems, lightweight torpedoes, sonar for high-speed vehicles, high-resolution sonar systems, underwater acoustic warfare systems, remote-controlled underwater systems, ocean technology and engineering, marine biosciences, marine mammal systems, underwater acoustic propagation [Pacific and Arctic oceans], ASW support for the Pacific fleet, and Arctic submarine systems. . . . The primary mission of the NUSC is to be the principal center for underwater weapon systems . . . sonar systems [hull-mounted and towed], submarine communications systems integration (including submarine antenna systems), underwater target systems, underwater acoustic propagation (Atlantic Ocean and Mediterranean Sea), underwater range technology and ASW support, Atlantic fleet.

Neither of these sprawling East and West coast research centers cuts into the domain of the Naval Research Laboratory, which concentrates—harder and harder—on basic and applied research of the physics of sound in the sea. As the Defense Department and the Navy elevated ocean acoustics among their blue-ribbon priorities, complementary research in physical oceanography, marine geophysics and oceanic biology became concomitantly critical. The effects of water motions, waves, weather, underwater topography, commercial shipping and undersea organisms attracted intense attention for their cross-connections to ASW technology.

The Mid-Ocean Dynamics Experiment (MODE I), jointly supervised by the Office of Naval Research and the National Science Foundation, was the first grand-scale effort of its kind to utilize modern computer and communications systems as a research tool. The results excited the Navy. They showed the existence of large, slowly rotating pools in the upper layers of the oceans that seemed to influence the way the oceans change in response to various weather patterns. They also showed that water temperatures at the surface and at depths of as much as 2,000 feet may be closely related. If this relationship turned out to be fairly common, the refinement of infrared sensors in satellites and airplanes surely would become a "must" endeavor among all the many in ASW.

Undersea listening devices and undersea weapons are tested at the Atlantic Undersea Test and Evaluation Center (AUTEC), the Navy's most secret and heavily guarded ocean laboratory. AUTEC, off Andros Island, the Bahamas, is roughly 15 miles wide, 100 miles long and more than a mile deep—one of the underwater trenches of the Bahamas group. At AUTEC, attack submarines sneak around against hydrophones; torpedoes and mines are tested; sonobuoys qualify on their signaling, and encapsulated, torpedo-firing mines are activated. Surface ships and aircraft, even, use the AUTEC range.

Presiding at this smorgasbord of submarine and antisubmarine systems, of research on the rampage, was Admiral Moran, Director of the Office of R,D,T&E of a Navy that was riding high, living up to its backhand reputation among the other services as the most proficient fund-raising organization in the world, fathoming the fathoms, putting the visions of Verne into the modern vernacular.

"The problem with R&D in the Navy today," said Admiral Moran, "is to figure out where we will be in the mid-1980s, which isn't so far away. We can see new technologies coming over the horizon from every direction, at an increasing rate of speed. Clearly there will be more than we can use. There already is. Systems and subsystems all over the place. When I was in ASW, I envied the Air Defense Command. They had a specific job to do and a specific number of airplanes to do it with. ASW is hard to define in neat terms. It's difficult to say that this is what I have to do and this is how I'm going to do it. Once, we tried to fly higher, fly faster, hit targets precisely. Now, we can go as high as the moon, go fast enough to escape the whole solar system, make the bang heard around the world. And now, enter a whole new set of technologies and problems. The electronics are amazing, so many advances, so many with unique characteristics, that the whole thing is just hard to comprehend. We have to try to do a commonsense job of incorporating them into our sensors, our weapons. We have to reject many of them, and yet, at the same time, we can't ignore any of them. We have to keep watching for the guy who comes up with the spectacular. We can never turn our backs on a screwy idea."

In the end, the judgment of whether or not an idea is screwy rests with the Directorate of Defense Research and Engineering, the top-level shop which reports directly to the Secretary of Defense about the achievements and the failures, the progress and the setbacks, the good work and the bad, in the laboratories and the testing grounds of the services and their contractors. Some changes were evident in DDR&E as a new team took over and began developing its reach into the years ahead.

8

The Worst
Case Mentality

Man is always trying to make nature do more than it can do at any given time. This is particularly true in defense technology, and we are never content with what we can do well, but are always pushing beyond the edge of what you might call prudent technology because we have to assume that if we can see better things to do, the other fellow will too. In some sense I believe we are running an arms race with ourselves because the United States has a much greater capability for technological innovation than our competitors. The situation is also better because the Soviet Union is now a somewhat more open society, and particularly because of our reconnaissance capabilities. We are no longer required to imagine quite as much. Obviously, our photographic capability does not let us foretell the future, but we at least know what the situation is at the present, something we did not always know in the past.

—Dr. Jerome B. Wiesner.

Things have changed for the worse since Dr. Wiesner spoke those words in 1969. The Soviets have swung back toward a more closed society; they have broadened their capacity for technological innovation, and now the arms race is on for real. The Soviets have become—in fact and no longer only in the fancy of the U. S. military—our strategic disputant. The degree to which our own interservice competition induced this is debatable, and perhaps not even, anymore, worth debating. It is enough simply to note the fact. It hurts the mind to watch, on both sides, the boundings of the hundreds and hundreds of strategic and tactical weapons systems, sub-systems and components, the thousands and thousands of projects in research and technology which are aimed at the inexorable improvement of familiar arms and the spectacular breakthroughs of futuristic arms. Long before this century has ended, we will take for granted the high-energy laser, its power source packaged to deployable size, as a blinder and a killer; remotely piloted aircraft, revolutionary now, as conventional strike and reconnaissance weapons; computer and sensor systems which will enable our air, ground and naval forces to find and hit targets all through the night, on all kinds of terrain and in the foulest of weather; aircraft, seacraft and landcraft of surpassing speed and maneuverability; weapons, perhaps lasers, to knock down missiles and satellites, and weapons, perhaps lasers and electromagnetic fields, for defending satellites. And more. If the laser was Buck Rogers' ray gun, the "flying belt" now in experimentation for the Marines and infantry was his means of propulsion. Not even Buck Rogers could have done some of the things the military is trying to achieve. In the deep, dark recesses of military research in the lands of the Rockies and the Urals, scientists are seeking the ultimate answer, called in whispers, "the G answer"—the means, likely electromagnetic, of defying gravity; of antigravity, which would make Model Ts of present-day rockets and mockeries of Mach-3 fighters. The G answer may be supplied sooner than we think, and we may not like its source. Its embodiment in those Unidentified Flying Objects has been enough of a cultural shock for the U.S. and, presumably, the Soviet air forces. But the G answer is so far out as to be a weapons warp, joined in that dimension by mind control and extrasensory perception, which are in the conjectural stage—at least—as military tools of the late twentieth century and beyond. For now, however, what we can tangibly foresee is more than enough for the mind, let alone the imagination, to handle.

It all comes to focus, if anywhere, in the Directorate of Defense Research and Engineering. At the mid-1970s, DDR&E, under new leadership, was trying to sort out the arrant arsenal of today and arrange more definitively the technological thrusts that will take us into tomorrow. "We no longer can afford," declared Dr. Malcolm R. Currie, the new director of DDR&E, "to play in the sandbox of all scientific areas."

To understand where we are going, it is instructive, first, to understand how we got to where we are today. And for this, we return to Dr. Wiesner, a central figure in the frantic fructifications and foul-ups of military technologies since World War II. Provost since 1966 of the Massachusetts Institute of Technology, where he has served on the faculty since 1946, Dr. Wiesner was Special Assistant to the President for Science and Technology and Director of the Office of Science and Technology in the White House from 1961 to 1964. An expert in electronics and ballistic-missile systems, he goes back, in his many consultantships and memberships in government agencies and advisory groups, to the years right after World War II when the cold war was joined. His recounting of that period helps to show us why we are where we are in defense research and development. It deserves the telling in his own words:

The 1950s were marked by very rapid technological change in all aspects of strategic warfare. In 1950 the thermonuclear bomb was just becoming a possibility, with the prospect of multiplying the yield per pound of nuclear explosive by a factor of about one thousand over that of fission material. The intercontinental bomber was just becoming an operational reality. Navigation systems adequate for long-range operation were just becoming available. Air defense missiles and short-range tactical offensive missiles were beginning to be feasible, but the long-range tactical offensive missile was still regarded to be technologically unobtainable, or at least so expensive and complicated that it had no place in a military system. Finally, the digital computer was just beginning to emerge as an important element in military control systems.

Every aspect of military technology was in a rapid state of change. Explosive power was multiplying, the speed and range of strategic military engagement was increasing vastly, and electronic systems were displacing man from operational and command positions. The dizzying pace of change was very disorienting both for the professional strategists and for the civilian leadership in the Executive Branch of the government and the Congress. Even the academic panelists who studied strategic problems and journalists interested in national security affairs could not keep up with the rapidly evolving situation. Rapid advances were also occurring in the military technology of the Soviet Union, and as a consequence a great deal of nervousness existed in the United States about the relative positions of the military capabilities of the two nations. During the 1950s this situation was exacerbated by the almost complete lack of knowledge about Soviet military technology in the United States, an intelligence gap which led to the conclusion— erroneously, as we later learned—that the development and deployment of United States' strategic weapons systems lagged behind those in the Soviet Union in a very dangerous manner. This intelligence gap was closed during the late 1950s when the Soviet Union began to permit considerably more travel within its borders, and American technical intelligence capabilities vastly improved. Also, continuing research and development efforts brought the new military technologies—rocketry, electronics, nuclear weapons and so forth—to a point of maturity from which it was no longer possible to make dramatic changes in the military capabilities of the strategic systems from one technical generation to the next, even though improvements in cost, reliability, operational ease and so forth justified continued development.

These two developments brought about a period of stability which began in the early 1960s and continues to this day. Obviously, the interesting question is whether such stability can be preserved in the face of new electronic developments, space achievements and other highly sophisticated new capabilities. In my judgment there is no immediate danger of this stability being upset—though some possibilities such as a deployment of an antiballistic system or MIRVs might force the equilibrium level for offensive forces to a higher level.

(Within months after Dr. Wiesner spoke those words, the U. S. military concluded that the Soviets were preparing to deploy an ABM system, and President Nixon made the fateful decision to deploy MIRVs. The stability had indeed been upset.)

Looking back again to the 1950s, Dr. Wiesner injected a wistful note: "There was an unbelievable amount of confusion in the planning for our strategic forces. All of this was, I think, further complicated by both the intensity of the cold war, the feeling we had that Stalin, if not madly irrational, could not be counted on always to act rationally. . . . Fear forced us to try to move at a technical pace which probably exceeded our capabilities to go from a conception or an idea to realizable weapons systems in a very short time. The history of that period is one, for those of us who lived through it, almost like a bad illness in the family. As I look back at the fears we had during that period, and at the frenzy with which we worked, and the failures that we encountered, I can hardly believe, now, that we, in fact, really did it. We had, as a result of the lack of any creditable intelligence information, and because of the intensity of the cold war, to make some assumptions which, in the end, turned out to be untrue."

Nothing has changed. The only intelligence which the Pentagon ever regards as creditable, in fact, is intelligence which says that the Russians are up to no good in developing better weapons for now, that they are always verging on breakthroughs in exotic weaponry which will break the back and the will of the Free World. Even if U. S. military and civilian intelligence were to agree—and insist—that the Russians are actually far behind us in military research and development, our own military R&D racers feel they could not afford to acknowledge this and slacken their pace. The Russians, they claim, are outspending the United States on military R&D by at least a couple of billion dollars a year. The U. S. military rejects, furthermore, the notion that all our intelligence people need do is to pry a little harder to determine the true nature and scope of Soviet R&D. The intelligence can never be good enough. It can never reveal what the U. S. military already fears it knows. This unrelenting apprehension of the Pentagon is the chief reason the U. S. military will never trust, for example, the 1972 SALT I agreement which limited the deployment of U. S. and Soviet antiballistic missiles. It is why the Pentagon immediately turned, after SALT I, to development of the "Site Defense of Minuteman" system, which is really an ABM. It is why the Pentagon operates on the theory of "the R&D hedge," which goes a long way toward explaining the arms race. In turn, the story of "Hen House," as told by Dr. John S. Foster,

Jr., when he was still boss of the Defense Directorate of Research and Engineering, before he recently became a vice-president of defense-contracting TRW Inc., helps elucidate the "R&D hedge."

"In the past two decades," said Foster, "we have in fact been able to rely on the R&D hedge. Let me give you an example. It is a story about a Soviet radar which we first detected in the late 1950s and which we have given the prosaic code name, 'Hen House.' Imagine, if you can, three football fields lined up end to end and standing on their sides. That is the size of the Hen House radar. It was so big that when we first found out about it, we were hesitant even to identify it as a radar. Much later we learned that it was far too powerful for most of the applications we could imagine. Assuming it was a radar, many argued that it made sense only as part of a detection, tracking and control network for satellites. The non-radar proponents even tried to make it into such things as a space communications system. The location of the first Hen House argued that, regardless of other intended uses, this equipment probably would form part of an ABM system. The precise role it was to play—and the other components needed to make a total ABM weapons system—were far from clear. In fact, these mysteries remain [into the 1970s] as additional Hen House and other radars have been deployed. We now know that the giant Hen House radars serve an important early warning and tracking function in the Soviet ABM system. They can, in the near term, provide the same radar coverage which we will have some eight years from now if all of the Safeguard [ABM] program is completed."

Two years after Foster told the story of Hen House, the ABM-limiting treaty was signed. But what he said next illustrates why the Pentagon does not trust the Soviets to live up to that treaty:

It is a puzzle to us today that they have a massive tracking capability and a minimal [antimissile] interceptor capability. Nevertheless, since interceptors can be deployed much more rapidly than the big radars, it is true that *an extensive ABM capability could be acquired rather quickly* [italics mine].

As we learned of the early Hen House developments in the Soviet Union, we decided to accelerate our R&D into penetration aids [for ballistic missiles]. As Hen House developments became extensive, we decided to deploy our Minuteman III and Poseidon systems which carry MIRVs. . . . The Hen House can teach us several lessons: the Soviets are good technologically when they want to be and, in some areas, they most certainly want to be; it can take us years to decide what, precisely, they are doing; and, finally, superior American R&D protects us from Soviet secrecy and surprises.

Foster left something out of his Hen House story, something which, as we have noted, he later revealed to a Senate committee under questioning; namely, that the Pentagon had decided to deploy MIRVs at least partly because the number of "aim points" in the Soviet Union had outstripped the number of warheads in the U.S. arsenal. No matter. The theory of the R&D hedge had been vindicated, in the minds of the military, by Hen House. Our MIRVs now stand ready to fly in nose-cone coops of their own. And we are developing maneuverable reentry vehicles (MARVs) too, because, in the words of Dr. Malcolm R. Currie, "they will be very difficult to intercept by classical ABM technology."

Dr. Malcolm R. Currie, lean, mid-forties, sandy hair trimmed modishly medium, turned out trimly in dark-blue blazer and light-gray trousers slightly flared, paced his E Ring inner sanctum right down the hall from the ballroom-size suite of the Secretary of Defense and told of his plans for the Directorate of Defense Research and Engineering. Currie had taken over DDR&E a short time before, succeeding Foster as only the fourth boss of defense research in the fifteen-year history of the post. Foster himself had accounted for eight of those years, showing remarkable resiliency in adapting to the policies of four Secretaries of Defense—McNamara, Clifford, Laird and Richardson—and in bridging the administrations of Johnson and Nixon. Currie's advent at DDR&E said something—in the professional backgrounds of the arriving and departing directors—about the changing emphasis of Pentagon research from the mid-1960s to the mid-1970s. Foster, formerly the director of the Lawrence Radiation Laboratory at

Livermore, California, had been a nuclear physicist, an atom man. Currie, however, had been a physicist-electrical engineer, an electron man, a laser man. "You could even call me," he said with a grin, "an ion man, a charged-particle man."

Currie's job would be to compose the complexities of military technologies into an arsenal of strategic and tactical weapons for any kind of war; most probably, if it came, for openers anyway, a war of electronics and counterelectronics, featuring computers in command, lasers as rangefinders and, not too many years away, lasers on the firing lines. As Currie said it:

> The next conventional war may well be one of electronics. We will invigorate the thrust of defense research and engineering on developing weapons for the suppression of defenses. Our big aims will be, one, locating targets and, two, delivering ordnance at a distance—by electro-optical, radar, lasers or infrared systems. The war in Southeast Asia showed—and the war in the Middle East confirmed—the importance of precision delivery through terminal guidance. The importance is enormous. When you come down to it, we would like for every missile, bomb or shell to kill its target. This would mean we could avoid making repeated attacks on a target by large numbers of aircraft or tanks or cannon. We would reduce the loss of life and equipment in our own forces. This class of one-shot-one-kill weapons is still in its infancy, but the first generation of the daytime electro-optical weapons—such as the TOW and Maverick missiles—has had outstanding success. Emerging from our laboratories right now are concepts of sensors which can extend this capability to night and to all-weather operations. Overall, we are giving special attention to expanded electronic warfare and to the use of remotely piloted vehicles for both reconnaissance and strikes against dense air defenses.

Quite an order. But in the environs Currie had come from, there was nothing especially fancy about it. It was simply technology on a fast track.

Currie held undergraduate and graduate degrees in physics and electrical engineering from the University of California, and had begun his civilian career—after service as a Navy flyer—as an instructor at Berkeley and at UCLA. He joined Hughes

Aircraft Corp. in 1954 as a member of the technical staff, specializing in research on such brain bogglers as traveling wave amplifiers and oscillators, electron optics, noise theory and physical electronics. Within ten years, he had risen to the directorship of the Hughes Physics Laboratory, to an associate directorship of all Hughes research laboratories, to a corporate vice-presidency and the directorship of every one of the labs, and, finally, to the general managership of the entire Hughes Research and Development Division, directing the business and technical activities of three thousand employees. His chief responsibilities rested in airborne radar, communications, lasers, infrared and electro-optical systems, and components and materials. In 1969, Currie left Hughes to become vice-president for research and development with Beckman Instruments Inc., of Fullerton, California. There, he broadened into the planning and marketing of instrumentation for physical, chemical, biochemical and biomedical research, physiological electronics and process control. After four years of this, he introduced himself at the River Entrance as the Pentagon's third most powerful personage (*the* most powerful, in the opinion of many, because the decisions of the boss of defense research and engineering are the ones that winnow the weapons that the Pentagon is all about).

On the way to the Pentagon, Currie had acquired nine patents as a result of his own research, and had several pending. The year that DDR&E was created, he had been named by a professional engineering society as the "Nation's Outstanding Young Electrical Engineer of 1958." Two years after that, the first operative laser was put together by Dr. Theodore Maiman of Hughes Aircraft, and Currie was there, in charge of the laboratory where it happened. He seemed a perfect fit with DDR&E, and it with him, as the Pentagon, in the mid-1970s, put the finishing touches of terminal guidance to the weapon-children of the thermonuclear era, and swung into the new age of Buck Rogers, into the dawning of death rays which someday may detonate or disintegrate ICBMs in space. But even though Currie could see this coming more clearly than most, he had little time, now, for conjecture about it. He had the immediate, pressing task of imprinting his own personality and leadership on a defense research establishment which practically had made an institution of Foster, and of rubbing off the tarnish that the Vietnam misadventure and highly publicized cost overruns had deposited on defense technologies. As Foster reminded Currie during the several transitional weeks that the incoming director commuted from California to look over the outgoing director's shoulder, the Vietnam war had done something else, too, which no one outside the defense establishment much recognized. Vietnam had been a testing ground for hundreds of items of equipment and weapons which signaled the new era of electronic warfare. They had been, for good or bad, exposed. The Russians knew of them, knew what they could do. The Russians thus were free to borrow from them, and, as Foster put it, "we have lost a margin of technological surprise."

"My goal," Currie told me, after Foster had gone and it was all up to him, "is to create in Congress and in the public a high degree of accountability in the ability of the Department of Defense to manage its programs. I want to establish a trend of a diminished number of imprudently accelerated programs. My whole object is to bring along enough weapons in research and development to give us a wide range of options—what Schlesinger calls 'a rich menu'—and then have the management guts to say, 'no' to those we can't use. Some of these weapons programs get started and never end. And I'd like to get across to everyone the fact that there really is civilian leadership in this department. The services are not going off by themselves. This is an awfully important fact to establish, because we are asking for more and more money in R&D, and we can get it only if we establish a sense of credibility. We must establish this before we can be accountable for the minutiae and before we can go on to a dialogue about the big issues. The fundamental issue, as I see it, is what is our national outlook on R&D? What does it contribute to our standard of living? Not just in defense, although defense certainly is far and away the biggest R&D user. I don't think this issue of the relationship of R&D to the nation's economy and to everything else has been thought through, and it desperately needs to be thought through. We're always discussing, and we must determine, the makeup of the world ahead, what will be the needs and what will be the technologies coming along to help us meet those needs. On the defense side, we must gather up all the information we can about this question and amalgamate it. We must foresee what conventional warfare will be like, for instance, and fit our plans for R&D squarely into what we foresee. No-body, of course, has a perfect crystal ball. But we can, I think, begin to define the thrusts of technology. In the last several years, as science and technology fell into disrepute, this nation, I believe, lost sight of the role of R&D. But now I believe we are seeing a reinvigoration of R&D and a new awareness of its role. The Mideast War and the Soviet missile developments demonstrated a need for greater flexibility on our part, in terms of our weapons options. The Mideast War also—and I consider this extremely important—restored confidence, to a very considerable extent, to the R&D community in this country. Some of the weapons and technologies which the defense R&D community—our own people, industry, the universities —have been looking at in the past were shown by the war to have become very important. Many of the technological thrusts which we weren't sure of were vindicated by that war, and this has given our scientists and engineers more confidence to go forward. Now, maybe we can put behind us the self-doubt and the second-guessing which in the past bred a lack of confidence in what we were doing. The war affected the non-defense R&D community, too. The energy crisis. What to do about energy of the future? The war, the Soviet missilery, the energy crisis, they all came to a hard-gut focus almost simul-taneously, and our perception of what R&D means to the United States immediately became more important to our fu-ture position with respect to the rest of the world."

Two weeks following this interview, Currie dispatched to Congress his whopping $9.4-billion budget for defense re-search, development, testing and evaluation. The great bulk of the money was spread across sixty-four major weapons systems which showed up in the defense budget. But there was a hunk, too, for more than 20,000 projects in research and exploratory technology related to the weapons of tomorrow as well as those of today. The R&D budget represented more than one-tenth of the entire defense budget and well over half of all federal R&D, including that of the National Aeronautics and Space Ad-ministration. Moreover, the defense R&D budget was nearly $1 billion higher than it had been the year before, marking the first time in several years that it had climbed above a fairly consistent level of the low $8 billions. When you added the R&D section to the section representing weapons production and maintenance, you came up with nearly half of the whole Pentagon outpouring, with personnel costs accounting for the remainder and climbing fast. This is why Currie stressed to me the necessity of close teamwork between himself and Arthur I. Mendolia, a former Dupont executive who came to the Pentagon simultaneously with Currie as Assistant Secretary of Defense for Installations and Logistics. I&L is the production side, the purchasing agent, of the Pentagon. Taking over where DDR&E leaves off, it supervises all procurement, plus the operation of military bases and the construction of all military facilities. Of the two shops, I&L manages money of much greater magnitude, but DDR&E is the exchequer of the evocative.

Before he is a scientist or an engineer, the boss of DDR&E must be an administrator-politician. He must control, and keep unclogged, his lines of communication with his principal deputy and with deputy directors for acquisition management, plans and assessment, research and advanced technology, strategic and space systems, tactical warfare programs and test and evaluation. Inside these broad administrative areas are dozens more, dealing daily and directly with the R&D shops of the services and defense contractors, with universities and think tanks. Under DDR&E's Tactical Warfare Programs office, for example, are assistant directors for air warfare, combat support, international programs, land warfare and ocean control. Woven into all this is the Weapons Systems Evaluation Group (WSEG), working in tandem with—and in the same building as—the Institute for Defense Analyses across the road from the Pentagon, and the Advanced Research Projects Agency (ARPA), which is independent of DDR&E in the hierarchical chart but inextricably allied in function. In his constant watch for new directions and trends in research and technology, the director of DDR&E depends mostly upon ARPA and the Defense Science Board, made up of twenty-four high-level university and industrial scientists and engineers, plus the chairmen of the separate scientific advisory groups of the Army, Navy and Air Force. The Defense Science Board is chartered as the Defense Department's senior technical advisory body and charged with advising the Secretary of Defense, through DDR&E, on scientific and technical issues. The man in the roost at DDR&E also chairs, ordinarily, the Defense

Systems Acquisition Review Council (DSARC), which checks the progress of the services' weapons development programs at preset milestones. In this role, Currie would wield—or yield—power with respect to the military. In other roles, too. Pivotal to his successful stewardship of the services is the quality of his working relationship with the civilian assistant secretaries of R&D in each of the military departments, who report directly to the Secretaries of the Army, the Air Force, and the Navy, and with the services' uniformed R&D bosses, such as the Navy's Admiral Moran, who report directly to their respective chiefs of staff. Somehow the top man at DDR&E, deriving his power directly from the Secretary of Defense but highly susceptible to being surrounded or outflanked by the military, must stay on top of it all, keeping the Services from pursuing pet projects at cross-purposes, watchdogging them for wastage, staying alert to the practices and research products of the plethora of industrial and university contractors, the "in-house" military laboratories, and the think tanks. It would be more manageable for the director of defense research if he were not a man on the go almost as much as he is a man on the do. He must traipse to Capitol Hill on demand of Congressional committees, and show up all over the country at military, industrial and academic symposia to make speeches about what's going on in defense R&D. Currie winced at the time away from the Pentagon that all the traveling would require, but he knew it would be necessary nonetheless. He wanted to reestablish, as he said, credibility, and the place to do that is out in public, the only place, in a democracy, where it counts. It would take some doing. Credibility has never been the long suit of a defense research establishment which plays a lot of hide and seek.

DDR&E was created in a 1958 amendment to the National Security Act expressly to watch over the R&D writhings of the services. Startled by the Soviets' launching of Sputnik in October 1957 and frustrated by the intensification of interservice rivalries over the development of strategic weapons in reaction to the rocket power which Sputnik had demonstrated, President Eisenhower presented Congress with a plan to strengthen the hand of the Secretary of Defense in making R&D decisions. ARPA came first, in 1957, to collate the services' basic research and take for them a collective view of the future. Then came DDR&E, embodying ARPA. The first director of this department-wide R&D establishment was Dr. Herbert York, who spent three years tentatively probing for power, and watching the Air Force emerge as the major domo of the Eisenhower-era strategy of "massive retaliation." York became deeply troubled by the treadmill of terrifying weapons which was set in motion in those years, and has devoted himself since then, in private life, to trying to slow it down. The second boss of DDR&E, under McNamara, was Dr. Harold Brown, who gave way to Foster in 1965 to take the historically more—but contemporaneously less—powerful post of Secretary of the Air Force.

In the McNamara years, the hypothetical power of DDR&E was almost absolute; more pervasive, even, than that of the Office of Systems Analysis. Together, the civilian commanders of those two shops were the chief executors of the centralization of control in the Office of the Secretary of Defense. Together, they called the shots about which weapons the services would develop for which missions. But soon after Laird and Packard took over, this changed. A Pentagon announcement of January 21, 1970, told it all:

> In line with the participatory management philosophy of the Secretary of Defense on weapons system acquisition, Dr. John S. Foster, Jr., director of Defense Research and Engineering, is reorganizing his office. In the past scientists and engineers in DDR&E have supervised the programs of the military services to the extent that in some cases the services have not felt that they had full responsibility and authority for the conduct of approved programs. The reorganization will reduce the amount of Department of Defense direction and guidance, and will result in a smaller staff at the Department [DDR&E] level. Most projects will originate in the services and be approved by the Department. But the primary responsibility for their conduct will rest with the Services.

Right down there where the R&D system works—or doesn't work—this was the announcement which signified the castration of civilian control as the premature remedy for the pains of its puberty. The military had won. Their programs no longer would fall to the cutting room floor at DDR&E or be savaged in the sanctums of the systems analysts. The services had persuaded Laird and Packard of their postulate that under McNamara, the weapons-selection process had been one in which computers whirred, lights flashed and printouts did the picking and choosing, in which these printouts were marched to the front office by budding civilian scientists in bow ties who stood at awed attention while McNamara manhandled the services' manhood. So the Pentagon retrogressed to the old days, when the services were free to define their missions in terms of the vehicles in which their troops rode and by the weapons which their troops fired. Everyone would have aircraft, missiles—even ships. The "military requirements" would be those which the services decided upon, and the "national requirements" would somehow have to fall into place as afterthoughts.

The civilian largesse of the Laird-Packard era at the Pentagon may have made some sense, and probably did pay off to some extent, in its deference to the services' better judgments of which weapons best suited their purposes. There was, still is, and always will be, in DDR&E and OSD, the insecure feeling among the civilians that the military men must know their business better than the civilians could ever know it, and that they should not be overridden without good and sufficient cause. Still, the civilians are the only ones who can draw the line between very expensive, very complex weapons which would be ideal for the military and those which are less costly and less complex but probably at least adequate. One example comes to mind. The difference between an engine which can power a fighter up to Mach 2.5 and one which can power it up to Mach 2.4 is one-fifth to one-fourth the cost of the entire fighter, and the fighter gains little in that extra squirt of speed. But to the military airmen, be they Air Force or Navy, to deny them that squirt is to do them—and this country—dirt.

Six months after Laird and Packard prevailed upon Foster to relax DDR&E's grip on the services, the blue-ribbon panel which Nixon had created to study Pentagon practices issued a report which advocated an even more drastic downgrading. It recommended that "the functions of the Director, Defense Research and Engineering, be allocated among three assistant secretaries of defense—Research and Advanced Technology, Engineering Development, and Test and Evaluation." This surely would have riven civilian control of research. The services would have divided and conquered. But nothing came of this recommendation, even though the arrival of William P. Clements, Jr., a member of the blue-ribbon panel, as Deputy Secretary of Defense had led to speculation that DDR&E's days were numbered. This speculation predated, and then was put down, by the subsequent appointment of James R. Schlesinger as Secretary of Defense and of Currie, whose celerity out of the chocks nipped any notion that he would stand for being a mere caretaker of a shop that was foredoomed.

As the months went by, Schlesinger began showing more than a little bit of McNamara in his concept of the secretaryship as it pertained to research and analysis. He clearly was trying to establish a middle ground between overcontrol and undercontrol of the military. Once marked for his "two and a half cheers for systems analysis," Schlesinger soon let the services know that two and a half cheers are superior to none. He upgraded analysis in the Department of Defense simply by appointing Leonard Sullivan, Jr., to be in charge of it, as director of the newly named Office of Program Analysis and Evaluation. Sullivan was no Johnny-come-lately, no mere bean counter, no whiz kid. He had been around, and he had demonstrated that he could not be pushed around. Since joining DDR&E in 1964, he had served as deputy assistant director and then director of combat systems, Tactical Warfare Programs; as deputy director for Southeast Asia Matters and, finally, as principal deputy director of the whole setup. He had been, in 1950, the first man ever to receive the graduate degree of Aeronautical Engineer—the engineering equivalent of a Ph.D. —at Massachusetts Institute of Technology. And he had spent fourteen years as a design and systems engineer in the aerospace industry. More than anyone else, Sullivan had been responsible for selecting the weapons and sensors which the Pentagon, caught off balance, finally pitted against the guerrillas and the jungles of Vietnam, and for spurring the services to develop those weapons and get them into action. So the services had felt his boot before, and they would be careful not to invite it again. Ex-Marine Sullivan had a reputation for saying straight out what he believed. One of the things he believed was that the Pentagon was risking pricing itself right out of an adequate defense. He had made many speeches about it, had dissertated to many interviewers about it, and now he was in better position than ever to do something about it. His style would help, too. A calm man, Sullivan, of solid mien. He could be sarcastic, but he was not known as a smart-ass. He seemed to march along smartly in the direction Schlesinger was taking—insisting on civilian control of R&D, but more as taskmaster than tyrant.

Schlesinger obviously faulted McNamara not for what McNamara had done but for what he had overdone. "I think it is fair," he told a group of companions at one relaxed gathering, "to say that when McNamara was in there, whether you agreed with him or not, he tried to present a rational and precise explanation of why we maintain forces. I think in many cases he was overprecise, that he had a degree of precision in his explanations that could not be practically sustained. But he was trying to be straightforward." His own attitudes would be guided, Schlesinger said, by "the extent to which the services get over their infatuation with high-cost, high-technology hardware that doesn't work. . . . Now, the whole weapons acquisition costs are so high. You have got the developers, the technologists, driving what you finally buy rather than a military mission drawing up and designing the equipment."

Still, Schlesinger seemed to share the conventional conclusion that the military had been made to suffer unduly under McNamara and that little had happened since, in the Nixon administration, to lift the pressure from the star-spangled psyches. He apparently failed to recognize that while all things warlike had come into disfavor in the United States during Vietnam, the services, during that period of poor public relations, had nevertheless succeeded in bending the Nixon White House and the Laird-Packard Pentagon pretty much to their will in the development and deployment of the very weapons whose high costs and oversophistication Schlesinger now decried. In the Tank, a MIRV is well worth the price of some public muttering; an F-14 or an F-15 a fair return for a few antiwar rallies, a Trident a decent tradeoff for a collegiate turndown of ROTC units. But Schlesinger chose not to make the equation.

"The first question I raise," he said, "is how do we treat our military. There has been a fair amount of abuse in using the Department of Defense and the military services as a whipping boy for all the frustrations of Vietnam and all the idiocies committed by the civilian leadership. A democratic nation gets about the kind of military establishment that it deserves, and if we continue to abuse these fellows and treat them this way, it is going to have consequences, I am not sure just what. I think that we have—to whatever extent it is a rough analogy —the isolation of the French military during the post-Algerian period. These people have been obedient to civilian direction, and we ought to be very careful to refrain from criticizing them doing what we would have regarded as very reprehensible their not having done. We want them to be responsible to civilian control, but that is the responsibility of the civilians."

At the end of Schlesinger's first year in office, he strongly recommended to the White House, and got, the appointment of Air Force General George Scratchley Brown as Chairman of the Joint Chiefs of Staff. It was said at the Pentagon that Schlesinger's sentimental favorite for the post would have been Army Chief of Staff Creighton Abrams. Schlesinger regarded Abrams as "an authentic national hero." But Abrams' health was failing even then, and he died a few months later. Brown was the obvious choice. Schlesinger held him, too, in great respect. Besides, Army generals had occupied the chairmanship for fifteen of the twenty-five years it had been in existence, and a Navy admiral, Moorer, had occupied it most recently. Brown became the first chairman from the Air Force since Nathan Twining in 1957-60. The significance of Brown's appointment lay, however, not so much in his orientation to the Air Force as in his orientation to R&D. He is the very first chairman of the JCS ever to have marshaled electrons as well as echelons, to have commanded technologists as well as troops. Unlike his predecessors, he had seen for himself, in his climb to the top through various commands, over the horizons of the world of superweapons.

A West Point graduate of 1941, Brown flew B-24 Liberators with the Eighth Air Force in Europe during World War II, including the bomber-busting, gut-shriveling raid on the Ploesti oil refineries over Romania on August 1, 1943. He won the Distinguished Service Cross on that one. The lead bomber and ten others in his group were shot down. Brown took command and led the remaining Liberators safely across the Mediterranean to Bengazi, Libya. In the Korean War, he commanded a fighter wing; in Vietnam, the Seventh Air Force. Along the way, he did a tour as assistant to the chairman of the JCS, and he came back to the Tank in full flower, as boss of the Air Force, in 1973. But it was his duty over the three previous years that made him unique, now, as the nation's top military officer: commander of the Air Force Systems Command, headquartered at Andrews Air Force Base just southeast of Washington, focus of bases, laboratories, testing centers and engineering complexes throughout the land, locus of all Air Force science and technology.

In mid-1974, the authoritative magazine *Aviation Week* devoted an entire issue to this vast domain of weapons development which Brown had left behind. "Systems Command," wrote Robert Hotz, the magazine's able editor, "has gone through three major cycles since its inception in 1952 as the Air Research and Development Command. The first was aimed at exploiting the revolutionary new technology that had begun to hatch in the waning years of World War II and eventually produced supersonic aircraft, atomic weapons and intercontinental ballistic missiles within a highly critical, competitive time frame. The second phase saw the refinement of this new technology, with major emphasis on improving management structures. Now, Systems Command has to grapple with both of these problems simultaneously, and it is developing new approaches to both advancing the frontiers of new technology and managing these developments within the strictures imposed by fiscal ceilings and the urgency of military necessities."

George Brown was in command at the very time that the grappling with both of the problems became gritty in the Air Force Systems Command. And he turned out to be an extraordinarily articulate exponent of technology, and of what it means to war machines. Consider his words of 1972:

> The impact of science and technology on strategy is almost infinite, since no strategy can really be postulated at all —or carried out—except in terms of the instruments that science and technology make available. Or will make available in the future. If the young David was no physical match for the giant Goliath, obviously his strategy had to depend upon the technology of the standoff missile. The technology was available, even though the science behind it—the laws of motion, ballistic forces, gravitation and all the rest—was

not perceived until many centuries later. The same is true of the standoff missiles—arrows, in this case—with which Henry the Fifth's outnumbered troops defeated a heavier and more mobile French force at Agincourt. The history of warfare has been a continuous exploitation of technology to increase the distance at which the engagement could be undertaken. Even so, in the end it has often come down again to a hand-to-hand engagement with a bayonet or rifle butt. The opening up of No Man's Land between opposing forces increased with the range of the big guns, both on land and sea, but again, they basically softened up the enemy preliminary to close-in engagement. In most cases, they were not in themselves decisive. The coming of the airplane, transcending for the first time all terrestrial barriers and obstacles and greatly expanding the speed of mobility, added an entirely new dimension to warfare. Here was a way to range far behind enemy lines to strangle the source of his warmaking potential, or to add swift and massive firepower at the very line of battle.

In each case, science and technology have enlarged the options of both tactics *and* strategy. And they have, by an abstruse formula handed down in 1905 in Switzerland, and an experiment conducted in 1938 in Germany, increased the destructive effects of explosive weapons by many orders of magnitude. In a parallel way, toys invented by the Chinese centuries ago, and experiments carried out here and in Europe beginning in the 1920s, have given a way to deliver those fantastic explosives over virtually unlimited distances. As one result of this intersection of technologies, it is possible for the first time in history for an enemy halfway around the world to take aim at your heart—and you will be dead in thirty minutes. Or he can shoot at you from beneath the sea—and your life expectancy is even less. Of course, you can do the same thing to him, and that fact gives rise to an uneasy sort of stalemate. Uneasy, because science and technology are not static in themselves; only the people behind them can make them static by refusing to proceed with research and development.

Unless all possible antagonists in this dangerous world agree with ironclad guarantees to halt military technology in its tracks, none of them can safely do so. It then becomes a question of which one is most successful in his pursuit of science and technology. If it is a power that is dedicated to peace and freedom and self-determination throughout the world, then the world will ultimately be peaceful and free. But if better scientific and technological efforts are achieved by others, there might be a different result. That, really, is what the technological race is all about—the true meaning of the impact of science and technology on strategy. The fundamental point is the question of *whose* science and technology impacts upon *whose* strategy. The obvious answer is that your own science and technology determines your own strategy—but that strategy is also profoundly affected by an adversary's science and technology. While it is true that the laws of science and the possibilities of technology are universal, it is also true that what you get out of them is directly proportional to the level, the quality, the continuity and the urgency of the effort you put into them. That is why there is so much alarm these days, in the Department of Defense and in the military departments, about the much larger expenditures and the more forceful momentum of Soviet military R&D. The USSR has been outspending us in this area by about three billion dollars a year. That three-billion-dollar differential is the cost of one whole year's R&D on *all* the major new weapon systems we are currently developing for the Army, Navy and Air Force.

Now that he had ascended, in 1974, to preeminence atop the Joint Chiefs of Staff, Brown obviously would generate maximum power for the military's eternal thrusting toward the doomsday machine. Late that same year, Brown very nearly sealed his own doom as chairman. During a seminar-type chat with students at Duke University, he remarked on the influence of the Israeli lobby with Congress in pressuring the Pentagon to keep supplying Israel with weapons which were becoming scarce in U.S. forces. But then Brown went too far. He said that the Jews "own, you know, the banks in this country, the newspapers. You just look at where the Jewish money is in this country." A local newspaper ran the story and the *Washington Post* and the wire services picked it up the following day. Brown was in trouble. Schlesinger and Ford slapped him down in public, and he apologized for his remarks, acknowledging that he had erred as to the extent of Jewish control of media and monetary affairs. Brown was permitted to remain as JCS chairman, but his image had suffered, perhaps irreparably, and he obviously would have to lower his voice. He also would be compelled to adjust a bit to the shifting back toward centralization of R&D under civilian control which was becoming slightly noticeable in the maneuverings of the Schlesinger-Currie-Sullivan team. To tighten the couplings between DDR&E and the services—and among the services themselves—Currie laid out a plan. "We will take," he told me emphatically, "a top-down management approach. In the past, it's been a bottoms-up kind of plan, program by program, starting with the services and ending with DDR&E. We also will begin aggregating missions that now cut across all the services. I plan to work jointly with the services in such mission areas as antisubmarine warfare, air defense, close support of ground troops and electronic warfare. I've drawn up a list of about fifty mission areas involving more than one service, and I will winnow this down to smaller, more manageable numbers as a starter. The mission of precision delivery of air-to-ground ordnance, by the way, is a good example here. No one can convince me that we need many different kinds of ordnance for this one mission. By pulling together the missions and the weapons we need for them, we will get a clearer view of technological needs and technological thrusts we want to concentrate on, and to decide what we feel will be important into the 1980s."

Back to antisubmarine warfare. Currie made plain his belief that the Navy ASW office had done a good job, but that DDR&E needed to step in more forcefully to help stir the stew of air, surface and subsurface ASW systems in the Navy's R&D pot. "ASW spreads through an awful lot of the Navy," he said. "The problem is how do you trade off among R&D investments. Should you develop a new helicopter, or go into a new surveillance system?"

The sensitivity of the services—and the alacrity of their reactions to any suggestion of reversion to civilian control—was demonstrated in this case. The publication of my magazine story setting out some of Currie's views, and containing his intention to involve DDR&E more strenuously in Navy ASW R&D, quickly triggered a sequence of phone calls from the

Pentagon's Flag Bridge to Stanley E. Peterson, assistant director of DDR&E for Ocean Control. The admirals testily wanted
to know just what the devil it was that Currie proposed to do.
Peterson, himself an electrical engineer and former submarine
officer, told them not to get excited, DDR&E would not try to
take them over. He emphasized to them, as Currie had to me,
and as I had in my magazine story, that DDR&E aspired not
to clash with the services over their missions but to form a
closer team that would operate on a clearer set of signals. All
very well. But the trouble was, as the admirals knew, that every
team must have a captain. And civilian Currie had become a
candidate for the captaincy.

At the end of a long day of prowling the Pentagon, I dropped
in on a top-level DDR&E official for one of those casual chats
which sometimes pay off in good ideas for articles but more
often simply serve to embellish insights. We fell to discussing
the services' thin skins.

"I guess I don't have to tell you," said my source, "that the
political power in this building lies with the uniforms. The
civilians can withhold the money that Congress appropriates
for the services, but that's a last resort and a negative power.
When that happens—very seldom—the teamwork comes to an
end. The services call the shots on the missions they want the
weapons to perform, and that's where their power lies. They
were afraid Currie would start making up his own missions for
their weapons. We told them we really couldn't care less about
doing any such thing. But we *do* care about what it will mean
when they keep wanting to make a plane go higher and faster.
We want to know: if it goes higher and faster, what does that
do to the mission? Do they need to keep adding technology to
perform the mission? Most of our reviews of the services' R&D
proposals are carried out in what we call the 'mission element.'
In years past, each service would come in by itself to present
its case. Now, we're conducting tri-service or bi-service reviews as much as possible. If the Air Force comes in to talk
about air-to-air missiles, Currie gets only the Air Force fragment. The Navy comes in two weeks later, and he gets Navy
fragment. When they come in together, he gets the whole
thing. It's taking them a little time to get used to working
together, but they don't seem to mind too much. So long as we
don't horse around with their missions. But that's bound to

come, sooner or later, and then we'll see. We're taking another tack, too. For example, we don't think it does us much good to know that the Navy or the Army or the Air Force is getting X, Y or Z for so many R&D dollars, or that this or that program is on track or off track in development, if nobody has ever really sat down and figured out what good all of it will do for the forces when they're out there fighting. So we give the reviews of technology a red-versus-blue flavor as often as we can. We stack up our technology against the Soviets' technology. We try to be objective about it, but it's hard to do. We try to stop adding technology onto our systems when we think they're enough better than the systems we'd be likely to have to fight against. But we can't be sure. We can never be sure. We don't know what the Soviets may come up with, or be coming up with, and we would be derelict if we left it to chance."

So Currie and his fellow civilians of DDR&E should get high marks for setting out to unscramble the services' R&D. Was it possible for them to succeed? "Yes, I believe so," said my off-the-record confidant, "although it's very tough when, really, the *veto* is the only civilian weapon, when *resisting* the pressure from the uniforms takes up most of our energies. It is very, very difficult for DDR&E—and for the Office of the Secretary of Defense—to do a *positive* thing. Look what happened to McNamara when he started shuffling weapons systems. Laird never fought that fight, really. We'll just have to see about Schlesinger and Currie. One thing, though. Currie has something going for him. He's a very straightforward guy. He levels from start to finish. Foster was more a manipulator. If he couldn't manipulate, he turned into a son of a bitch. There's something else, too. When we have a difference with a service, we almost always have allies right inside that service, because of the internal competition for R&D dollars. And it's getting fierce. If we've given the Navy a hard time in the morning, we might get a sub rosa visit or a phone call from one of the admirals in the afternoon telling us to hang in there, we're on the right track. The Navy guys have to be more careful about that sort of thing. The Air Force guys don't give a damn about it in general. They do their infighting more out in the open. They're more loosely structured."

Not long after Currie took charge of DDR&E, the Center for Strategic and International Studies at Georgetown University published a report on "U.S. Military R&D Management" which could not—so far as Currie was concerned—have been better timed. It said in part:

> Decentralization, which has been a recent objective, may well have gone too far. The principle is fine, but in practice, all of the performers—military, civilians, contractors, Congress—must cope with their own persisting problems that work against successful decentralization. When there is trouble, the Office of the Secretary of Defense must step in and make national decisions. But OSD won't know about trouble in time, unless it is intimately involved in the R&D process. There will always be a balance of some kind between the powers of the high civilians in OSD and the military and civilian managers in the services. The pendulum may have swung too far toward decentralization.

This was no shallow study. It had taken three years. The panel in charge of it had been composed of ten men of savant stature in the military-university-industrial R&D milieu. Among them were retired Vice-Admiral William F. Raborn, the original director of the Polaris program, later the director of Central Intelligence, and now a vice-president of Aerojet General Corp.; Dr. Frederick Seitz, president of Rockefeller University, former chairman of the Defense Science Board and former president of the National Academy of Sciences; Dr. Rodney Nichols, a vice-president of Rockefeller University and former assistant director of DDR&E; Dr. Thomas B. Cook, vice-president of Sandia Corp. and a member of the Air Force Science Advisory Board. These men and their companions wrote conventionally in their study that the United States needs to shore up military R&D "as a hedge against miscalculations in arms control agreements and as a guard against technological surprise." But they also wrote that this "does not necessarily mean greater procurement of weapon systems." They recommended less secrecy in R&D "in the interest of efficiency," killing shaky R&D programs more quickly and ruthlessly, subjecting contractors to harsher penalties if they don't perform up to snuff, and closing or limiting Defense Department laboratories when they cease to serve a useful role. Although the panel applauded Pentagon attempts to straighten out the R&D procurement tangle, it concluded that many of those attempts had been counterproductive, even strange. For example:

A logical plan has evolved, but in practice it seldom, perhaps never, has been followed from beginning to end. Existing projects such as the F-14 were not started along the new paths. Managers adapted some ongoing projects where they could, but adapted the plan where they could not. They made some arbitrary decisions when overruns loomed. Some of the decisions were very interesting. On the AX [A-10] close-support plane for the Air Force, for instance, cost estimates began to grow alarmingly, so the Office of the Secretary of Defense put an arbitrary limit on the cost-per-plane of production models. The Air Force and the development contractors were told to bring in cheap prototypes, with costs under the ceiling, or forget the whole project. The R&D world will be watching for the final production results.

Ironically, the A-10, an attack plane which probably will be a slow-flying patsy for surface-to-air missiles despite its heavy armor, became threatened, shortly after the R&D report came out, by the Enforcer, which the Defense Department quickly shot down. As Richard J. Levine summed it up in the *Wall Street Journal*:

It can take a lot to shake the Pentagon's weapons-building bureaucracy out of its accustomed ways—more, apparently, than even the formidable ingenuity and persistence of aircraft designer David B. Lindsay, Jr. Mr. Lindsay, who is also a wealthy Florida newspaper publisher, has been trying for three years to interest the Defense Department in his design for an attack aircraft to provide close support to ground troops. He has built a rugged little warplane, called the Enforcer, that packs a potent punch, carries a bargain-basement price tag, gets high marks for performance—and leaves the Pentagon cold. Designer Lindsay has run into one bureaucratic roadblock after another. He has failed to persuade the Pentagon to give the Enforcer a full-scale test flight, much less consider buying it. "I'm totally frustrated," he says. "We aren't selling anything. We're just trying to get the plane tested. The Defense Department has given up knocking the airplane and now says there's no requirement for it." The apparent reason for official coolness [wrote Levine] is simply that the military brass fears that the Enforcer would show up, or even threaten, such pet projects as the Air Force's new A-10 attack jet and the Marine Corps' vertical liftoff Harrier; those planes, which are designed for the same close-support role as the Enforcer, are more costly and complex. "The services are closing every door they can," says a staff member of the Senate Armed Services Committee. "The Enforcer is too practical and too cheap to appeal to them." And so the prototype plane, developed entirely with funds put up by Mr. Lindsay and Piper Aircraft Corp., sits in lonely storage at Vero Beach, Fla., far from the wild blue yonder.

Levine and others who wrote about the Enforcer weren't building it up out of a clear blue sky. Pentagon officials conceded in private that the turboprop plane, with 75-millimeter recoilless rifles mounted on its wings, was surprisingly effective. The Navy became quite interested in the Enforcer, but the Air Force, in protecting its A-10, demanded of the Pentagon's top civilians that they tell the Navy to back off. And that, according to one of my best sources in Navair, is exactly what happened. "We aren't," said my source, "even allowed to mention the Enforcer. It's plugged up. It's gone."

In the Naval Ship Systems Command (now called the Naval Sea Systems Command) lay another lesson for the military technologists that keeping it simple can result in making it good, even spectacular. "The Application of Ferro-Cement to Planing Hull River Boats" was the unexciting title of a paper written for Navships by officers and sailors whose on-the-job R&D in Vietnam struck a sweet chord. Back in 1970, these Navy men were seeking a replacement for fiberglass patrol boats. They needed a shallow-draft craft that could make 20 knots quickly from a cold start, and cruise at about 15 knots for hours on end. They decided to build one with ferro-cement, a common housebuilding material. After much trial and error, they found that unwashed river sand made tough cement. They turned it into ferro-cement by infusing chicken wire, cured it with burlap and wet paper towels, and formed it into a twenty-four-foot hull. They braced the hull inside with angle irons, pasted some wood here and there on the exterior, and affixed outboard motors. They painted eyes and teeth on the bow, put their prototype *Viper* into the Saigon River, and skimmed merrily off at the amazing speed of 26 knots. Total cost of materials: about one thousand dollars.

Jerry-built riverboats, however, are not the stuff of long-running defense R&D contracts or of snugger relations between DDR&E and the defense industry. As the Pentagon tried desperately to cope with the soaring prices of technology in the inflation-ridden national economy of the mid-1970s, the arbitrary cost ceilings which it began imposing on the development of weapon systems began cracking contractors. "Problems with industry," reported the Center for Strategic and International Studies, "have grown. There have been disquieting signs of a rift between the Department of Defense and defense industries. The Lockheed near-bankruptcy and the Grumman threat to discontinue production of the F-14 without price relief were the results of Pentagon, as well as company, mistakes. Growing segments of the industry may try to move out of defense work for less risky—and perhaps greener— pastures." Even so, the report acknowledged that the Pentagon had no choice but to decelerate or deny many programs. "The Soviet Union," said the report, "is moving fast on a broad front, and there are critics who worry that our newer systems, when they come, will already be obsolescent compared with those of the Soviet Union. This panel would accept that risk, however, in order to gain tighter control over the R&D process." Then came the usual caveat: "Our defense R&D has not kept pace with Soviet efforts, even though Pentagon spokesmen have warned about the possibility of losing technological leadership. It is not all the Pentagon's fault. The Congress has consistently voted less than asked for defense R&D. The Pentagon objective has been modest—simply to preserve relative positions between U.S. and Soviet R&D. But we have lost ground."

A few months following the report, CIA director William E. Colby, who later would deny the Navy's claim that the Soviets were preparing to take over the Indian Ocean, rode his limousine down the George Washington Parkway along the south bank of the Potomac, across the river, and up to Capitol Hill.

There, he told the Joint Economic Committee that the Soviet Union had more than doubled its military-space research and development budget in only a dozen years—from one-sixth of the total military-space budget to one-third. "These increases," Colby asserted, "clearly were connected with the several new strategic systems now in development and which were tested, especially during the past nine months." In summary, he said, the United States and the USSR were spending about equal amounts for military procurement, but the USSR was spending at least one-fourth more than the United States for military R&D. Ominous. It also turned out that the Russians had shelled out vast amounts to build dummy surface-to-air missile sites to confuse American bomber crews. U.S. analysts called these "Potemkin sites"—more than eight hundred of them, complete with fake launchers, radar, revetments and vehicles —after Marshal Potemkin, the eighteenth-century architect of false-front "villages" in deception of Catherine the Great. It was getting so you couldn't tell when a SAM was a flim flam; a Hen House, Mickey Mouse.

In May 1972, the United States and the USSR signed an agreement called "Cooperation in Fields of Science and Technology." American companies immediately began preparing to exploit a golden Russian market in years to come. Delegations of Soviet technologists began tramping around the plants of the giants of U. S. industry, notably those of the aerospace and computer companies, with an eye to the technologies that they might want to take home. Executives of Lockheed, Boeing, McDonnell Douglas and others flew to Moscow to discuss the possible sale of their commercial jumbo jets. The Russians were intensely interested in these planes. While they obviously knew how to build such big transports, their manufacturing processes still were too primitive to permit mass production at costs that would be competitive in world markets. So what they wanted was not the American planes so much as the American manufacturing technologies that would enable them to mass-produce comparable planes. They also wanted a computerized air-traffic control system comparable to the one then being utilized by the Federal Aviation Administration. The State Department and the Bureau of East-West Trade, which had been created in the Commerce Department specifically to help American companies peddle goods, services and technolo-

gies behind the Iron Curtain, were extra nice to the prospective Soviet customers. But the Defense Department got the
wind up. To the military, it was obvious that computer and
production technologies sold to the Russians for commercial
purposes could just as easily be used for military purposes. In
the absence of clear signals from a Nixon White House which
kept trying to hawk both to and at the Soviet Union, Currie
concluded that the time had come to crack down. He came
across the river one winter noontime in 1973 to address a research and development symposium of the National Security
Industrial Association, lobbyist for a plenitude of high-powered defense contractors, and laid it out for them.

"Let me inject a note of caution," he said. "The Soviets have
become critically aware that their great deficiency is not in
scientific knowledge but rather in production technology.
They apparently feel that they can close neither pivotal gaps
in their military capability nor gaps in their general economic
growth, both domestically and worldwide, until they acquire
a manufacturing technology comparable to ours. This applies
particularly to high technology areas such as integrated circuits, computer software, aircraft, engines, avionics and specialized instruments, to name a few. We therefore see what
appears to be a carefully designed Soviet approach to acquire
production technology, increasingly in the form of complete
turnkey plant operations in these critical areas. Soviet negotiators are well organized and briefed to deal individually with
our industrial firms as a monolithic customer offering tantaliz-
ing visions of future markets. The very characteristic of our
free-enterprise system makes it receptive to this sort of approach. The problem is compounded by our sometimes naïve
acceptance of the availability of vast new markets. I would urge
you to be wary of some of the commercial and balance-of-
payment advantages because, in my personal opinion, the market may be significantly less than advertised, the difficulties of
doing business extensive, and the ability to pay questionable.
I believe this is an issue of national importance. We need clarifi-
cation of national policy, and I will work toward that end."

He had, in fact, already begun, simply by making the speech
and putting the contractors on notice that they might incur the
displeasure of the Pentagon by selling out, as it were, to the
Soviets. Currie had powerful help in Congress, where Cold

Warrior Senator Henry M. Jackson led the trade-dampening brigades. And so, influenced additionally by the subsequent Mideast war, the Soviet missile testing, the Kremlin's policy of restricting emigration of Soviet Jews, and the negative turn of negotiations on limiting strategic weapons, Congress and the administration hunkered down to the old way of doing business with the Russians, meaning doing hardly anything at all. Currie could relax a little. He had bought some time. Détente had been denied, at least for the time being. So had trade in technology. The Pentagon had won the round. As 1975 began, all bets were off on U.S.-Soviet trade. Congress had agreed to give the Kremlin favored treatment in trade only if the Soviets, in turn, agreed to loosen restrictions on the emigration of Russian Jews. The Soviets, in retaliation, angrily renounced previous trade agreements with the U.S. East-West trade had taken a U-turn for the worse, but not necessarily in the eyes of the Pentagon.

After the Nixon-Brezhnev arms-control summit had produced little more than posturing on both sides, I went back to my files in search, again, of clues as to where the apparently ambivalent administration of this President who had pledged "a generation of peace," yet who was brandishing military power as the way of achieving—and risking—it, might be at all consistent. My perusal took place during the period when the White House tapes on the Watergate affair became public, laying naked one conversation between Nixon and the men around him in late 1972, in which he had said of the North Vietnamese: "Those bastards are going to be bombed like they've never been bombed before." In my files, under "research and development" was a 1968 speech by then-candidate Nixon. Warning of "possible breakthroughs by the huge Soviet research and development establishment" into dimensions of weaponry which would plunge the United States into pusillanimity, Nixon declared that the United States was "short-changing its scientific community, risking the opening of a research gap between our effort and that of the Soviet Union." And he pledged a national policy that would nourish science and technology in all fields, not just in defense, to power us up to peace and prosperity.

Karl G. Harr, Jr., clicked the picture into place in September 1974, after Nixon had resigned. Harr, president of the Aero-

space Industries Association, had been uneasy for a long time
about the softening of Pentagon-industry relations in R&D,
and about the protectionist wall which the Pentagon had
bricked around technologies which the industry—rightly or
wrongly—believed would do no harm if dispensed east of the
Elbe and the Urals. But the problem, said Harr, went deeper
than that. Where R&D was concerned, he said, "we must immediately create within the government an adequate focus of
authority." He continued:

In addressing this question, I should state that something
has been troubling me. Nearly two years ago, at a time when
the decline of support for our technological progress was
becoming evident, we proponents of technology were heart-
ened by an historic event. On March 16, 1972, for the first time
in history, a President of the United States delivered a message to Congress on the burgeoning importance of science
and technology to national progress. That message called for
a national commitment to actions designed to stimulate support for research and development and technological innovations in the private sector. Also for actions strengthening
collaboration between federal agencies and state and local
governments, and for actions to promote cooperation between the United States and other nations in science and
technology. Sadly, one has the right to ask today: "Where's
the action?" Many of those who in 1972 looked forward to a
new national policy and a new impetus to science and technology view the years since that Presidential message as
being no less than a disaster. By 1973, for example, the National Aeronautics and Space Council, the Office of Science
and Technology, and the President's Science Advisory Committee were abolished by the White House. Studies by the
Domestic Council and by White House task groups, drawing
upon the technology-applications ideas of all major federal
agencies and from industry, disappeared into the archives of
bureaucracy. In place of a central focal point for national
policy and thrust in science and technology, accountability
for programs—along with generally inadequate funding—
has been spread among the National Science Foundation,
the National Bureau of Standards, the Department of Commerce and the Department of State. All of these agencies are

highly regarded in their special areas. But individually, none of them can be responsive to a national policy which—in effect—does not exist.

Currie had said it too: national policy on research and development had to be thought out, defined and set in motion. The United States was, and would be, only as strong as the technologies which sprang from its R&D—in energy, defense, transportation or whatever. But Currie could not afford to mark time while the new administration of Gerald R. Ford coped with the lacks and confusions of policy, as in science and economics, and with the contradictions of policy, as between national security and foreign affairs, which Nixon had left behind. The defense R&D chief was confronted by overwhelming problems in his own bailiwick which did not brook procrastination. Inflation, which Ford right off the bat called the nation's "deadly enemy," was eating up the buying power of the defense budget, most particularly that portion in R&D. So Currie made some quick fixes. He tinkered with the development timetables of the B-1 bomber and SAM-D missile programs, and made plain that he intended to juggle some other big systems as well. These maneuverings on multi-billion-dollar weapons made, if not really any immediate difference in costs, at least some headlines about the apparently sound approach of DDR&E. Nearly unnoticed, however, were Currie's scramblings on other fronts. His success at these would be crucial to the vitality of defense R&D for many years to come. They had to do with the care and feeding of basic research and exploratory development, with solidifying the mushy relationship between the military and the mathematicians and physicists whose formulae and sometimes forlorn laboratory forays are forerunners of the weapons of the future. Currie had said, too, that the Pentagon could no longer afford to play in the sandbox of all scientific areas. But neither could he afford to let all the sand trickle out of the box.

9

The Death
Ray Dawns

Let there be lights in the firmament of the Heavens—
—Genesis 1:14

At a Christmas holiday party in 1972 I moseyed up to an old acquaintance who works for the Pentagon's Advanced Research Projects Agency. "Long time, Ed," I said, carefully affecting insouciance. "Been busy? I hear you guys are really going all-out on lasers." He dead-panned me. "How's the family?" he said. Then he winked.

A month later into 1973, the following story moved on the Associated Press wire:

The United States is planning a stepped-up effort to produce a "laser bomb," a nuclear weapon that would be simpler and smaller but as powerful as the hydrogen bomb, it was disclosed yesterday. The planned new thrust to perfect such a weapon was revealed in a one-sentence footnote in the Nixon administration's proposed budget for the Atomic Energy Commission. A laser bomb would be an H-bomb in which the intense heat of a laser beam—perhaps the most concentrated and powerful form of light in the universe—would be used to trigger the hydrogen explosives. Present

H-bombs require detonation of atomic bombs to trigger them. A laser-triggered hydrogen device used as a bomb or in the warhead of an intercontinental ballistic missile would be simpler, smaller and cleaner from the standpoint of releasing radioactivity than an H-bomb triggered by an A-bomb. Research aimed at building a laser bomb has been underway for at least five years. But the $34 million earmarked to be obligated by the AEC for such work in fiscal 1974 represents the largest sum ever assigned in a single year.

By this time, the Pentagon's research and development of low-energy lasers to guide bombs and missiles, and to pinpoint targets and their ranges, had long since surfaced. Indeed, laser-guided weapons were used with devastating accuracy in the latter days of Vietnam. Now, laser triggering of H-bombs was coming to public attention. Still securely cloaked, however, was the research being done by ARPA and all three military services on the high-energy laser. This is the death ray that abruptly will upset the balance of today's offensive and defensive tactical and strategic weapons, superseding all of them as the penultimate defender and destroyer, capable of turning men into messes of mush, their machines into molten metal.

The Pentagon does not like to say it that baldly. Throughout the research establishments of the military, officials concede the intensification and the potential import of their work on high-energy lasers. They say, however, that they have such a long way to go, so many problems to overcome, that there is no justification for anyone becoming breathless about beholding Buck Rogers and his ray gun just yet. The laser power source is a sticker, for one thing. It takes tremendous electrical power to generate a laser beam that will be hot enough to disintegrate metal—so much power that today's generators are too large to be deployed in aircraft or—dare we mention?—satellites. Deep in their intellects, though, these men know that it is bound to come, that they will succeed in packaging these power sources for portability. It always does come. Technology always teases, then triumphs. So the question is not whether it will happen, but when and where. In the United States or in the Soviet Union. As always.

Military research on high-energy lasers is no recent, rush-rush affair. In 1966, at Kirtland AFB, New Mexico, the weapons-testing center of the Air Force, a gas laser, powered by 5,000 watts and beamed through a 44-foot tube, burned through firebrick in five seconds flat. The distance between the laser-tube aperture and the firebrick was of almost no importance. A high-energy laser beam is as hot at 100 miles, or you name the distance, as it is at 10 feet. If it is shot in a vacuum. Or in, for example, space. The atmosphere degrades a laser beam as the range increases. The heat and speed of the beam cause plasma to build up around it, diffusing and weakening it. This problem of "thermal blooming" is a major one for the ray-gun researchers. That they will surmount it is certain. They already have begun to do so.

Even now, in 1975, the Air Force is counting on outfitting the doublesonic B-1 bomber, scheduled for production in the late 1970s unless its costs shoot it down, with a laser for self-defense. A laser power package small enough to ride the B-1—a plane no bigger than a Boeing 707 transport—would certainly be small enough to ride the cavernous C-5A transport, the KC-135 tanker, the B-52 bomber and the commercial jumbo jets. These planes can climb to where the atmosphere is relatively thin. Up on top, they could spin a web of laser beams to ensnare incoming missiles and bombers. Searchlights with a sting.

The suggestion of such a scenario evokes cringing, looks of pain, hollow laughter or ridicule at the Pentagon. "Dreamer," they scoff. But such dreams have long since passed from the subconsciousness to the consciousness of military R&D, and they are forbidden in official conversation because, for now, they are better left unsaid.

Who ever envisioned that the radar born of World War II could be refined to see over the horizon? Research aimed at this achievement began in 1949. Less than twenty years later, the Pentagon made public its development of new, ultra-powerful radars that can peer halfway around the world, monitoring missile firings inside the Soviet Union just seconds after the missiles leap skyward. As it will, inevitably, with high-energy laser weaponry, a research breakthrough made over-the-horizon radar suddenly possible and practical. It came in 1962. Scientists and electrical engineers on ARPA's "Project Defender" contrived an "S-band tube"—a radar transmitter to provide high energies of between 2,000 and 5,000 megacycles, at wavelengths of 5.5 to 15 centimeters, that could be bounced off the earth's ionosphere about 100 miles up and reflected back, at an enormously wide angle, to earth. Laser beams, too, can be caromed, using mirrors. Mirrors reflect light, and lasers are light itself, traveling at 900 million feet per second, pencil-thin, piercing, deadly.

The research and exploratory development of high-energy lasers—and the improvement of low-energy, range-finding, target-selecting, bomb-steering lasers—stood at the top of the list of Defense Directorate of Research and Engineering priorities in 1975. Lasers headed the list not only because of what marvels they had shown and what wonders they promised in weaponry but because the Defense Department was very worried that it had slighted laser research, perhaps irredeemably, in the past, and had better get cracking. The research had been going on for a long time, back into the 1950s, but its Pentagon funding had been—considering its portent—rather casual and spotty. Until 1973, the gist of the heavily censored testimony of defense research officials on Capitol Hill was that progress in high-energy laser technology was disappointing and slow. Then the progress seemed to pick up, along with the funding. In 1973, all three services asked Congress to give them substantially more money than they had requested for lasers in the budgets which they already had submitted for that year. Piecing together the few details that the services provided publicly to justify their moves, it became apparent that they had decided to begin "demonstration" phases of ultrapowerful-laser technology. The Navy set out to build a shipboard laser laboratory to find out how—or how well—lasers could defend ships against missiles and aircraft. The Army and Marines planned to install high-energy lasers on vehicles, as antiaircraft weapons and, presumably, as weapons against tanks and personnel carriers. The Air Force, already a step or two ahead of the other Services, had in mind using a KC-135 as a testbed of the laser as a defender of the bomber. The magnitude of the Army's laser budget amendment did not surface. But the Navy, which had asked for $12.4 million, now wanted half again as much, or about $18.5 million. The Air Force beefed up its budget request from $22 million to about $30 million. These increases presaged a trend. In 1974, total funding for high-energy laser-radiation research stood at about $94 million. In 1975, it jumped to about $120 million, with the Air Force absorbing about $40 million and the remainder almost equally divided among ARPA, the Navy and the Army. In terms of the total defense R&D budget, $120 million is piggy-bank change. But in terms of its rate of increase in just a few short years, laser-weapon research spending had begun to zoom. A shadow had appeared, however, and was spreading; the shadow of insufficient funding of the "technology base"—the potfuls of research and exploratory development programs in governmental and industrial laboratories and in universities, the seedbeds of the weapons of the future and of improvements of weapons just recently put into the field. The technology base was where laser weapons and the whole galaxy of sensing, range-finding, targeting and remote-controlling electronics had begun to sprout. If kept in the shade, it would turn fallow, its sprouts would fail. So, Dr. Malcolm R. Currie, chief of the Directorate of Defense Research and Engineering, moved to cast back the shadow. Let us set the stage.

The year before, the report on "U.S. Military R&D Management" of the Center for Strategic and International Studies reasserted a criticism which had been intensifying ever since the defense research establishment began slighting basic research in favor of emphasis on Vietnam gadgetry and the evolution of strategic nuclear weapons. True, laser sensors and other products of electronics technology had come to the forefront in Vietnam. But there was concern that these might have been brought along too quickly, too precipitously, without the constancy of research which would assure their continued development. And there was no doubt that research of high-energy lasers had been neglected during the Vietnam years. The Center for Strategic and International Studies had this to say:

We are concerned about the [money] appropriations to the early stages of the R&D process—to research and exploratory development. Clearly the bulk of the available funds must be saved for the system-development stages, because those projects require great expenditures. But, despite the concern about the long-term technology competition with the Soviet Union, the funding of early stages has not been significantly enhanced. Added money has been requested disproportionately for the "D" end of the process, rather than the "R." Indeed, DDR&E management attention appears to be focused too much on advanced development stages. This, of course, is where the public and Congressional criticism comes, but DDR&E should not neglect the smaller, and less controversial, research stages. In the long run, the entire pattern of defense R&D should tilt toward more exploratory work across a very wide front and away from development of so many costly systems.

For its trend away from basic research and exploratory development, for its newfound scorn of "hobby shopping," and its insistence on the immediate "military usefulness" of research projects, the Defense Department really had no one to blame but itself. The trend was set nearly ten years ago, just as Vietnam began frustrating the American military technologies of that time, by "Project Hindsight." This was the Defense Department's first attempt to get facts that would resolve how it should apportion R&D dollars to assure the highest payoff in improved weaponry and military equipment; whether to leave military-financed research free to follow its own leads or to hitch it to the enhancement of the technologies of the here and now. The "Hindsight" analysts also sought to find out whether government laboratories had been as productive as those of industry. They selected fifteen major weapon systems then new to the field—for example, the Mark 46 torpedo, the C-141 cargo plane and the Bullpup air-to-ground missile—and examined all subsystems and components of these. In each case, the analysts asked: What scientific knowledge or new technology from the past two decades contributed to advances in this weapon? Where was the work done? What motivated the creators? How was the research initially financed? By industry or the military? As they went along, the "Hindsight" teams of scientific and engineering specialists identified research and development "events" which had made distinctive contributions to the systems. One such, in the evolution of the C-141, for instance, was the development, starting in 1949, of the titanium-aluminum-vanadium alloy used in the compressor blades of what was eventually to become the aircraft's engines. All told, the "Hindsight" hunters isolated 556 "events" involving 1,025 main contributors to the development of the fifteen systems. Industry had accounted for about half of the 556, defense laboratories for about two-fifths, universities for about one-tenth, and nonmilitary government labs and foreign labs for the miniscule remainder.

"Project Hindsight" concluded that while defense laboratories had contributed substantially to weapons development, their relative importance had been declining, though not necessarily to their discredit. The reason, said the report, was that during the twenty-year period considered in the study, "the national scientific and technological community essentially quadrupled in strength" while the in-house laboratories had grown hardly at all. The most decisive conclusion of "Hindsight," however, was that the contributions of science to the military since World War II were greatest when the research had been directed to fulfilling specific military needs. The authors acknowledged that the military, at the time of the study, still was continuing to benefit from the undirected, basic research that had taken place three or more decades previously in nuclear physics, relativity, thermodynamics, optics and electromagnetic theory, among other fields. But while this basic research had paid off, "the fact," said the Hindsighters, "remains that the contribution from recent undirected science to the systems we have studied appears to have been small." They wrote that they did not question the value of basic scientific research, but only meant to emphasize that scientists more quickly solve problems, and the military more quickly puts their solutions into actual weaponry, when the military identifies the problems on which the scientists are put to work. "Hindsight" also concluded that advances in military weaponry do not usually come about through single, spectacular breakthroughs in research, but through the aggregation of many innovations. And it found that, ordinarily, a decade or more must go by before enough innovations "collect" in a radically improved weapon design. For example, transistor technology gets all the credit for having cut the size of the electronic components in the brain pans of planes and missiles. But without the companion development of ancillary technologies such as tantalum capacitors, printed circuits, the nickel-cadmium battery and others, transistor technology in itself would have made for only a marginal measuring down—far from today's miniaturization—of electronic components.

In the fall of 1973, seven years after the "Hindsight" report, the Defense Department teamed with its R&D contractors in another look back through the development of modern weapons to determine where they had begun and what had gone into them. This examination, however, bordered on the frantic, and was born of desperation. It was undertaken by industry on the demand of Currie, who was moving, as we have noted, to preserve the defense technology base. It had to do with something called "Independent Research and Development," or "IR&D." At seminars and through his speeches, Currie told the defense contractors that they had better start managing their IR&D programs more efficiently and help him document the legitimacy of those programs. Otherwise, Congress would withdraw the money that it had been giving the Pentagon to keep the programs going. For Congress was challenging the Pentagon and the industry to prove that IR&D projects, which fill no immediately perceptible military research purpose, were worth the half billion dollars that the Pentagon spends on them every year. The IR&D issue evoked yawns outside the Pentagon, the industry and some quarters of Congress, but in those circles, it was a gut issue, of much moment for the future of the technology base.

IR&D covers the private research and development performed by industrial companies in the hope that it will lead to technology deserving of either defense contracts or commercial sales or, in the best of all situations, both. The companies spend about $600 million a year on such research, but charge off most of this to the Pentagon as overhead on other defense work for which they already are under contract. The Pentagon budgets this money, and reimburses the companies. Through the years, the Pentagon and the companies have contended that the IR&D work very often contributes, eventually, to improvements of weapons technology, and thus deserves sustained Pentagon support. The companies say that they could not afford to continue executing IR&D if they were not permitted to charge it off. They also say that without IR&D, the underpinnings of defense technology soon would crumble, even though the IR&D of the moment may not have any clear-cut relationship to a current military mission or weapon program. Finally, the companies take the position that if they were denied IR&D funding, they would have to quit bidding for Pentagon contracts because they would lack the money to continue updating the technologies which had made them competitive in the defense market in the first place. The Defense Department stands with them all the way. Currie called IR&D "absolutely crucial to the technology base." But Congressional critics see it quite differently. They call the Pentagon reimbursements a slush fund which the companies use to enhance their commercial product lines, or simply pocket. In 1973, at the request of Senators William Proxmire, John Stennis and Thomas McIntyre, the General Accounting Office undertook an investigation of IR&D practices. The GAO had looked into IR&D before, but never in the depth of the investigation which GAO began just about the time Currie took over at DDR&E. So Currie had to move quickly.

In mustering the defense industry to counterattack, Currie suggested that the companies come up with hard evidence of how IR&D had paid off, through the years, in military hardware. To cover his flanks, he also appointed a committee within the Defense Science Board to conduct an IR&D investigation of its own and report back to him how well the companies were managing their projects, and how justified they were in charging off its costs to their defense contracts. He professed objectivity in this, and considering his personal curiosity level, he probably was, to some extent. But no one really expected that the DSB would foul its own nest by finding too much wrong with IR&D. Currie was counting on favorable findings from the DSB, and also on gleaning several striking examples of IR&D payoff from the defense contractors. He knew of one such example already: lasers, which Hughes Aircraft had begun researching with its own money back in the 1950s, and had brought to beam, in various forms, both before and while Currie was with the company. Avco-Everett, United Aircraft and Northrop also had invested heavily in laser research. The Pentagon had not funded this research at the time, partly because defense scientists had not been persuaded of its ultimate success, partly because the Defense Department had been far more excited about the R&D of nuclear weapons than it had been about the R&D of laser electro-optics. Not until much later were defense contracts awarded to several companies for the beginnings of R&D on lasers as they would someday apply to the defense arsenal.

At Currie's urging, three trade associations representing

more than 400 defense contractors—the Aerospace Industries Association, the National Security Industrial Association and the Electronics Industries Association—went to work in 1973. To come up with examples of IR&D payoff and to articulate the industry's argument for Pentagon support of IR&D, they formed a team headed by T. J. Murrin, executive vice-president, defense and public systems, Westinghouse; Irving K. Kessler, executive vice-president, government and commercial systems, RCA; and Thomas G. Pownall, president, Martin Marietta Aerospace. In May 1974, this team held a breakfast press conference at the Mayflower Hotel in Washington to make public its 300-page report, replete with examples of major weapon systems, subsystems and components which had sprung, years ago, from researchers in industrial laboratories using company funds. Among these were lasers, of course, and integrated circuits, sonars, helicopters, short-takeoff planes, sensors, spacecraft-and-missile heat shields, radar altimeters, radar, navigation systems, parts of ship-defense missile systems, hydraulic valves, electronic countermeasures, the Harpoon missile and many others. It was obvious, in the report, that IR&D had been especially rewarding as the sire of submarine and antisubmarine systems, along with aircraft. All told, the recitation by industry of the wonders that IR&D had wrought seemed persuasive enough at a glance. But the question remained: would Congress consider it so? The General Accounting Office investigation would extend into the spring or summer of 1975, and its results would probably make the difference on Capitol Hill. Currie knew full well that the tenuous nature of IR&D and its peanuts status as part of a $10.3-billion-plus defense research budget in 1975 made it an attractive target for Congress. The lawmakers are reluctant to rip into major weapons systems, but they relish making a token show of thrift by rejecting programs of seemingly obscure import. IR&D funding had become even more vulnerable in 1974 and 1975 when inflation began wracking the defense budget as a whole and it became obvious that something would have to give. But more later, in the final chapter, on that.

Cogent to the IR&D controversy was the long-running argument over the effectiveness of government laboratories. Should DDR&E, ARPA and the services rely on them more or less? Congress consistently has favored more reliance, in the notion that the in-house laboratories are less expensive and can be fine-tuned more harmoniously to the needs of the military. But the opposing point of view is that industrial laboratories, because they stay on top of the commercial and defense markets for the products of their research, are less likely to be dilatory in their R&D, more likely to build purposefully on the technologies which they already have going for them—and for the Pentagon. "The market orientation," said the report of the Center for Strategic and International Studies, "makes it more likely that every avenue will be explored in implementing new technology by industrial laboratories. This aggressive marketing of laboratory results is likely to lead to a much earlier realization of the problems and opportunities associated with new developments. Industrial laboratories tend more to carry a project through to the prototype stage because industry is interested in the final payoff. This means that a variety of technical and managerial skills are focused on each particular program."

The trouble with this point of view is that the marketing syndrome may suborn scientific research, as contrasted with the development of marketable technology. Too much emphasis on the pertinent, not enough on the possible. No one ever knows for sure which fields of science could lead to novel weapons of the future. The best the Pentagon can do is to try to stay abreast of the stupefying spectrum of science, and this, say those who worry about overreliance on industrial laboratories, is best done in government and university labs, where pauses for reflection and explorations of the exotic do not pummel anyone's profits. Indeed, the research contributions of the more than one hundred government labs and test centers to weapons systems have been impressive through the years. They include the beginnings of the Sidewinder, Shrike and Walleye missiles, proximity fuses, caseless ammunition and, on the humanitarian side, the heart pump. Government labs are credited with having outshone their industrial counterparts in carrying out the crash research that adapted weapons and tactics to the Vietnam War. Among their products were night vision devices, the 175-millimeter artillery system, frozen blood, antimalarial drugs, advanced helicopter technology, antipersonnel weapons such as the gravel mine—and laser-guided bombs. Government scientists and engineers do other things, too, that their better-paid peers in more richly funded industry cannot be expected to do: give the Defense Department more objective guidance on overall research progress and goals; investigate materials, techniques and ideas with a degree of detachment and catholicity that would be unsupportable in the profit centers, and—not least—train officers in the technical concerns which have become almost as important to military careerists, nowadays, as combat command experience.

Dr. John L. Allen is a graduate of one of those laboratories. A quarter-mile walk down the third-floor, E Ring corridor from Currie's command suite in DDR&E is a door bearing the legend, "Deputy Director, Research & Advanced Technology." That is where Allen works, and what he is. DDR&E officials always seem to run slightly behind their appointment schedules, so Sherry, Allen's sandy-haired, full-figured receptionist (DDR&E receptionists seem to run to the highly attractive) offered me coffee, and I chatted with Air Force Colonel John J. McCambridge, Allen's military assistant. He noted that only about 17 percent of the R&D budget was being spent for basic and exploratory research, and he lamented, like everyone else in Allen's bailiwick, the unknown but probably dire effect of annual Congressional cuts of a few million here and there on such work. Those millions would have broadened the technology base. Then Allen strode into the antechamber, stuck out a hard hand, and ushered me to the conference table in his office. It was our first meeting. He had been on the job less than a year, but he had spent virtually his entire adult life in military-related science and engineering. Now in his mid-forties but looking ten years younger, mostly because of his fit-looking physique, clear countenance, and full head of dark hair, Allen had just come off nearly three years as the Naval Research Laboratory's associate director for electronics. He had served on the Defense Science Board committee which studied, and recommended, the development of lightweight fighters. In the early 1950s, he spent four years in the Air Force, mostly as an instructor at the Air Force Radar School and at MIT's Lincoln Laboratory, which since World War II has been preeminent in radar research. Allen enrolled at Pennsylvania State University upon leaving the Air Force, and was graduated in 1958. By the end of the following decade, he had picked up a master's degree in electrical engineering and a doctorate in communications biophysics, both at MIT. He returned to Lincoln Laboratory, and founded its "Array Radars Group." Now, he was leading DDR&E's drive to shore up the technology base, and he had a problem.

"We've suffered a big erosion of funding," he said, brushing a speck off the "Thank You for Not Smoking" sign on the table. "In terms of real-world dollars, we're doing only 60 percent as much basic research and exploratory development as we were doing ten years ago. On a graph," he said grimly, "this would be called the 'going-out-of-business curve.' A big fraction of development money has gone into the big weapon systems. But a lot of it has gone elsewhere in the government. I'm a little bit sad to see that national policy—or the absence of it—has been to put basic research elsewhere—to a large extent, in the social agencies. I'm not knocking the social agencies. But we shouldn't forget something: Military research is very important to the civilian economy too. It has given us plastics, composites, electronics. It has given us, in fact, the whole airline industry and a twenty-billion-dollar aircraft industry. The Department of Defense paid the bill to pioneer us into the jet age. Now, other nations are applying the research base that we built up, to compete with us in selling the products of that research base. But we can't just sit and complain about the erosion of the technology base, and blame the world for it. What we have to do right here is to exercise a real scrutiny and make crunchy decisions on what to stop doing. There is a great reluctance to bite the bullet on some of these issues."

QUESTION: "Now that guidance and control seems to have progressed so far, will there be a letup of R&D in that area?"

ALLEN: "We have come a long way in guidance and control. But most G&C systems are fairly new. You can probably look forward to about twenty more years of evolution in them. They are still coming right out of the technology base. Development of guidance-and-control electronics is an example of what happens as a technology matures. The expertise gravitates from the defense side to industry—if the technology has turned out to be profitable. Radar is another example. The technology began in the military. Now, industry is outstanding in R&D of radar for conventional weapons. If you look at all of the work, industries and defense labs each get about 40 percent of the technology base R&D. And about three-quarters of the technology base lies in six main areas. Weapons get about 20 percent; electronics, 18 percent; vehicles—air, sea and land—11 percent; materials—fiberglass, composites and the like, you wouldn't have the fiberglass sailboat had it not been for the Polaris program—12 percent; biomedical sciences, 8 percent; and environmental sciences—oceanography, geodesy studies and so forth—about 8 percent. We're finding that the fallout from oceanography is very heavy. It's also visible. What we've got to do in the Defense Department is to make technology more visible. It's hard for the man in the street to understand, for instance, why what is in the F-14 makes it more valuable than the F-4."

Lasers, of course, ranked high among Allen's priorities in research and technology. He acknowledged his excitement, too, about infrared imagery—"We now can 'see' in a different wavelength band from ten years ago"—and about how new low-power lasers coming along, happily, "just happen to be in that same wavelength band." Obviously, the combinations of infrared and laser seek-and-see systems promised 20/20 night and foul-weather vision for U. S. hunters and targeters in the immediate future, with great significance for submarine detection. Allen mentioned something else, too, that especially stimulated his imagination: "The Navy is working on superconductivity propulsion, based on a twenty-year-old physical principle. The exploratory development now is geared to making a unit that can provide useful power for ships."

Superconductivity is achieved when you take strange combinations of metals and deep-freeze them in a process known as supercooling. When they get down near absolute zero, they become superconductors. They lose their electrical resistance and generate electricity at very close to 100 percent efficiency. It is a very expensive process, for now. The cryogenics—the freezing mixtures—are delicate and costly. The metals which make up the alloys, such as niobium, mercury, tantalum, vanadium and iridium, are rare. But who seriously doubted that the technology could be mastered, or the costs accommodated? Moreover, it takes little imagination to foresee that the bulky superconductivity power-refrigeration unit being developed by the Navy will someday become small enough for aircraft, which by then, because of the electronic supersophistication of their flight controls, no longer will need wings or tails, and will have the speed and the silhouette of, say, flying saucers.

Somewhere, sometime, long ago, a genius or two or three discovered and defined the physical principles which progenerated yesterday's, today's and tomorrow's weapons. A favorite arguing point of Pentagon research types is that any jet plane flying today is the product, actually, of propulsion research which began in the 1930s—in Germany, by the way—and that if the cost of all jet-engine research everywhere in the world over all those years were factored into the price of each plane, the price would be out of sight. So, really, the price of weapons cannot be measured, and is meaningless. But they could make an even better point: the research goes back even farther than the 1930s, clear back to the discovery of the laws of action-reaction, of force, of thermodynamics and aerodynamics, of gravity—to Newton under the tree and to all his supercranial cousins, wherever they happened to be when lightning, or the apple, struck. Today's apple trees are in the universities, and the Defense Department, in the mid-1970s, was harvesting them only haphazardly. The thinkers and researchers of academia were in no danger—unlike their counterparts who stick to the evolvement of technology—of rediscovering fire or reinventing the wheel. They were exploring, or had the brains and facilities but no money to explore, such exotics as mind control, extrasensory perception, biofeedback—parapsychology in all its permutations. To the military, booming along with bombers, missiles, submarines and electronic sensors, these were phantasmagorical fields of research. But would they always be? Would the day come when the Pentagon would have to seize, for example, on the utility of mind-to-mind communications, of mind-from-mind interceptions of enemy communications? There was much talk that the Russians, with a big head start, were already deep into military research of parapsychology, that they had tried transferring thoughts to and from their cosmonauts, that the names of their experimenters would someday be as synonomous with the extrasensory as Pavlov's is now with the conditioned reflex.

Back to the here and now. It was forbidding enough to U.S. defense officials that the Russians' basic research in areas that we already could fathom, and would need to field, apparently was outdistancing the Americans'. "It concerns me," said Admiral Moran of Navy R&D, "that there have been three Nobel prizewinners for research on lasers, and two of them were Russian." The other, Dr. Charles H. Townes, shared the Nobel Prize in physics in 1964—for research in quantum electronics in the 1950s that led to lasers—with Soviet scientists Nikolai G. Basov and Aleksander M. Prochorov. Where had Dr. Townes done his work? In an industrial or government laboratory? No. At Princeton.

Nurturing basic research obviously had become a national, not just a defense, problem. The National Science Board appointed a twelve-member panel to study the interaction of science, technology and society in the United States. In 1972, the panel reported that the national commitment to "high-risk" basic research had become increasingly inadequate since 1968. It defined this kind of research as that which has "a low probability of producing results and yet promises results, if achieved, of such significance that the projects are deemed worth the risk." In the same period, the General Accounting Office dug into the scope of defense basic research, and came to the same conclusion. GAO found that not only was innovative research on the wane, but that there was an appalling divergence among the top Defense Department and military R&D overseers as to just what is meant by "basic research." If you can't define it, you can't do it, said GAO. "The director of the Defense Advanced Research Projects Agency," reported GAO in a letter to Defense Secretary James R. Schlesinger, "also has stated that research has become too application-oriented, and that now even basic research is expected to be directed at some end product. He felt that the Department of Defense was making very few contributions to new technology. In fact, the director stated that ARPA, which was expected to be an independent and innovative source for the introduction of new technological concepts into the defense establishment, was becoming too application-oriented. More specifically, ARPA is supposed to conduct high-risk, high-payoff research in areas where defense technology appears to be falling behind. The agency, however, does not review the services' research programs to determine whether there is an adequate balance between innovative and evolutionary research. Instead, it reviews the service programs to identify 'gaps' in the technology which it can fill. The director told us that when such areas are identified, the research does not necessarily have to be innovative. The emphasis is to fill the gaps in the technology."

A few years back, ARPA officials petitioned the Defense Department for permission to begin contracting with universities and other, offshoot experimental centers for the beginnings of defense-related research in mind control, biofeedback and the like. If you can believe the very few people at the Pentagon who even acknowledge that this happened, the ARPA men were told to forget it and, furthermore, to keep quiet about even having proposed it. For one thing, supposedly said the powers at the Pentagon, it would be political suicide for the Defense Department to ask Congress for money to start monkeying with mind control. Good Lord, can you imagine the reaction on the Hill? For another, where is the military usefulness in it? "Well," the ARPA petitioners reportedly said, "the Russians are into it, and we should have an R&D hedge. We should be able to defend against them." No go, said the decision-makers of Defense. Or so it would seem. Time will tell.

Again, away from the exotic and back to real life. For all the technological successes of government and industrial laboratories, the uneasy feeling kept building up in the Pentagon that defense research is bound to atrophy unless it can be transfused again by academia, unless there is a return to the pre-Vietnam era when MIT, Cal Tech, Harvard, Princeton, Stanford and another dozen or so titans of theoretical mathematics and physics worked wholeheartedly and unabashedly in the weapons culture. The relative aridity of the defense-universities relationship of recent years has tended also to dessicate the not-for-profit Federal Contract Research Centers. These think tanks, most valuable for their expertise in systems analysis and engineering, often served as the conduits between the cerebrators of the universities and the pragmatists of the Pentagon. Four of the ten think tanks currently under Pentagon contract—and receiving only about 2 percent of all defense research money—are laboratories actually affiliated with universities: Johns Hopkins Applied Physics Laboratory; Pennsylvania State Ordnance Research Laboratory; University of Washington Applied Physics Laboratory, and MIT's Lincoln

Lab. Others, such as Stanford Research Institute, Systems Engineering Corp., Aerospace Corp., IDA, RAND, the Center for Naval Analysis and Analytic Services (ANSER), are independent of university administration, if not of university scientists. They are more directly tied, for the most part, to the military services, and deal in the engineering and systems analysis of weapons-cum-strategies.

In the waning summer of 1974, the military, industrial and university members of the Defense Science Board took themselves off to the Naval War College at Newport, Rhode Island, for a week or more of brainstorming with one another and with key representatives of the country's R&D community from far and near. Currie packed off, too, to spend some time with them. "We are muddling through," he told me the day before he departed, "with the universities. I'll explore the problem with the DSB, and I will start addressing myself to it when I get back. I feel very strongly about our relationship with the scientific community. It's a vital coupling. Our support of university work has been seriously eroded. It hasn't become bad enough that I think the world will end tomorrow, but it's not good. It's something that could keep on deteriorating, almost imperceptibly, until we wake up some day and find that we've finally lost something precious. We're all—ARPA, DDR&E and the services—contributing only about $250 million a year to the universities, and we've got to turn that around. I think we can. We've gone through a turning away by the universities from defense research, but there are signs that this trend is ending. The professors and administrators seem to be more willing to discuss the problem now. The students don't seem to have the very rabid feelings of the Vietnam years. I view this as an opportunity. We'll think it through, and go to work, reestablish strong ties."

So Currie had made a start at shoring up two shaky foundations of defense technology—IR&D and the universities. He could talk, meet, travel, think and encourage until the tropics froze over, however, and none of it would do him any good unless he had more money. This is precisely what he tried to get for the technology base in his $9.4-billion budget. And no sooner had it landed on Capitol Hill than there was Currie, right behind it, making his most important move of all, trying to justify it. Where did he begin?

By taking his request for money for high-energy laser R&D out of his briefcase and making it *the* example of how he was trying to coordinate the services' research, and of how important the research was.

The previous year, 1973, when Currie had been on the job only a few months, the Armed Services and Appropriations committees had expressed concern that the services were duplicating their research of low-energy laser target-designating and missile-guiding systems. Both the Army and the Air Force had been conducting separate programs to develop "smart" missiles guided by laser beams, of the sort that had been used in Vietnam. Currie made a decision, and put the Air Force solely in charge. Now, he emphasized to Congress that the high-energy laser program, too, would be well-integrated almost from the start.

He testified: "I have a very simple picture that I think of in terms of illustrating the power of systems based on this technology. We spend a great deal of money and effort in the Defense Department making various types of missiles, with their guidance systems and the platforms that launch them, to carry—in essence—packages of explosives from the platform to the target. These explosive carriers represent the most intricate and expensive parts of our weapons arsenal, of our tools of modern warfare. The laser, in contradistinction, consists of a device in which one has a controlled explosion, and one converts that explosive energy to the form of light, which is transmitted instantaneously at the speed of light to the target, therefore, prohibiting any evasive action.

"The high-energy laser program started out in ARPA. ARPA was the instrument by which the original research and the discoveries were fostered. We have established what we call the 'High-Energy Laser Group.' This is a department-wide group which consists of the program managers in the high-energy laser efforts in the services, as well as outstanding experts, largely from academia, who continually review the program as a whole. One of the more recent members is a representative from the Atomic Energy Commission's Lawrence Livermore Laboratory. The director of the AEC's Los Alamos Scientific Laboratory's laser division attends the meetings too. HELG provides the mechanism by which I can watch the balancing of the programs—I can understand them—and from which we can depart in emphasizing one aspect or the other." Currie also spread out for the Armed Services committees the several single-spaced pages of security regulations surrounding high-energy laser work. These left no doubt that the work compared, in the looser but still hardly lighthearted security atmosphere of today, with that of the World War II Manhattan Project, when it came to keeping secrets and punishing those who failed to keep them."

At one session of the Senate Armed Services R&D Subcommittee, there was this give and take which showed how laser weapons were catching the fancy:

SENATOR THOMAS J. McINTYRE, CHAIRMAN: "During my recent visit to the Pratt and Whitney Corporation in Florida, which is one of the major companies involved in high-energy laser applications, I was told that technology is running ahead of the money available, and that more money could be applied to take earlier advantage of what has been learned. Do you agree with that?"

CURRIE: "Yes. In general, I share a concern that enough of our total resource in the high-energy laser area is not going to technology but to the applications of that technology. It is a very highly subjective area . . . and I am reviewing the entire Defense Department tri-Service and ARPA effort in high-energy lasers from this point of view."

McINTYRE: "This subcommittee has a reputation for applying bandaids to some of the requests you make. I will tell you right now that if you find that we are not spending enough money on the laser—as a layman, I have a feeling that it [deleted]—so I don't want to impede it; here, I believe, is the name of the game—if you need more than you are now asking for laser development technology, don't wait for a supplemental budget request, come in and tell us about it."

CURRIE: "I am not bashful, and I will take you up on that offer."

McINTYRE: "How much additional money do you think you can effectively use in fiscal year 1975?"

CURRIE: "We are faced with an interesting problem in the high-energy laser field [deleted], and the cost of pursuing each one of these developments is increasing so rapidly that the whole thing could go topsy-turvy. We are increasing the budget [deleted] this year. I want to hold to that until we can really get our bearings."

After considerably more dialogue, with McIntyre continuing to offer a blank check for Currie to fill in, and with Currie saying let's see where we stand first, McIntyre capped the colloquy as follows:

"I think that we would be much more attuned to increases in laser technology than we are to some of the other areas, particularly in strategic-weapon areas that pop up against the ABM treaty. So much for that."

No one made the connection, at least not in print, but something intriguing had happened, meanwhile, over at ARPA. Dr. Peter O. Clark had taken over as chief, Laser Technology, Strategic Technology Office. He had been at Hughes with Currie. Doing what? High-energy laser and optics technology research. He had been a key man in the advancement of laser radar technology, too, and he had written several technical papers, and held three patents, on laser devices. He had been a laser man all the way—one of the new-new breed. His work in electrical engineering and physics leading to his doctorate at Cal Tech had been concentrated on lasers and laser devices. Truly, the atom men were moving to the rear at the Pentagon. The royal purple adorned the beam.

Through the spring of 1974, the Senate Armed Services Committee held a round of hearings covering all Defense Department programs in electronic warfare, Remotely Piloted Vehicles, antisubmarine warfare and high-energy lasers. At the end, the committee reported:

"Electronic warfare embraces every aspect of military operations and poses a major challenge to our industry. The ability of our offensive equipment to reach and destroy enemy targets depends in large measure on the effectiveness of our electronic warfare capability. In the same manner, defensive electronic warfare equipment may well determine the ability of our forces to survive an enemy attack. Remotely Piloted Vehicles already have proven their value, and promise to be a relatively inexpensive way to perform important military missions which today must be conducted with manned aircraft. Antisubmarine warfare is the name of the game in maintaining our control of the ocean lines of communication and insuring the survivability of our fleet."

And on top of all this, asserted the committee: "High-Energy Lasers promise a revolutionary change in future weapon systems which may alter the very concepts and tactics of warfare."

So captivated was the committee by lasers, pilotless planes, undersea sensors and the like, so relieved and refreshed was it to be turning to something besides wearisome, worrisome nuclear weapons for a change, that it actually chided (McIntyre had provided the cue) Currie for not having requested enough money for the technology base where all these new-generation weapons were germinating. This surely surprised Currie. He thought, even, that he had asked for maybe a little more than he was likely to get. The committee also fed back to Currie something he already knew:

"We urge the Department of Defense," said the committee report, "to exercise more foresight and better judgment in the decisions made regarding what research and development programs to propose each year. This should insure more favorable consideration by the Congress. Future authorization requests for R&D must emphasize those technologies and weapon systems which are critical to our future survival."

At Kirtland AFB in the Manzano Mountain foothills near Albuquerque, the high-powered laser already had taken to the field. No one in authority would confirm them, but reports persisted, and proliferated, that laser beams already had zapped a few drone planes out of the sky. The Air Force researchers were concentrating hard on their field tests. At the beginning of 1974, the CIA had handed the military its estimate that the Soviets were spending the equivalent of $1 billion a year on laser-weapon R&D. The only consolation—a small one —in this was that apparently the U. S. was far ahead in the low-energy laser field. Laser-guided bombs and missiles were becoming commonplace in the U.S. arsenal. The trick to them was relatively simple. In its nose, the bomb has a device which detects a laser beam. It spots the light that the beam reflects from the target, and adjusts the bomb's steering vanes accordingly. The bomb heads straight toward the point of laser reflection. In Vietnam, the laser was aimed from another plane, not from the bomber or attack aircraft. This technique became prominent during the devastating B-52 bombing of Hanoi-Haiphong in December 1972, but it had been employed, not so publicly but just as spectacularly, beforehand. The previous spring, two helicopters used laser target-designators and wire-guided missiles to destroy about fifty targets—at least half of them, moving tanks—in one day of the battle for Kontum in the South Vietnam highlands. The targets were illuminated by the infantry. All U.S. fighter and attack planes, helicopters and new tanks now are being outfitted with laser target-designators. Targetseeking lasers now being installed in attack planes not only will permit the pilot to lock onto targets at ranges of ten miles or more but also will control his cockpit radar display of the target and its range. The planes, in short, will be self-contained laser systems—finding, tracking and destroying the targets.

In contrast to the laser-guided bomb, its television-guided cousin is just as accurate but more complicated and more expensive to field. The bomb has a small TV camera in its nose. A crewman focuses this camera on the target. When the bomb is dropped, the camera guides it to the target on which the camera maintains its bead. TV-guided missiles use essentially the same technique. The Navy Walleye missile and the Air Force Maverick missile, which showed its mettle during the Arab-Israeli War of 1973, are guided by television. The Navy Bulldog missile (the old Bullpup grown up) is laser-guided. The TV-steered members of the new "smart" family of bombs and missiles are even more likely than the laser-guided versions to go blind in bad weather. But advances in R&D of infrared "imaging" systems probably will help overcome this problem.

Combining low and high power may be the key to the laser as the kingpin defensive weapon of the future. United with radars, lasers instantly would get the drop on any targets that the radars spot. They would be trained along the radars' lines of sight at continuous-pulsed low power, which would be transformed into kill-level power the moment the radars pick up incoming targets. As soon as the radars would spot and fix, their lasers would "shoot," at 186,000 miles per second. This would mean instantaneous detection and destruction of bombers or missiles—unless the bombers or missiles can slip through or under the radars, or kill the radars first. In this is the new arms race, and the runners already are up the track.

So quick is the laser that only one, tracking and beaming on radar, could pick off descending multiple warheads in miniseconds. The lasers' swiftness of strike would permit defenders to detonate missiles far down-range from the missiles' targets. In tests, high-energy lasers already have burned through the nose cones of missiles built to withstand the scorching, searing heat of reentry from space.

"I regret," a high-level Pentagon official let drop one day, "that we may someday go into space with lasers." He left the implications unsaid, and changed the subject abruptly. He may have been thinking of lasers that would defend early-warning, surveillance and reconnaissance satellites against attack. The Russians have been said for years to have tested a satellite-killer system. Laser purists point out that putting aboard satellites the bulky power generators currently and prospectively available for intense, weapon-level laser energy is—and probably will be—out of the question. But others say the purists are begging the question, underrating the technology, being persnickety. Whatever, there would be other uses in space for lasers of slightly lesser power: for one, seeking out ballistic-missile submarines by measuring the water that they displace as they range the oceans at shallow—in relation to their hunter-killer counterparts—depths. Ocean surveillance even now is one of the principal pursuits of the orbiters of both the U.S. and the USSR. The U.S. Navy is using airborne lasers to measure the heights of waves. It is a foregone conclusion, given the onward and upward thrust of all technology, particularly of laser and space technology, that the lasers of the future will fly ever higher above, and look ever deeper into, the seven seas.

L.A.S.E.R. stands for Light Amplification by Stimulated Emission of Radiation. It is, simply, intensely concentrated light. Ordinary light is but a small part of the whole spectrum of electromagnetic radiation, which ranges from ultra-low frequency through the communications wavelengths, through the radar wavelengths and beyond, with the wavelengths growing shorter, through infrared, visible light, ultraviolet, x-rays, cosmic rays and, finally, gamma rays. The laser, using electrical power to stimulate and concentrate light rays through a medium—a solid, a gas or a chemical—has only one, extremely intense, "coherent" wave which, as its colliding photons chain-react and proliferate, builds up into a continuous or pulsating beam. One laser beam could carry 100 million communications channels—far more than all telephone and radio channels now in use. The astronauts used laser beams to televise and radio-transmit their messages to Houston. Laser beams, because they are superfocused, assure highly secure transmissions. And because they flash at 900 million feet per second, they are reflected to their sender, who may be using them to fix artillery and missile ranges, before he releases the button that he pressed to release the beams. Their time-distance margin of error means not a whit; on the human scale of measurement, the lasers are errorless. Their civilian uses, from surgery to welding to three-dimensional photography, even to laser-ranging canes for the blind, are practically without limit. And it is mainly at Kirtland AFB that their limitations as weapons are being overcome.

In 1969, the Defense Department decided that the time had come, if it had not already passed, to let loose the laser. ARPA set up a supersecret, tri-Service project code-named "Eighth Card," centered at Kirtland's Weapons Laboratory. It remained secret to all outsiders for more than a year. Then it began to surface. Bits and pieces of information over the next couple of years made it clear that Kirtland's laser researchers had long since overcome the problems of the physics of converting the laser to a weapon; they were into the design engineering phase, trying, as one of them told *Air Force* magazine, "to get a highly controlled beam of light out from inside a very explosive box where all these forces are at work. There is no obvious or easy way of doing this. We, therefore, protect the various tricks of doing the job, which are as significant as the tricks you worried about when you put the first atomic bomb together."

Three years later, in September 1973, the following Associated Press story moved on the wire out of Albuquerque:

"The first laser assembly and maintenance facility for military aircraft in the United States will be at Kirtland Air Force Base overlooking Tijeras Arroyo, a spokesman said today.

" 'The Air Force is pursuing a high-energy laser research program to determine the feasibility of using lasers for a variety of military applications, including weapons,' the spokesman said.

" 'We want to see how a laser beam moves through the air and what happens to it,' he said.

"The multimillion-dollar Advanced Research Technology Facility is expected to be completed next year. The spokesman said the arroyo is more than 8,000 feet wide and the site was chosen to enable the facility to use the south bank of the arroyo as a backstop for transmitting laser beams."

The plan for construction of the Advanced Research Technology Facility was legitimate news. But Buck Rogers' boys at

Kirtland had long since found out how a laser beam moves through the air and what happens to it—and to anything it strikes.

Six months later, there was a hint that the "thermal-blooming" barrier to the beam-as-a-weapon was showing signs of surmountability. The hint came from the Navy, when Dr. Peter Waterman, one of its top R&D men, testified before the House Appropriations Committee. According to the hearing record:

QUESTION: "Is the highest priority requirement in the Navy for a laser defense weapon against antishipping missiles?"

DR. WATERMAN: "[Deleted.]"

This was followed by an exchange on the effects of weather on lasers. Most of the colloquy was censored, but did contain Waterman's concession that "one of our worst problems, of course, is the atmospheric moisture." Then:

QUESTION: "[Deleted.]"

WATERMAN: "We feel it will operate under those conditions and that we will be able to hit the target and transmit enough energy to damage it fatally."

The likelihood was that the censored question of the committee member had to do with the Navy's research in overcoming thermal blooming, the plasma that builds up around a laser beam when it is drilled through air, clear or foul. The likelihood also was that Waterman's response had been motivated by the Navy's new emphasis on R&D of chemical lasers, as contrasted with previous R&D of gas-dynamic lasers. The chemical laser radiates in shorter wavelengths, and its energy is far more resistant to absorption by air or moisture, which obviously is prevalent, often in the form of fog, on the oceans. The efficiency of chemical lasers—the ratio of power generated to power used in generation—is extremely high. Their recent advent, according to researchers, represents a leap of a light-year from the old ruby ray of yesterday, and means that the laser now is almost ready to shoot to kill.

The beauty of the laser, in the eyes of its military beholders, is that it will be a "clean," discriminating weapon, not a weapon of mass destruction, obviously one for the defense, not the offense. It will disintegrate or incinerate or melt individual targets—planes, missiles, tanks, men—one at a time—and only if they themselves are threatening. The laser's deployment as a defensive weapon consequently—or so the theory goes—will discourage the other side from deploying and launching the nuclear weapons of mass destruction which he knows the laser would neutralize. This argument is compelling up to a point. But it ignores the offensive potential of the lasers of the future for detonating nuclear warheads on their home grounds, for wiping out fleets of bombers wherever they are sheltered, for disrupting the radar defenses and communications networks of nations in a first strike. It ignores, in short, the plain fact that no weapon can ever be described as purely defensive. If it kills it is, ipso facto, offensive in nature, and certain to be regarded as such. Moreover, one side's deployment of lasers for the defense might well evoke the other side, in desperation, to challenge the efficacy of those lasers early in the game, using, perhaps, laser countermeasures along with conventional nuclear weapons. Having developed laser-guided weapons, the Pentagon's R&D establishment has been toiling for some time now to develop countermeasures. So has the Soviet R&D establishment been toiling. One way to foil a direction-finding laser beam is to beam another laser at the wrong target and misguide the missile or bomb away from the beam that it is supposed to follow. How do you counter this? By training the missiles and bombs to follow only the beam of a particular laser—by coding its pulsations. Which adds a big, new dimension to the military art of codebreaking.

The modern mural of the martial arts has electronics as its master motif. Electronics made possible the precise guidance of nuclear missiles and warheads, and will make possible, through lasers, the precision of their pulverization. The wars —or war—of the future will be electromagnetic. The bloody Arab-Israeli affair of 1973 drove this home to the planners of the Pentagon, who still, at a time of oil-and-economic crisis for the Western nations, keep their sights trained on the Middle East, where the next war may very well begin. The last one served up some lessons.

10

The
Electronic Landscape

The President of the United States takes pleasure in presenting the PRESIDENTIAL UNIT CITATION to TWENTY-SIXTH MARINES (REINFORCED), THIRD MARINE DIVISION (REINFORCED) for service as set forth in the following citation:

For extraordinary heroism in action against North Vietnamese Army forces during the battle for Khe Sanh in the Republic of Viet Nam from 20 January to 1 April 1968. Throughout this period, the 26th Marines (Reinforced) was assigned the mission of holding the vital Khe Sanh Combat Base and positions on Hills 881, 861-A, 558 and 950, which dominated strategic enemy approach routes into Northern I Corps. The 26th Marines was opposed by numerically superior forces—two North Vietnamese Army divisions, strongly reinforced with artillery, tank, antiaircraft artillery and rocket units. The enemy, deployed to take advantage of short lines of communications, rugged mountainous terrain, jungle and adverse weather conditions, was determined to destroy the Khe Sanh Combat Base in conjunction with large-scale offensive operations in the two northern provinces of the Republic of Vietnam. The 26th Marines, occupying a small but critical area, was daily subjected to hundreds of rounds of intensive artillery, mortar and rocket fire. In addition, fierce ground attacks were conducted by the enemy in an effort to penetrate the friendly positions. Despite overwhelming odds, the 26th Marines remained resolute and determined, maintaining the integrity of its positions and inflicting heavy losses on the enemy. When monsoon weather greatly reduced air support and compounded the problems of aerial resupply, the men of the 26th Marines stood defiantly firm, sustained by their own professional esprit and high sense of duty. Through their indomitable will, staunch endurance and resolute courage, the 26th Marines and supporting units held the Khe Sanh Combat Base. The actions of the 26th Marines contributed substantially to the failure of the Vietcong and North Vietnamese Army winter-spring offensive. The enemy forces were denied the military and psychological victory they so desperately sought. By their gallant fighting spirit and their countless individual acts of heroism, the men of the 26th Marines (Reinforced) established a record of illustrious courage and determination in keeping with the highest traditions of the Marine Corps and the United States Naval Service.

(Signed) Lyndon B. Johnson

Khe Sanh was a long time ago, as measured by the headlong development of the electronic battlefield in all the years since. And yet Khe Sanh played an unrecognized part in the beginnings of this new and futuristic battlefield. To begin the story, let us take a more recent war, where the world's two superpowers probably are in their keenest and most dangerous competition.

On Yom Kippur, October 6, 1973, a combined Egyptian-Syrian force of more than 100,000 infantry and 2,000 tanks ripped into and rode rearward a partially mobilized Israeli force of about 400 tanks and 5,000 infantry in the Sinai Desert and on the Golan Heights. By the time a cease-fire had been forged, on October 24, the Israelis had gouged back into the Golan and into Syrian territory. On the Sinai front, they had established a bridgehead across the Suez Canal, thrusting their American-built M-60 tanks across and beyond the canal in armored tactics that would have made Patton proud, and nearly surrounded the Egyptian Third Army of 25,000 men. But the Israelis had been bloodied badly. Their weapons, mainly American, had been matched—in some cases, overmatched—by the Russian tanks and antitank and antiaircraft missiles which the Arabs had aimed against them. Especially by the surface-to-air missiles. It looked, for a week or so, as though the Israelis would be routed. Foreheads were furrowed at the Pentagon.

Throughout the combat, featuring what military historians now claim were the fiercest armored engagements in the history of warfare, the daily and twice-daily briefings in the Pentagon press room not far from the River Entrance were tense affairs. How many planes and tanks have the Israelis lost? Can they win this one? How many Russian ships are on the move in the Mediterranean? Is the U.S. Sixth Fleet moving in? Can you confirm reports that the Russians are staging an airborne division for deployment to the Syrian front? How many F-4s are we sending Israel? How many tanks? How many missiles? Can you confirm reports that the Israelis have nuclear weapons? Can you comment on reports that the Russians are sending the Arabs nuclear weapons? The answers were vague. No one at the Pentagon was certain or confident of anything. Not until the final week of the fighting, when the Israelis turned it around, did the details begin filtering out. The United States had severely depleted its own forces of fighters, attack planes, tanks and surface-to-air and antitank missiles in a massive airlift and sealift resupply of the Israelis which added up to, in the end, about $2 billion. The Russians had done the same, and their weapons had turned out to be hellishly effective. This depressed the men of the Pentagon, although it should not have surprised them. (I wondered at the time about the anomaly of the Pentagon's previous claims of how good the Russian weapons were, and its consternation at finding out that those claims were well-founded.) What shocked the Pentagon just as much, however, was the refusal or the reluctance of NATO nations to let U.S. cargo planes use U.S. bases in Europe as refueling and trans-loading stops on the way to the combat zone. Without the cooperation of Portugal, which from the beginning permitted U.S. planes to use the U.S. base at Lajes, the Azores, the resupply which spared Israel probably could not have been brought off. Our European allies had decided that the continued supply of Arab oil—with winter coming on—was more important momentarily than military and political little-brotherhood with the U.S. Even though the bitter resentments which this situation roiled on both sides of the Atlantic were shortly suppressed, the implications for the future of a militarily melded Western world were—and remain—ominous.

This, however, was a problem the Pentagon had to leave to the politicians and statesmen. To the military men in the Tank, and to the civilian hierarchs in their E Ring suites, the shifting sands of the Middle East had exposed some nasty nuances of weapons and tactics, which compelled the immediate reexamination of American forces and weapons and a heightening of the research and development of the battle arrays of the future.

Most dramatic among the Mideast surprises were the SAMS —the surface-to-air missiles—against Israeli attack aircraft. SAMs accounted for all but a few of the more than one hundred planes that Israel lost, most of them in the first week of the fighting. Back in 1971, the Soviets finished equipping the Egyptians with a geographical belt of these missiles which extended twenty miles beyond the west bank of Suez. The Israelis paid little heed. Still flushed with the success of their virtually unimpeded air and tank strikes in the Sinai in the six-day war of 1967, the Israelis had lapsed into the old mistake of preparing to fight the next war the same way they had fought the last one. This was not to be. Now, the Egyptians— the Syrians, too—had Soviet SAMs in great variety. But more than that, the Soviets had taught them how to synchronize these SAMs not only on the defense but on the assault. There were three radar-guided SAMs—SA-2 for high altitudes, SA-3 for medium level and SA-6 to intercept the attack planes on their low-level runs to target. Laced into the networks of these missiles was the short-range, heat-seeking SA-7 Strella, carried by infantry afoot and fired from the shoulder, or by tracked or wheeled vehicles, and the radar-guided, tractor-mounted, quadruple, 23-millimeter ZSU-23 antiaircraft gun. When the Egyptians attacked across the canal, their infantry and armor took along the gun and the heat-seeking missile. They also took along—and this is what confounded the Israeli pilots more than anything else—the radar SA-6 batteries, moving them forward alongside the armor and the infantry on the assault, providing a protective umbrella right on, not behind, the lines. They also moved some SA-2 and SA-3 batteries. The Arabs did something else too. They forsook the old tactic of firing radar-steered antiaircraft missiles one at a time. They fired them, as had the North Vietnamese toward the end of that war, in salvos. A fighter-bomber might elude one, but probably not two, and almost certainly not three or more. The Israeli pilots found these missiles coming up at them in clusters of seven or eight at a time. To cap their consternation, the Israeli pilots were not equipped with the electronics needed to jam the SA-6 radar, and the Arabs had a field day. In the end, the Soviet SAMs were defeated, destroyed. Suicidal air sorties took some of them out. But the Israelis smashed most—to the satisfaction of Army men in the Pentagon—with tanks. It took a blood bath. If only they could have been jammed from the air. If only the Israelis had been warned of their advent on the battlefield. Where were the electronic countermeasures that could have accomplished this?

As Arthur Hadley summed it up later in *New Times Magazine:*

> Victorious through a combination of tank-shock action and tactical airpower in the Six Day War, the Israelis spurned complex electronic equipment, missiles, artillery, night-fighting equipment, all of which are bulky, complicated, expensive and were not necessary before. Instead, the Israelis chose to be "lean and mean," shunned the sophisticated weapons in favor of speed, firepower, reliability and bombload. But the Egyptians had no intention of fighting the last battle again. Convinced they couldn't take Israeli pilots in the air, they gambled on controlling the air above the battlefield with modern missiles. Convinced they'd be beaten by the Israelis in tank-to-tank battle, they gambled on knocking out Israeli tanks with sophisticated missiles. In doing this, they created the "mid-intensity battlefield," where electronic wizardry and precision weapons make it increasingly difficult for men and machines to live and fight. ... The irony is that it was the Egyptians, the less technically oriented society, who opted for new weapons. Without an air force, they control the air over the battlefield. Without tank battles, they destroy Israeli tanks.

Hadley and others also pointed out that the Egyptians owned the night. Their Soviet equipment ran heavily to the night-fighting, infrared variety. Israel lacked it. Nor did the Israelis have, until late, the laser-guided U.S. smart bombs which, early on, would have permitted them not only to smack targets from the air despite the SAMs but also to find and destroy the Suez Canal bridges which the Egyptians covered with dense black smoke for miles around as they crossed into the Sinai.

The first week of the war produced a spate of news stories

and commentaries from the battlefront concerning the imminent demise of the tank as a weapon of modern warfare. There
was good reason. In that week, Israel lost an estimated five
hundred tanks of British and American make to Soviet-
designed Snapper, Swatter and Sagger antitank missiles. All
these were wire-guided, ranging up to about three thousand
yards, launched from armored-infantry vehicles. Arab aircraft
seldom attacked Israeli tanks. The Russian-built T-54 and T-62
tanks were mostly outgunned and outmaneuvered by the hell-
for-leather Israeli tankers. So the Arab missiles were the weapons chiefly responsible for all those burned-out hulks of Israeli
tanks which dotted the deserts on the Egyptian front and in the
stony hills at the Syrian border. This aroused anguish at the
Fort Knox armor center and among the Army generals in the
Pentagon who had been pushing for several years and were
still at it—despite difficulties of cost and technology—to develop a new Main Battle Tank for the U.S. arsenal. The *New
York Times* for example wrote of the Mideast war:

> Infantry armed with modern antitank missiles can fight
> armor to a standstill and is on its way to restoration as "the
> Queen of Battles." The effectiveness of such infantry against
> tanks and the steady development of mobile, accurate sur-
> face-to-air missiles offer a second important lesson: the tank-
> and-fighter-bomber team, which has ruled most battlefields
> since 1940, has been eclipsed as the decisive tactical forma-
> tion. Soldiers and airmen are asking whether the missiles
> that proved effective in this war may not be the forerunners
> of simpler, even more lethal weapons.

In consequence of the savage toll taken of its tanks early in
the combat, the Israelis messaged the Pentagon that their need
of fighter-bomber replacements and electronic countermeasures was equaled by their need of the same type of antitank
missiles that were threatening to undo them. The Pentagon
was in position to respond. The cargo decks of the C-5s and
C-141s shuttling to Israel were stuffed with U.S. Army TOW
(which stands for tube-launched, optically tracked, wire-
guided) and U.S. Air Force Maverick TV-guided missiles. The
Israelis rushed these into the field, and used them with devastating results in the counterattack on the central front of the

Sinai. The C-5s and C-141s also sped the guided, air-to-surface Shrike and Walleye missiles east of Suez. On October 16, Israeli tanks closed in on the canal and roared across, the infantry following after, and headed straight down the road toward Cairo. In the north, amid a crescendo of bazookas, missiles and tank guns, Israeli armor had already beaten back the Syrians. Both Arab nations finally had been left with no choice but to take on the Israeli armor with armor of their own, and to put their own tanks on the line against missiles which the Israelis now deployed. And the war—for 1973—was over. The tank as a weapon had both won and lost. It had been shown up as perhaps more vulnerable than expected. But in the Israeli counterattack, it had done the job it always has been expected to do. So what were the tacticians left to think?

Brig. Gen. Kenneth Hunt, deputy director of the London-based Institute for Strategic Analysis, summed up, in *Air Force* magazine, the prevailing analysis: "The antitank missile has made its first real mark on the battlefield, and infantry now has, for the first time, a weapon effective at both short and long ranges against the heaviest tank. This does not, of course, mean that the day of the tank has ended. This missile is a defensive weapon, and a tank is still needed for offensive operations. But the balance has swung against the tank, which has dominated the battlefield since World War II. What is needed now is a mixture of missiles and tanks (with some missiles mounted on tanks), according to the tactical requirements. If the emphasis is on defense, then more missiles will be procured; if on offense, then more tanks. But cost is a factor. The inventory in Europe must be examined afresh in the light of Israel's experience." One way of looking at the cost factor is that a new tank costs a half-million dollars; a TOW missile, $2,000.

After the sand had settled, the U.S. Air Force claimed that Israeli airpower had been decisive. But the U.S. Army did not buy this. Its spokesmen noted that not until Israeli tanks had wiped out or wasted Egyptian surface-to-air missile batteries on both sides of the canal was the Israeli air force free to attack as it pleased, as it had planned. The only patently bad news for the U.S. Army out of the Yom Kippur war was the Israelis' disdain of slow-moving helicopters as gunships. The United States had employed attack helicopters with sometimes deadly effect in Vietnam. But there, they were not menaced by fire from air or ground of anywhere near the ferocity which would have befallen them in the Middle East. And even over South Vietnam, where U.S. control of the air had been near-absolute, thousands of helicopters had been downed. They might be of some use at night, said the Israelis, who had picked off almost a half-hundred Arab choppers, but in the daytime, they said, the helicopter is a sitting duck. Withal, three cheers for Israeli armor and infantry.

The Army always has been the most unglamorous of the services, and, during and since Vietnam, a four-letter word in the civilian lexicon. As Professor Vincent Davis wrote in *Naval War College Review* a few years back: "A fundamental fact seems relatively clear: Americans do not personally like to fight in wars, especially and most particularly as members of ground forces. Indeed, Americans have greatly and often passionately —sometimes even violently—resisted personal participation in combat and have used various means, including political efforts, to avoid circumstances that could require such participation." This is why the betting was against the success of the all-volunteer army when it began as an experiment in recruitment in the early 1970s, and why many believe that if the concept does come off, we will have created a monster, an amoral army of mercenaries who will be easy pickings for power politicians. Perhaps. This resistance of Americans to ground combat also accounts in great measure for the upsurge of the new technology of electronic warfare, of one-shot, one-kill weapons, to cut down the slaughter of infantrymen, be they Army or Marines.

Taking nothing away from the sailors and airmen, the infantryman, the tanker and the artilleryman fight a completely different, much more demoralizing kind of war. Talk to the senior officers, now at the Pentagon, who fought in Vietnam, and you will note the difference. There is no exhilaration in the recollections of a rifleman. Air combat, while often deadly, has its thrills and its high-flown exploits of machines and men. Ground combat, deadly for greater numbers almost everywhere they turn, in its fevers and shivers as well as in its shots and shells, has only those thrills which grow out of sustained individual horror. Especially was this so in Vietnam. Much has been made of the fact that the Army and Marines lost far fewer men, in proportion to the numbers who fought and the total

years of their fighting, than either lost in Korea. But this over-
looks some points. For one, swift helicopter evacuation from
the battlefield and modern surgery saved thousands upon thousands of "grunts" who came back to civilian life terribly disa-
bled and, in many cases, ignored. It belabors the obvious to
note that a sizable number, maybe a majority, were black. For
another, the infantry tactics of Vietnam—Khe Sanh notwithstanding—alone were enough to drive doughboys to drugs,
which they did. In Korea, as in all previous wars, the infantry
soldier had at least the small satisfaction of knowing that when
he went on the assault, he was after something tangible—the
high ground, the hill, and that when his platoon or his company got up on top, it would dig in and defend. A mile a day
might be enough of an accomplishment to keep a man going.
In Vietnam, infantry outfits engaged in "search-and-destroy"
sweeps of the hostile countryside which will become infamous
in military annals for their futility. Stories abound in the Army
circles of the Pentagon of entire squads and platoons being
worn down and wasted in search-and-destroy operations—
over the same terrain, day after day after day—which never
went anywhere to stay, and settled nothing; of squadmates
betting one another on who would return and who wouldn't;
of bets defaulted by the dead; of heroin and booze bolstering
the living. The U.S. Army is determined never to try to fight
that kind of war again. It hustled electronics into the field in
Vietnam to give its infantry a better break, and this did have
some effect, as we shall see later in this chapter. When they look
back on the debilitation of Vietnam and the carnage of Yom
Kippur, the U.S. generals know what they will need for the
next one. Several months before his death in 1974, Army Chief
of Staff Gen. Creighton Abrams put it into perspective:

"When I entered the service, only thirty-eight years ago, it
was largely a horsedrawn army. The battlefield has changed.
We have had to assimilate radar, jet aircraft, nuclear weapons,
helicopters, missiles, computers, satellites—to mention only a
few. Knowing that the future promises even greater changes
gives us powerful incentive to keep up. Every lesson we have
been able to dig out of the Mideast war fully reinforces our
faith that we are headed in the right direction. The proliferation of antitank weapons means that new tanks must have a
lower silhouette, improved agility and better armor protec-

tion. Infantry must possess a degree of mobility comparable to tanks. It must have protection from small arms and artillery fire, and it must be able to fight mounted when required. Air defense weapons must provide a protective umbrella over the fluid battlefield. Mobility, firepower and teamwork are still the keys to victory. We must assure that American soldiers are not surprised on some future battlefield by a technologically superior enemy. The Mideast War provided an opportunity to compare our progress with that of the Soviet Union. We had a unique view of Soviet weapons systems in action. The Soviets have made significant progress in a very short period of time. What we have learned has helped us refine our requirements for modernization, especially of the forces deployed to Europe. We need, as a matter of urgent priority, an improved family of tactical nuclear artillery weapons to provide the field commander the precise ability to inflict damage on his enemy with greatly decreased collateral damage to nonmilitary targets.

"And," said General Abrams, "in what is perhaps the least understood aspect of modern conflict, we must strive to increase our electronic warfare and night-fighting capability."

One afternoon at the Pentagon I talked with Army Lt. Col. John A. Klose, who had commanded a chopper outfit in Vietnam, and with Norman R. Augustine, about the new directions of the Army. We discussed the Army's "Big Five" of new weapons in development—the SAM-D (air) defense missile system, the Main Battle Tank, the mechanized infantry carrier, the attack helicopter and the huge transport helicopter. Klose, a friendly man, bridled a bit when I suggested that the helicopter was all done. "Oh, sure," he said, "the old argument about what happened to the horse cavalry when the machine gun came in. I don't think it applies to the helicopter. We had trouble with the Cheyenne because it became too complicated and cost way too much. The new one should work out better. What everyone forgets in the vulnerability argument against helicopters is that we're designing it to take advantage of the terrain, for agility as well as speed. It will pop up from behind trees, from gullies, fire its missiles and pop back down again. Hide, shoot, run, hide. I'll tell you, we ran exercises against West German tanks, and scored kill after kill against them. When we were done, their commanding officer told us he'd been skeptical about helicopters, but we'd sold him."

Maybe. Then Augustine, who is assistant secretary of the

Army for Research and Development, took over the conversation. Born in 1935, he is another of the new breed of youngish technologists calling the plays at the Pentagon. He earned undergraduate and graduate degrees in aeronautical engineering at Princeton, joined the University's James Forrestal Research Center, and then worked as a research executive for Douglas Aircraft in California. He came to the Pentagon in 1965 to work, first, in the Strategic Defensive Systems side of the Defense Directorate of Research and Engineering, and then as DDR&E's assistant director for Tactical Missiles, Ordnance and Land Warfare. After a hiatus which he spent as a manager of missile and space engineering with LTV Corporation in Texas, Augustine returned to the Pentagon to take the top civilian Army R&D job in 1973, less than a month before the Yom Kippur war broke out. Tidily, Augustine became the Army's chief contact with Currie of DDR&E, where Augustine had worked during the Vietnam years. He talked, now, about the comeback of the infantryman.

"You've heard the saying," he said, "that the Air Force and the Navy man their equipment, but the Army equips its men. Well, that's what it's all about in our shop. The individual soldier is still the heart of the whole show. I guess it's fair to say that the tank is still the heart of the Army. But the individual man now has become a formidable fighting machine. He's got the missiles. He's a threat to the tank, to the airplane, to the helicopter. He can deliver heavy firepower against all these, just as the helicopter—with its guided missiles—can deliver against the tank. With the antitank weapons of the past, sending the infantryman up against a tank was like hunting bear with a shotgun. Now he has the Dragon missile. It makes him a tank *hunter*, for the first time. He can carry it along with him and fire it from the shoulder. It has better accuracy and it's far more lethal than the 90-millimeter recoilless rifle. It can kill anything inside the ranges that a platoon normally operates. All he has to do is aim it through a scope, fire it and keep his sight on the target until it hits. Its sensor automatically holds it on the line of sight. The signals are transmitted through a wire, just like the TOW. What we had in the past were artillery, air and infantry in support of tanks, and artillery, air and tanks in the attack of tanks. Now we've got the infantry in the attack part of it too."

So much for what the infantry could fight with if the Russians struck across the Elbe tonight. But what about the years ahead?

"There lie the tough choices," Augustine said. "As Mal Currie says, we have to continue to develop a wide range of weapons, but we have to decide which offer the most substantial jumps ahead. We must look for a laser, not to give us half again as much power, but five times as much power. The risks are greater. You might get nothing. But wars are won or lost, not by a 20 percent better weapon but by—the best example—an atomic bomb. Can you imagine the reaction in this country if Sputnik had been a *military* surprise? Back to the laser. There is no question that the day will come when it's a weapon. And I'm not talking about the twenty-first century. We'll see it. The laser rifle is a possibility, but it is some time away. Consider what comes first—lasers to designate targets for the infantryman. The laser fixes the target and he kills it. Or the artillery shell rides the beam and kills it. One shot. He won't need to carry all that ammo. An infantryman carrying a very small radio and a laser designator will have on command the firepower of a whole army. Optics, too. The use of optics in guidance is just beginning to blossom. Optics will permit us, for one thing, to stabilize tank guns no matter what the tank is doing. The tank can be going over very bumpy terrain, and the optical sight keeps its gun on the target all the time. Optics permit us to fight at night. Lasers, optics, electronics, the whole package, they mean at least as much to the Army as they do to the air people. This whole defense business we're in really started with the aerodynamicists. But in recent years, relatively few big decisions in defense research have been driven by aerodynamics, or even by propulsion. They have been driven by electronics. And this is where the Army is today."

For a look at how the stage was set, let us go back to a time shortly after the United States decided to wage full-scale infantry and air war in Vietnam, and to the Jasons.

My first encounter with the Jasons came during work on a magazine article about the Institute for Defense Analyses in 1966. One of IDA's divisions was called, simply but meaninglessly, "Jason." That was nearly all the information I could glean from the tight-lipped IDA types. What I did not realize then was that the Defense Department and IDA had clamped down on revealing the group's full membership and activities because the Jasons, for the first time, had turned their attention to Vietnam. They were, and still are, a group of forty to fifty of the best brains in theoretical physics and mathematics which the universities of this nation have to offer. These men, then mostly in their thirties, teamed up in 1959 at Los Alamos. Among the founders reportedly were Marvin L. Goldberger of Princeton, Keith Bruechner of the University of California at San Diego, Kenneth Watson of the University of California at Berkeley, and Charles H. Townes, Nobel laureate-to-be for his work on the quantum electronics of the laser. They and several others on university faculties believed that they owed the national security effort the part-time benefit of their combined brainpower. Things looked bleak for the United States at the time. The Russians had launched Sputnik, and there was "the missile gap." Remember?

For housekeeping purposes, the Jasons worked through IDA, which took care of their budgetary and administrative needs. Townes, in fact, was an IDA officer. In practice, however, the Jasons reported directly to the new Advanced Research Projects Agency in the new Defense Directorate of Research and Engineering. They received from ARPA something like $500,000 a year, later on, when their work really got hot, whey they began theorizing about the antiballistic missile, about strategic policy, and—most germane to our narrative—to the "Electronic Battlefield." At first, they took the name "Sunrise," as suggested by the Pentagon. Years later, Goldberger reported that they changed the name to Jason at his wife's suggestion. Sunrise sounded like a love song, or a shaver.

Goldberger had worked on the Manhattan Project. Afterward, he studied for his Ph.D. in physics at the University of Chicago under Enrico Fermi. A little later, Murray Gell-Mann, destined for a Nobel prize in 1969, joined the Chicago group, as did Harold Lewis and, as a graduate student, Richard L. Garwin, who afterward joined the faculty of Columbia. All were among the original Jasons. So was Dr. George B. Kistiakowsky, a native Russian chemist who worked on the A-bomb and then served as science advisor to the Pentagon and the White House. Dr. Gordon J. F. MacDonald of the University of California served simultaneously as a Jason and as IDA's vice-president for research in the mid-1960s.

In his book *Think Tanks*, Paul Dickson wrote in 1971:

The Jasons . . . spend much of their spare time, certain weekends and all of their summers thinking about warfare for the institute [IDA] on a consulting basis. Each summer they and their families are whisked off to a remote resort where, under heavy security, they engage in intense group thinking on defense matters. Although the names of some of the members of Jason are known [such as Norman M. Kroll, who heads the Physics Department of the University of California at San Diego, and Edwin E. Salpeter, Professor of Physics and Nuclear Studies at Cornell], many are not. IDA's policy is to guard the list of Jason members.

Reported *Science* magazine in 1973:

"Finally, Jason became a club in a purely social sense. While the physicists rolled up their shirt sleeves with generals at such scenic spots as La Jolla, California; Woods Hole or Falmouth on Cape Cod; or the Bowdoin College campus in Maine, their wives and children would be establishing themselves on the local beach for the summer. . . . On one occasion in the early 1960s, some of the wives collaborated in producing a supper-club series of skits titled, 'Review from the Bridge,' featuring a mock striptease number to the tune of a song, 'My Heart Belongs to IDA.' "

Life was good. Science and defense made a happy marriage. Then came Vietnam and the misadventures which strained the wedlock. In 1966, four Jason professors wrote a secret report analyzing the possible use of tactical nuclear weapons in the stubbornly spreading war. They were Robert Gomer and S. Courtenay Wright of the University of Chicago, Freeman Dyson of the Institute for Advanced Study at Princeton and Steven Weinberg of Harvard. Their work was printed in March 1967 as IDA Report No. HQ-66-5220. On February 12, 1968, according to an account in *The Nation* of April 15, 1968, "an anonymous phone call to the Senate Foreign Relations Committee touched off nationwide rumors that the United States was planning to use tactical nuclear weapons in Vietnam." The account continued:

The call was received by Carl Marcy, staff director of the committee, who later told the press that the caller suggested the committee should find out why Dr. Richard L. Garwin of Columbia University had been sent to Vietnam. Garwin was described in the call as "a tactical nuclear weapons expert." The following day, public information officers at the Pentagon explained that Garwin and two associates had been sent to Southeast Asia to appraise "the effectiveness of new weapons," but that "the new weapons have no relationship to atomic or nuclear weapons of any kind. . . ." A colleague at Columbia, professor of physics Leon M. Lederman, told the campus newspaper that the Pentagon had sent Dr. Garwin to Asia to study the feasibility of installing "some electric gadgets" which could serve as "technical aids toward deescalation."

This would have been the electronic barrier which Defense Secretary Robert S. McNamara was proposing to build between North and South Vietnam—to detect infiltrators in the event of a truce, and the passage of troops in the event of an invasion from the north. ARPA already had set up elaborate facilities in Bangkok, Thailand, for research on "counter-guerrilla surveillance systems," including work on infrared systems developed at the University of Michigan. We were seeing the origins of the electronic battlefield, and the Jasons were fathering it.

"In 1966," reported *Science* magazine, "some Jasons and other intellectuals, principally in Cambridge, decided to do something on Vietnam. Roger Fisher of the Harvard Law School [and later inventor of the television program 'The Advocates'] wrote John McNaughton of the Office of the Secretary of Defense in January suggesting an electronic barrier. Meanwhile, a group of Harvard and MIT scientists suggested to McNamara that they establish a general technical working group on Vietnam, and received his blessing. The result was an intensive ten days of briefing with McNaughton, Maxwell Taylor, John Foster, and others, and, for the intellectuals, according to one, 'everybody and his grandfather.' They were held at the Dana Hall School for Girls in Wellesley, Massachusetts."

Then the Jasons got with it. Their several study groups on the different aspects of the barrier proposal met at the University of California at Santa Barbara in the summer of 1966. Among them, according to *Science*, were Henry W. Kendall of

MIT; Frederick Zachariasen of Cal Tech; William A. Nieren-
berg of the Scripps Institution of Oceanography; Gell-Mann;
Lewis; MacDonald; Garwin, and Seymour Deitchman of IDA.
They suggested sowing sensors and "button bomblets," which
would set off sensors if tromped upon, throughout an 80-by-15-
mile strip along the Demilitarized Zone and the border between Laos and North Vietnam, at the start of the Ho Chi
Minh Trail. These sensors, if activated, would send for strike
aircraft and simultaneously detonate gravel mines already
planted throughout the strip. But as *Science* recapitulated the
fate of the electronic barrier (same old story): "As a result of
infighting among the military and the Office of the Secretary
of Defense on implementation, it [the barrier] was only installed on a piecemeal basis."

The irony of the Jasons' research and analysis of Vietnam
problems and prospects was that the scientists probably were
scorned unfairly by their dovish colleagues in the community
of the academic elite for having played along with the Pentagon in perpetuating the war. Most of the Jasons were now
getting on toward their mid-forties, and their younger peers,
especially, had come to regard them as jeremiads. Actually, as
it turned out, the Jason analysis of tactical nuclear weapons in
Vietnam had led the scientists to conclude that those weapons
should *not* be used. But the Jasons could not reveal this conclusion to the outside world because their work was so highly
classified. Their proposal of an electronic barrier was aimed at
helping bring about a cease-fire—or so the Jason participants
now claim—as much as it was at creating a killing zone. Several
of the Jasons quit working with the Pentagon, in fact, when
they became persuaded that the Johnson and Nixon administrations really were interested in the barrier—and in all the
electronics being introduced to Southeast Asia—more as weapons than as means of achieving and monitoring a cessation of
the fighting. Kistiakowsky was among the Jasons who jetti-
soned the Pentagon.

Amid all this, the Jasons seemed to decline in influence and
presence in defense research circles. When its budget was cut
in 1971, IDA cast the Jasons loose, seemingly to drift apart and
away. But there was less to the severance than met the eye. The
Congressionally imposed construction of IDA's funds had
made it impossible for ARPA to keep on showing the Jasons'

half-million dollars a year as a line item in IDA's budget, so ARPA simply moved the Jason account into the administrative budget of the Stanford Research Institute at Menlo Park, California. This happened in 1971, and the Jasons have continued to thrive. SRI itself is deeply involved in benign research and analysis of economics, life sciences, urban and social systems, management systems and other types of socioscience compatible with the antiwar climate of recent years. But SRI's range of research in defense-related fields remains spectacularly spectroscopic: tactical and strategic weapons; communications; naval warfare; ultrasonic imaging; optics and holography; on and on. Here is SRI's own list of its research topics in electronics and radio sciences alone; microwave theory devices and techniques; laser radar systems; laser and microwave countermeasures and intercept receivers; environmental meteorology and climatology (altering the weather, as we shall note later in this book, is now a prime pursuit of defense research); radio propagation effects of nuclear explosions and electromagnetic pulse; laboratory studies of electromagnetic waves and plasmas (remember the lasers' "thermal blooming"?); optical and radar propagation; radar and radio effects of Auroras; reentry physics; satellite and rocket instrumentation; high-frequency ionospheric propagation; high-altitude chemical phenomenology; over-the-horizon radar; remote sensing of storms and sea state.

Enough? Obviously, the Jasons should be quite comfortable in the folds of SRI, doing only ARPA knows what about the weapons of the future.

"The Jasons are still very, very influential and still in demand by ARPA," a senior think tank official told me toward the end of 1974. "But we need a new group of Jasons. Younger men. The original group hasn't changed much at all. It was formed because its founders were young and full of get up and go about helping national security. They were bothered by the fact that in the late 1950s and early 1960s the Pentagon was getting all its scientific advice from only a few of the hawkier, stodgier types like Dr. Teller. Now the Jasons are getting just as conservative. They're in their late forties and fifties for the most part. They won't let the younger scientists come in— those who might want to, and there are more of those than you might suspect. This has created a lot of jealousy and friction between the Jasons and the outsiders on the university faculties. Inside the Jasons, too. Unless they get new blood, I wonder how much longer they can keep it up."

However the Jasons may fare, they probably will be annotated, in the final analysis, not so much for their work on missiles and antimissiles as for their studies of electronic warfare, which embraces the whole of submarine detection and tracking, countermeasures, lasers—anything and everything which puts electrons, ions and photons to work in weaponry. The sequel to the Jasons' electronic barrier, the electronic battlefield, is part of electronic warfare. It is of the future because its potential for evolution of technology and revolution of warfare is almost infinite. It already had shown to advantage in Vietnam, where the Americans took the first step toward fighting wars less with bodies, more with beepers that bring on the bombs from the air or anywhere.

The electronic battlefield comes down to all kinds of possible variations on the basic system of sensors and electronic-guided weapons which the Jasons had devised for the "McNamara Wall." It might more accurately be called "the automated battlefield," for it all depends on Air Force, Navy and Army computers receiving, processing and transmitting the signals and strike orders generated by the sensors. This battlefield began to come into being in Southeast Asia in 1967. "Igloo White," the Air Force sense-and-strike system in Laos, was among the first. Commanding Igloo White was Brigadier General William J. Evans, once a fighter pilot, who in 1973, wearing a second star, took charge of research and development in the Office of the Air Force Chief of Staff at the Pentagon. Along with Igloo White, the Army and Air Force strewed, through 1968 and 1969, at least a dozen other sensing systems in the countrysides of the bamboo villages and oxcarts. *Washington Monthly* magazine characterized these as having "the most colorful and obfuscating menageries of code words and project names since Captain Video went off the air—to name a few, Dual Blade, Tomcat, Duffle Bag, Tight Jaw, College Eye, Infant, Grasshopper, Pave Knife, Command Bolt and Igloo White. The hardware that belongs to these names includes antipersonnel mines, laser-guided bombs, night vision devices, cluster bombs, 'people sniffers' [or chemical detectors which

react to enemy body odors], thermal imagers which react to
body heat, button-size bomblets and seismic registers which
pick up the thump of trucks or troops on the move."

By the time of the *Washington Monthly* article, in 1971, the
segment-by-segment deployment of the automated battlefield
in Vietnam, Laos and Thailand had become public knowledge.
Tucked away in crannies of the cavernous Pentagon budget, it
had been supersecret to the extent that it had been kept even
from the Armed Services Committees for more than two years.
In that period, ARPA and the services had spent more than $2
billion on it, and had involved enough industrial, think tank
and university R&D contractors in it to form an army of their
own. Washington correspondent Warren Burkett, who may
have been the first reporter to break the story, reported that in
January 1970 more than eight hundred defense contractors
turned out for a Pentagon briefing on the automated battlefield
as it was and would be, and more than twice that number of
contractors failed to gain admittance for lack of space. Finally,
in 1971, the Defense Department accepted the Senate Armed
Services Committee's urgent invitation to come testify about
the battlefield. As the *Washington Monthly* described the Christmas morning session in part:

"The Pentagon brought down some of its newly developed sensors to the hearing and laid them on the table, all the
MAGIDS, MINISIDS and MICROSIDS, for the senators to
see. The whole presentation was something like a rerun from
Mr. Wizard, with the gee-whizzing lad sitting at his knee,
bedazzled with the glories of modern science: Senator Goldwater: 'Does that beep at regular intervals?' General Deane: 'Just
when it detects something, but right now, because there is so
much disturbance here, it keeps beeping. . . .' "

Burkett previously had written the following descriptive
account of what was going on in Southeast Asia:

> Deep in Laotian jungle, communist mechanics tuned mu-
> nitions-laden Russian trucks. Tonight the cargo would slip
> another notch down the Ho Chi Minh Trail toward South
> Vietnam and Cambodia. Seconds later the truck, parked un-
> der the triple-layer jungle canopy, exploded with bombs,
> mines and shells. Black smoke, laced with fire, boiled over
> the tops of the trees. Screams of the dying mechanics were

heard by U.S. airmen flying high overhead in an unarmed EC-121 reconnaissance plane. Nearly a hundred miles away, near Thakhek, Thailand, American intelligence officers heard the carnage go on for hours. Delayed-action bombs and hundreds of tiny land mines, some called "Dragon's Teeth," chopped down men trying to extinguish fires and salvage truck parts. Eventually RCA's "Command Mike III," Sandia Corp.'s "Air-Delivered Seismic Intrusion Detector (ADSID)" and Honeywell's "Magnetic Intrusion Detector (MAGID)" fell silent. Another North Vietnamese truck stop had been abandoned.

However, thousands of other such "unattended ground sensors" continue to sound off across Laos, Cambodia, North and South Vietnam. Buried right up to their radio antennas, camouflaged as jungle vines, these "bugs" catch the sounds, vibrations and magnetic-field effects of trucks, men, guns and supplies moving in a post-monsoon attempt to restock Vietcong and North Vietnamese combat areas. Since the first of the year [eleven months], by Air Force estimates, more than 1,000 trucks have gone up in flames, early victims of the electronic battlefield tactics being developed by the U.S. Army, Navy and Air Force.

Such tactics are expected to sustain the armed forces through the next 15 years at smaller combat strength. . . .

Accompanying the air development has been a similar night vision, radar, infrared, light-amplification and sensor program for Army and Marine units on the ground. Half the sensors are now used by the troops of South Vietnam. American fire bases are so heavily watched by these devices that only one-third the number of combat troops are needed for defense and scouting patrols. And base commanders say they can control nearly twice as much territory. This hedges President Nixon's commitment to reduce U.S. ground forces in South Vietnam to below half their peak of 500,000. . . .

It is one feat to detect the movement of supply trains and blow them up. It is quite another feat to detect a massive infantry assault in the dark and fog of predawn and, because the sensors have warned you, blow them back. Three years before the electronic battlefield came to public attention, one small part of it was put to the acid test in Vietnam.

In December 1967, the North Vietnamese regulars were deployed in heavy strength throughout Northern "I Corps" area —85 miles from Hai Van Pass in the south to the border of the DMZ in the north, 45 miles from the China Sea in the east to the Laotian border in the west. Along the eastern DMZ the enemy had a division of three infantry regiments. On the east coast he had the 270th Infantry Regiment—three infantry battalions, an artillery battalion and an antiaircraft battalion. In the area bounded by Gio Linh, Con Thiem, Cam Lom and Dong Ha—an area known as "Leatherneck Square"—he had the 27th Infantry Battalion of four rifle and heavy weapons companies. In the area west of Quang Tri, the North Vietnamese had marshaled about 3,250 infantry; west of Hue, about 1,400 infantry. There was another infantry battalion between Ca Lu and Khe Sanh. And this area was the only one in all Vietnam, at the time, where the North Vietnamese had deployed their best artillery—more than 100 tubes of 130-millimeter guns and 152-millimeter howitzers.

At the turn of the new year, 1968, it became apparent that the North Vietnamese troop movements had a focus: Khe Sanh, where the U.S. 3rd Marine Division had positioned only one of its nine infantry battalions which occupied the I Corps area. There was another Marine battalion between Hai Van Pass and Hue. The remainder of the division was divided between Hue to the south and the DMZ to the north. Combat patrols out of Khe Sanh kept getting into fiercer, more frequent firefights. A buildup. So the 3rd Division began reinforcing Khe Sanh. On January 27, 1968, the Khe Sanh complement stood at four battalions of infantry plus a battalion of 105-millimeter howitzers, a battery of 155-millimeter howitzers, five tanks with 90-millimeter guns. By now, the Marines had concluded that two enemy divisions had moved into the Khe Sanh area. On January 19, a Marine combat patrol surprised an enemy force moving onto Hill 881-N at Khe Sanh. "The patrol was reinforced by two rifle companies," commented the Marine division commander who later took charge at Khe Sanh, "and the argument became quite vigorous. This action continued until dark when our forces withdrew to their permanent positions. We could not afford to have them out on a limb 2,000 meters beyond our most advanced combat outpost on Hill 881-S."

The official Marine Corps account of "The Battle for Khe

Sanh," which contributed mightily to cracking the enemy's Tet offensive of 1968, has this to say about that division CO:

> One incident in November 1967, which was to have a tremendous effect on the future of the Khe Sanh combat base, was the arrival of Major General Rathvon McC. Tompkins at Phu Bai as the new commanding general, 3rd Marine Division. . . . In addition to being an extremely able commander, General Tompkins possessed a peppery yet gentlemanly quality which, in the gloom that later shrouded Khe Sanh, often lifted the spirits of his subordinates. His numerous inspection trips, even to the most isolated units, provided the division commander with a first-hand knowledge of the tactical situation which would never have been gained by simply sitting behind a desk. When the heavy fighting broke out at Khe Sanh, the general visited the combat base daily. Few people were to influence the coming battle more than General Tompkins, or have as many close calls.

The general's subsequent account of what happened at Khe Sanh shows the sides of him which the official report mentioned. It also shows that his Marines took advantage of advance warnings from two sources; one traditional, the other a new type. What follows is General Tompkins' partial recounting of the siege of Khe Sanh:

> And now, on 20 January, at Khe Sanh there occurred one of those fortuitous chances that make the expression "the fortunes of war" something more than a tired cliché. At 1400 hours on that day, First Lieutenant La Thanh Tonc of the 14th AA Company, 5th Battalion, 101st Regiment, 325th Division, approached our lines waving a white flag. He revealed to our interrogators not only the dispositions of the two assault regiments of the 325th but also the general plan of attack. An officer courier flew in to my Command Post from Khe Sanh with the interrogation report. We studied the information. I decided that we would accept it as valid. We had nothing to lose and stood to gain a great deal. I recalled that sometime before, at Dak To in the Highlands, a similar event had occurred, and the Army commanding general had received valuable information. The Army staff tended to

believe the information was too good to be true and should be discounted. The commanding general ruled otherwise, and events vindicated his judgment. I wondered if history would repeat itself on us.

The North Vietnamese attack which began on January 21 did indeed conform to the deserter's information. The village of Khe Sanh fell. The Marines withstood a twenty-four-hour mortar and artillery barrage on their combat base outside the village, but finally were surrounded and placed under siege. On February 5, after two weeks of incessant shelling, the North Vietnamese infantry began probing the Marine positions under cover of artillery and rocket fire. But they were being monitored. Let General Tompkins take it from there:

It was in this attack that the sensors proved their great worth to Khe Sanh Combat Base—in their role as information-gathering devices. Throughout the dark of February 2 through 4, the sensors reported large troop movements along a ridge to the northwest of Hill 881-S. . . . My intelligence and communications personnel knew little of sensor accuracy and reliability, and I knew even less. And so, I embraced the theory that it would be folly to become erudite in one's ignorance—therefore: believe that which the sensors purport to say. Thus I concluded that at least two battalions of infantry—or an equivalent number of porters—had reached a point 3,000 meters to the northwest of Hill 881-S, that they had come from the direction of the known location of the 325th Division. Dawn came without further developments—or confirmation, for that matter.

From the late evening of 4 February onwards, more and more puzzling things occurred. First, the sensors along the north-south portion of the ridge to the west of Hill 881-S began to give tongue vociferously in the same intensity as had their neighbors on the northwest portion the night before. Second, the latter began to sound off again. Third, the hitherto silent southern portion of the ridge, running from west to east, reported movement in the same strength as had the other sensors, but only along one section of the ridgeline. . . .

By one hundred hours on 5 February, all sensors fell silent.

Expecting more information, I sat back and waited. Then I slowly entered a state of inward panic. I could not prove that which I was beginning to believe. The forces had either moved off the line of sensors and the ridges away from Hill 881-S—therefore, no danger—or they were moving towards the hill—therefore, grave danger, especially in the thick mist. I plumped for the second explanation. The risk was too great to ignore. . . .

The North Vietnamese rate of march is four kilometers per hour over easy ground and two kilometers per hour over rough. The last sensor report from the south had occurred at 0100 hours. It was now past 0200 hours. We should fire at 0230, when the enemy should have reached this point here on the map on its march north to Hill 881-S. The enemy will be in regimental column, battalions on line, interval 100 meters —standard NVA regimental tactics for night attack. Therefore we should place a target block 500 by 300 feet square meters about the anticipated enemy position, fire 350 rounds of light and medium artillery into it, and copper-bottom our bet by adding a 1,000 meter curtain of fire at each end of this east-west block to the south of the hill—200 rounds of 175-millimeter fire—in the event that the enemy outsmarted us by attempting a double envelopment.

At about 0230, eight batteries of artillery fired over 530 rounds into and along the curtains of the block. We had no confirmation at all that we had hit anything. The enemy still had half an hour to march to reach Hill 881-S. 0300 hours came and went without further sign of their presence. I concluded that even if we had not struck them fair and square, at least we had informed them clearly that we were aware of their existence and, consequently, they had aborted the attack. Nevertheless, something continued to bother my mind. Despite my concern, the general euphoria which by that time had permeated the CP prevented me from remembering the one or two facts which hitherto had escaped my attention. At about 0445 those facts were violently brought to mind.

The enemy, attacking in two-battalion strength, assaulted Hill 861-A. The missing two battalions had been signaled by the sensors, and, to my shame, I had completely forgotten them. I assumed now that those two battalions had left the ridge near Hill 881-S, swung north of the hill, and had occupied their attack position to the northeast of Hill 861-A, from where they made their assault.

The rest is history. Once more, Marine NCOs and other ranks made up for the mistakes of the alleged brains of the staff—as they have done throughout our history. There is no proof, naturally, of any connection between those sensor impulses representing a possible two battalions on the northwest ridge and the units which attacked Hill 861-A. Only one battalion actually made an appearance on the hill, and it, as you will remember, met a revolting fate. The second battalion, if there was one, was attended to by one hour of shelling and air strikes, which landed on all possible assembly-reserve areas at the base of the hill. Subsequent information suggested that a second battalion actually did exist, but that it never had an opportunity to take its place in the line of battle.

It is very easy to reason backwards. Sensor information can be very deceptively inviting in this regard. I like to think that all I have told you is precisely as it happened, but I cannot be sure, and will never really know until the North Vietnamese actually tell us.

For whatever it is worth, the major assault on the combat base, during the night of 29 February to 1 March, was signaled in precisely the same way as had been the hill attacks. And we were ready for them.

In the several years which have elapsed since General Tompkins' Marines broke the North Vietnamese regulars at Khe Sanh, the electronic battlefield has been refined to the point where, now, his sensors might tell him not only how many people are out there in the mist, where they are moving, and what he could expect, but even call down fire on those people through a computer. They would have come in handy along the Suez and in the Golan hills in October 1973.

The electronic battlefield, if defined strictly in the context of ground combat, is only one piece of electronic warfare. Immediately after the Yom Kippur war, the U.S. Army boosted electronic warfare even higher on its wish list of weaponry. It intensified its development of defensive electronics for helicopter and ground forces, and of more specialized electronic countermeasures hardware for specific combat situations. Reported *Aviation Week:*

The role of the Army Security Agency [ASA], the service arm traditionally invested with responsibility for collecting and analyzing military signal intelligence [Sigint], primarily strategic in nature, is enlarging as a consequence of the new emphasis on electronic warfare. With an anticipated larger role, reinforced ASA brigades will operate on tactical levels in the field, giving direct electronic warfare support to other Army units as well as more general support for rear-echelon positions. ASA aviation companies operating light aircraft will be assigned missions of locating hostile emitters at greater accuracies, at longer ranges and with less hindrance from the terrain than is possible with ground-based receivers. They also will perform critical countermeasures or jamming missions.

Radar-jamming equipment also stood high among the newest, most secret American technological treasures for which the Israelis began shopping within weeks of the Yom Kippur war—just in case there is, as there may well be, a next time. Israel's military leaders had their eyes on the Navy EA-6 Prowler, a variation of the A-6 attack jet, equipped with an electronic pod and a computer for distorting the multifrequency radars of surface-to-air missiles. Beyond the Prowler, however, for jamming, for air strikes, for reconnaissance, even someday for dogfighting, lay the unmanned planes. These RPVs (Remotely Piloted Vehicles) were being developed by all three U.S. services for a myriad missions, under the aegis of ARPA. The U.S. sent the Israelis some primitive models— simple drones—in the Yom Kippur war. But the Israelis would want the more sophisticated models coming along. These would be made to order for the military needs of militarily undermanned nations which have no bodies to spare. The unmanned plane, in combination with—and part of—sensor-activated, automatic firepower from land, sea and air, will be the *pièce de resistance* of what the U.S. military now calls IBCS —Integrated Battlefield Control System. The advent of these precisely controlled robots of the skies truly promises to eliminate humans from combat, to make of warfare a match-up of machines and electronic devices which the military and civilians alike will watch on the tube, complete with instant replays and halftime highlights. Should we live so long.

11

The
Mach II Robots

During the Vietnam War, an Air Force drone airplane landed in the Gulf of Tonkin. An Air Force helicopter was sent out to retrieve the drone and the pictures which its camera had taken of enemy target areas. As the chopper hovered, its engine failed, and it plopped into the drink near the drone. The chopper's three crewmen piled out, swam to the floating drone, and clambered atop it. They sat there, squeezed together on a fuselage barely long enough to accommodate them, until they were spotted by a Navy patrol plane, which signaled their position to a Navy ship. The ship came by and picked them up. After they had come aboard, a ship's officer said to them: "Tell me, how the hell did all you guys get into that little airplane?"

By now, no one in the military services would ask such a question. The drone is fast coming into its own. Now gone beyond the mere drone in sophistication, these unmanned airplanes are called RPVs, for Remotely Piloted Vehicles. They are the objects of swiftly accelerating research and development by all three services and the Advanced Research Projects Agency. They are, quite literally, the wave of the near future in warfare. Although the R&D was still in its infancy at the mid-1970s, it had progressed far enough to convince even the most skeptical among the men who wear the wings of the military that pilots, long before the end of this century, will have become misfits in cockpits.

In June 1974, preparing to conduct a fleet amphibious exercise in the Atlantic off Norfolk, the Navy asked the Air Force to become involved. Would the Air Force fly a few of its unmanned reconnaissance planes over the beach, to let the Navy see how effective they could be? Glad to, said the Air Force, but you'll have to pay the costs. The Navy agreed. The results, according to the participants of both services, were spectacular. But the Air Force put on a performance not on the program. It stuck a TV-guided Maverick missile on one of the unmanned planes, attacked the fleet and scored a ship-kill, as recorded by telemetry monitoring. This was not really surprising to those in the know. Two years earlier, a Firebee unmanned plane had zoomed down from 50,000 feet straight into and through the Terrier missile defenses of the frigate *Wainwright* off the Atlantic coast. If the Firebee had fired a high-explosive or nuclear missile, or if it had taken the warhead all the way by itself, there would have been no *Wainwright* left.

In the summer of 1971, on the coast of southern California, a Navy pilot settled into his cockpit, started his engine, taxied his fighter to the runway, and took off over the Pacific. He was intercepted, head on, by a Navy F-4 Phantom. In less than a half minute, he had turned inside the Phantom and taken up a sure-kill firing position on the Phantom's tail. He had whipped into position so tightly and at such speed that if he had been sitting in the plane, he would have been blacked out by his own body weight. But he had been sitting in a cockpit on the ground, flying a Firebee by remote control. Over the past few years, many such tests have taken place, and the results have always been the same: the manned plane is no match for the RPV. The RPVs can outturn, outfly and elude the fighters and their missiles. Fighter pilots remained skeptical, however, because the tests were rigged in the RPVs' favor. Their remote controllers had been able to keep the RPVs, and their opponents, in sight, and they had joined the dogfight with the manned fighters in range of their TV-camera vision. RPVs, said the fighter pilots, will never be dogfighters until they can scan the skies the way a pilot can. But the pilots must have sensed that the technology of optics no doubt will bring into being the unmanned plane of unlimited vision. It is only a matter of time. When this happens, the pilotless plane will have attained the ultimate: an air-superiority dogfighter. Meanwhile, the RPVs have shown what they can do in other missions for which pilots no longer will be needed in the immediate future. Some of those missions, notably the low-level runs against surface-to-air missile batteries, the pilots might prefer, indeed, to forgo.

Drones have been around a long time; clear back, in fact to the "war to end all wars." They are direct descendants—in mission, if not in technology—of the Bug, a World War I biplane designed to be stuffed with high explosives and flown on its own until it crashed, hopefully somewhere near the target. The Bug was fueled to fly as far as a predetermined number of engine revolutions would be needed to take it to the target area. When the engine died, the Bug became a bomb. It was tested, but never sent forth in combat. In World War II, Hitler's V-2 rockets, the progeny of Peenemünde, were quasi-drones. There were others, too. The B-24 bomber which exploded and killed Navy Lt. Joseph P. Kennedy, Jr., was among them. He was to have bailed out over England after setting the bomber on a remotely controlled course to Germany. Something went wrong. In the Pacific, the U.S. also used some B-29s on remotely controlled bomb runs.

The most common drones are the target drones, which have abounded over test ranges since the 1950s. Only since the 1960s, however, have these air-launched planes taken on the refinements of radar reflection and computer-programmed flight characteristics which permit them to simulate particular aircraft. One Firebee drone can play the part of a Soviet Backfire bomber or a Soviet Flogger fighter, depending on the radar silhouette, speed and maneuverability contrived for its mission of the moment. Only rarely do the target-practicing American pilots and antiaircraft missile batterymen actually shoot down the drones. Electronics aboard the target craft record the hits or misses according to how close the missiles come.

The best-known drone is the Firebee. Ryan Aeronautical Co., which built Lindbergh's *Spirit of St. Louis*, produced the first Firebee in 1951. The latest version, the Firebee II, is powered by a turbojet engine and can carry enough fuel to fly at supersonic speeds for more than an hour. The Firebee is only one of nearly two dozen drone models produced by Teledyne Ryan Aeronautical, Northrop, Beech and Rockwell International for target practice by all three services. But target practice is old hat. The world of the drone widened when the Air Force discovered that the Firebee was a dandy device for shooting pictures as well.

Even before the Russians shot down the high-flying Lockheed U-2 and captured its CIA pilot, Francis Gary Powers, in May 1960, Ryan Aeronautical and Boeing had proposed building reconnaissance drones for the Air Force. Ryan's concept was called "Red Wagon"; Boeing's, "Blue Scooter." In the diplomatically messy aftermath of the U-2 affair, President Eisenhower agreed to stop sending manned reconnaissance planes on photo missions over the Soviet Union. He had an out. Destiny seemed to have smiled upon the drone. But the Air Force decided, instead, to move ahead with development of another manned recon plane, the SR-71 Blackbird, product of the same Lockheed R&D "Skunk Works" which previously had devised the U-2. Six years later, on May 9, 1966, a Blackbird high over China's Sinkiang Province monitored a nuclear explosion. President Johnson knew about the blast within minutes. And within a few hours, he also knew, from data collected by the spy plane, that China had set off not an H-bomb, as had been feared, but an A-bomb. This Blackbird was an early version of the plane which, in 1974, set a transatlantic speed record. When the Blackbird came to the fore, in 1960, Boeing withdrew its proposal to build an RPV reconnaissance plane for the Air Force. Ryan Aeronautical's proposal was shelved, too, at the Pentagon. Then, two years later, during the missile crisis, came the turning point. An Air Force U-2 was shot down over Cuba. Its pilot, Major Rudolf Anderson, Jr., was killed. President Kennedy wanted to know why Anderson's mission could not have been flown by a drone. He was told that in the entire Air Force inventory, there were only two drones which might have been capable of casing Cuba from on high. So Kennedy told McNamara to have the Air Force come up with some more. The Air Force began converting Firebees to the high-altitude mission.

Over the next few years, the Chinese had plenty of practice taking pot shots at reconnaissance drones. In the Pentagon, among the few officials who knew what was taking place, it was called "Chinese William Tell." Finally, in 1964, the Chinese downed a Firebee. By now, there are parts of at least three U.S. reconnaissance drones on display in Peking. Hanoi's War Museum features others. No one talks about "Compass Arrow" any more at the Pentagon. This was the name given to the project of drone surveillance—including the "reading" of radars—over China. "Compass Arrow" came abruptly to an end when President Nixon began laying plans for his mission to Peking in 1971. Still, it had taken no time at all to establish the pilotless planes as superb in reconnaissance over China, Vietnam, Laos and Cambodia, at altitudes up to 70,000 feet and down to a hundred. More than 1,000 drones, most of them built by Teledyne Ryan, were delivered for recon combat duty in Southeast Asia. They flew 2,500 sorties. Combat pilots, thrown a bit off balance by the drones' sweeping intrusion, called the drones' area of operations the "Tonkin Gulf Test Range." For all their value, the unmanned craft did cause a certain amount of clutter. One time, the Navy was compelled to announce its error in having proclaimed the kill of a MiG-21. Inspection of the fragments of the downed aircraft revealed that a Navy F-4, in trying to protect an Air Force C-130, had shot down the reconnaissance drone which the C-130 "mother ship" had been controlling. This was nothing to shrug off. The drones were delivering. Time after time, they brought back pictures of targets and of target damage from missions which theretofore had cost the lives of the crews of conventional reconnaissance planes. In Congressional testimony of January 9, 1973, just after the thunderous B-52 bombings of Hanoi and Haiphong, Admiral Thomas H. Moorer, Chairman of the Joint Chiefs of Staff, revealed that all the bomb-damage photos had been taken by drones, buzzing North Vietnam under clouds only as high, sometimes, as hundreds of feet. "If you noticed," said Moorer, "every picture I showed you had the word 'drone' on it, and most of these pictures were taken at [deleted] feet, far too low to conduct bombing. That was the reason I showed you more than one picture of the same target, because the drones are so close to it that they cannot get all the targets in one photograph." The drones had been Firebees, specifically designed for the Air Force "Compass Bin" low-level reconnaissance project in Southeast Asia.

Had the North Vietnamese not indicated that they would come to terms in 1973, their homeland might have been subjected to the first air strikes in history by unmanned bombers. The Air Force stood ready to launch these remotely controlled aircraft, which by then were called "drones" only out of habit. Their technology had far outstripped the drone designation. Their "pilots" no longer needed to keep them in sight from the ground or from a following aircraft. Now fitted with television cameras, they could be controlled from hundreds or thousands of miles away by an operator who saw on his TV screen, simultaneously, the images of ground and air which the cameras in the RPVs were photographing. Signals and pictures between pilot and plane could be relayed through manned aircraft, such as the new Airborne Warning and Control System (AWACS) plane now being developed by the Air Force, through satellites or through other, high-loitering RPVs. Some communications problems still had to be overcome, but they were mere details of a technology which had been mastered in the main. It was the very same technology, predicated on the miniaturization of electronics, which had led to the development of TV-guided and laser-guided "smart bombs" and missiles, already used, with gratifying precision, in Vietnam. Most of the publicity attendant upon their deployment had been focused on the way they had picked out military targets in the environs of Hanoi and Haiphong. But six months earlier, in May 1973, a 2,000-pound "Hobo" (Homing Bomb) had obliterated a bridge just north of Hanoi which had withstood repeated onslaughts of conventional bombs. Now, in 1973, the unmanned aircraft, too, could be armed with TV-guided missiles, and sent north, far beyond the retinal ranges of their ground and air controllers. On their first bombing run, they would have revolutionized air warfare. The next war will bring that first bombing run—and that revolution.

Several events led up to the Air Force readying the RPVs as bombers, and to the Pentagon's recognition of the all-robot air force as a future practicality, not a pipe dream. In the spring of 1970, the Air Force Systems Command and RAND convened a symposium at Santa Monica, California, of more than one hundred military and civilian experts in the technology of remotely controlled planes. All three services and the National Aeronautics and Space Administration were represented, along with representatives of several companies and, besides RAND, the other Air Force think tanks: MITRE Corp. and Aerospace Corp. Five panels were formed. Each was assigned to study the problems and prospects of sending RPVs on a different combat mission—interdiction, close air support, air superiority, reconnaissance and surveillance, and electronic jamming of enemy missile radar. One panel dealt exclusively with the command, control and communications problem. Three months later, everyone got together again to report. The chief conclusions were that the potential was vast and that the few problems probably were surmountable. The specialists foresaw RPVs as the first wave of air strikes against heavily defended targets; to draw the fire of surface-to-air missiles, and to seduce interceptors into the air. This would open the targets to the manned fighter-bombers, and expose the interceptors to the manned fighters trailing the RPVs in the attack. The RPVs would be ideal for jamming, too, either by "nulling" the enemy's direction-finding antennae or by cluttering his radar with chaff. The eye-opener at the Santa Monica symposium, however, was the conclusion of the air-superiority panel that technology would allow for RPV fighter planes, armed with rockets, guns and, later, laser guns, capable of turns and dives which would "pull" twelve times the force of gravity and easily defeat any enemy pilot who tried to stay with—or away from —them. The key to their success in all missions lay in refining the techniques and the electronics of remote control. The main elements of this control already existed in military or space systems. Video cameras and zoom lenses provided the essential optics. Electronic command, tracking and telemetry systems, tailormade for drones, were taking on added sophistication almost by the day.

Within months of the Santa Monica exploration of the future roles of the RPVs, the Firebees were taking on the Phantoms, and providing solid evidence that pilots may not be required to clear the air.

In January 1971, David Packard, then Deputy Secretary of Defense, directed the establishment of a top-level "defense suppression" program. It was an emergency effort. Antiaircraft guns and missiles were downing far too many American planes in Vietnam. Too many American pilots were checking into the "Hanoi Hilton." The new Pentagon program contained many elements, but principal among them were the RPV and the "smart" bombs and missiles, taken separately or together. A few months after the Packard directive, the Air Force, Navy and Army set up a technical coordinating committee to pool information on the progress and problems of their fledgling RPV programs. At that point, the Army and Navy had relatively little to report, having only just begun. But the Pentagon intended not to let the littlest scrap of any service's research become a leftover. Mainly, the tri-service committee was assigned to "program definition"—coming to conclusions about how you fight wars with unmanned planes and what it will cost you to do so.

In January 1972, one year after Packard's directive, the preliminary testing of the RPV attack bomber, a defense-suppression weapon if ever there was one, came to an end. RPVs had launched Mavericks, Hobos and antiradar Shrikes, scoring bull's-eyes on targets in the Mojave Desert, and even against hillside caves. These tests were unpublicized at the time. In hindsight, they almost certainly were the reason for Dr. John L. McLucas's assertion in mid-1972 that the Air Force was "on the threshhold of utilizing RPVs for selected strike missions." McLucas, Undersecretary of the Air Force at the time, was to become Secretary in 1973. He will be remembered, some day, as the man who did the most to push the Pentagon and its reluctant pilots into the age of the pilotless plane.

A half-minute glance around McLucas's suite in the Air Force realm of the Pentagon's E Ring was enough to show where his love abided. Models of unmanned planes—long-winged, stubby-winged, sleek of fuselage or squat—stood, it seemed, everywhere. I was accompanied, at this interviewing session, by an Air Force brigadier general, deskbound at the Pentagon, who had been a fighter pilot in World War II and Korea and who had, I thought, the perfect fighter pilot's name: Slade Nash. The general also exhibited the typical fighter pilot's attitude toward RPVs: the slight smile which said don't get carried away; the occasionally raised eyebrow which meant prove it to me; the impatient shifting of body whenever McLucas uplifted the RPV as a future air-to-air interceptor. By the time of this interview, in May 1973, Nash had come, however, to the realization that air defenses now were a thousandfold more ferocious than any previously encountered by the bomber and attack pilots of his generation, and that the RPV would be a welcome ally of, so long as it did not preempt, the fighter pilot. The following November, in the Middle East, those air defenses would startle the world, and speed the deployment of the RPV.

Right off, how did McLucas size up RPVs? "I think," he said, in accents North Carolinian, "they are terrific. We're actually just beginning a ten-year cycle in their R&D. In ten years, their dogfight role could be realistic. We can put on the dogfight with the manned plane as a stunt today, but we've still got to get it accepted as a concept, train people in it, and develop the tactics. The surface has just been scratched. We're making headway, but we've still got to convince everyone in the Air Force that it's the way to go. It's coming. It used to be very hard to find a four-star Air Force general who would accept the RPVs. But now there are several who do, including the commander-in-chief of the Tactical Air Command. For other missions, for strike and recon, they're already here. It wouldn't surprise me if we're in full-scale production of RPVs for those missions in four years."

McLucas became Air Force Undersecretary in March 1969, already well-practiced in the ways of the Pentagon and its peripheral spheres. He had just been president and chief executive officer of MITRE Corp. and had served in the early 1960s as Deputy Director of Defense Research and Engineering for Tactical Warfare Programs. He was another example of how the same basic cast of Pentagon players keeps popping up on stage or in the wings in switches of starring and supporting roles. A native of Fayetteville, North Carolina, McLucas was graduated from Davidson College in 1941, earned a master's degree in physics at Tulane University in 1943, served three years as a Navy officer, spent one year at the Air Force Research Center, Cambridge, Massachusetts, and then took his doctorate in physics at Pennsylvania State University. He came to DDR&E in 1962 following several years as an electronics industry executive. He left DDR&E in 1964 to become Assistant Secretary General for Scientific Affairs at NATO headquarters in Paris. Truly a technocrat, McLucas, but of philosophical and diplomatic bent. He seemed more adept than most at seeing how all the pieces fit, and this trait, along with his persistence, helped him push RPVs to prominence through the pilot politics of the Air Force. He was helped, too, by events.

We met next at a luncheon in the Pentagon, where McLucas, the host, and by then Secretary of the Air Force, discussed with four news magazine correspondents what his service might have learned in the Yom Kippur war just then ending. The conversation ranged over many topics. When someone suggested that the heavy loss of planes to missiles might have brightened the future of unmanned aircraft, McLucas leaned back, deployed his napkin, and asserted with obvious satisfaction: "It certainly did."

That the Air Force finally got serious about RPVs can be attributed also to the growing interest of General George S. Brown, who became chairman of the Joint Chiefs of Staff in 1974. More than a year earlier, from his command post at the Air Force Systems Command, Brown ordered up another study of the possible missions of the unmanned craft. While he was taken with the technology of the RPVs, Brown had yet to become fully convinced of their practicality in combat. At an earlier discussion of RPVs with their boosters from RAND, Brown had thanked the think tankers for their presentation of the superperformances which the RPVs had in store, but had said: "You still haven't shown me how they will win a war." Now, he set out to find out. On May 9, 1973, ten generals, the cream of the Air Force commands, met at Wright Patterson AFB, Ohio, to begin a six-month study of RPV missions. These were the commanders who would oversee the development of RPVs in the real world, or not at all. They had no predilection to science fiction, no patience with planes that might not pan out. Their study was to be an outgrowth of a preliminary analysis by Teledyne Ryan and Northrop, each of which the Air Force had awarded $300,000 in late 1971 to explore, among other things, the relative advantages and disadvantages of recoverable and expendable RPVs. The companies had worked through the Tactical Air Command. And as McLucas had noted, Lieutenant General William B. Momyers, the CO of Tac Air and himself a fighter pilot, had become persuaded that the unmanned planes were worth a good, hard look. At Wright-Pat, the high-level committee, headed by Major General John J. Burns, chief of Air Force Operational Requirements and Development Plans, assigned various parts of the study to a forty-one-member staff composed of officers from all Air Force commands. Their job: correlate the technical capabilities of the RPVs with the actual missions of the Air Force, and report to the generals, finally, whether the RPVs demanded urgent development, whether they could wait, and what they would cost.

It may seem strange and confusing that the Air Force kept studying the roles of the RPVs even after the craft had proved their worth in reconnaissance, and actually had been prepared to take on the strike mission in Vietnam. And it is, unless you work at the Pentagon. The Pentagon almost always operates this way. Weapons can be devised which work very well, or promise to, in combat, and yet, after the combat ends, are set aside while the services plunge ahead with what they know best how to do: keep evolving highly expensive weapons which belong more to the past, but which give the military the feeling of security derived from tradition, and the defense industry the big dollars that come from assured production. While the results of the Air Force generals' RPV study were not made public, enough pieces surfaced to indicate that they had turned thumbs up for RPVs in reconnaissance, electronic jamming and possibly—just possibly—strike missions, but that they remained convinced that there was no place for the RPV as an air-superiority interceptor in the foreseeable future, if ever. The Air Force grounded its continuing skepticism about the RPV as an attack bomber in the notion that the large numbers of unmanned planes which would be needed for such missions could not be coordinated effectively from remote-control stations. They would not have the flexibility of flight patterns needed to elude enemy fire. They would not be able to judge the situation and adjust to it, the way pilots can, during quick-time combat crises. And while the RPVs presumably would cost much less than manned fighter-bombers, the heavy losses which they might incur on strike missions against defended-to-the-death missile batteries would make their costs prohibitive, taken altogether. What it all came down to, perhaps oversimplified, was that the Air Force had seized on the RPV for unglamorous reconnaissance and electronic missions, but had slighted the RPV for all missions which it might perform as an actual weapon, as a fighter or a bomber. At the Pentagon, the customers wore wings, and they weren't buying. Not yet.

Hurting and destroying the enemy would be left to the planes with pilots in them. Hurting and destroying the enemy is the glory, as well as the gore, of war; it is the stuff of the legends and the lore of war—and of the big money for the weapons makers. Until the Pentagon decided to turn the RPVs into weapons, not just into scouts of the skies, the defense industry, save the companies which specialized in them, could hardly afford to become enthusiastic about their future. The profits would remain in the planes that the pilots flew. But then, just as the RPV began cooling off in the Pentagon's hobby shops, the Arabs struck Israel.

In less than two weeks of fighting, the Israelis lost more than a hundred American-built attack planes to Egyptian and Syrian surface-to-air missiles. Immediately, the RPV moved up smartly once again toward the top of the Pentagon's priorities as a "defense-suppression" weapon, as an attack plane. By the end of the three weeks of Mideast combat, the prospect of fielding RPVs armed with glide bombs and missiles for stand-off attacks against antiaircraft missile installations and armor had become downright compelling to the pilotless-plane pro-crastinators along the Potomac. American-built TV-guided missiles and glide bombs had savaged the Arab forces. The Maverick, the Walleye and other weapons of this nature had destroyed over a hundred and fifty Arab tanks in one week. The Israelis conceded that they had been remiss in not order-ing drones from the U.S. years beforehand. They would have used swarms of drones as attack planes against the surface-to-air missile nests, in concert with the TV-guided missiles. At one time, they had considered buying U.S. drones. But they had abandoned the idea because they continued to believe that manned planes could manage to pierce the missile umbrellas. They had made a mistake, which the U.S. Air Force now could turn to its own advantage and, consequently, to the Israelis', the next time out. The Yom Kippur war had showed conclu-sively that missiles costing only a few thousand dollars apiece can destroy, in days, dismayingly large numbers of jets costing double-digit millions apiece, plus their pilots, on whose lives price tags are difficult to affix. In the final days of the war, the Israelis reportedly did send some drones into battle. They bought small numbers of these craft directly from U.S. manu-facturers—not from the U.S. Air Force—and flew them, via El

Al, to the battlefront. They were used, according to reports, as decoys to bait Arab SAMs. If the SAMs could not be jammed, at least they could be flimflammed. By drones, better late than never.

The Germans probably were the first to use electronic countermeasures—to escape the British blockage and radar scrutiny of the warships *Scharnhorst, Prinz Eugen* and *Gneisenau* in Brest harbor during World War II. The Germans interfered with British radar signals only slightly at first, in low key, scarcely intrusive. Over a period of time, they gradually intensified the interference. The British radar operators came to regard the interference as normal background noise. When the German ships broke for the English Channel, the Germans jammed all British radar save one, and the British, by then so accustomed to the interference that they considered it normal, did not believe what the unjammed radar was telling them about those movements on the water. The three ships dashed free into the North Sea.

In 1943, it was the turn of the British. Approaching Hamburg, RAF bombers dropped strips of metal chaff which reflected radar signals spuriously among those being reflected by the bombers. Airborne ECMs were born. By now, electronic countermeasures have become so sophisticated and specialized that much of the Pentagon's research is devoted to electronic counter-countermeasures (ECCMs) to nullify the enemy's countermeasures. In keeping with Newton's third law of motion—to every force or action there is an equal or opposite reaction—every new countermeasure educes another counter-countermeasure, and so on. Jam the jammers. Jam the jammers of the jammers of the jammers . . . There was a time when jamming equipment was built into aircraft. Now, the equipment is being packaged in pods which are slung under the wings. This permits interchangeability of pods for particularized missions. Some jets, like the Navy EA-6B Prowler, which the Israelis coveted after the Yom Kippur war, are designed to do nothing but jam. But the Air Force has converted F-105 and F-4 fighter bombers to fly "Wild Weasel" missions, aimed at nothing more nor less than the destruction of radar missile sites and radar warning systems. The computers of the "Wild

Weasel" planes are supposed to tell the pilots how to dodge the missiles as they make their low-level attack runs against the missile emplacements. This tactic was used in Vietnam, and the pilots of the Wild Weasel planes today are among the most enthusiastic proponents of RPVs for strike-jamming missions. Israel had neither Wild Weasels nor RPVs.

When it came to the Soviet SA-6 Gainful missiles which felled Israeli F-4s and A-4s so furiously, the United States found itself back to Square One in the game of ECMs and ECCMs. The SA-6 radiated a coordinated web of five separate signals, one each for detecting, locking onto and tracking the Israeli attack planes; the other two, for guiding the missile to, and destroying, the planes. The signals were divided between two radars, each ferried by a separate vehicle rolling along with the Arab armored columns. The Gainful had not been used in Vietnam. Coming across it for the first time, the U.S. Air Force could not tell the Israelis how to jam it. So the Israelis had to take out the SA-6 batteries the hard way, with armor and aircraft. Drones delivering bombs and missiles, or confusing or overwhelming the SA-6 radar in great numbers, like hivefuls of hornets, could have made all the difference in Israeli losses and in the duration of the war. By not having anticipated the SA-6, and in not having RPVs at the ready, the U.S. Air Force, too, demonstrated that it tends to live in the past, until evicted by events.

Many months after the Yom Kippur war, McLucas reflected on its relationship, and that of the Vietnam War, to the development of strike RPVs in the Air Force: "We went through a lull in pushing their development after we decided not to use them in Vietnam. We had showed in tests that they could be used on strike missions. But we would have needed many more of them than we had available. We would have had to go into large-scale procurement. The RPVs were winding up in R&D, but the war was winding down. Then, to have something like the SA-6 come along in the Middle East can give you quite a bit of heartburn. You may learn how to deal with the SA-6. But what about the SA-9 that you may see some day? So the Middle East put the emphasis back on standoff weapons. It refocused attention on the RPV."

Money for the development of defense-suppression weapons, including guided tactical missiles, glide bombs and strike drones, accounted for a sizable chunk of the $6.2 billion supplemental budget which the Defense Department rushed to Congress after the Yom Kippur war. The unpiloted attack plane finally had taken off inside the Pentagon. None too soon. The Arabs had used another Soviet antiaircraft missile, the shoulder-fired, heat-seeking SA-7 Strella. To be effective, this infrared-homing missile had to be fired from behind the attacking aircraft it was intended to hit. The Strella was hit-or-miss. But both the Americans and the Soviets are feverishly trying to develop heat-seeking antiaircraft missiles which can take planes head-on. The advent of such missiles would be especially ominous. They could be jammed only with great difficulty. They might indeed mark the end of the large, piloted attack jet. The smaller, dart-and-destroy RPV would be needed in a hurry.

Air Force R&D funding of pilotless planes doubled from 1973 to 1974. In that period, RCA's Missile and Surface Radar Division announced that it had completed the design of guidance and control, sensors and all other electronics needed for a new generation of RPVs. Among other things, this portended a breakthrough on the problem of one remote operator controlling and coordinating more than one unmanned craft in the attack. Now, it seemed, one operator, sitting in a command plane or in a darkened room on the ground, watching a wall-size console, could fly a couple of squadrons against densely packed or widely dispersed nests of ground-to-air missiles.

As the Air Force revved up the strike-mission RPV, its "Compass Cope" program was already well advanced. This involved competition between Teledyne Ryan and Boeing for a contract to produce long-wing RPVs, similar to configuration to the U-2, which would undertake reconnaissance from altitudes up to 80,000 feet. The first Boeing prototype crashed on landing in 1973. Under the command of its remote operator, it sideslipped just above the runway and caught a wing. This pointed up one of the two principal pursuits of RPV research and development: how to recover the planes, and how to make sure that the communications between them and their remote operators cannot be jammed or jiggered.

Colonel Charles E. Kenney was in charge of coordinating Air Force RPV research at the Pentagon when we talked. "Retrieval," he said, "is our biggest problem right now. We're working on automatic landing systems. The question is, at which point in the command-and-control loop does the automatic landing system take over from the human controller."

The Air Force does not want to waste its RPVs, even though they will cost much less than manned planes. The Compass Cope reconnaissance versions will be the costliest, ranging up to $2 million or so apiece. Most varieties, however expensive, are being designed to return and land after their missions, if only to save the electronics equipment aboard. In modern warfare, that equipment has taken on not only the duties of man but his salvage requirement as well. Unless they can be landed, the RPVs must be recovered by helicopters either from the water or in the air. Air recovery relies on parachutes. The RPV's chute has a main canopy and, extending atop this, a smaller "engagement" canopy, which has metal ribs and looks, from inside, something like a bird cage. The helicopter catches this canopy with three hooks. The main chute then falls away. This permits a metal cable, which had circumscribed the main canopy, to straighten out, linking the RPV directly to the helicopter. The helicopter then reels in the RPV just like a fisherman. In a combat situation, involving many RPVs and helicopters, this technique would be difficult. It would resemble a shad run in the sky.

"We're trying to get away from helicopter recovery," said Colonel Kenney. He had come a long way, already, with RPVs. They had become his specialty at the beginning of the 1970s, at the Air Force Systems Command, at the right hand of General Brown. Kenney had concentrated on the strike-mission RPVs firing laser-guided rockets. "The Compass Cope planes will be wheeled, so it will be normal to land them," he said. "But the strike drones could land in a number of ways—wheels, or maybe with a combination of chutes and air cushions. We'll have some RPVs, probably, that we won't have to land. We call them 'tactical, expendable decoy systems.' Their whole mission will be to make the enemy fire his SAMs, and let the fighter-bombers come in. I tell you," he said with a smile, "the guys who flew decoy in the Vietnam War are very enthusiastic about this. We may be able to produce expendable drones for no more than about fifty thousand dollars apiece."

Kenney was most emphatic about the Air Force not crossing RPV missions with the Army, which had begun winging into a less extensive but no less revolutionary RPV program of its own. Would history repeat itself? Would the Air Force and the Army continue, with unmanned planes, their eternal jockeying for primacy in the mission of close air support of ground troops? "We're avoiding it like the plague," said Kenney. "It's dumb to do business that way in this day and age. We've had enough of that."

When RPVs began catching on, around late 1971, there was considerable speculation that before the end of the decade, the Air Force might have more long-range RPV bombers than the four hundred B-52s then in its arsenal. Even if this were attainable, the Air Force would never admit it. Such a prospect would be just another political drawback to the B-1 bomber, which was bucking turbulence enough. In 1974, at a session of the House Defense Appropriations Subcommittee, General Brown, Secretary McLucas and Representative William Minshall of Ohio discussed the proposition of the RPV as a global weapon:

MINSHALL: "Why could not an RPV do the same job that a B-1 could do, for all intents and purposes?"

BROWN: "Well, from the work we have done with RPVs to date, we know they can do many things that a manned system in the past has done. . . ."

MINSHALL: "Do not misunderstand me. I am not trying to put the B-1 out of business. I think it is a great concept. I am for it. But I would like to look ahead a bit."

BROWN: "But we have a long, long way to go with an unmanned aircraft to perform some of these functions at very long ranges, and we have not demonstrated that sort of thing. We of course have done some tests with unmanned vehicles carrying a missile, with an optical system to guide the missile to the target, and so on. But we have not done any very long-range work like you suggest. Nor do we have any plans to do it in the immediate future."

MINSHALL: "I just wonder—if you can get to a target without a manned crew, say even with a standoff weapon, why could you not do the same thing at even a longer range with a remote pilot on the vehicle?"

BROWN: "I am not sure we know how to do it yet. I do not know what the technical problems are, but it is not in our program. Perhaps someday it will come to where it is all done mechanically, without man. But the functions that must be performed by the crew during penetration, for instance, to handle the electronic warfare problem, require judgment: to react to situations which would be extremely difficult to anticipate and counter through automation."

McLucas: "Could I add a word to that? I claim to be one of the strongest proponents of RPVs."

Minshall: "You do?"

McLucas: "I do. I think they have a great future in the Air Force and maybe in some of the other services too. But it seems to me it is sort of an intermediate case between the rigid missile system and the very flexible B-1 case. By the RPV technique, you bring a man, a pilot, into control. So that for those things that he knows about, he can take account of with the RPV. But for those things for which he does not have the right sensors on board the RPV, he will not know about them. To that extent, he is not as flexible. As you go through RPV development, you can introduce more and more of the capabilities that a man would have if he were there. All of these things require proving and testing. We are doing quite a bit of this right now —and have been for the last two or three years—and it is not completely inconceivable to me that in another ten years or so, we might have more or less duplicated a lot of a man's capabilities. But certainly we are not there yet, and will not be for a long time. All of this still leaves you with the question of getting the communications loop closed between the man on the ground who is in control and the vehicle itself. These links can be made reasonably secure, but there is always that question about whether they would be interfered with."

Making the communications links secure was the job of the Advanced Research Projects Agency. ARPA also was working on a computer that "thinks." The connection, and its implication for future long-range RPVs (or would they be called CPVs for "Computer Piloted Vehicles"?) was becoming obvious.

In the fall of 1974, the Army awarded its first contract for development of ten prototype "mini-RPVs." These aircraft, about six feet long, with wingspans of seven or eight feet, will buzz battlefields at low altitudes or loiter up to 12,000 feet, seeking targets and signaling for and directing artillery fire. Someday, said Major Jack H. Clifton, the airborne ranger in charge of coordinating the Army's RPV project, the pilotless planes will serve not only as forward observers for the artillery but as artillery themselves. "They will be," he said, "rounds with wings." The Army calls them "Kamikaze" drones, and they will be built, by Pentagon standards, dirt cheap—no more than $50,000 per plane. The Army will confine its RPVs to what it calls the FEBA, the forward edge of the battlefield, and no more than twenty-five miles beyond, strictly as part of division artillery. The Artillery Center at Fort Sill, Oklahoma, is the focus of the Army RPV program. Apart from the Kamikaze models, the reconnaissance and fire-calling RPVs in the Army's future present a problem of landing which may be even stickier than that of the Air Force. Operating up front, the Army craft will not have access to runways. They will have to be returned to small clearings. But they will not be, like those of the Air Force, jet powered. Army propulsion R&D was being concentrated on propellors and small engines of the sort that drive chain saws, washing machines and lawn mowers. Thus the recovery problem will not be compounded by the need to maneuver a jetcraft to landing. The Army probably will launch its RPVs by catapult, and recover them in nets similar to those used on aircraft carriers. The Army was planning autopilots for its RPVs, plus built-in, computer-programmed flight patterns which ground controllers could bring into play on radio command. The artillery's RPVs will use lasers to designate targets for the big guns and missiles to the rear, or carry small warheads and small TV cameras, and hunt and kill, all of a piece.

"We intend to use these birds as integral parts of our artillery units," said Major Clifton. "We are trying to remove the individual, as much as possible, from the battlefield."

The Navy, starting from behind the Air Force and Army, began working with both services in the late summer of 1974 on development of RPVs of all shapes and sizes: miniplanes to find and fix tactical-range targets for frigates and guided-missile destroyers; maxiplanes, based aboard carriers, which would fly high and loiter long, scanning the seas for the enemy up top and underneath, warning of missiles and planes on the way; midiplanes, of weights up to about three thousand pounds, to be launched from amphibious assault and amphibious command ships, and, in the 1980s, from the big, swift, hydrofoil surface effects ships. These RPVs would make the guerrilla fleets of the future even quicker to kill. Again, retrieval is the rub, especially when the RPV comes home to the smaller ships. The Navy does not want to have to fish for its Firebees.

The Senate Armed Services Committee hearings on RPVs in 1974, contained the following exchange between Senator Thomas J. McIntyre and Vice-Admiral William J. Moran of Navy R&D:

McINTYRE: "You state that the Navy in the long term is looking toward a new dimension for naval warfare, such as space technology, faster, more agile surface platforms, and missile standoff capability. Would you consider the use of remotely piloted aircraft as a new dimension?"

MORAN: "I think the RPV is well within the definition of a new dimension. We have gone through a long evolution in the aircraft business where we are now all involved in buying airplanes at a very impressive price tag per airplane. We put a lot of effort in trying to get that number down in all of the services, and we have not been too successful. A part of the cost of that airplane is having the man in it—and the safety that needs to go with him, and the rating and the experiments and tests that have to be accomplished before we will put a man in the plane and send him off. The RPV allows you to shortcut that much of the investment. For the kind of things where an unmanned device can do the military job—the job that we used to ask a manned airplane to do—the RPV is in fact a new dimension."

It all seemed plain enough. The RPVs promised to cut costs dramatically. They would not need cockpits, cockpit instrumentation, armor, ejection systems, air conditioning, oxygen systems and pressure controls. Some could be built of materials much less expensive than metal, if they were to be sent out, anyway, on kamikaze missions. These would require only the simple techniques needed to build model airplanes and sailplanes, which the long-wing versions for high-altitude surveillance do indeed resemble. Even the landing gear of the RPVs destined for retrieval would be far less complicated, and costly, than those of the manned aircraft. As McLucas summed up the economics: "If a manned aircraft costs $3 million, and we sustain an attrition rate of only 1 percent, we lose $30 million for every 1,000 sorties. On the other hand, even if an RPV cost $500,000 to do the same job, we could withstand an attrition rate of 6 percent and still break even, on a purely economic basis."

For the time being, the services seemed to be doing their best to keep RPV costs as austere as possible, and to avoid duplicating planes and missions. The temptation to get too fancy or too far-flung is always, however, there. The Pentagon proclaims Spartan intentions for its spending on the development of all big weapon systems, and nearly always gives in to the glut of technology. In the case of the RPVs, ARPA's research already boded ballooning costs, for it was advancing, in the mid-1970s, toward horizons well beyond mere remote control, toward fully automated flight, toward the "digital airplane." This would involve the interactions of command computers and their smaller cousins aboard the planes, permitting the planes to "know" their positions at all times, to head and maneuver, to perform in all kinds of weather. As noted in a previous chapter, these planes also will have dispensed with hydraulic and mechanical controls. Their control surfaces will be actuated by electronics. They will not even look like airplanes; more like flying saucers. They will be able to go anywhere and do anything, and they probably will be taken along, in the twenty-first century or even before, as intersolar or interstellar sojourners. What remarkable scouts they could be out there. If you believe in flying saucers, what remarkable scouts they already are, right here. Whose, is another question.

Returning to the here and the now and the near at hand, Robert Barkan, a former Bell Telephone Laboratories engineer, summed it up colorfully and musingly in *The New Republic:*

> So, in the 1980s, enemy warplanes will be met by hundreds of RPVs equipped with rockets, missiles, and laser ray guns, swarming around their larger but slower adversaries like bees attacking a bird. Later, pilots will be put back in the planes. But the pilots will be computers, programmed to recognize a target and destroy it. Humans will play a minimal role, perhaps merely giving orders such as, "Go. Shoot. Stop. Return." . . . War will increasingly become a contest between machines—which do not bleed, die, get addicted to drugs, shoot their officers or refuse to fight. A pilot flying an

RPV bombing run from a swivel chair in an underground control center doesn't look out his cockpit window at the death and destruction below, and wonder, "Why am I doing this?" He doesn't watch the flak coming up at him and swear that he'll never fly again. He feels no more compunction than the engineer who designed the machine.

After—or along with—the computer-piloted craft will come still another specie of RPV. Only, the "R" will stand for "Robot." This robot at the throttle and stick will have a computer which will remember all the details of all the instructions of all the missions its plane must perform, and which will be programmed to execute these details in accordance with the combat situations which it sees before it. It will see those situations via its senses, which, through combinations of optics, radar and infrared technologies, may indeed make it a more accurate and quicker-reacting observer than man. It will have arms and hands, legs and feet, to manipulate the controls. It will be able to climb into, and out of, its plane. Possessed of microminiaturized vitals, it will be small enough to ride midget machines. No one will ever have to ask: "How the hell did all you robots get into that little airplane?"

While the RPVs of successive generations may wind up costing as much as the world, the relatively low prices of developing and producing their "now" generation promised the Pentagon near-future relief from the rapine costs of their piloted cousins. And this, more than their military potential, was the reason they had finally captured and were holding the attention of the crash-helmet set in the Pentagon. Not only would their production costs be much lower; they obviously would be less expensive, too, of maintenance and storage. As Colonel Kenney put it: "What RPVs offer, under a tightening budget, is the 'surge' capability. You can turn them out at a steady pace, and if war comes, you have them sitting in sheds, ready to surge. You can get this surge capability for minimum annual investments."

In 1974, Secretary McLucas combined a trip to Wright Patterson with a labor-of-love speechmaking appearance in nearby Dayton, Ohio. He addressed a new organization of a new breed of enthusiasts called the National Association for Remotely Piloted Vehicles. This was their first symposium, titled, "RPVs in the 1980s," and McLucas, appropriately, was their first keynote speaker. After thanking the conventioneers for their moral and political support, and assuring them that RPVs finally were for real in the Air Force, McLucas turned candid about where the leverage lay in promoting the future large-scale production of the unmanned planes. "By far the most important reason why we in the military are interested in the RPVs," he said, "is to achieve a significant cost advantage over comparable manned aircraft systems. Here lies the key to greatly expanded use of RPVs. We must exploit the cost advantage."

The timing could not have been better. The climate was perfect for such exploitation. For as 1974 drew to a close, the wildly inflated Defense Department budget had become an instrument of self-infliction, and the military's high-priced manned aircraft and other weapons had become wolves at its own doorstep.

12

The
Rope Merchants

It is an unfortunate fact that we can secure peace only by
preparing for war.
— John F. Kennedy

It is sometime in the early 1980s. The President sits tensely
at his command console in the underground Situation Room
at Fort Richie, Md. The Soviet Union, in a 48-hour blitz-
krieg attack, has seized West Berlin. One thousand Allied
soldiers have been killed. Now, the Kremlin has turned the
wounded and POWs over to West Germany—and notified
the United States that as far as it is concerned, the episode
is closed. The President demands that the Soviets withdraw.
The Kremlin refuses. The President is determined to im-
press on the Russian leaders that he means business—that
they are risking nuclear war. He orders up a television picture of a hydroelectric plant in a remote Russian region.
Satisfied that a mini-nuke blast there will cause minimal
civilian casualties, he sends out the signal to launch a single
ICBM. Then, on a TV screen in front of him, he watches as
the hydroelectric plant is destroyed.
— "Visions of the Next War," *Newsweek*, April
22, 1974.

Toward the end of 1974 I set out to write an article on how
the nation's runaway inflation was ravaging the B-1 bomber

program and threatening to abort it even before the first test plane took to the air. The article was shaping up even more dramatically than I had imagined. In 1970, when the Air Force awarded the B-1 development contract to Rockwell International, the cost of building 244 B-1s well ahead into the 1980s had been estimated at $11.5 billion. Now, it stood at $18.6 billion. This meant that the average cost of each projected plane had climbed to the astronomical proportion of more than $75 million. As I patrolled the Pentagon in pursuit of the story, Lady Luck flopped into my lap. In the course of our conversation on the plight of the B-1, a high-level official drew a piece of paper from his desk, handed it to me, and said: "Right here is one of the most important stories you'll ever write out of this building. It could be the beginning of the end. It makes me think of Lenin's old saying, something like, 'When the capitalist countries hang themselves, we will sell them the rope.' "

Were the Russians about to drop the bomb? No, but maybe they would never need to. On the piece of paper which the defense official slipped me were lists of numbers. They represented the rates of inflation rampant which the Defense Department Comptroller had circulated to the military services, for the services to employ as guidelines in preparing their weapons procurement and research and development budgets for fiscal year 1976. The numbers told a story that was staggering and ominous. When their import had sunk in, I suggested to the man who had given them to me that my magazine should headline the story: "Here Come the Rope Merchants." My article, which appeared in the "Washington Outlook" column of *Business Week*, went as follows:

> The defense budget that will be sent to Congress next January will top $100-billion and then some. The main reason for the huge increase over this year's appropriation: For the first time, the Pentagon intends to budget realistically for inflation and let the costs fall where they may. Inflation was seriously underestimated in this year's budget. Planners at the Pentagon and at the Office of Management and Budget factored only a 3.5 percent estimate into the costs of major programs. But the actual rate has ballooned to 11 percent for procurement and 8.2 percent for research and development, testing and evaluation projects. It has robbed the current

budget of $6 billion in buying power. Congress has cut $5 billion more. Defense Secretary James R. Schlesinger doesn't intend to get trapped the same way again next year. The fiscal 1976 budget is being calculated on the assumption of eye-popping inflation rates for the next few years.

The story went on to spell out those numbers, year by year. They showed that inflation, now eroding the whole United States economy, was expected to escalate the costs of weapons in the next five years, through 1980, by at least half again as much as the overwhelming levels to which they had already soared. My story noted that the Pentagon would reveal these costs in presenting Congress, for the first time ever, with a five-year projection of the defense budget. The story ended: "But the enormous cost increases that inflation already has brought about will surface much earlier. In about two weeks, the Pentagon will report to Congress on how prices of major weapons have ballooned so far this year."

Indeed the Pentagon did. The report was a shocker. It showed that rip-roaring inflation had driven up the costs of forty-two major weapons programs, in only three months, by $16 billion—to $143.6 billion. So it finally had arrived. The crisis that the Pentagon had been warning about for several years, and could no longer fend off. The price of national security finally had gone up to a level that might be too high to pay. If unchecked, the escalated defense costs would blow the super-heated national economy apart, and already threatened to do so. It was painfully obvious that no longer could the defense budget accommodate the costs of all the people and weapons which the services had insisted all along they must have to keep the United States secure. Unless the Pentagon cut deeply into its costliest weapons systems—on its own or on orders from new President Gerald R. Ford—its next budget would stand at about $104 billion, an increase of $15 billion over the amount that Congress had just finished appropriating. Something had to give, and the choices would be all bad in the E Ring.

Within days after the story broke and swept through the media, Schlesinger held his first press conference in three months. "We are very concerned about the impact of inflation," he said in classic understatement. What worried the Defense Secretary and all his subordinates was that the Soviets

would gain a big and possibly insurmountable edge in weaponry as the United States scaled back or killed the production
and development of the big guns of its present and future
arsenal. In private, Pentagon officials for the first time seemed
wasted of will. Dispensing with the customary caveat that fate
somehow would stand on the side of the Western World, they
gloomily discussed the likelihood that the Soviets needed only
to wait a short time longer until the United States and its
equally beleaguered European allies priced themselves out of an
adequate defense. They noted, moreover, that unbridled inflation, stimulated by oil prices, could cause a depression in Western Europe and lead to the overthrow of governments friendly
to the United States. At his press conference, Schlesinger emphasized that the Soviets, who he wryly noted "do not need a
national consensus" in allocating funds for national security,
were beefing up their military budgets at "a rate of increase of
3 percent a year in constant rubles, well beyond their own pace
of inflation." Defense correspondent Cecil Brownlow's story
on the situation—typical of most—started out: "U.S. defense
posture will revert relatively quickly from 'second to none' to
'second to one' if the White House or Congress decrees that the
Defense Department must absorb spiraling inflation costs over
the next five years, according to top Pentagon officials." But
Schlesinger hung in there. "I don't think we will let it happen," he told the press.

The question was how possibly to avoid letting it happen.
Schlesinger decided right off that he would not order the services to rip any weapon system right out of their forthcoming
budgets. But he would buy time by ordering them to stretch
and juggle the development and production of some. Again the
question: Which ones? Slowing them down would only add to
their inflationary costs in future years and would risk rendering them technologically obsolete before they were ever deployed.

The next Pentagonian to hold a briefing on the inflation
invasion was General George S. Brown. It was his first press
conference in the three months since he had become chairman
of the Joint Chiefs of Staff. Brown acknowledged that he was
"not confident" that the military could maintain the stupen-
dous status quo of weapons systems. "I think you will find," he
said, "that there will be changes in the program that will be

rather significant." He said these were being worked out among the Joint Chiefs, Schlesinger and other top civilians in procurement and research and development, and would surface in early 1975. The budgetary buzz saw had caught the entire Tank in a position of relative unpreparedness. Brown had had more than a year's experience, as Air Force Chief of Staff, in this strategic sanctum of the Joint Chiefs. But Admiral James L. Holloway, 3rd, had been Chief of Naval Operations for less than six months; General David C. Jones, Air Force Chief of Staff for only four months, and General Fred C. Weyand, Army Chief of Staff for only two weeks, following the death of General Creighton Abrams. The Pentagon had just announced, in fact, that the new Main Battle Tank being developed by the Army would be named the "Abrams" in honor of this widely respected general who had served as Patton's lead-tank commander in the war for Europe, as commander-in-chief in Vietnam, and as Army Chief of Staff. The attachment of his name immediately personalized and should have popularized the new tank that was in the works. And yet the tank program stood out as a prime example of the inflationary bind that the Pentagon now was suffering: its costs had soared from an estimated $2.3 billion in 1970 to $4.3 billion by the end of 1974. Shortages of steel and of the huge castings for hulls and turrets also had slowed production, and increased costs, of the M-60 "Patton" tank which would remain the Main Battle Tank of the Army and Marines until the "Abrams" came along, and which had been ferried to the Middle East by the several hundreds during and after the Yom Kippur war. So prices, shortages and the shipments to Israel had left the Army sadly in arrears on "Pattons," and sorely in jeopardy on "Abrams." It would be left mainly to General Weyand, an infantryman rather than a tanker, and the first non-West Pointer (University of California) ever to become Army Chief of Staff, to find a way out of the entanglement of tanks.

During those days of depression both fiscal and psychological at the Pentagon, Leonard Sullivan, Jr., assistant secretary of defense for program analysis and evaluation, put it on the line at a symposium of the National Security Industrial Association in Washington. Britain, he said, "must either remove forces from NATO or give up protection of its sea lanes" in order to offset the savagery of its own inflation. Japan, France,

Italy and even West Germany were hurting too. "The whole free world," Sullivan asserted, "is in a slow process of unilateral disarmament in proportion to inflation." In the United States, the tiger appeared about ready, finally, to catch its own tail, and chew itself to death.

The inflation that beset the nation and its military establishment in 1974 and 1975 was the direct result of the Johnson administration's failure to raise taxes early enough to help pay for the Vietnam War. Johnson wanted the war and the Great Society at the price of one. Finally he proposed an income surtax. But Congress delayed in enacting the surtax, and it stayed on the books only long enough to show how far short it fell of fighting off the inflation which had long since begun. The cost of weapons began going up, up, up. The defense business community, by and large, tolerated the war which was reaping it record profits. Then the Nixon administration took over. Up still more went the weapons costs—the costs of fighting the war and of preparing for future wars, of arming to disarm. No new taxes. On April 30, 1973, *Time* magazine declared: "A long string of danger signals began to blink more insistently last week. The message: Like a runaway freight train, the economy is hurtling forward at an inflationary speed that could send it off the rails into a recession next year." Twelve days later, *Business Week* weighed in with an editorial, and took out a full page ad in the *New York Times* to spread its word more widely. Headlined, "An Urgent Plea for New Economic Policy. Now!" the editorial called for an emergency surtax, and charged: "The Nixon administration has lost its grip on the economy. It is driving the U.S. into a superheated boom that inevitably will end with a paralyzing recession."

Then came the Soviet wheat deal, high food prices, the Yom Kippur war, high oil prices, energy shortages—and the full-blown inflation which had been sown in the failure of two administrations to face the fact, among others, that weapons do not come cheap and do not accept credit cards. And now, that same inflation finally had become a threat to the weapons which had fathered and fed it through most of the previous decade.

One autumn afternoon at the Pentagon, just as the story of breakneck inflation was breaking in the press, Dr. Malcolm R.

Currie, director of defense research and engineering, took sick. In view of the events, well he might have; for it was in his bailiwick, again, that the tough choices would have to be made in culling weapons and weapons-to-be. Currie's illness, however, was plain, old appendicitis. He was taken to Andrews Air Force Base Hospital for surgery. Unaware of this, I checked into his office to ask him for comment on the inflation story. His secretary and his top aides said that he felt so deeply on the subject that he might be willing to discuss it from his hospital bed. And he did.

"We have a hard-guts sense of concern—a long-term, crushing, brutal problem," he said. "I am deeply concerned about the contrasting long-term trends in U.S. and Soviet R&D efforts. We know the Soviet R&D effort is increasingly effective. They are fielding some excellent, high-technology weapons systems, in large numbers. We saw them used against our weapons in the Middle East, and when they were used well by the Arab side they were very effective. The Soviet R&D effort is massive any way you measure it, and growing. Our defense R&D effort is shrinking in the squeeze of national priorities and inflation. There is no way that the United States can retain its vital advantage in quality over Soviet weapons in the long run if this trend continues. And we live in an era when it has been amply demonstrated that one, key new weapon can be decisive."

That same week, a Gallup poll showed that 44 percent of the American people believed the United States was spending too much money for military purposes. As for the remainder, only 12 percent felt the spending was too low, 32 percent said it was "about right," and 12 percent had no opinion.

"It really comes right down," said Sullivan, "to this: Is inflation getting serious enough so that we have to reconsider our whole defense policy? We're verging on it. Even if the rate of inflation starts to drop, the prices will stay high. So inflation may come down, but prices won't."

It would be up to Currie and Sullivan, mainly, to confront the cutting edge of the problem. It was an old problem, and it had been talked about for years and years. But now it demanded action. Which weapons do you choose? Do you push ahead full speed with all those weapons systems already in production? With those, such as the B-1 and Trident, well advanced in development and about ready for production? If you do this, do you sacrifice spending on the technology base which will provide the weapons of the future? Do you draw in your research and spend your money on improving the weapons you already know about? Do you prepare to fight the next war the same way you had been preparing to fight it since the last one? What kind of war will it be? Nuclear and global? Conventional and limited? Both? Currie knew full well that there was no margin for sacrifice in the funding of the technology base. In 1974, inflation, all by itself, had eaten away every penny—and more—of the increased funding which he had budgeted to beef up that base. In consequence, basic research and exploratory development of new weapons was not only stagnating but shriveling.

There were plus sides to all this. In the past, by fudging the impact of inflation in its budgets, the Pentagon had put itself and its contractors into the bind of being criticized for cost overruns which had been induced by the inflation which the Pentagon had tried to ignore, and for which it had not budgeted. Now, Congress would get, perhaps for the very first time, an honest Pentagon budget, showing the costs as they really were expected to be. Even more important, the inflation crunch might finally force the Department of Defense to crack down on the services, to winnow their "wish lists" of weapons because they no longer had any other option. For the sake of sparing the technology base, maybe an Air Force or a Navy fighter plane could be shelved; the Air Force A-10 close-support plane or the Army attack helicopter could be grounded; a choice could be made, at least for the time being, between Air Force development of the new airborne ICBM, which was test-launched from a C-5 in October 1974, or that of the B-1; between bringing on the Trident submarine or backfitting the new, longer-range Trident missile into the Polaris-Poseidon boats, where the missiles would nestle quite nicely; between a new tank or a modernization of the current tank. The glut of weapons had been the direct result of the unchecked gluttony of the services, and maybe now, given the grimness of the times, the services would have to become leaner, harder, firmer, emphasizing teamwork rather than tautology of weapons and missions. But think how this would affect the defense industry, where marginal companies always seem to be saved by a new Air Force, Navy or Army mission concept which affords them contracts on major weapons which expand, but do little to elevate, the arsenal. And then think again. These contracts mean big money and lots of jobs. Congress cries about them but can't do without them. The technology base is a poor relation. Whose Congressional district cares about, or knows about, the technology base? How many generals and admirals give a damn about it, either, down deep?

Much was made at the Pentagon in 1974 about the whack that Congress had taken at the defense budget for fiscal 1975—the budget which had been prepared prior to the onset of the inflation invasion. Congress appropriated nearly $83 billion for the Pentagon to spend, and gave the Pentagon authority to contract for an additional $6 billion. The cut from the funding which the Pentagon had requested came out to about $5 billion. But the other side of the coin was that this was the biggest appropriations bill ever passed by Congress; it nearly matched the combined total of $85 billion in ten other appropriations bills which Congress, up to that point in 1974, had passed for the nondefense sectors of the government, including space. No major weapons were eliminated or even gouged. The bill exceeded the defense appropriation of the previous year by $3.6 billion. It included $205.5 million for twelve F-111 and $100 million for twenty-four A-7D aircraft which the Air Force had not requested and did not want. It contained $3 million for continued research on binary nerve-gas weapons which the House, at one point, had threatened to outlaw. It funded Schlesinger's "Counterforce" nuclear-missile development to the hilt. It provided $45 million for the Safeguard antiballistic missile and $118 million for development of the "Site Defense of Minuteman" ABM coming along as Safeguard's successor. It appropriated $3 billion for Navy shipbuilding, including $1.7 billion for Trident; $445 million for B-1 development—and $138 million for twenty-five A-10 close-support Air Force planes and $18.5 million for close-support Army helicopters. The bill had a lot or a little something for every defense contractor you could name or find.

As 1974 drew to a close, it became obvious that if any major surgery were to be performed in the forthcoming $100 billion-plus, inflation-ridden Pentagon budget, Schlesinger was awaiting orders from the White House to force him to perform it.

He had no intention of cutting that budget much on his own, and it was the President, not the Secretary of Defense, who had what Sullivan called "the excruciating problem."

Schlesinger was counting on Ford not forcing a deep defense budget cut. He had good reason to believe that Ford was not disposed to do so. The new President had served many years as a staunch pro-Pentagon member of the House Defense Appropriations Subcommittee. In his very first address to his old cohorts on Capitol Hill, Ford had served notice that while the national belt needed to be tightened, it had no notches to spare around national security. Schlesinger, whose relations with Ford were far from comradely, felt the point needed emphasizing, however, and he chose Ford's anti-inflation "Economic Summit" meeting of early October 1974 to challenge Ford to follow through. "If we continue to reduce our military establishment," Schlesinger said, "let us do so consciously, accepting secondary status consciously, rather than through a continual erosion of the resources available to the department. The United States aspires to retain military power second to none, and we will not be able to do it on 4.5 or 5 percent of the Gross National Product. The defense share of the GNP has declined to about 5.6 percent in the current budget year. . . . Détente rests on a worldwide military equilibrium which is undergirded by the forces and the leadership of the United States. If the United States drops the torch, there is no one else to pick it up."

Schlesinger had come to believe that Oswald Spengler, author of the work *Decline of the West,* had been an optimist. The Defense Secretary's way of trying to redress what he perceived as evidence of that decline in his own domain was to become more militant on all fronts. In a speech before the National Security Industrial Association, Schlesinger told the contractors: "Ironically, some voices have been raised to suggest that technological advance be terminated. Indeed, I might sympathize with such suggestions, were Andrei Sakharov charged with the direction of military R&D in the Soviet Union. Unfortunately, as is only too obvious, he is not."

In that same speech, Schlesinger saved his choice sarcasm for Congress, which had cut to $700 million the $1.45 billion he had requested for military aid to South Vietnamese forces. "There remain among us," said Schlesinger, "those who, in Churchill's

words, are decided only to be undecided, resolved to be irreso-
lute, adamant for drift, solid for fluidity, all-powerful for impo-
tence. . . . The South Vietnamese have done the job. Our
assistance to Saigon has declined. Outside aid to Hanoi has
increased. A small state, beholden to us, still struggles to survive, but we have neither the temerity to sever its lifeline nor
the resolution to pay the relatively small be necessary price to
assure its continued existence. Rather, we have chosen to put
an ally on the military equivalent of starvation rations."

This was a touchy subject in more ways than one.

The first sign of rupture between Ford and Schlesinger had
appeared back when Ford was Vice-President. Then, Ford let
it be known that he thought Schlesinger had done a poor job
of selling Congress on the need of heftier aid to South Vietnam. Schlesinger did not reply directly. But nothing if not
contrary, he, in turn, let it be known that the preoccupation
of the Nixon White House with finding a way out of Watergate
—at a time that Ford still was vigorously defending Nixon—
wasn't much help to him on Capitol Hill. "If I were to say that
there was no effect from Watergate, I would lose my reputation
for candor," Schlesinger said. When Nixon's resignation appeared in the offing, insiders at the White House and the Pentagon were saying that Ford had come to believe that no
Secretary of Defense could have salvaged all the aid to Vietnam, and that Schlesinger was a sure thing to stay on under
Ford. But something else had happened to make everyone
wonder once again. As *Washingtonian* magazine reported:

> On the morning of Friday, August 9, Secretary of Defense
> James Rodney Schlesinger flashed a message to all American
> military commanders around the world notifying them that
> Gerald R. Ford was the new Commander-in-Chief of the
> United States and that "he will have the fullest support,
> dedication and loyalty of all members of the Department of
> Defense." His message to military commanders was in a
> sense routine, as was the simultaneous Pentagon announce-
> ment that U.S. forces remained on a "normal alert status"
> during the transfer of power from Richard M. Nixon to
> President Ford. This was the kind of public action Dr.
> Schlesinger, a meticulous man, would be expected to take at
> the peak of the Presidential crisis. What was not publicly

known was that between Wednesday and Friday of the critical week, Schlesinger, a man who doesn't believe in taking
even the most minimal risks, had set in motion a series of
secret precautions against the danger that Nixon, in an act
of desperation, might order an irrational move by U.S.
forces somewhere in the world so that a sudden emergency
would defuse the growing pressures of his resignation.

As the *Washingtonian* writer Ted Szulc pointed out, there
was nothing to suggest that Nixon had anything of the sort in
mind. But Schlesinger was taking no chances. A few days
following the event, he held a "backgrounder" with reporters
who regularly cover the Pentagon, and told them what he had
done. The story broke. It smacked of *Seven Days in May*. Immediately, as the *Baltimore Sun* reported it: "Several high-ranking officers said privately they were insulted and shocked by
the inference that elements of the military might be responsive
to unauthorized or illegal orders reaching them through some
circumvention of the chain of command." Still, there were
reports that some elements of the Air Force, in particular, so
deeply resented the forced resignation of the President who
had bombed Hanoi, who had managed the release of American
prisoners of war (nearly all flyers), that they might have done
something extraordinary to show their allegiance to that President in his hour of humiliation. While there may have been no
connection, General David Jones of the Air Force was the only
member of the Joint Chiefs of Staff to make a speech, during
those dire days, reminding the military that its duties must
stand apart from politics. The fascinating thing to Schlesinger-
watchers, however, was that his action had put him in an
awkward position—not that he cared—and that Ford moved
fast in the aftermath.

The President called a Cabinet meeting on Monday, August
27, following the weekend of the stories about Schlesinger's
alert. After the meeting, Ford detained Schlesinger for a face-
to-face talk, and then snappily issued this statement: "I had a
meeting today with the Secretary of Defense. We discussed the
matter. And I have been assured that no measures of this nature were actually undertaken." There was no elaboration on
what Ford meant by "measures" or by his saying that they
were not "actually undertaken." There the matter rested. Un-

easily. Talk of a putsch or a coup receded from the Washington consciousness even faster than Nixon himself. A new Commander-in-Chief was in charge. The services would stand by him. And he, it was obvious, would stand by them. In this, Ford and Schlesinger—the one cozying up to Congress, the other not caring a fig what Congress thought; the one hopeful of conquering inflation and restoring national confidence, the other cynical and combative about it—were bound in an alliance of purpose, if not of palship. They would share the pastorate of the Pentagon, at least through the period when Ford would need all the stability he could summon in a Cabinet and a government already too long in the turmoil of turnover. General Alexander Haig, former Army Vice-Chief of Staff and Nixon's White House chief of staff, was on his way to Europe to command U.S. forces there. NATO Ambassador Donald Rumsfeld was on his way back to take Haig's job. Columnist Jack Anderson reported that Rumsfeld, a former colleague of Ford's in the Republican ranks of the House, really was destined, sooner or later, to supplant Schlesinger at the Pentagon. Nixon had been preoccupied with foreign affairs and with Watergate, diffident about economics and—toward the end—about defense. Ford would be just the opposite, leaving foreign affairs to Kissinger and concentrating on economics and defense; especially, as the months rolled by, on defense. Military columnist R.D. Heinl provided the background and the clue. He wrote:

When the great Pacific typhoon of Dec. 18, 1944, rolled the U.S.S. *Monterey* 30 degrees on her beam-ends, it came within a flicker of taking Lt. Gerald R. Ford, USNR, down to Davey Jones' locker and preventing the United States from having a President who knows national defense from the keel up. Lt. Ford, scrambling topside to his battle station at the height of the gale, lost footing on the rain-drenched, wind-lashed flight deck of the light aircraft carrier, slid like a toboggan toward the raging sea, and was only halted at the deck's edge by a strip of coaming that prevented his joining five men lost from the *Monterey* and more than 800 in the Third Fleet. After that, with 10 battle stars on his Asiatic-Pacific campaign ribbon, the rest of the war was an anticlimax for the man destined to become 38th President of the

United States and the fourth consecutive World War II naval officer to occupy the White House. The practical grounding in war, followed by more than two decades as one of the hardest-working members of the House Defense Appropriations Subcommittee, results in a new President whose knowledge of the intricacies and complexities of the common defense is probably not surpassed by any predecessor in this century, save Dwight D. Eisenhower.

Ford's first speech was full of familiar rhetoric: "A strong defense is the surest way to peace. Weakness invites war, as my generation knows from bitter experience." It also contained the familiar overture to the Soviets, pledging strong U.S. support of the SALT talks and of détente. It was a honeymoon speech, and then Ford precipitously pardoned Nixon and the honeymoon was over. Then the President and Kissinger, in one-two time, made speeches which carried the hint of a threat to the Arabs that the United States would not stand indefinitely for their oil-price blackmail. Some of the edge was taken off those speeches by Schlesinger, who, at a press conference, emphasized that the United States had no intention of sending troops to confiscate any oil fields in the Middle East, and that, furthermore, he was not even aware of any military contingency plans—if indeed there were any—to do any such thing.

It later developed that Ford had instructed Schlesinger to play cool counterpoint to the President's hot-sounding theme. At the White House, Ford was overheard telling Schlesinger: "It was a pretty harsh speech, but it had to be given." So the President and his Secretary of Defense were using the old tactic of planting a seed and then covering it. That seed would take nourishment from the spreading notion that the final solution—if oil countries remained recalcitrant—would be to go in and get the oil.

At his press conference, Schlesinger also contradicted other top people in the Pentagon who were saying in private that the United States might raise the price of its weapons to the oil-producing nations in retaliation against their economic blackmail. "It would be inappropriate," Schlesinger said, "to use military sales as leverage in those [oil-price] discussions." In this lay heavy irony. For if the United States ever would have to fight in the Middle East, it would be confronted by a vast and growing arsenal of its own weapons, some of them the newest and best of its own technology. At the turn of 1975, Kissinger clinched for an armed-camp world the notion that Middle East intervention by the United States was a live possibility. It would happen, Kissinger told *Business Week,* only if the oil-price policies of Iran and the Arab oil-exporting countries threatened the U.S. economy with "strangulation." The feeling grew in Washington, however, and was strengthened by an American Enterprise Institute report on "Arms in the Persian Gulf," that the oil nations might be jacking up their prices in order to get the billions they needed, not to nourish their people but to fatten their military arsenals—with the most modern and the costliest U.S. weapons that their money could buy.

In 1973 and 1974, Shah Mohammed Reza Pahlevi of Iran ordered from the United States a gigantic array of ground and air weapons valued at $3.5 billion. As we have noted in a previous chapter, these included eighty F-14 fighter planes, which Iranian pilots would learn how to fly and fight with, courtesy of the U.S. Navy. As we also have noted, an Iranian bank was among those which lent Grumman Corp. $200 million to keep Grumman's production of Navy and Iranian F-14s from dying for lack of dollars. Iran also had bought F-4 fighters, C-139 transports, TOW antitank missiles and Bell attack helicopters which the U.S. Army had deemed too expensive, and which were superior to any attack helicopter in the U.S. inventory. Now, the Shah was eyeing the new lightweight fighters and the Airborne Warning and Control System (AWACS) aircraft being developed for the U.S. Air Force; the DD963 destroyer just going into production for the U.S. Navy. Why not? Iran, the Pentagon had maintained, is our friend, our ally, our proxy protector of the Persian Gulf. Under a 1959 agreement, the United States is committed, in fact, to "take such appropriate action, including the use of armed forces, as may be mutually agreed upon," to help defend Iran. It makes sense then, said the Pentagon, for the United States to arm Iran so that the U.S. would not be forced into involvement in Iranian wars. Now, however, in the oil crisis, the "ally and friend" theory was beginning to look shaky. No sooner had Ford spoken of possible retaliation against the oil-producing nations than the Shah, in Australia, expressed his strong resentment of Ford's veiled threat and reminded Ford that he, in this particular squabble, stood firmly on the other side.

Not only Iran. Saudi Arabia had ordered $582 million worth of U.S. weapons and training aids in the previous year. Among them were F-5E fighter planes—short-range but highly maneuverable; great dogfighters—and Navy patrol boats. The Pentagon was devising for the Saudis a naval modernization and base-building program, plus a plan to streamline the Saudi national guard. Who protects the oil fields in Saudi Arabia? The Saudi national guard. Then there was Kuwait, which already had bought about $19 million worth of U.S. arms, including F-8 fighters which had performed so unexpectedly well in Vietnam. Kuwait was considering another order of about $400 million for a wide range of weapons featuring ground-to-air Hawk missiles.

It was a hot and bubbly mixture out there around the Persian Gulf. Iran stood in league with the Arab nations on the matter of oil prices to the United States. But Iran and Iraq were at each others' throats, too. All the Arab nations, most notably Kuwait, were leery of the Shah's large fleet of air-cushion ships which could whisk to the other—Arab—side of the Gulf. What it came down to was that the Imperial Iranian Armed Forces were strong enough to take on just about anybody, and maybe, someday, they would. The sales of U.S. arms to Iran meant much more than big income for U.S. defense contractors or a boost to the U.S. balance of payments; they meant the deep involvement of U.S. policy in the military future of Iran, whatever that may turn out to be. There were so many purposes in the Middle East that it was hard to trace their crossings. And so, in a seller's market, the United States simply went ahead and sold. The Pentagon and State Department had estimated that foreign cash sales of arms in the year from July 1973 to July 1974 would amount to $4.6 billion. They turned out to be $6.6 billion. Figuring in credit sales and guarantees of future sales as well, the total climbed to $8.3 billion. This was double the amount of the previous year. In less than four years, the dollars coming back to the United States from weapons sold abroad had magnified sixfold. The Middle East, including Israel, accounted for a lot of this; Europe, too, of course. But the United States had found new customers south of the border as well.

Since the 1960s, it had been the policy of the United States that arms should not be sold to nations which, in Washington's wisdom, might better spend the money to uplift their citizens; which did not need the weapons; which would only use them to make more trouble in a world already overarmed. This policy applied to the Middle East to some extent, but had been pegged mostly to Latin America. There, the nations were armed mostly with American equipment bought cheap after World War II. At the turn of the 1970s, however, Northrop Corporation had developed the F-5E Freedom Fighter (later to be designated, more discreetly, the International Fighter) tailored specifically for the foreign market, most especially the not-so-affluent nations. Because of U.S. policy, Northrop was blocked from selling these planes to Latin America, where a number of countries, including Peru, had expressed interest in buying them. The French were active in the Latin American market, as were the Russians. Finally, in 1972, Peru ordered a batch of French Mirage fighters, thus foreclosing, possibly forever, any order from Northrop.

In June 1973, President Nixon, whose campaign of the year before had been boosted by extra-generous donations from Northrop executives, exercised the pragmatic approach which characterized his foreign policy. He lifted the ban on sales of U.S. weapons to Latin America, specifically authorizing the sale of Northrop F-5E fighters to Argentina, Brazil, Chile, Colombia and Venezuela. At the time, Chile was under the Marxist government of Salvador Allende, whose election the CIA had tried to undermine and whose overthrow the CIA was even then trying to mastermind—all with the knowledge and backing of Henry Kissinger, then Nixon's national security advisor, and of Nixon himself. Why would the United States want to sell modern fighter planes to an unfriendly government which had maltreated U.S. corporations on its soil? Because the sale might somehow provide the United States with diplomatic leverage. Moreover, the Soviets had offered Allende MiG-21s, and the presence of Russian fighters certainly would have spread the Russian influence in Latin America. Finally, Allende, as the United States had good reason to believe, would not be around forever, and the salesman who waits is lost.

Three months later, the Allende government fell to a military coup, and Allende, by official accounts, shot himself dead.

The new Chilean dictatorship faced threats from two quarters: one, the legions of Allende supporters, whom it repressed; the other, neighboring, socialistic Peru, which now had the Mirage fighter and fighter-bomber, plus the British Canberra jet bomber, and which had ordered Soviet tanks to boot.

On October 6, 1974, the State Department of President Gerald R. Ford announced that Chile had ordered eighteen F-5E fighters at $60 million and thirty-six A-37B close-support attack jets—built by Cessna and used in Vietnam—at $10.8 million. The Chileans also were in the market for modern M-60 tanks to countervail the Russian armor in the Peruvian forces. All the Chileans had, at the moment, were venerable U.S. M-41 and M-48 tanks, and old British Hawker-Hunter fighters. Peru said it had no intention of attacking the Chileans, in any case. But if it had, the time obviously was now, not later.

In Washington, it did not matter that Nixon had gone. Realpolitik still reigned.

It was a seething, sanguinary world that Ford faced. The Turkish-Greek war over Cyprus cost the life of U.S. Ambassador Rodger P. Davies only a month before the State Department's announcement that modern U.S. weapons now had made their wedge in Latin America. Aside from its divisive impact on NATO and the bitterness which it left the Greeks in their assessment that Ford had tilted toward Turkey, the savagery on Cyprus had pointed up the problem of U.S. nuclear weapons abroad. More than seven thousand of these weapons had been stockpiled in more than one hundred special ammunition sites in Europe, including Greece and Turkey. The Pentagon said they were fail-safe, but the feeling persisted that terrorists, or governments, somehow could manage to field them. Just having these weapons in hostile hands would be enough of a horror. The United States also was developing miniature nuclear warheads to replace the large, "dirty" warheads now spread across Europe. Called "tactical" or "battlefield support" nuclear weapons, those now in place are much more powerful than the 20-kiloton atomic bomb which blew up and burned Hiroshima. The new ones would sacrifice nothing in power at the end of their long-range rides aboard Lance or Pershing artillery missiles. Sounding a familiar theme, General Andrew J. Goodpaster, who later was replaced by Haig as Supreme Allied Commander in Europe, contended that the smaller warheads coming along could be used to attack a greater variety of military targets with less threat to civilian populations. But the warheads would be coming from both sides, now. When the United States introduced tactical nuclear weapons to Europe during the Eisenhower administration, the Russians did not have any. Now they do. By the thousands. Let Schlesinger take it from there:

> In NATO's early days, the United States enjoyed a clear superiority in nuclear forces. This allowed early NATO strategy to be based on the "tripwire" concept, by which conventional ground forces in Europe were designed to serve primarily to trigger nuclear retaliation by the United States against a Warsaw Pact attack. Now, as the Soviet Union reaches nuclear parity with the United States, deterrence will be strongly reinforced if we maintain a balance of conventional as well as of nuclear forces. This clearly does not mean that we no longer require a nuclear deterrent. Nor does it mean that the American nuclear commitment to the security of the Alliance has been outdated. The commitment is firm. But it does mean that our nuclear forces may no longer carry the same dominant weight in the balance of deterrence that they did in an earlier period, and this places a higher value on NATO's conventional military capabilities. Thus, maintenance of a strong conventional capability is more than ever necessary—not because we wish to wage conventional war but because we do not wish to wage any war.

Schlesinger, the hortatory logician, definitely did not sound like a man who saw a way to cut the defense budget. A buildup of nuclear weapons only meant the need of a buildup of conventional weapons too. And in the $104.7 billion defense budget which Schlesinger slammed into Capitol Hill in February 1975, this is exactly what he proposed doing through 1976 and beyond. Ford was with him—all the way.

Ford and Schlesinger now were counting on the sag in the U.S. economy as a big help in pushing their massive defense budget through Congress. Inflation, which always militates against additional government spending, seemed to be slowing somewhat. The recession, however, was deepening. Unemployment was high. Thus the administration and Congress, in a quick switch, were putting the accent on stimulating the economy rather than on restraining it. They differed drastically on how to provide the stimulus, however. Ford's way was through a big shot of defense spending. But Congress, heavily Democratic and the most outspokenly anti-Pentagon of modern times, favored spending more generously, instead, on public works and income maintenance programs, where Ford wanted to hold the line. This battle, with the defense budget the main battleground, would be waged through most of 1975, culminating in final voting on defense appropriations bills around October or November. In the late winter and spring months of 1975, Schlesinger defended his budget time and again —always, as usual, with "no apologies" for its size—before congressional committees. He did not commit himself full-time to this effort, however important it was. There was much other business for him to tend, including the nation's forces of nuclear missiles.

Any notion that the Ford administration might ease up in testing strategic weapons while negotiating with the Soviets was dispelled by the thunder of an intercontinental rocket motor over Vandenberg Air Force Base, California, on October 25, 1974. That day, Secretary of State Kissinger arrived in Moscow to lay the groundwork for Ford's arms-limitation talks with Brezhnev in Vladivostok the following month. Détente, lately derailed, seemed to be coming back on track. But on that same day, the U.S. Air Force conducted its first test of an air-launched intercontinental missile. At 20,000 feet, a 43 ton Minuteman I missile was pulled free of the rear cargo door of a C-5 transport by parachutes puffy enough to fill the sky. As the missile fell, the parachutes pulled its nose cone into the upright position, and its motor ignited. By the time it had descended to 8,000 feet, the missile's motor had built up enough power to thrust it spaceward. It reached 20,000 feet, its motor died, and it arced into the ocean off California. The test proved nothing from the standpoint of progress on the big R&D problem: how to guide an air-launched ICBM to its target. But in showing that a Minuteman could be fired from aloft, the test was more convincing than all of Schlesinger's speeches, Congressional testimony and press conferences of the preceding months about the intent of the Pentagon to provide the President with more "strategic options." The test showed that Schlesinger—and now Ford—meant it. The test was a sky-borne signal to Moscow that the Nixon administration's policy of peace through warheads was still being hotly pursued; that the United States would continue to test for war while it talked of peace (just as the Russians, simultaneously, were doing); that there would be nothing do-goodie about any détente; that the new wayfarer in the White House was at least as much a warrior as the one before him, who had been brought down not by war but by Watergate, not by combativeness but by corruption.

Departing Moscow, Kissinger flew to New Delhi, where he urged India, newly the possessor of nuclear weapons, to cooperate with the United States in trying to prevent their witless wildflowering throughout the world. Relations between New Delhi and Washington had been strained since 1971, when the United States supported Pakistan against India in a war which Pakistan lost, and which the citizens of Bangladesh, created in its aftermath, had paid for in famine and death. Kissinger's speech to the Indian Council of World Affairs was hailed as conciliatory. It seemed to enhance the prospects of an eventual meeting between Ford and Indian Prime Minister Indira Gandhi. But only days after Kissinger had departed New Delhi on another of his do-it-alone diplomatic dowsings for peace in the Middle East, the U.S. Seventh Fleet dispatched a carrier task force into the Indian Ocean to play Teddy Roosevelt's old game off India's shores. True, it was anybody's ocean to sail. But the Indians had expressed resentment of the U.S. ships showing the big stick in the past. So the timing of the task force followed the usual pattern of extending the hand and then clenching the fist, stroking the back and then chopping the neck. That same week, Senator Stuart K. Symington, second-ranking Democrat on the Senate Armed Services Committee, made a speech before the United Nations in his capacity as one of three members of Congress in the U.S. delegation to the UN General Assembly. He noted that the United States now had a nuclear weapons stockpile equivalent in firestorm power to 615,365 "Hiroshima-size" atomic bombs, and that both the United States and the Soviet Union were building up their nuclear arsenals "each day of the year." Said former Air Force Secretary Symington: "One miscalculation, one sudden terrorist activity, one paranoid leader, could set the spark to a world-wide nuclear holocaust. There are now six members of the nuclear club—six scorpions in the bottle instead of the original two—and as each month passes, it becomes more probable that soon there may well be twenty scorpions in the same bottle. At that point, what a few of those scorpions decide could make little difference."

With the Palestinians continuing to foment fear of another war in the Middle East, and shortly to receive a hearing before this same General Assembly, the worldwide proliferation of conventional weapons, courtesy of the United States, the USSR, and several other nations too, also had become a major cause of concern. On this subject, a Navy admiral decided to speak out.

Rear Admiral Julian Lake, a former fighter pilot who had commanded the very first operational F-4 squadron back in the 1960s, told me one day in late November 1974, that he was "concerned and frustrated," and had decided to "let it all hang out." By now, Lake was vice-commander of the Naval Electronic Systems Command. NAVELEX, as we noted in a previous chapter, has to fight hard inside the Navy for every cent it gets. Lake, particularly, was feeling the pinch. He was in charge of all Navy testing of electronic countermeasures against surface-to-air missiles of the sort which had devastated Israeli planes in the Yom Kippur war of 1973, and he was decidedly unhappy about the way things were going, about the money he had to work with. He charged his superiors in the Defense Department and in the Navy with "apathy and a reluctance to lay it on the line." He said they were moving too slowly to learn how to jam SAMs, and underfunding his testing program, at a time when the Pentagon was preoccupied with its money-gobbling strategic missiles, ships and submarines, and its bewildering assortment of aircraft. The very costly Air Force test shot of an airborne Minuteman had taken place the week before we talked.

On the record, and at some risk to his career, Lake declared: "There are too many, more pressing demands for dollars. Unfortunately, these demands are not being resisted. Electronic warfare, despite what you may have been told, is the first thing to get skimmed off when the money crunch comes around. Electronic countermeasures have a psychological disadvantage: they don't go 'bang.' They are hard to understand. As soon as the shooting stops, they become victimized in the budget. We would rather spend money to practice dropping bombs or shoot missiles. As a result, a lot of hard-learned lessons of the Yom Kippur war are being ignored. And when the shooting starts again, where will we be? We suddenly will need those ECMs."

Lake, however, did not confine his concern to Soviet SAMs. "We're mesmerized by the Russians, by responding to Russian missiles," he said, "but there are all kinds of missiles around. A lot of countries have our own Hawk missile now. We ought to be finding out how to fight against it. The Saudis have it. Iran has the latest version of it. The French Crotale missile is all around, too. We aren't facing up to the fact that we may have to fight against them. We don't really need a lot more R&D on our ECMs. We understand most of the things we have to deal with. We have many ECMs which do different jobs, but we need to make total systems out of them, package them, buy them, and test tactics with them. All it takes is a decision on top to spend the money. This is called 'leadership.' "

In the Defense Directorate of Research and Engineering, there was strong reaction to Lake's charge of neglect of electronic countermeasures. John M. ("Rusty") Porter, DDR&E's assistant director in charge of all "defense-suppression" R&D, including work on ECMs, had this to say:

"It's not a matter of apathy. It's a matter of not having enough money to go around. Every conversation in this building anymore gets down to money in a matter of minutes. We have the big, ongoing systems like the B-1 and Trident. We have inflation and overruns. We have more funding requirements for more money than we've got. The dollars are just not readily available for support items like ECMs. We're not ignoring the problem. We're struggling with it all the time." Porter also disagreed with Lake's argument that the Pentagon had been slow to develop and test ECMs against new enemy missiles like the Russian SA-6, which neither the United States nor Israel figured out how to jam during the Yom Kippur war, or like those newer models which might be encountered the next time. "There is nothing," Porter asserted, "that we have reasonable intelligence about that we can't jam or degrade—and that includes infrared as well as radar missiles." Porter agreed with Lake that ECMs could use more funding. But he pointed out that Pentagon spending on research and development of ECMs stood at $212 million in fiscal 1975, a jump of $79 million over the level of fiscal 1973 and of $56 million over that of fiscal 1974. "We would like to have about $256 million in fiscal 1976," he said, "but we'll be lucky to get it."

All this was enough to make you wonder. Was the United States in shape to drop a Minuteman missile within a hair of a Soviet silo, and yet in no shape to succeed in a limited war? For all its fancy R&D of the weapons of the future, were its fighting forces and weapons of the moment up to snuff? Except for those of mass destruction? Did Ford really have any options? Would the Pentagon become a poor farm?

And so it goes on. None of this is to suggest that the Soviets were being, or will be, more reasonable or tractable. In the course of writing and researching this book, I studied several of a series of books under the general heading, *Soviet Military Thought*, as translated into English. Among them were *The Offensive, The Basic Principles of Operational Art and Tactics*, and *The Problems of Contemporary War*. They caused me to quail, not because of their militancy, which at times made Schlesinger and the Joint Chiefs sound like pacifists in comparison, but because the writers, in their slavishness to all things Soviet, steeped their militancy in the familiar sanctimony of evangelists who would just as soon kill for their cause, and who have no doubt that it is their God-given right to do so. The tone of the Russian military writings reminded me of an incident on Capitol Hill in the early 1960s, during the heated early era of civil rights debates. The late Senator Olin Johnston of South Carolina took the floor to warn of the evils of racial integration. He was followed by his fellow South Carolinian, Strom Thurmond, whose speech far surpassed Johnston's in anti-integration intensity. Johnston listened for a few minutes, then headed for the cloakroom off the Senate floor. There, he told a group of reporters: "The difference between Strom and me is that ol' Strom really *believes* that crap." And so it is with the Soviets, in their post-Hungary and post-Czechoslovakia protestations that they prepare only for peace, and have no designs on anyone else.

So the buildup —Vladivostok notwithstanding—goes on. On both sides. But not far away is the day that the United

States and the Soviet Union may find, in their stalemate, that they have lost control of the situation. Besides them, China, Britain, France and India have nuclear weapons. China was expected to test-launch its first intercontinental missile in 1975. U.S. intelligence sources believe that ten other nations could develop atomic weapons, given their scientific resources. Among them is Iran. In fact, nearly any country which determines to become a nuclear power, at the expense of its commonweal, probably could do so. The prospect of this proliferation through the remainder of the twentieth century is what caused the editors of the *Bulletin of the Atomic Scientists* to move the minute hand of the "Doomsday Clock" on their cover three minutes closer to midnight in 1974. As Neville Shute set out the scenario two decades ago in his novel *On the Beach:*

> As tensions mount in Southern Europe, Albanian warplanes drop nuclear bombs on Naples. Tel Aviv is destroyed by a nuclear attack from an unidentified country. Egyptian atomic bombs devastate London and Washington. China, the Soviet Union, the U.S. and Britain are drawn into war. Soon mushroom clouds cover nearly the entire planet.

Other kinds of cloud forms may come first. Both superpowers continue to pursue the development and production of nerve gases that kill in a twinkling. And they are concentrating research on techniques for spreading clouds of liquid fuel over battlefields, exploding those clouds, and causing heavy blast damage to troops and equipment. The Soviet Institute of Chemical Physics in Moscow is the focus of the Russian research. American research is dispersed among all three services. Much of it is aimed at using fuel-air-explosives to detonate minefields on land and in the ocean. In 1973, General Brown, then Air Force Chief of Staff, mentioned explosive clouds of fuel among "significant changes in weapons systems" which the Air Force anticipated before the end of this decade.

In July 1954, the Air Force Space and Missile Systems Organization (SAMSO) turned twenty years old. SAMSO had come a long way since first it set up shop in an abandoned schoolhouse in Inglewood, California. Its sole mission back in 1954 was to come up with an intercontinental ballistic missile. Having achieved this and more, SAMSO now has reached much farther out. For space is where the Americans and the Russians have trained their sights. You will be able to perceive more about the pace of the superpowers toward peace—or war—by watching not what Ford and Brezhnev say, or what they sign, or how they treat their defense budgets in the aggregate, but how intensely their military establishments compete for the upper hand in the outer reaches. Unmanned satellites of both sides already account for all but a few of the more than 600 now in orbit. About 320 are American, 240 Russian, and the rest Australian, British, Canadian, French, German or Japanese. Some serve civilian communications and weather-watching purposes, but most have a military mission—communications, reconnaissance and surveillance, early warning of missile attacks and the like. During the Yom Kippur war, for example, Russia launched four military reconnaissance satellites and retrieved each quickly in order to process its film. U.S. weather satellites, using both visual and infrared sensors, gave the Air Force detailed, up-to-date information of conditions over North Vietnam, and permitted precise planning of air strikes. After the Mideast war of 1973, the Soviets began launching a series of military satellites programmed for intelligence-monitoring operations. Through the end of the year, their Plesetsk base had boomed into orbit 77 satellites with military missions, 9 more than it had in 1972. By mid-1974, the Soviets were compiling data every day from 72 tactical military communications satellites. And they apparently, by now, were putting primary emphasis on photo-reconnaissance spacecraft to monitor the comings and goings of the U.S. fleet and the activities at fleet shore stations.

"I want to emphasize," said Air Force Secretary John L. McLucas, "that the Department of Defense does not operate and experiment in space merely because space is there. Nor are we developing space systems to threaten the security of other nations. In fact, under the Space Treaty, the United States has agreed not to place weapons of mass destruction in outer space or in orbit around the earth. Rather, we are using the medium of space to increase our alertness to danger and to assist in maintaining an effective deterrent posture. Our space activities are the result of continuing reviews of our national defense needs and the medium where they can best be satisfied, be it land, sea, air or space. . . . A major use of the space medium is to provide us early warning of missile attack and detection of nuclear explosions which take place above the ground. In the case of early warning, we need to know where the missile attack originated, how many were involved, and what their trajectories and projected impact points are. Moreover, we would need this information under all weather conditions, on a global basis, and as rapidly as possible. For these reasons, we have several systems devoted to the early-warning mission, including different types of ground radars as well as space sensors. We have developed satellites which can detect and track intercontinental ballistic missiles and submarine-launched ballistic missiles almost from the moment they are fired. In addition, these warning satellites can detect nuclear explosions above the ground. Ultimately they will replace the current satellites which monitor the atmospheric nuclear test ban treaty."

Note carefully that the Space Treaty forbids, as McLucas said, only weapons of mass destruction in global orbit. Note also that the sharp line which the Eisenhower administration drew against military influence in the U.S. space program long since has been obliterated.

"This dichotomy," said *Aviation Week*, "didn't even last until the first successful U.S. satellite was launched by an Army-developed Jupiter intermediate-range ballistic missile booster." In an editorial calling for an end of "the official government hypocrisy about our nonmilitary space program," the magazine said in part:

The civilian space program operated by the National Aeronautics and Space Administration literally would never have gotten off the ground without the use of boosters developed for military IRBM and ICBM roles. Even today the bulk of all operational satellites, military and civilian, is launched by Thor, Atlas and Titan boosters developed by the Air Force. The NASA manned space flight program depended from the start on a strong military input both from the astronauts, who were all military-trained test pilots, and the program managers. When Apollo was in its post-fire crisis, NASA called on Gen. Sam Phillips and a contingent of more than 40 key military research and development officers to revitalize the program and successfully land men on the moon. . . ."

The pollen of all NASA programs is wafted across the Potomac to the Pentagon. The Air Force is "monitoring" NASA's space shuttle, which in 1974 was about halfway along its eight years of R&D, and will take an active part in the R&D—and the use of the shuttle—in the end. Another NASA program which has captured the fancy of the military is that of the half-ton robot, a mechanical man with arms and hands, laser-television vision, wheels and a computer brain. Someday it may roam on Mars, or anywhere on earth or in sky that men dare not go.

In 1964, Defense Secretary McNamara asked the Air Force to devise a way of arming satellites with nuclear weapons for their defense against Soviet satellites which might also be armed in kind. The Air Force plan, called Program 437, still sits on the shelf to which it was consigned by the subsequent treaty banning nuclear weapons in space. It sits there impatiently. In heavily censored testimony before the Senate Armed Services Committee in 1974, Air Force Secretary McLucas said: "We have come quite close, in many instances, to deciding to do it. But we have never actually decided to do it because it is quite expensive, and we just are not sure that it's necessary."

Is the Pentagon uncertain of the need for the antisatellite system because it does not consider the Soviets a menace in space? Or because, if it holds off awhile, the high-energy laser, which technically is not a weapon of mass destruction, will be available for intersatellite or satellite-missile warfare? Whatever, it now has become obvious that even the "cleanest" combat in space would threaten and probably destroy all life on planet Earth.

In September 1974, Dr. Fred C. Ikle, director of the Arms Control and Disarmament Agency, warned that a barrage of hydrogen explosions, down close to the earth or in space above it, could shatter the ozone layer in the stratosphere that protects all earthlife from the undiluted ultraviolet rays of the sun. Highly concentrated ultraviolet light rips apart the protein molecules which are the basis of life. Ozone—heavy oxygen, with three atoms instead of two—absorbs ultraviolet light. So man's mastery of a form of light called the laser could lead, through its use as a weapon to detonate nuclear missiles, to his destruction by another form of light, straight from the sun which has sustained his life on earth.

Can the arms race in space be stopped? Consider that mastery of the air has always been a military imperative, leading in turn to mastery of land and sea. He who controls space will control the air. The military is concerned with today's, not tomorrow's, dangers.

He who controls the climates also will control the air—and all else, too.

In 1968, Dr. Gordon J. F. MacDonald, a geophysicist and an early member of the Jasons, left his post as vice-president for research of the Institute for Defense Analyses. He also published a little-noticed analysis of the potential for meteorological warfare. Among the prospects he listed were: manipulating temperatures by shooting into the upper atmosphere materials that either would absorb sunlight from above, thus lowering temperatures below, or intercept heat being radiated from the earth, thus raising the earth's temperatures; setting off crushing underwater explosions at the edges of the continental shelves, thus causing tidal waves or earthquakes; opening, with rockets, holes in the ozone layer thirty miles up, thus admitting —in effect, aiming—ultraviolet rays over selected parts of the planet. Dr. MacDonald, who later became a member of the White House Council on Environmental Quality in the Nixon administration, made it clear that his article was speculative only, that he was by no means advocating the alteration of the atmosphere. But when reports began surfacing four years later of Air Force-CIA rainmaking over Southeast Asia, it turned out that the stuff of Dr. MacDonald's speculations had been a staple of military R&D as far back as 1963. The weathermen of the Pentagon actually had predated the "Weathermen" of the anti-Pentagon by a good many years. Research on ways of warping the weather had come together at the Cambridge Research Laboratory, Hanscom AFB, Massachusetts, under the aegis of the Joint Chiefs of Staff but with CIA participation and the direct approval of the Johnson and then the Nixon White House.

In March 1973, the Federation of American Scientists asked Nixon to own up officially to U.S. weather modification in Southeast Asia. The Federation, which included twenty-one

Nobel laureates, said in part: "There are many different kinds of geophysical warfare which, if they were to be engaged in by ourselves and by opponents, would be to the clear disadvantage of mankind. The use of weather modification as a weapon of war is an opening wedge to the use of climate modification, the inducement of earthquakes, and other still more terrible methods." Did this sound familiar? It should have. Among the members of the Federation, and one of its foremost spokesmen on this issue, was none other than Dr. MacDonald, who by then had left Nixon's Council on Environmental Quality. Like so many scientists over so many years, he was trying to keep the military from practicing what he himself had postulated. At a press conference in Washington, MacDonald was asked whether he knew for sure that the United States had waged weather warfare in Southeast Asia. In response, he cited references in *The Pentagon Papers*, which had been surfaced by Daniel Ellsberg, to a "Project Pop Eye" which had induced rainstorms, through cloud-seeding, over the Ho Chi Minh Trail in Laos.

Not until a year later, however, in March 1974, did the Pentagon finally admit to having deemed it necessary—if not nice—to fool with Mother Nature over Laos, North Vietnam and South Vietnam, from 1966 through 1972. Defense Department officials made the admission at a briefing of the Senate Foreign Relations Committee. They said that the cloud-seeding project —in conjunction with the emplacement of electronic and chemical sensing devices—had succeeded in stanching North Vietnamese infiltration down the Ho Chi Minh trail, especially in the summer of 1971. But they denied allegations that their cloud seeding had been responsible for the devastating flooding of North Vietnam in the fall of that year. The Pentagon people pointed out that cloud seeding had been the object of civilian R&D for many years, and that the military had simply found it to be compatible to the cause of the war. What they did not emphasize was that the "technology" has now proceeded to the point that not just rainshowers but torrents can be triggered, that entire continents can be targeted for catastrophic cloudbursts.

During the Senate debate of 1974 on the military procurement bill for fiscal 1975, Senator Gaylord Nelson of Wisconsin introduced a floor amendment prohibiting weather modification as a weapon of war. The Senate passed it, but it was deleted in conference with the House. A short time later, the Senate Armed Services Committee asked Dr. Stephen J. Lukasik, director of the Pentagon's Advanced Research Projects Agency, whether the Defense Department was pursuing any R&D that might be contrary to the intent of the Nelson amendment.

"There is no such work in ARPA," said Dr. Lukasik, "but I am not familiar in detail with the totality of activities in the Defense Department. To the best of my knowledge, there is nothing going on in the Department that is in conflict with that amendment."

The committee then asked Lukasik to look into the matter and provide a statement for the record. The statement, when it came, was a masterpiece of what-do-I-mean. As the record of the committee expressed it, "the information follows":

"Department of Defense research in weather modification is entirely unclassified and does not involve any unique techniques not known to the civilian community. Research is pursued to develop means for protecting military personnel and resources and to prevent technological surprise. This research is thus not contrary to the intent of the amendment referred to."

What it came down to was that the Senate committee actually had no power to force the Pentagon to account fully for its actions with respect to an amendment which had not become law. And the Pentagon did not. It is questionable, in fact, that the Pentagon would have responded fully even if the amendment had become law. There is plenty of precedent for the Pentagon not having done so, and never having been challenged.

In mid-October 1974, the Soviet Union introduced a little-noticed draft convention at the United Nations "banning the modification of the environment and the climate for military and other purposes incompatible with the interests of international security, the well being, and health of people." More specifically, the Soviets proposed outlawing all modifications by man of "the surface of the land, the floor of seas and oceans, the earth's interior, water, the atmosphere, or any other elements of the natural environment." This would include, they said, cloud seeding or any other means of inducing precipitation or redistributing water resources; artificial engendering of seismic waves; creating electromagnetic and acoustic fields in the ocean; disturbing the natural heat and gas exchanges between the hydrosphere and the atmosphere, or the heat and radiation balance among earth, atmosphere and sun.

To the Pentagon, this was nothing more than a typical Russian ploy. Whether the Soviets were ahead or behind in the research and development of ways to prostitute the elements, they stood to gain. If they were ahead, the enactment of prohibitive international law would permit them to stay ahead. If they were behind—as was probably the case—they could simply break the law and work to catch up. The latter hypothesis presupposed, of course, that the Pentagon would not break the law, and would disband its R&D. Any way you look at it, the "R&D hedge" once again was being brought to bear. But whether it is weather, missiles, warheads, fighter planes, submarines, radar, computers, electronic countermeasures, electronic warfare, lasers, guidance and control, unmanned planes, submarine listening devices, satellites or whatever, the global game of one-upmanship must go on. Wars would be neat and clean: weapons against weapons; robots against robots. Man's ability to create foul weather would be accompanied by his development of weapons which could hunt and kill just as effectively in foul weather. His exploration of the oceans and of space already had turned into his military exploitation of them. And all the while, man was removing himself, through his development of seeing-eye, surgical-strike, multifarious machines, from the physical encounter, the spilling of guts, which has made him think twice about face-to-face combat. He would abandon the bayonet but not the bomb. He would fight from a console but not from a foxhole. He could become, in consequence, much less afraid to fight. He might even be willing—or forced—to spend a trillion dollars or three trillion rubles on national defense in less than the next decade, just for the privilege. In the end, he would finally have quit talking about, and done something about, the weather, and he would have no place left to hide—not in the night, not in the earth, not in space, not even on Mount Ararat.

Nearly five centuries ago, Leonardo da Vinci, maybe the greatest technologist of them all, wrote:

There is nothing on earth that would have so much power either to harm or benefit man ... if it were true ... that by such an art one had the power to disturb the tranquil clearness of the air, and transform it into the hue of night, to create corruscations and tempests with dreadful thunderclaps and lightning flashes rushing through the darkness, and with impetuous storms to overthrow high buildings and uproot forests, and with these to encounter armies and break and overthrow them, and—more important than this—to make devastating tempests, and thereby to rob the husbandmen of the rewards of their labors. For what method of warfare can there be which can inflict such damage upon the enemy as the exercise of the power to deprive him of his crops? What naval combat could there be which should compare with that which he would wage who has command of the winds, and can create ruinous tempests that would submerge every fleet whatsoever? In truth, whoever has control of such irresistible forces would be lord over all nations, and no human skill will be able to resist his destructive power. The buried treasure, the jewels that lie in the body of the earth, will become manifest to him; no lock, no fortress, however impregnable, will avail to save anyone against the will of such a necromancer. He will cause himself to be carried through the air from East to West, and through all the uttermost parts of the universe. But why do I thus go on adding instance to instance? What is there which could not be brought to pass by a mechanician such as this? Almost nothing, except the escaping from death.

Acknowledgments

and Sources

I wish to acknowledge the advice and encouragement of authors Joseph C. Goulden and William D. Hickman; the excellent files of author and former McGraw-Hill colleague Warren Burkett and of colleague Herbert W. Cheshire; and the sage counsel of Ray Connolly, Washington bureau manager of *Electronics* magazine.

Trains of thought, conclusions, and speculations in this book are my own. All quotations, except those attributed to documents, testimony, speeches or publications, are the result of my own reporting, which pervades the book. I wrote newspaper or magazine articles on the topics of each chapter and relied heavily on my own notes. Basic documents from which I drew extensively are as follows:

The Budget of the United States Government, fiscal years 1974, 1975, and 1976.

Annual Defense Department Report, Fiscal Year 1973, Secretary of Defense Melvin R. Laird.

Annual Defense Department Report, Fiscal Year 1975, Secretary of Defense James R. Schlesinger.

Annual Defense Department Report, Fiscal Year 1976, Secretary of Defense James R. Schlesinger.

The Department of Defense, Program of Research, Development, Test and Evaluation, Annual reports by the directors of Defense Research and Engineering, fiscal years 1973, 1974, 1975, and 1976.

United States Military Posture for Fiscal Year 1975, by the Chairman of the Joint Chiefs of Staff, Admiral Thomas S. Moorer, USN.

United States Military Posture for Fiscal Year 1976, by the Chairman of the Joint Chiefs of Staff, General George S. Brown, USAF.

Nomination of James R. Schlesinger to be Secretary of Defense, Hearing before the Committee on Armed Services, United States Senate, June 18, 1973.

Hearings before the Senate Armed Services Committee:
  Part 1, Authorizations, Feb. 5, 1974.
  Part 2, Authorizations, Feb. 7, 19, and 22, 1974.
  Part 5, Research and Development, Mar. 4, 7, 8, 14, 15, and 18, 1974.
  Part 6, Research and Development, Mar. 22, 26, 27, and 29; Apr. 1 and 2, 1974.
  Part 7, Research and Development, Apr. 4, 5, 12, 16, 23, 25, and 26; May 2, 1974.

Hearings before the Senate Armed Services Committee: Part 3, Authorizations, May 8, 9, 15, and 16; June 7 and 8, 1973.

Department of Defense Appropriations for 1975, Hearings before the House of Representatives Defense Appropriations Subcommittee:
  Part 1, Jan. 29–Mar. 2, 1974.
  Part 2, Mar. 7–Apr. 1, 1974.

Report Authorizing Appropriations for Fiscal Year 1974, Committee on Armed Services, United States Senate, Sept. 6, 1973.

Report Authorizing Appropriations for Fiscal Year 1975, Committee on Armed Services, United States Senate, May 29, 1974.

Report Authorizing Appropriations for Fiscal Year 1975, Committee on Armed Services, House of Representatives, May 10, 1974.

Department of Defense Appropriation Bill, 1975, Report of the Senate Committee on Appropriations, Aug. 16, 1974.

Department of Defense Appropriation Bill, 1975, Report of the House Committee on Appropriations, Aug. 1, 1974.

Department of Defense Appropriations for 1974, Hearings before a House Appropriations Subcommittee: Testimony of Vice Admiral Hyman G. Rickover, June 19, 1973.

Diplomatic and Strategic Impact of Multiple Warhead Missiles, Hearings before the House Foreign Affairs Subcommittee on National Security Policy and Scientific Developments, July and Aug. 1969.

U.S.–Soviet Commercial Relations: The Interplay of Economics, Technology Transfer and Diplomacy, Report by the House Foreign Affairs Subcommittee on National Security Policy and Scientific Developments, June 10, 1973.

Weapon Systems Acquisition Process, Hearing before the Senate Armed Services Committee, May 12, 1972.

Strategy and Science: Toward a National Security Policy for the 1970's, Hearings before the House Foreign Affairs Subcommittee on National Security Policy and Scientific Developments, Mar. 1969.

Military Applications of Nuclear Technology, Hearing before the Subcommittee on Military Applications of the Joint Committee on Atomic Energy, Apr. 16, 1973.

Close Air Support, Report of The Special Subcommittee on Close Air Support of the Preparedness Investigating Subcommittee of the Committee on Armed Services, United States Senate, 1972.

The Process for Identifying Needs and Establishing Requirements for Major Weapon Systems in the Department of Defense, U.S. General Accounting Office, Oct. 23, 1974.

Status of Selected Major Weapon Systems, U.S. General Accounting Office, May 31, 1974.

Program Acquisition Costs by Weapon System, Department of Defense Budget for Fiscal Year 1974.

Program Acquistion Costs by Weapon System, Department of Defense Budget for Fiscal Year 1975.

Program Acquisition Costs by Weapon System, Department of Defense Budget for Fiscal Year 1976.

Report to The President and the Secretary of Defense on the Department of Defense, by the Blue Ribbon Defense Panel, July 1, 1970.

    Appendix A: *Mechanisms for Change; Organizational History.*

    Appendix E: *Staff Report on Major Weapon Acquisition Process.*

    Appendix F: *Staff Report on Operational Test and Evaluation.*

    Appendix N: *Staff Report on Joint Chiefs of Staff Decision-Making.*

Jane's Weapon Systems 1973–74, Edited by R. T. Pretty and D. H. R. Archer, Jane's Yearbooks, London, England.

Free World Tactical Missile Systems, General Dynamics Electro Dynamic Division, May 1971.

Acquisition of Major Weapon Systems, Report to the Congress by the Comptroller General of the United States, Mar. 18, 1971.

Dictionary of Weapons and Military Terms, by John Quick, Ph.D., McGraw-Hill Book Company, 1973.

Setting National Priorities: The 1974 Budget, by Charles L. Schultz, Edward R. Fried, and Alice M. Rivlin, The Brookings Institution, Washington, D.C., 1973.

Setting National Priorities, the 1975 Budget, by Barry M. Blechman, Edward M. Gramlich, and Robert W. Hartman, The Brookings Institution, Washington, D.C., 1974.

Chapter 1

p. 1, Parable, *The Autobiography of Benjamin Franklin and Selections from His Other Writings,* edited by Nathan G. Goodman, The Modern Library, New York, 1932, p. 201. (As cited by Charles J. Hitch in his book, *Decision-Mak-*
ing for Defense, University of California Press, Berkeley and Los Angeles,
1965.)

p. 3, Pike, Speech to Armed Forces Management Assn., Washington, June 7, 1973.

p. 11, F-111, *Air Force* magazine, June, 1973; San Diego *Union,* Feb. 25, 1973; *Aviation Week & Space Technology,* Apr. 30, 1973; *Time,* Dec. 4, 1972.

p. 16, A-10 and Clements, *Armed Forces Journal,* Mar. 1973; Washington *Post,* Feb. 26, 1973.

p. 16, A-7, Senate Armed Services Committee Report, Sept. 6, 1973.

p. 17, Weapons costs, General Accounting Office Report, *Cost Growth in Major Weapon Systems,* Mar. 26, 1973.

p. 17, Staats, Speech to The Society of Experimental Test Pilots, Beverly Hills, Calif., Sept. 28, 1973.

p. 19, Schlesinger, Transcript of meeting with McGraw-Hill executives, Sept. 18, 1973.

Chapter 2

p. 27, MiG and Phantom, *U.S. News & World Report,* May 9, 1966.

p. 29, Carl and Thach, *Aerospace Daily,* Oct. 9, 1968.

pp. 30–31, Navy planes and pilots, *Armed Forces Journal,* Apr. 1974.

p. 42, Packard, *Policy Changes in Weapon System Procurement,* a report by the House Government Operations Committee, Dec. 10, 1970.

p. 43, Packard, Washington *Daily News,* Sept. 18, 1969.

p. 46, Packard, *Time,* June 21, 1971.

pp. 42–47, Packard philosophies, *Government Executive* magazine, Sept. 6, 1969; *Wall Street Journal,* Dec. 12, 1969.

p. 49, Clements and Maurin, Dallas *Morning News,* May 13, 1973.

pp. 50, Perot, *ibid.*

p. 50, Clements and Flax, *Aviation Week & Space Technology,* May 14, 1973.

p. 52, Clements and committees, Memo from Clements to the Secretary of the Navy, June 8, 1973; testimony before House and Senate Armed Services committees, June 1973.

p. 53, Clements and Pentagon, press conference, June 13, 1973.

p. 53, F-14 and Sparrow, *New York Times,* June 22, 1973.

p. 56, Bellis and engine, Washington *Star-News,* May 16, 17, and 31, 1973; Washington *Post,* May 17, 1973.

p. 58, Shah and F-14, *Wall Street Journal,* June 12, 1974.

p. 60, Grumman loan, Statement of Grumman Corp., Oct. 3, 1974.
p. 65, Mideast dogfights, *Armed Forces Journal*, Apr. 1974.

Chapter 3

pp. 77–85, JCS and War Rooms, Defense Department fact sheets, Apr. 1965 and Aug. 8, 1973; *Commander's Digest*, Dec. 20, 1973; *Army* magazine, Feb. 1968 and Apr. 1970; *Orbis*, Fall 1969; *National Journal*, Feb. 5, 1972; *Air Force*, Apr. 1966; *Time*, Feb. 5, 1965.
p. 87, Johnson–McNamara–Goodwin *et al.*, Washington *Post*, June 15, 1969.
p. 92, Moorer documents, *Transmittal of Documents from the National Security Council to the Chairman of the Joint Chiefs of Staff*, Report by the Senate Armed Services Committee, Feb. 6, 1974.
pp. 96 and 101, Soviet shots, *Aerospace Daily*, Dec. 3, 1973, and Jan. 28, 1974.
p. 101, Brookings, *Setting National Priorities: The 1975 Budget*, Blechman, Gramlich, Hartman, the Brookings Institution, May 1974.

Chapter 4

p. 108, Schlesinger, Transcript of interview with Time, Inc., executives, Sept. 12, 1973.
p. 108, Schlesinger and AEC and Llewellyn King, Washington *Post*, Jan. 8, 1973.
p. 117, Schlesinger and stamina, Speech to National Jaycees, Arlington, Va., Dec. 15, 1973.
p. 121, Schlesinger and Jackson, Time, Inc., interview.
p. 129, Scoville, *The New Republic*, Mar. 30, 1974.
p. 129, FAS, Federation of American Scientists Public Interest Report, Feb. 1974.

Chapter 5

p. 136, Johnson and DNA, Testimony to House Armed Services Committee, Mar. 12, 1974.
p. 139, Lapp, *The New Republic*, June 21, 1969.
pp. 140–145, Minuteman, *Saturday Review*, Aug. 30, 1969; *Time*, June 27, 1969, and Feb. 11, 1974; *Newsweek*, May 1, 1972; Air Force Fact Sheet, Dec. 7, 1965; *Armed Forces Management*, May 1970; *Bulletin of the Atomic Scientists*, Jan. 1970; *New York Times* magazine, May 4, 1969.
p. 147, ABRES, *Jane's Weapon Systems*, 1973–74.
p. 148, McIntyre, Speech to Electronic Industries Assn., Washington, D.C., May 1, 1974.
p. 152, Phillips and MX, *Air Force*, Mar. 1973 and Jan. 1974.
p. 153, NAVSTAR, Report of Director, Defense Research and Engineering, Fiscal Year 1975.
p. 153, Plymale, *Aerospace Daily*, Jan. 30, 1974.
p. 158, Cruise missiles, Washington *Star-News*, Aug. 15, 1973; *Aerospace Daily*, July 11, 1973; *Ocean Science News*, Mar. 1, 1974.
p. 159, Missile contracts, *Aviation Week & Space Technology*, May 6, 1974.
p. 160, Schultz, *Air Force*, Aug. 1974.

Chapter 6

pp. 169–172, Submarines, *Nuclear Powered Submarines*, Atomic Energy Commission, Nov. 1964; *Underway on Nuclear Power*, U.S. Navy, 1969; *Polaris-*

Poseidon Fleet Ballistic Missile Weapon System, U.S. Navy, 1968; *U.S. Navy Atomic Submarine Lineup,* General Dynamics, 1969.

pp. 174–177, Strat X and ULMS, *Electronics,* June 12, 1967; San Diego *Union,* Apr. 16, 1967; *Armed Forces Management,* May 1970; *Air Force/Space Digest,* June 1968.

p. 185, Laird funding, Annual Report of the Secretary of Defense, Fiscal Year 1973.

pp. 184–198, Congress, *Congressional Quarterly,* Mar. 28, 1973.

Chapter 7

p. 193, Rickover and Todd, *Business Week,* May 18, 1974.

p. 196, Venturer, *Navy* magazine, July–Aug. 1970.

p. 197, Mark 48, *Ocean Science News,* Apr. 1, 1973.

pp. 201–203, Soviet fleet, *Navy,* July–Aug. 1970; Washington *Star-News,* July 8, 1973; *U.S. News & World Report,* Mar. 12, 1973; *The Defense Monitor,* Center for Defense Information, Apr. 1974 and Sept. 1974.

p. 203, McIntyre, Speech to National Security Industrial Assn., Apr. 10, 1973.

p. 205, Giant sub, *Wall Street Journal,* Mar. 15, 1972.

pp. 210–211, ASW, *Armed Forces Journal,* Oct. 19, 1970; *New York Times,* Jan. 17, 1974; *Ocean Science News,* Feb. 8, 1974.

p. 214, SASS, *Ocean Science News,* Feb. 8 and 16, 1974.

p. 215, NAVELEX, *Electronics,* Oct. 9, 1972.

p. 217, AUTEC, Chicago Tribune, Oct. 15 and 22, 1967.

Chapter 8

p. 219, Wiesner, House Foreign Affairs Committee hearing, Mar. 11, 1969, on *Strategy and Science: Toward a National Security Policy for the 1970's.*

pp. 221–223, Wiesner, *ibid.*

p. 223, Foster and Hen House, Speech to American Newspaper Publishers Assn., New York, Apr. 23, 1970.

p. 229, Currie funding, Defense Department Budget, Fiscal Year 1975.

pp. 231–232, DDR&E, Blue Ribbon Panel Report, 1970.

p. 235, Schlesinger and McNamara, Time, Inc., interview, Sept. 12, 1973.

p. 235, Schlesinger and military, *ibid.*

p. 237, Brown, *Impact of Science and Technology on Strategy,* Speech at Air War College National Security Forum, Maxwell Air Force Base, Ala., May 1972.

p. 245, Ferroboat, Washington *Star-News,* July 15, 1973.

pp. 249–251, Harr, Speech to World Affairs Council of Orange County, Newport Beach, Calif., Sept. 10, 1974.

Chapter 9

pp. 253–256, Laser funding, *Aviation Week & Space Technology,* Nov. 8, 1971, May 14, 1973, and Sept. 2, 1974; *New York Times,* Sept. 13, 1973; *Air Force Times,* Sept. 5, 1973, and Oct. 23, 1974.

p. 254, Lasers-list, Speech by Lt. Gen. Robert E. Coffin, deputy director of DDR&E for Acquisition Management, to DMS, Inc., symposium, Rye, N.Y., Mar. 5, 1974.

pp. 260–262, IR&D, *Technical Papers* and *Position Paper on Independent Re-*

search and Development and Bid and Proposal Efforts, Aerospace Industries Assn. of America, Inc., Electronic Industries Assn. and National Security Industrial Assn., Mar. 1974.

pp. 273–276, Laser descriptions, *Soldiers* magazine, May 1973; *Air Force*, Dec. 1970; San Diego *Union*, Dec. 1973; *American Legion* magazine, Oct. 1972; *U.S. News & World Report*, Oct. 1, 1973.

p. 277, Chemical lasers, *Aviation Week & Space Technology*, Jan. 21, 1974.

Chapter 10

Accounts of the Mideast War were drawn from many sources. The basic document was the Report of the Special Subcommittee on the Middle East of the Committee on Armed Services, House of Representatives, Dec. 13, 1973.

p. 287, Abrams, Testimony before Senate Armed Services Committee, Feb. 22, 1974.

pp. 290–296, Jasons and Think Tanks, *Science*, July 23, 1971, and Feb. 2, 1973; *The Nation*, April 15, 1968; *Electronics*, June 12, 1967.

pp. 298–303, Khe Sanh, Testimony of Maj. Gen. R. McC. Tompkins before Senate Armed Services Committee, Nov. 19, 1970.

p. 304, jammers, *Electronic Warfare* magazine, Jan.–Feb. 1974; *Aviation Week & Space Technology*, July 29, 1974, and Oct. 15, 1973.

Chapter 11

pp. 308–309, Drones, *Armed Forces Journal*, May 17, 1971; *Time*, Sept. 11, 1972; *U.S. News & World Report*, May 20, 1974.

p. 311, Symposium, *Air Force*, Oct. 1970.

p. 315, RPV study, *Astronautics & Aeronautics*, Apr. 1973.

p. 320, R&D funding, *Electronics*, July 31, 1972.

p. 323, Army, *Aviation Week & Space Technology*, July 1, 1974.

p. 327, Robot, *New Republic*, Apr. 29, 1972.

Chapter 12

p. 331, Weapon costs, Department of Defense Selected Acquisition Report (SAR), Oct. 1974.

p. 337, Appropriation, *Congressional Quarterly*, Sept. 28, 1974.

p. 339, Ford and Schlesinger, *The New Republic*, Apr. 1974.

pp. 343–344, Arms sales, Schlesinger annual report, Fiscal Year 1976.

p. 353, Fuel cloud, Associated Press, Sept. 5, 1973.

p. 356, Arming satellites, *Air Force*, May 1974.

p. 357, MacDonald, *Unless Peace Comes; A Scientific Forecast of New Weapons*, edited by Nigel Calder, The Viking Press, 1968. A chapter, *How To Wreck the Environment*, by Gordon J. F. MacDonald. Reprinted in *Weather Modification*, a report by the Senate Foreign Relations Subcommittee on Oceans and International Environment, Jan. 25 and Mar. 20, 1974.

p. 357, FAS, petition and letter to President Nixon, made public by Federation of Atomic Scientists, Mar. 1, 1973.

p. 358, Pentagon admits, *Science*, June 1974.

p. 359, Soviets and UN, Record of UN General Assembly proceedings, Oct. 21, 1974.

p. 360, da Vinci, reproduced from *The Myth of the Machine*, Lewis Mumford, Harcourt, Brace & World, Inc., 1966; 1967; p. 291–292.

Index